Russia and Soul: An Exploration

RUSSIA AND SOUL: AN EXPLORATION

Dale Pesmen

Cornell University Press

ITHACA AND LONDON

First published 2000 by Cornell University Press
First printing, Cornell Paperbacks, 2000

Printed in the United States of America

Library of Congress Cataloging-in-Publication Data

Pesmen, Dale, 1959–
    Russia and soul : an exploration / Dale Pesmen.
        p. cm.
    Includes bibliographical references and index.
    ISBN 0-8014-3739-3 (cloth : alk. paper) — ISBN 0-8014-8709-9 (pbk. : alk. paper)
        1. National characteristics, Russian. 2. Russia (Federation)—Civilization. 3. Social psychology—Russia (Federation) 4. Interpersonal relations—Russia (Federation) I. Title.
    DK510.34 .P47 2000
    947—dc21

                                                                    00-009678

Cornell University Press strives to use environmentally responsible suppliers and materials to the fullest extent possible in the publishing of its books. Such materials include vegetable-based, low-VOC inks and acid-free papers that are recycled, totally chlorine-free, or partly composed of nonwood fibers. Books that bear the logo of the FSC (Forest Stewardship Council) use paper taken from forests that have been inspected and certified as meeting the highest standards for environmental and social responsibility. For further information, visit our website at www.cornellpress.cornell.edu

Cloth printing   10 9 8 7 6 5 4 3 2 1
Paperback printing   10 9 8 7 6 5 4 3 2 1

Contents

IV AUTHORITY

V TOGETHERNESS

VI CONCLUSIONS

Dedication and Acknowledgments

To the people who taught me about generosity and helped write this: Michael Wasserman, Tania Fel, Steve Coleman, and my friends and acquaintances in Russia. To my parents, Allen and Enid Pesmen, and to everyone who encouraged me to say what I wanted to say.

I am indebted and grateful to professors Paul Friedrich, James W. Fernandez, Victor Friedman, Raymond Fogelson, and Anna Lisa Crone, as well as to Daphne Berdahl, Krisztina Fehervary, Sarah Krive, Martha Lampland, Alaina Lemon, Stephanie Platz, Jennifer Rayport-Rabodzeenko, Mark Steinberg, and Marko Zivkovic for support, readings, and suggestions.

Thanks to editor-in-chief Frances Benson of Cornell University Press, the press's readers, especially Nancy Ries, as well as Candace Akins and Carolyn Pouncy.

Thanks also to the Omsk State Music Theater, the Omsk Academic Theater of Drama, New Turners Theater, the Milwaukee Repertory Theater, the Omsk Department of Culture, and the kind people who worked at coffeeshops where this was written.

Note on Transliteration, Translation, and Names

I use the Library of Congress system for Cyrillic transliteration except when there is another commonly accepted English spelling for a name. Wierzbicka (1992) has shown that "*Soul* can always be translated into Russian as *dushá,* while the reverse is not true." One goal of this study is to examine this somewhat untranslatable *dusha.* For these reasons I often use the noun *dusha* (pl. *dushi*), a related adjective (*dushevnyi*), as well as the adverb *dushevno* rather than translating them as "soul," "soulful," and "soulfully." For the same reasons, I do not usually italicize dusha, but treat it as an English word. I do italicize it when I am referring to the word itself. When I do translate *dusha,* I usually translate it as soul rather than as *the soul*; it is more accurate for a number of reasons that will become clear.

Most previously unpublished translations from Russian, unless otherwise noted, are mine. This book owes a great deal to Michael Wasserman's linguistic expertise and inspiration.

Although a number of my Omsk friends deserve to be thanked by name, I use pseudonyms to refer to all individuals whom I interviewed or to whom I refer, with the exception of public figures (such as politicians and entertainers) I did not know personally and one whom I interviewed on tape and who said I was welcome to cite him.

Glossary

I have tried to define terms the first few times I use them; I include here only terms not glossed in subsequent uses.

babushka, grandmother
bezdushnyi, cruel, soulless; n. *bezdushie*
biznes, *biznesmen*, business, businessman
blini, thin pancakes
blat, "credit" or "pull" with or through relatives and acquaintances
byt, everyday life, mode of life
chastushki, four-line folk limericks, sung
CPSU, Communist Party of the Soviet Union
dusha, pl. *dushi*; adj. *dushevnyi*, adv. *dushevno*, soulful; see Introduction
glubinka, the provinces; lit. the depths
Komsomol, Young Communist League
krut- and words based on it, see Chapter 8
kul'tura, "culture," *kul'turno*, "cultural" or "cultured"
ledokhod, spring ice procession downriver
meshchanstvo, petty bourgeois lifestyle or personality
muzhik, peasant (m.)
nachal'nik, boss, supervisor, superior; *nachal'stvo*, the bosses, management
narod, the people
nekul'turnyi, without *kul'tura*, uncultured
obida, offense or soul-injury, degradation and hurt; *obidno*, It's offensive, hurtful
oblast', region, province
obman, *obmanyvat'*, deception, to deceive; *obmanuty*, deceived
obshchenie (v. obshchat'sia), communion, communication, interaction, intercourse

otklik, a response, an answer; *otklikat'sia*, to respond or answer

pel'meni, dumplings

perezhivat', *perezhivanie*, *perezhivaniia*; living through things, pouring your soul into them, intuiting, suffering, caring; to experience / experiences

pirozhki, pies with meat, cabbage, potato, mushroom, or other filling

podskazat', (nominal form, *podskazka*, a hint), to hint or prompt

prostor, vast expanses, open space, lit. and fig.

razmakh, swing, sweep, (wing)span, scale, range, dash. Big, not small or petty, gestures

russkaia dushá, "Russian soul"

samogon, homebrewed alcohol, usually above 40%

sistema, the System

sovok, jaded, crude Homo Sovieticus (pl. *sovki*); see Chapters 2 and 11 footnotes

ty, you, familiar

ugoshchenie, food offered a guest; *ugoshchat'* (verb), to treat someone, offer hospitality

venik, leafy broom used in *bania*

vy, you, formal and plural

zadushevnyi, *dushevnyi razgovor*, "soulful" conversation

Russia and Soul: An Exploration

PART I

SITUATING SOUL

Introduction

Is soul a thing?

> About dusha—well now that, if you will, is the most complicated
> question you can ask.
>
> Yurii Yur'evich, Omsk, 1992

The Depth of Meaning and the Meaning of Depth

The morning after the Soviet Union's sudden death in December 1991,
a frivolous headline quipped: "I woke up and—Hello! Soviet Power
is no more!"[1] In the military industrial city of Omsk, southwestern
Siberia, however, for many ethnic Russians, Ukrainians, and others, the Soviet Union's demise was clearly being faked. Life was too tough to waste energy on politics anyway. Many people assumed "They" were fooling
around, trying to pull something off, probably getting rich, at "Our" expense. When "They" had gotten what they wanted, the USSR would just as
suddenly reappear.

In October 1992 most of Omsk was still unconvinced. The city found itself immersed in an odd anniversary of the Revolution. Stiff, filthy red laundry flew right alongside new red, white, and blue flags, unhealthily metamorphosing into a questionable "democracy." This mess, all this flapping
together in the air of wheeling, dealing, and the brave new politic of rob-
bing each other blind, challenged so much that it was hard to take in even
visually.

People tried to "take it in." The USSR's passing slowly began to be described by many in terms of injury to dusha, pain in the soul, as negotiating
social changes in dusha (*v dushe*) and with dusha (*s dushoi*). The enigmatic
Russian soul is a widely known romantic cliché, but that year one woman
told me: "Before, when we thought about dusha (soul), we were philosophically wondering what to do. But now we've started asking it simply, deeply.

[1] *Ia prosnulsia, zdraste! / Net sovetskoi vlasti!*"

3

Now we're *really* starting to think about soul." A young businessman said "We've changed a lot. Something's really happened with that—that dusha of ours."

This is one of a handful of non-Soviet ethnographies that focus on Russians during and just after perestroika. I first went to Omsk in 1990, as an interpreter for a theater staging an American musical about a bar on the Florida coast (cool project for a Siberian winter). I made friends and returned repeatedly to do fieldwork through 1994. I was there both in January 1991 when this "closed" military industrial city quietly "opened," allowing foreigners to obtain visas, and almost a year later when the USSR disbanded. I lived with families in the city and spent time in villages and at dachas.

This is also an ethnography of Russian *soul*. Cliché that it is, many aspects of what is exoticized as the deep Russian soul are widely shared by Americans and Western Europeans. And interestingly, many Americans and Western Europeans often relate soul itself to Russia. When cultures have been intimately related, such similarities can be powerful heuristic tools. In English, for example, soul, like the Russian word *dusha*, may relate to an indescribable "inner world," an expansive, authentic "life force," and essences of people, places, groups, and other things. Soul and dusha both often relate to compassion and suffering and are invoked in contexts of resistance to modernity, materialism, and hierarchy. They are felt to be centers that can be corrupted and deviated; they may be complex and simple, exposed or muffled; they may harden, soften, open, and close. They may be listened to or heard (or not). Feeling "deeply" is an important indicator of soul, yet things may end up "so deep" that *nothing* about them is experienced. Healing truths are often believed to emerge from these depths, increasing what may be called *life*. And alongside their spirit of capitalism, many Americans and Europeans share a "Russian" sense that certain kinds of resistance or rebellion can bring soul back into consciousness, again, increasing "life."

In the Epilogue I give many examples of similarities between dusha and, for example, the English-language "soul." There are also many differences between them. Examining exact relationships between Russian and other versions is a job for an intellectual historian; but I do show resonances between habits and images of soul that indicate many non-Russians' continuing engagement in a worldview related to the one I describe in Russia.

"The conceit of the West deserves our mockery," says a character in a novel by Russian author Alexander Zinoviev (1982:32–33), deriding outside attempts at understanding Russian soul. Talk about dusha often corresponds, as Wierzbicka (1992) writes, to what has been called Russian national character. Although Russians often discuss their own national character, others' diagnoses of it have been ridiculed since at least Dostoevsky's time. Russian soul is what, in Russian and Soviet books, films, and folklore, idiotically romantic foreigners write about. I discuss this derision in several chapters, but I must also say that I think there's something to it. Many of us would resent having our "mentalities" summarized. It also seems uninteresting to even *see* people as "having" mentalities. In an effort to think about people more generously, I have tried to pay more attention to the surface of things, to what we *can* see. The more I did this, the more vividly I saw how believing in two of the elements I mention above, *depth* and *centralization*, comes to organize life and meaning.

In this book I question imagery of depth and explore some ramifications of believing in such imagery. I show how, faced by the fragmentation and incomprehensibility of 1990s Russian time and space, individuals wove images of soul and other highly valued "wholes." Such pictures of rich, vast entities, "infinitely" deep, alive, and meaningful (or allegedly "too" deep and meaningful to express), form part of creative integrations of individuals and groups. But however persuasive, as images of humans they are grossly simplified and thus in somewhat bad faith. What's more, their reliance on vague rhetorical gestures in the direction of something huge and authoritative supports the hegemony of size, strength, and power as valuable criteria. The creation of wholes and souls is continuous with how ethnicities and classes and so-called blood ties are discovered, politicized, set up against others, and sometimes taken to the extreme of all that and made violent. Identities created by exaggeration, conflation, and generalization and felt to be authoritatively real are made to be manipulated.

So what can anthropology do?

By describing everyday life in a universe in which there was Russian soul, I focus on what I call its *metaphysics*: its explicit and implied elements and workings. I reflect on how souls people described to me were obtained, what was "for" and "against" them, fed and starved them, according to what laws; under what conditions dusha was apparent and what made it vanish; dusha's connection to various kinds of life; what a person with soul could be like; how soul was related to various powers and "other worlds"; its relation to consciousness, and some implications of all this for space and time. Ethnography showed that soul was, in early 1990s Russia, invoked and involved in sacred and profane situations that it molded and that modified it. Ethnography helped me examine in great detail some fictions and realities of believing that people "have" reified, centralized life forces. Soul can be seen as what human flexibility and incoherence look like or what they become when molded by belief in a model of the center, of depth.

Discourses of dusha and other souls claim to describe realities behind or underneath the appearances of everyday signs of the self. The reigning ideology assures us that there *are* "deeper" realities and that it's important for us to reach for them or coax them out. But I would like to question the assumption that there is some superior, more valuable reality behind the appearances and that our thought should be oriented in that direction. What if the signs, shaped by beliefs, are all we have?

Perhaps, in other words, surfaces are better than we think. Bakhtin implies that we cripple ourselves by seeking essential truths, that it is precisely their *absence* that "obligates us to attend so carefully to particulars in their immediate, responsive network of relations" (Emerson 1996:117–18).

This book examines having a deep, valuable center in order to *question* these categories. But writing an ethnography about something is very different from attacking it from a philosophical or psychological perspective. Eagleton (1996) has said that Adorno dreamed of "the dialectical feat of a thought faithful to the opacity of one's subject matter." This ethnography tries in many ways to take into account how enmeshed we are in our "cultural" beliefs.

Parallels between Russian and other "souls" suggest that this ethnography may be a useful tool for critically examining some aspects of our everyday metaphysics. But our flexibility, great as it is, is limited by local habits that theory is unlikely to have arms long enough to get at. What can this sort of questioning be worth?

Although one can't help but be complicit with these habits, if one becomes convinced that they are, philosophically or aesthetically, not entirely admirable, one may be able to withhold some of the wholeheartedness of one's collaboration to withhold some of the sense that, since we live by these models, they are the true laws of the universe.

Late and Post-Soviet Soul: Alive and Well?

Stigmas associated with romanticism and clichés seem to be one reason why scholars have widely ignored soul's meanings and values in contemporary Russia.[2] Some Russians and others dismiss Russian soul as a hackneyed notion irrelevant to tough, millennial post-Soviets. Some mourn it, implying that whatever it was died. Some figure good riddance. In all these cases, Russian soul's vitality is assumed to have disappeared. Russian soul was certainly a myth, notion, image, consoling fiction, trope of romantic national self-definition, and what romantic foreigners came to Russia for. But my attention was drawn to dusha as how individuals did things and what they did; soul seemed to be a vital, changing repertoire of options and practices that evoked and mediated actions, interpretations, and change, at least during the early 1990s.

The term *perestroika* (restructuring) was used during the Soviet era to refer to the need to rebuild parts of society. Although Mikhail Gorbachev had

---

[2] Exceptions are Wierzbicka (1989, 1992) and Boym (1994:73–88).

referred to perestroika for years, in 1986 he applied it to a new project of revitalizing communism by democratizing governance, decentralizing planning, making state enterprises self-sustaining, and establishing competitive private enterprises. This perestroika included foreign policy changes such as disarmament and international cooperation in dealing with environmental issues (Wilson and Bachkatov 1992:169–70, Corten 1992:101–2). Perestroika, Gorbachev said, would affect "all aspects of social life . . . Perestroika is a big word. I would equate it with the word revolution" (Tucker 1987:157).

A major aspect of this revolution was about talk: *glasnost'*. Glasnost means voicing or making something known. It was not a new word either; it had been used since at least the 1850s (Corten, 1992:51, Wilson and Bachkatov, 1992:84). Solzhenitsyn had called glasnost the only bitter medicine that could cure the mortally ill country, and Gorbachev used the term well before the 1980s (e.g., 1987 2:7). Initially applied to cultural life and the press, during perestroika glasnost became a call for "openness in every part of life."

Initial changes demanded more and more reform; the worsening economic situation and new liberties led to ballooning criticism of how "the System" treated its people and to brutal challenges to Soviets' understandings of themselves, their pasts, and their futures. It also led to the disappearance of the country they had been born in and for most, the intensification of their poverty. A joke defined glasnost as being able to open one's mouth but not having anything to put in it (Corten 1992:51).

In 1985–86, in his speeches and articles, Gorbachev not only began to revitalize the terms perestroika and glasnost, but, I found, dramatically increased his use of words that referred to psyche, spirit, and soul.

Before I go on I must stress that in everyday life many uses of *dusha* did not mean much of anything to the person who said them; "Like hares, they are so like the ground they sit on, that it requires a sharp eye . . . to make them out," as a nameless writer (T.D. 1925:720) said of dead metaphors. Uses of *dusha* could be as invisible as the *hands* in "hands down." It seems unfair to disturb their privacy. If I sometimes point them out, it's because like hares, they could jump. This revitalization could have happened at any time,[3] but it happened very often in the early 1990s. An interlocutor image-wrestling over symbolic capital, gesturing or claiming to gesture at something she or he felt to be relatively nonverbal, would reach out, grab a word, term, idiom, or other "conversational prefab" (Attinasi and Friedrich

[3] For example, a friend told me that a neighbor boy had been scaring her nephew with their sheep. My friend told her nephew to tell the boy that jokes like that rub him [his dusha] the wrong way, *Takie shutki mne ne po dushe*. He paused, and then, using the form of statements such as *Druzhba druzhboi, a sluzhba sluzhboi* (Friendship's friendship, but a job's a job) to revive my friend's expression's sleepy dusha, agreed: "Right! Soul's soul and a ram's a ram;" *Dusha dushoi, a baran baranam*. Those sheep were separate. Sheep—separate from his dusha.

1995:33–34), and breathe life into it. Sometimes it woke up, sometimes it didn't.

For example, spirit (*dukh*), as in "the spirit of communist ideals," was well-used during the Soviet era, but Gorbachev began to use it in what he called "the spirit of newness." In speeches during the eight years before perestroika, I found that he had mentioned *dukhovnyi* (spiritual) potential, heritage, interests, needs, culture, and development each about once, and spiritual life twice. Then, *at the 1986 Communist Party Congress alone,* he used *dukhovnyi* to modify at least *fifteen* nouns, many more than once, emphasizing *dukh, dukhovnyi,* and even dusha in headings and titles. He prioritized spiritual transformation: perestroika of all spheres of life begins with *psychological* perestroika. Although Gorbachev had referred to "psychological perestroika" since at least 1978, in 1985–86, instead of the odd limp gesture at restructuring one's attitude to work, he began lavishly offering synonyms and subcategories, being almost analytically specific about how this sharp break or turn in minds and moods was "one of the hardest perestroikas." Gorbachev had formerly used *dusha* in canonized expressions for "the bottom of his heart" and for members of the population (*dushi naseleniia*). At the 1986 Congress, however, he passionately stated: "It is bad when politicians are blind not only with their eyes but with their souls," and went out of his way to call the essence of a political collaboration its dusha.

This renaissance of the term *dusha* was not limited to political rhetoric. Although "Russian soul's" vitality was supposed to be long gone, many Russians and others spent their openness energetically blaming centuries of leaders (including Gorbachev himself and other engineers of perestroika) and other entities for injuring that precious soul. Dusha was said to be dying, murdered by the West, by the Soviet and post-Soviet powerful, by attempts at a market economy, by everyday life. Even some "optimists," new businessmen, and young people agreed something was being lost, although, perhaps, necessarily.

In 1991 *Komsomol' skaia pravda* titled an article about money with: "It's time to think about the soul of the population." This pun on the term for population member or serf revitalizes the "soul" in the fixed expression (as does Gogol's title *Dead Souls*). The same paper headlined an October 1993 article on conflicts between Yeltsin and Khasbulatov with: "Dusha has been flayed bloody." Uses of *dusha* in fixed expressions aside, everyday talk featured much more constant reference to it than people noticed. A college teacher was surprised, she said, to find that in a recent essay assignment "not a *single* student had managed to avoid using that word."

During the following years, souls of many kinds were actively found, negotiated, reproduced. The ethnographic aspect of this book shows how in early 1990s Russia soul was invoked and involved in sacred and profane situations, ambivalently treated, mocked, and revered, how "it" was used to create, manipulate, and exploit cultural capital, during the course of which "it" was itself modified. Again, though, I'm also exploring how soul is and is not a thing.

Researching Soul

In various cultures, what have been translated as "souls" have been described as vital principles located in body parts; seats of conscience that inspire acts; protective, benevolent, and/or dangerous entities; and cores of spirit. Souls come from an almighty spirit, the earth, or genies; they may be received as a gift, by conquest, or by choice; some people have traditional methods for obtaining souls (Riviere 1987:429).

Trying to say something about the far from fully formed and understood situation in which I participated in Omsk, trying to respectfully discuss what others were living through, I begin with none of the above categories. In fact, early on I stumbled on the most incorrect way to ask about dusha: to treat it as a *thing*. This not only masked dusha's (relation to) meaning but had a paralyzing effect, like asking an American "What's human psychology?" As a friend said, "The idea of dusha is hard to express with some sort of single definition, as hard as answering 'What's love?' "

When I first noticed that dusha in everyday life and talk encompassed many concepts of soul, I wondered if the idea was to look for meanings of *dusha*. I soon realized, however, that a value associated with romantic Russian soul, the alleged impossibility of exhaustively defining or knowing it, its legendary unfathomability, had surprisingly significant angles to it, and that no one set of meanings could be definitive. Even when subtly formulated, searches for definitions alone won't work on a term like *dusha*.

Another legitimate reason for Russian disdain for attempts to "explain" dusha and for how dusha is characterized as generally impossible to understand is that in many ways "Russian dusha" was a deceptive lexical item: not just a notion, image, or entity but an aesthetics, a way of feeling about and being in the world, a shifting focus and repertoire of discourses, rituals, beliefs, and practices more and less available to individuals.

So how to circumvent the trap of asking what soul *is*?

One way was to investigate soul as how people *did* things. A number of practices were considered "definitive" of Russians: when tenth-century Prince Vladimir had to choose a religion for Rus', says the Primary Chronicle, he declared Islam out of the question because the use of alcoholic beverage was central to Russianness. The steam baths were a site of pre-Christian religiosity, one of the "twin pillars of Russian culture" cited in an eleventh-century legend (the other pillar being the Church; Condee, 1996). I deal with drinking, steam bathing, and other "souls" that have more to do with what *happens* than with what people *have*.

Another way was to focus on adjectives people used to describe dusha (like deep, inexplicable, and mysterious), what meaning those adjectives had, and how they meant what they meant.

I look at how individuals flexibly manipulate images and practices, adapting them to contingencies and relating them to one another.

In general, however, this problem of not wanting to direct my interlocutors to narrowly define dusha or to define it as a thing forced me to devise an idiosyncratic way of structuring an ethnographic interview. I compiled a long list of paired terms that, over time, I had noticed were commonly used and highly charged in certain kinds of talk. Although I did ask questions about life history, Omsk, and moral, religious, and cultural issues, as well as questions touching on issues people talked about "at table," most of the interviews were built on these paired terms. I simply offered two words or phrases and asked for people's own associations to them. The fact that the words were paired did not pressure people to see them as opposed; pairs that some people responded to as oppositions evoked utterly nonbinary associations from others. This led to surprisingly nuanced, relaxed, lively conversations that rested on stories and examples from people's experience. A few examples are: business/dusha; everyday life/dusha; other world/this world; friendship/business; art/dusha; character/dusha; deep/dusha; hope/dusha; education/dusha; communication/dusha; conscience/dusha, and body/dusha. I also quoted references to soul from popular books and recounted recent Omsk experiences of my own, asking for help in understanding them, help I really needed.

I conducted over fifty hours of interviews with individuals between eleven and seventy-five years of age, twelve female and fourteen male. These were workers, craftspeople, teachers and engineers; my village friends worked on a State farm. Most of these people's salaries were less than subsistence-level, and soon even that was often not paid. Some were unemployed; a few worked for private firms. Older people had tiny pensions.

Although I introduce each "character" in the book as she or he begins figuring importantly, for reference, here is a partial list of people I cite or mention often. Not all of these are people I had formal interviews with, and not all individuals I interviewed are listed here. Only a few of the people I refer to here by pseudonym did I seek out for an interview; most were just members of my expanding circle of acquaintances who agreed to be interviewed on tape. An important household is that of Anna Viktorovna, a retired teacher, her son Grisha, a craftsman, and his wife Nadia, a receptionist. Grisha's coworkers, craftspeople and highly skilled laborers, appear now and then, such as Masha, a mother of two young children. Other important voices are those of engineers Zina and Andrei Orlov; Lara, a married teacher in her forties; Mila, a single office worker in her thirties; Oleg, a married, KGB-trained businessman in his twenties, and his younger, single friend Anatolii. Yurii Yur'evich, a regional public prosecutor and Aleksandr Ivanovich, in middle management of a theater, figure prominently. Evgeniia

Pavlovna, a retired teacher, and Maria Fëdorovna, a retired seamstress, make appearances. Others are Petrov, a middle-aged former regional "partocrat," Vera, a theater administrator and mother, Maxim and Lena, writers in their forties, Vitya, a preteen boy, Svetlana, an institute student, and Kazannik, a former people's deputy who was teaching law in Omsk in 1992 and was later briefly attorney general under Yeltsin.

In a village I stayed with Zhenia and Tamara, State farm workers in their thirties, and their children. Zhenia called himself, his parents, and his grandparents peasants. Every Omsk city resident I cite at any length, even highly educated ones, had close ties to villages and/or small towns; the parents of some still lived there. Andrei Orlov, an engineer, was born and starved through World War II in a remote village.

If in many societies the soul is rarely or never the object of metaphysical discussion (Riviere 1987:426), talk related to dusha was an integral part of it. At what could be night- or afternoon-long sessions at table, a form of intense communication was often an explicit goal. My interviews became analogous to this "sitting," and if the first responses I got could be stiff or formulaic, the ensuing conversations were usually creative and mutually rewarding. This book is full of voices of thoughtful people who are, in Nancy Ries's words (personal communication, 1999), "very experienced at being Russian," trying hard to put into their own words, "local theory," if you will, something about how they live in the world. They tried, energetically and in earnest, to formulate descriptions of their world for themselves and for me.

Many people mournfully alleged a decrease in such talk, dated anywhere from the revolution to the present. After interviews some people thanked me, and we thanked each other: "We used to talk like this much more." One friend called the talk we had just taped "a great psychological workout." Another man told me hyperbolically that if people had talked like that more during the Soviet era, many of that period's travesties would never have happened.[4] In other words, if the careful observation and representation that characterizes my friends' statements was sometimes initiated by me, it was not foreign to them. Their exclamations after our "interviews" confirm that, at the least, the activity we had just engaged in had a respected place in their scheme of things. They were also quite good at it.

For many reasons, Russian soul is discussed more when foreigners are around or in earshot, but most media I draw on here were really addressed to Soviets; radio, television, newspaper, and magazine discourse and popular literature and nonfiction dealt with dusha and spiritual issues with astounding frequency.

Besides interviews, I took copious notes on other conversations with

---

[4] I also heard the Soviets blamed for damaging soul by virtue of officially discouraging talk about it and use of the word.

scores of people, and two groups of college students responded to my questions at length in writing. I recorded radio and television shows, and used maps, letters, newspaper articles, films, and prerevolutionary, Soviet, and post-Soviet literature and nonfiction. Over the course of perhaps two years I painstakingly indexed this material according to a growing, constantly modified list of Russian and English words and phrases important in everyday 1990s speech and media discussions of national and individual character, moral issues, power relations, history, and interpersonal relationships. The final list consisted of about 250 terms that guided me in the writing of this book.

The terms that first struck me as salient turned out to belong to a semiotic repertoire of great tenacity and authority that "extends the meanings of [its constituent] . . . symbols" (Friedrich 1996a). So although Russian soul is, as it is called, a myth, a notion, an image, a consoling fiction, and a nationalist trope, it is also *ways* in which people did things and *what* they did.

It has been very hard to reduce all this material to a linear narrative for the purpose of making a book, particularly when its dozens of dimensions of cross-referentiality are one of the grounds of the book's validity. The unusual texture of this book is part of my argument—it tries to resist in form what it argues against philosophically.

My categories can be seen as "places" where the dusha worldview has left its trace on the meaningful landscape. These categories reflect each other. Even their implied presence in a text or situation influences formal properties of and people's assumptions about that text or situation. Thus the formalist notion of the dominant, a "focusing component" that "rules, determines, and transforms" other components (Jakobson 1987:41–42), is more apt than "theme." Dusha and depth, organizing principles I use to examine perestroika life, can dominate a speech act, performance, work of art, or image without themselves being present. They may lurk in other terms, in a tone of voice, in a gesture, expression, or pause. Voices representing particular points of view or philosophical positions (Coleman 1999 on Bakhtin 1981) were available to be opportunistically used by individuals in specific contexts. I am looking at discourse as communication within and between people, not as a "system" (that is, in Bakhtin's, not Foucault's sense). This is also complex and hard to represent.

In an attempt to approach this interconnection of phenomena respectfully and represent phenomena in some of their contingency, I decided to repeatedly return to them in different contexts rather than trying to "catch" and run them into the ground in definitive analyses. Similarly, the texts and events I include show a mixture of peasant, intellectual, aristocratic, and more widespread elements. It wasn't one of my goals to try to analyze what was what, though I sometimes do.

Each chapter presents situations and stories from my notes, from hearsay, and from the media and literature, and introduces people whose words or actions helped me think about these issues. The themes and images that serve as chapter beginnings tend so often to be tropes of each other that, for example, expansiveness, chaos, alcohol, other worlds, centers, and music may carry associations to all of the others in part of what Stites (1992:5–6) calls a "rich interconnection" that allows Soviet audiences to "decode effortlessly the various quotations, allusions, and symbols that recur so frequently." These elements have persisted through styles and movements in art, politics, and everyday life.

Trying to make an utterly coherent thing out of all this would have just reduced it. Even a really *good* explanation or model can only do so much. But if each understanding, image, or theory has its limit, there's always a next moment. This challenges us to expand our tolerance for different kinds of interrelation between successive observations, impulses, and pictures. Stites (1992:5–6) notes that elements of national character and Soviet tradition were constantly, sentimentally voiced, accompanied by equally "genuine" "impious jokes, underground satire and mockery." I like this "equally genuine"; mockery and satire do not usually undermine another moment's sentimental earnestness because people—even anthropologists—are not coherent. This may be one of our greatest strengths. Works of theory or ethnography presented as argued or organic wholes have still been in some sense collaged together from an anthropologist's creative, analytical and observational episodes. Neither logical formulas nor romantic, organic, or spatial unities are great tropes for the pictures we can make with the material we're fortunate enough to have.

This book's complexity is iconic of the complexity of my object—the life of soul is at least that complex. Trying to write this ethnography would have felt like walking a razor's edge between complicity and senselessness had I not kept questioning my method and tools while using them, trying to find categories that more precisely suited my subject.

As I can only say "apparently" and "people said" so many times in an effort to make my own voice stand out from voices in which I immerse the reader, I want to again stress that the cosmology I am describing is what I *found*. It is, of course, in ways I have no control over, the cosmology I live by, but I am *not* presenting this picture in a spirit of admiration, only of compassion. Detailed ethnography with an emphasis on what people actually did and said they experienced, ethnography that sticks as close as possible to phenomena, is one of my tactics to question as respectfully as possible the realities and moralities of depth and centeredness. It's hard to know how to intelligently and respectfully criticize something with which one is complicit. But respect is indispensable, because crude opposition is the dumbest form of collaboration.

Because context is all-important to performances and powers of dusha, I have not tried to filter out anomalies, idiosyncratic events with no statistical significance, ideological tirades delivered for my edification, or lies. I examine a texture of life that, for those living it, indiscriminately combined elements of many genres, provenances, and derivations.

I have also not chosen topics according to what seemed uniquely "Russian." For one thing, objective cross-cultural uniqueness is rarely a factor in something's meaning. In addition, "Russianness" and "Russian" are vague, changing entities in a number of ways.

First of all, among the many contexts that have woven into the meaning of *dusha*, nationalism is still strong. Dusha is still conceived of such that Russian dusha makes sense but, for example, Jewish soul, Turkish soul, Tatar soul, and Ukrainian soul usually do not sound right to Russians. If, in the West, "Slavic soul" has often been synonymous with or subsumed by "Russian soul," Russians themselves often stretch the boundaries of "Russian" to approach "Slavic," "Orthodox East European," or even post Soviet bloc.[5] Though Russian dusha may be broadened to "Slavic soul" and, as I will demonstrate, it may be found or said to exist in any individual, it tends to be associated with only one ethnic group. By the 1990s, however, the bounds of this ethnic group were unclear.

Many factors contributed to increasing indeterminacy as to exactly what "Russian" meant. Over decades, write Schnirelman and Komarova (1997), many Russians became increasingly alienated from the culture and state in which they had formerly been the majority. As they dispersed and were dispersed through the USSR, central Russia became less a center of and for "Russians." The state both campaigned against Orthodoxy and, in the name of building a homogeneous Soviet community, encouraged Russification of non-Russians. Individuals whose parents were identified as belonging to other ethnic groups became Russian by passport, and this identification often became more than one of convenience. As a result of such processes, by the time the Soviet Union dissolved, who was Russian and what that meant had also become fuzzy. And, some felt, in need of definition.

Was a Russian someone with "Russian soul"? This is even less clear. The idea of Russian soul reflects an educated intelligentsia-formulated image, not of the Russian intelligentsia but of peasant Russia. Some members of the nineteenth-century intelligentsia challenged themselves to "get" souls by, as Cherniavsky (1969:204) writes, dissolving themselves in these masses, "imbued with compassion, brotherly love, and suffering." But the fact that formulations of collective soul are steeped in intelligentsia images of the folk and that views of the Russian character as drawn to "elemental humanity" have often been reproduced as "national character" without ex-

---

[5] Interestingly, in the context of *russkaia dusha*, contrasts and similarities indicated by Russians between Russia and other nations typically referred to Europe, America, Central Asia, Africa, and the East. East Europe hardly existed on the map of loci useful for defining (Russian) dusha.

amining the practices involved, does not mean that imagery of Russian soul was not in fact shared across social groups.

By the late Soviet era, many aspects of dusha were shared. After the revolution, the intelligentsia, always a fuzzy sort of class,[6] became fuzzier. "Soviet culture" was by design homogeneous, and although this plan was only partially realized, the cultural gulf between masses and elite was narrowed (see Hingley 1977:267). Stalin-era embourgeoisement also cut across social and income classes (Dunham 1990:4–5). In my experience, differences in understanding and use of the word *dusha* were much more evident between individuals and situations than between "classes." By the early 1990s, in some contexts, it was a given that all "Russians" who had not *lost* soul *had* it. It still implied simplicity and suffering, but was usually independent of class, except in emphatically power- or status-related contexts; "cultured" intelligentsia (the people who first rhapsodized about the idea) were often seen as having soul.

Later in the book I discuss more ways in which "Russian" and "dusha" were smudged and flighty categories, and refer to "Russian" and "soul" with these indeterminacies in mind. Purely semantic, national character, and mentality studies, in contrast, assume a coherence I try not to assume. These approaches, which I discuss in a concluding section, vividly point out undeniably present phenomena, but they all buy into soul's deceptive thingness. One may certainly observe "typical behaviors," but even if every single "Russian" said and did the same thing, describing these people as "having" national character would miss, mistreat, and misunderstand their individuality. It is more accurate to look at how souls' blurring, infectious practices relate to the meaning of *dusha*.

An Incomplete History of Russian Soul

Russian *dusha* is etymologically tied to breath and air, as is *dukh* (spirit), and is related to Judeo-Christian notions of soul and other vital principles. Dusha can imply a range of senses of spirit and of what gives life to flesh.[7]

---

[6] In the nineteenth century, Brooks (1984:214) writes, breakdown of villages' insularity encouraged people of all cultural levels to ask what it meant to be Russian. This coincided with the rise of romantic imagery of the simple, philosophizing Russian peasant in literature, philosophy, and social thought. In the Soviet Union, "intelligentsia" could refer to "anyone engaged in non-physical labor . . . a person with a liberal education . . . [or] persons critically disposed to the existing economic and political order" (ibid.:20–21; see Pipes 1961 and Mirsky 1949:321–22). Hingley (1977:227) cites a historian saying that in 1967 10,676,000 Soviets could be classified as intelligentsia. My Omsk friends were not all intelligentsia by any definition, and peasants among them shared aspects of dusha culture with my most educated urban informants.

[7] Dal''s Russian dictionary (1880:503–4) notes that spirit (*dukh*) and soul (*dusha*) are listed separately only "for convenience." *Dukh* is "a fleshless resident of the spiritual world. . . . Re-

Anna Wierzbicka finds three meanings for *dusha*: one religious or quasi-religious, a second more everyday, and a complex "emotional, moral, and transcendental" meaning, though, she says, it is often not clear which is intended (1989:53–54).[8] Souls I found in Russia involved what have been treated as issues of personhood (an interactive notion); self (more reflexive) and identity (an enduring sense or image of self), including nationalism and collective identity (Romantic/idealist folk psychology, which posits a group mind or soul).[9] Issues of purity and pollution are also involved.

Those historians who care seem to agree that the image of a mysterious, enigmatic Russian soul was, by the mid-nineteenth century, very important to Russian intelligentsia. "Unconscious yet strongly felt" ideas, protest against the West, and a sense of mission are some characteristics of this soul (Williams 1970). By deriving antitheses to "Western" rational articulation, precision, delimitation, reserve, calculation, reflection, and predictability, Russian nationalists described Russian national character as featuring strong feelings, the inexpressible, the unlimited, the hyperbolic, the spontaneous, the unpredictable, the immeasurable, and the unmannered (Rogger 1960:268–70, Greenfeld 1992). Hans Rogger (1960:1, 6–7) suggests that eighteenth-century concerns with national identity, values, character, and destiny—later informed by the Napoleonic wars, Russians' residence abroad, German Romanticism, and the writings of Herder, Schelling, and Hegel—gave birth to Russian nationalist thought. After Peter's reforms, Russians began to consider their relationship to Europe and propose specifically national values in the imagery of the peasant village, "the microcosm of Russia. In the confrontation of good and bad, of town and country, Russia and the West, the heart was ranged against the head, true feeling against convention, nature against art" (ibid.:137).

Williams (1970) agrees that "the concept that Russians had certain advantages over the West precisely because they were backward" dates to the eighteenth century, but suggests that the idea that *Russians had soul* and the term "Russian soul" itself became popular only later, with the government's breakdown and the emancipation of the serfs. Williams points out that although by the late 1830s "the idea that the West was dying of soullessness

---

lating this word to a human, some imply his soul, others see in soul only that which gives life to flesh, while they see the spirit as the higher spark from God, reason and will, or a striving toward the lofty." *Dusha* is a "spiritual being enlightened with reason and will; . . . the person with spirit and body; . . . a human being without flesh . . . the vital quality of man imagined separately from body and spirit (in this sense it is said that animals have a soul)." See also Peterson 1992:752–53.

[8] According to Wierzbicka (1989:41–5), among other differences, *dusha* is distinguished from English *soul*, French *âme*, and German *Seele* by its high frequency and wide scope of use.

[9] Meanings Mauss (1985) describes appear in dusha talk, which refers to religious representations, what individuals are and desire to be, character, roles, "true face," personality, psychological being, self, consciousness and perceptions, "beings possessing metaphysical and moral value," and "a fundamental form of thought and action" (see Mauss 1985:22, Fogelson 1982:72, and Carrithers 1985).

had caught on," there was no "adequate phrase to express the idea that Russia had the potential for a glorious future."

The philosopher Chaadaev, in his 1836 *Philosophical Letter*, asked whether Russia had its own history. The eventual answer, Williams shows, was that Russia's unique contribution was her literature. "When Lermontov died, [the critic] Belinskii wrote that he had the 'soul of a Russian poet.' " If Belinskii's words, Williams (1970:573–87; see Cherniavsky 1969:194) writes, reflected the language of German Romanticism and Idealism, the idea reflected his own quest. In 1842 Belinskii described Gogol's *Dead Souls* as "as broad and sweeping as the Russian soul." Williams calls this "literary compliment" the coming of age of "the Russian soul," a term later elaborated by Dostoevsky, who is still a synonym for Russian soul internationally.

Older (and) non-intelligentsia notions of dusha and Russianness are very hard to get at. Although both nationalist and everyday uses of *dusha* at first seem unrelated to Orthodoxy, there are substantial links. It is worth noting that the Russian Church had attributed great importance to the irrational since medieval times. For the nineteenth-century population, Brooks (1984:214) says, "To be Russian was to be loyal to the tsar and faithful to the Orthodox Church." For the lower classes dusha may well have belonged primarily to the Church at some point, at which it would not have been used as richly as it later came to be. This may be confirmed by how a book on Russian folk beliefs mentions dusha only in a creation story, as a pure thing which the Devil cannot give but can only pollute (Ivanits 1992:131–32). If, as Steinberg (forthcoming) writes, plebeian writers were "obsessed" with "the nature, social place, and moral significance of the individual," they seem to have used words other than *dusha* to discuss these issues. But dusha did appear occasionally in folk songs, and I must stress that there is a yawning gap in scholarship on older, non-intelligentsia and folk uses of *dusha*, so I cannot take (nor am I interested in taking) a position on any ultimate genesis of Russian soul.

It has been argued that toward the turn of the century the Russian soul "myth" began a drawn-out death (Cherniavsky 1969:227, Brooks 1984:217, Williams 1970:587). In Soviet schools and in general, dusha was directly attacked as obsolete superstition about immaterial spirit. This denial of dusha's existence included controlling public use of the word (for example, in the press). It did appear, however, in contexts of Soviet projects of re-"engineering the human soul"[10] and, Wierzbicka (1989:45) writes, in both the Stalin era and later years loyal communists often used *dusha* and *dushevno* to refer to moral and psychological aspects of a person, including of Stalin himself.

---

[10] Jochen Hellbeck (1998) argues that the Revolution may well have primarily targeted dusha, citing Stalin-era accounts of writers trying to "analyze the soul."

The scientific term *psikhika* (psyche), promoted during the Soviet era as a replacement for *dusha,* never caught on; *lichnost'* (self, person, personality, individual) fared better. At the time of the revolution, *lichnost'* denoted, Steinberg (forthcoming) writes, an "inward nature and personality" that entitled people to freedom, "a sacred, moral self that transcended narrow individualism," as well as a critique of whatever "degraded" or "insulted" it. It is clear to me, however, that during the Soviet era this *lichnost'*, officially sanctioned, lost its freshness, what Steinberg calls the powerful subversive potential inherent in speaking about inner life. In the early 1990s the word my friends used for these purposes was *dusha.* People did not often choose to discuss *lichnost'* except in narrowly psychological contexts. They did not cite it among the many things they insisted were "one and the same" as dusha. They did not imply that it was undergoing the same tormented processes as dusha. It was dusha, at least in the early 1990s, that condensed Russianness, Russian history, and mystical, social, and philosophical notions of self, soul, identity, and personhood, interwoven with ritual and sentiment. Dusha's early descriptions had become "multivocal nodes of interconnection" (Turner 1969:42–43) involved in flexible practices. I show how many meanings and rituals tied to Russianness and Sovietness revitalized and transformed during perestroika were mediated by dusha.

Organization of this Book

This book has six parts, consisting of chapters and short stories. In terms like those my Omsk friends used, each chapter begins with something "in," affecting, "coming out of," or associated with some power of Russian, Soviet, or post-Soviet dusha.[11] Each chapter has its take on soul: situations and activities where dusha was important or often mentioned; categories, images, and tropes relating to it. In the first part I sketch the times, places, and conditions in which my Omsk friends were living. The second part examines things presented as "against" and "for" soul: first, a chapter on some ways in which the everyday world was discussed and treated as lousy and destructive; then a discussion of what might be good for soul and what was good about it. The third part, "Everyone Wants Something, but Only through Someone," touches not only on money and, as a friend called it, the exchange of potatoes but on many forms of what that friend called the exchange of human warmth in situations such as drinking together and figuring out who's with whom and who's like whom. The next part, "Authority," treats metaphysical, spatial, and political "bosses" in the late to

---

[11] "Soviet" and "post-Soviet" dusha are not common terms but an outgrowth of my research.

post-Soviet situation. In part five I continue exploring kinds of "together-ness" and coherence. Finally, I present a range of conclusions: connections between this study and previous thoughts on Russian "soul"; a philosophi-cal summary; and support for my claims that there are resonances between many non-Russian souls and those I describe in Russia.

This book is an ethnography of part of 1990s Russia and part of dusha; it is also a preliminary attempt to poke at some basic assumptions shared by many people who never call themselves "Russian" but assume they have souls.

O.M.S.K.

Omsk and Its Images

> Siberia. We have none of that natio—natio—natio—nalism.
> There were a lot of Tatars here. *A lot*. But they and the Russians
> lived in harmony [*dusha v dushu*].
>
> Anna Viktorovna, Omsk, 1992

Omsk is a major Siberian city, with a university, institutes, museums, theaters, orchestras, and huge factories. Because this chapter is meant just to sketch the scene, I shamelessly elaborate on some things (including history, population, environment, and dwellings) to the exclusion of others.

In 1579, the Stroganovs sent the Cossack Ermak on a campaign against the Sibir khanate, during which he passed through what later became Omsk region. In 1714, Peter I sent an expedition to southern Siberia to scout a location for a military stronghold; Omsk fortress was founded in 1716 near what is now the Kazakhstan border, at the confluence of the Irtysh and Om rivers. Omsk became a city in 1804. In 1892, railroad tracks were built east and west from Omsk. Today its agricultural region covers 53,000 very flat square miles.

Several friends joked that OMSK was an acronym, for *Otdalënnoe Mesto Ssylnikh i Katorzhnykh*, "Remote Site of Exiles and Hard-Labor Convicts." Another man earnestly related the name (derived from that of the river Om), to a mantra. A third reported hearing on the radio that soon, after the end of the world, it would be on the nearby banks of the Om that a new civilization arose.

Dmitri Mendeleev (1834–1907), a Tomsk-born Siberian, predicted an "irresistible eastward shift" of Russia's mean center of population. The "new center of Russia" was an imaginary spot just northeast of Omsk, at 55° N.

This imagery sparked a furious conservative reaction which continued after the scientist's death: " 'There was a Russia of Petersburg,' wrote one critic indignantly, 'but there can be no Russia of Omsk' " (Hauner 1990:152–53). On one hand, Omsk's provinciality and location in Asia are problematic for a "cultured" Russian city. On the other, being Siberian can be a source of pride; Siberia is imagined as an extreme version of much of what is considered Russian: greater expanses, warmer hospitality, etc., and so Omsk was often imagined as more "Siberian" than it is and as lying farther north than it does.

Provinciality is positively and negatively valued in both the capitals and the provinces: provincials were considered more soulful, less "civilized." Omsk residents (*omichi*) often portrayed their city as one of apolitical people absorbed in getting by. At a time of apocalyptic rumors about civil war it was joked that if there was a revolution the news would reach Omsk in several days. "Everything," one man said, coopting a remark about people who get jokes very slowly, "gets here later, like to a giraffe's head. In Moscow the slightest thing makes people go out on the street; they have someone to perform for. In Omsk no one hears you." Others said there would never be war in Omsk (at least for the rest of the summer) or that its role would "come later, like after the Revolution."

The revolution was quiet in Omsk, but in 1918, Admiral Aleksandr Kolchak (1873–1920), commander of the White Army in Siberia, took Omsk from the Soviets, intending to make it the capital of his White Russia. Omsk was retaken by the Red Army in 1919. Kolchak's plans for Omsk were a romantic theme during perestroika.

In 1905–11, when Stolypin encouraged peasant migration to Siberia, the population of Omsk region began to grow. During 1930–35, farms were collectivized; at one point the region had four hundred collective and State farms. During and after World War II, military factories were evacuated to Siberia and new ones built, as a result of which the city was closed to foreigners and its population increased more than tenfold (from 100,000) by its 275th anniversary in 1991, when the region was opened and State farms were incorporated.

There was a sharp increase in crime during perestroika. A 1997 Russian government report (Associated Press, May 1997) claimed that between 1989 and 1995 deaths rose by 40 percent in Russia and births dropped by 60 percent. A public prosecutor I interviewed, alleging a twofold rise in murders and attempted murders in Omsk region between 1981 and 1991, blamed "dusha, spiritual decline."

Omsk was hard to romanticize, which made its few legends important. A friend wrote in an excited letter that Jules Verne mentioned Omsk in a story. Dostoevsky's 1850–54 imprisonment in Omsk's "Dead House" is often described as the period when he came to know Russian soul through his suffering and his contact with the Russian people, the *narod*. His suffering in Omsk was often presented to me, as it is in the Omsk Dostoevsky Museum and in outside accounts, as the foundation for his soul's development from talent into genius: "All [his] creative work following . . . Omsk was . . . 'elevation into world symbols of his . . . experience acquired exactly there, in the world of outcasts' " (Leifer 1984, citing a Soviet literary critic). Dostoevsky apparently had a similar opinion. On being released from the Omsk stockade, he wrote his brother (February 1854) that "These years will not have been fruitless. . . . How many folk types I am bringing out . . . how many characters! . . . It is enough for volumes. What a strange people."

As the epigraph indicates, Omsk's population was heterogeneous.[1] A friend's mother was ethnic Ukrainian and his father Chuvash; their passports called them Russian. It had been desirable in interactions with the Soviet bureaucracy to be Russian by passport, and such things could sometimes be arranged, but many of these people considered themselves Russian in other ways as well. Though Soviet census figures are notoriously skewed, for lack of alternatives I am including some.[2] In 1989 the official population of Omsk region (city, towns, and rural areas) was 2,141,909 (1,148,485 in the city). By 1992, according to the regional statistician, the population had grown by 25,000. This growth continued as an influx of refugees from Central Asia offset losses of ethnic Germans, Jews, and others. After the city was officially "opened" to foreigners, increasing numbers of tourists, business people, technical specialists, and representatives of religious organizations appeared. Chinese came by train from Harbin on business or buying trips. Omsk began hosting an international marathon.

Names of villages and districts in Omsk region were often named for the resettled population, invoking other places in the former USSR. Villages were also often characterized by a salient group of residents: "a German village." A teacher in her forties said:

> I'd say that in Siberia there was, maybe, a concentration of culture—they exiled Decembrists here. Omsk was where a lot of exiles were sent. They stayed in Omsk. Later they developed Siberia, industrially, scientifically. Again the best people came here from the capitals. And they didn't get crude here, because they didn't have to fight so hard for their existence. These great expanses . . . that says a lot, a lot for Siberia.

Another teacher, now retired, Anna Viktorovna, a small, modest, spirited woman in whose kitchen I spent days, if not weeks, and whom I al-

---

[1] According to the speaker quoted in the epigraph, Omak managed its diversity well. The expression *"dusha v dushu"* (literally, dusha into dusha) is a common phrase meaning that people are "tight," get along "naturally." The idea that people get along "like fish in water" would be close.

[2] The census gives the regional Russian populations as 1,720,387, and German, Ukrainian, Kazakh, Belorussian, and Tatar as between 134,199 and 49,784. Reported Chuvash, Jewish, Estonian, Latvian, Mordvin, Polish, Armenian, and Azeri populations ranged from 2,000 to 5,600.

most never saw outside that kitchen, was describing the vastness of the Omsk region, stuck between two even larger spaces: to the south Kaza-khstan, to the north and east the rest of Siberia. She described it as a con-tinuum: steppe and forest steppe with their fine wheat fields; marshes and bogs, part of the world's largest connected swamplands, over two million square kilometers blanketing western Siberia with cranberries and lin-gonberries and people in high rubber boots (against cold and snakes) gath-ering them with combs; and finally, the taiga, with its pines, fir, cedars, and deciduous trees, including occasional birches and ashberries,[3] and its huge anthills, my height. She told me how a person's dusha doesn't lose its dukhovnost', spirituality, when it interacts with nature, how strawberries can be found near birch groves, how the vitamin-rich stone berry grows at the edge of wooded areas where sunlight comes in. As Anna Viktorovna was dutifully listing fur-bearing beasts in the forest: red squirrels (with brushes on their ears) that turn grey-white in winter; fox, lynx, bear, polar fox, hare (in winter white with black-tipped ears, grey in summer), moose, giant red mosquitoes, biting flies . . . an announcer on the radio rhythmi-cally enumerated great Russian writers. We both noticed and laughed long and hard.

I first saw the changing landscape Anna Viktorovna described to me one November when I traveled 297 km to Tara, a city of 40,000 founded in 1594. Driving north, we soon passed the dark, lush zone of resorts and pines in otherwise open steppe. Two-thirds of the way, the road winding up the west side of the Irtysh iced over. The opposite bank, where the taiga eventually begins, stood higher. People were ice fishing in tents, though, un-usually, the Irtysh had not yet completely "stopped." There were no bridges in the north. My companions talked about falling through the ice and about near-drowned children.

Times of Year

Fall is mushroom season. Evgeniia Pavlovna, another retired grand-mother, told me that Muscovites used to come to Omsk just to pick mush-rooms and berries, but that now it is too polluted. Mushroom picking is part of autumn conversations and later ones, when the prepared mush-rooms are offered at meals. Mushrooms are marinated and salted for at least forty days, the same amount of time after a death that wakes are held. Lara, a teacher in her forties and—though she did not love her new obliga-tion to grow, collect, and preserve food—a consummate provider, gave me

[3] Rowan or ashberry trees (*riabina*) can be orange, red, or "black-fruited." People use the berries for "high-vitamin" tea. I was told that one cannot eat city ashberries because they ab-sorb toxins so well.

dried mushrooms still on the thread. She had "more than she could ever use."

In the fall, banks of poplar down get deep. The air is full of it. It gets in one's eyes, nose, and mouth; people comment on the poplar being the stupidest possible tree to plant in a city. Then, by mid-October, you turn out your lights one evening and see that it is snowing out, hard. People say that if it doesn't snow on the Feast of the Veil (*pokrov'*; October 1 in the Julian calendar), it will be warm for two more weeks, though "Everything is so mixed up that probably these things don't hold any more."

Everyone is salting cabbage and going to the dacha to wrap up the trees and berry bushes so they don't die. By early November, you notice that the Omka is already solid, the last water path coated over; the Irtysh still has islands of ice floating north and barges going the other way.

During the early 1990s, a thick coat of ice covered the city streets and sidewalks all winter. People walked holding elbows. Young men, especially, slid more than walked. Some wore felt boots, though some found this countrified. Fur hats were worn by almost everyone. Omsk was the Siberian Cossack center; Cossacks occasionally wore uniforms, tall hats, and boots. Elaborate, internally lit ice-block castles and cities were built in parks, featuring giant Grandfathers Frost, granddaughters Snegurochka, and ice hills down which children and playful adults slid on a piece of cardboard if they had no sled and on their behinds if they had no cardboard. In the evening young people gathered around the New Year's tree and danced to loud Russian pop music from speakers on a truck.

After Christmas (January 7) comes Epiphany. The "Epiphany frosts," a cold snap, is awaited and discussed. On sunny, cold (at least −20° C) days, there might be a tender, gentle light—gentle because of snow, made high in the air and suspended in silver crystal clouds, sparkling thinly, light-dust. Cold weather is good; winter thaws were called a new, dirty phenomenon, unhealthy and menacing.

At one winter meal, a woman in her thirties playfully announced that she had to admit something: she prefaced it by saying that it was really Russian character (*kharakter*), genetics (*genetika*): they know they oughtn't to do it in Siberia, but children lick metal outside in the wintertime. Everyone started laughing about how in winter, "when it got so cold that the snot froze in our noses and birds fell out of the sky," knowing they shouldn't and that it would hurt, they would lick a doorknob, skate blade, or metal fence; and how, when their tongue stuck, they ran home with it bleeding and hanging down to *here* (somewhere in the chest area). The woman kept repeating that she still really wants to lick metal sometimes "for dusha."

Common winter birds were magpies, titmice, and sparrows. Very cold weather was hard on the littlest birds, fluffed very low in balls on the street, on vents, even on meat at the market.

In April the two-meter-tall *KHUI* (PRICK), written neatly by foot in the snow under a bridge, broke up.[4] It marked the onset of the annual north-bound (downstream) ice procession (*ledokhod*). People came to watch and maybe drink vodka, watching sunlight falling on ringing, crashing ice-bergs. If they passed at night, there was just din, moving glow, cold air blowing. "You watch and *rest.*" The swell, roar and tinkle of ice blocks nudging each other downstream makes you a little seasick, but calms you down.

Around late April, a cooling-off "always follows the *ledokhod.*" A few flakes of snow fall, the weather is clear and bright. On "Clean Thursday" some people clean their apartments. Pussywillows disappear after Willow (Palm) Sunday; roses and the first tulips are sold at underpasses.

One May Day, Zina and Andrei Orlov and I drove tiny cherry and male and female sea buckthorn[5] seedlings to their remote, newly acquired field on a dirt road. We saw a crested steppe bird, a lapwing, and holes on the road that boys try to flood gophers out of. We planted carrot seeds and onion bulbs, and "privatized" compost from an unmarked field. We found a wild apple tree and replanted it. They said if I planted trees I'd come back. We tied the tiny sticks to stakes with strips of rag, but the wind still bent them over. We stood the dog in tumbleweed smoke to de-tick him (en-cephalitis). He gets hormone tablets but he still jumped all over Zina.

People talked about leaves appearing as something that really mattered. Before the leaves opened one could go to birch stands, make campfires, and drink birch juice until one couldn't anymore. Like fresh water but fresher. Some people make kvass, a slightly fermented drink made with dark bread, out of birch juice. Birches look different in spring than in winter: there isn't that intolerable, inverted weightless white in white snow, grounded only by the darker sky. Embedded in varied gray and hay tones, though, their color-lessness still seems supernatural.

Outside the city, it is a long way between villages and towns. A man in his twenties cited a song: "Steppe and more steppe," to say how boring it was as opposed to trees (for the soul). Steppe is subtle; unlike mountains, it gets breathtaking slowly. Colors range from iridescent yellow-green strips to vast, pale, tender, even dry grayish-green fields with black crows. This stretches in no rush to horizon roughened by a line of trees to protect fields from the wind. The trees are bitter green black firs or pines or white birch,

---

[4] Khui, the standard "three-letter word" on fences and dirty vehicles, is more obscene than English glosses prick or cock, even in the 1990s, when a certain devaluation of such lexicons was afoot. A man enters a meat store and asks for beef. The clerk tells him that there is no meat but that she could sell him porcelain. The man points out that there is a sign on the front of the store that says "Meat." She answers that you can't always believe what you read: "In the yard of the building where I live there's a shed. On it is written *khui*. And what's inside? Fire-wood."

[5] Sea buckthorn (*oblepikha*), *Hippophae rhamnoides*. An orange berry that grows in prickly clusters on trees originally "from the East." It is prized for its "vitamins" and other qualities.

where berries and mushrooms grow. There are power lines and a quarry in all that flatness, where children swim and men fish with a net. If you know the landscape, you can pick out the solitary tree where the village your mother was born in stood until it became obsolete in the State-farm system and was plowed over. Lara and I, planting potatoes, saw feathery steppe grass, little purple irises called cuckoo's tears, and buttercups, called "chicken blindness," not to be kept in a house where hens sit on eggs.

I was walking home one light spring evening. Light hit the confluence of the two rivers so that the Irtysh was pale oxide green and the Omka clay brown. Suddenly, violent billows of dust made everything disappear, lungs and eyes ache, stiffened fabric, turned the evening into a hellish grey-brown glow. I thought it was the end. Nicknames for Omsk during spring and summer, funny in their irreverent resemblance to real town names like Petropavlovsk and Murmansk, were Vetropylsk (from *veter*, wind; and *pyl'*, dust) and Mukhosransk (flies and shit). I was told that dust storms were rare, but there was another the next day. "Nothing protects us from the steppes." Then it turned cool and rainy, mist blew around the barges and came into the city, and apple blossom, lilac, and bird-cherry (*cherëmukha*) perfumes took over.

For weeks people said that as soon as the bird-cherry flowered it would cool off. You cannot plant bird-cherry trees near a house, as the household head will die when the roots reach the house. The berries are hard; the brown, rich flour makes muddy pies and rough, flavorful cakes.

People walked to and from commuter boats with shovels, garden plants, and heavy sacks. Barges hauled mountains of lumber or coal; freighters with flammable tanks passed, decorated with both the Soviet hammer and sickle and the Russian tricolor. Tour boats circulated, at times the only place in town to buy beer. It was light until midnight, and campfires burned on the river beaches and islands; people bathed, men and boys fished thigh-deep. The restaurant door banged as drunk men and women came out to fight. At three A.M. a motorboat sped somewhere.

People sit for hours by the river and in parks. Grandmothers complain on benches. Wagtails wiggle their rears, pecking a dusty bald spot in the grass. Nearby, a scrap of paper's laborious beginning cursive dictates in neat trochaic feet: "If you farted once already, go ahead and fart again," a member of a class of Russian verse that includes: "If you took a crap, you maggot / pull the handle on the toilet." When I showed it to friends, they delightedly said I'd found genuine proof that the mysterious Russian soul was alive and well in today's youth.

Trash urns in parks have sparrows. Young and middle-aged couples kiss on benches, the woman on the man's lap. Drunks drink, sleep, or sit in pairs. Young men share cigarettes, sell beer or drink it. Women talk. Couples with baby carriages sit. People with dogs sit. Children draw on the sidewalk. In the morning an older person exercises stiffly and energetically.

People spread out clothes, toiletries, and hardware to sell; volumes of Dale Carnegie, detective stories, folk medicine, and astrology; Algerian figs, sweet rolls, white rolls with playful shapes or poppy seeds, mineral water, and, one day, little Central Asian apricots. A kiosk selling pirated cassettes thumps out an accented English "Don't gimme no shit." A scarved grand-mother blinks, taps a foot. Kiosks sell American flag T-shirts. Ads for insur-ance companies have supplanted most socialist slogans on buildings.

An Experimental City

> Omsk is an experimental city. They built an oil refinery and people survived; a plastics factory, a tire factory, did nuclear test-ing upstream, added a chemicals complex, some of us are still kicking . . . but it's OK—if there are still people left, in a year they'll gas them.
>
> Local joke

On a weekend or evening the air might suddenly become unbreathable. People outside at the time developed coughs and chest and throat pain the next day. This was a *vybros,* discharge from the factories. Stories also leaked out as to how discharges and accidents happened. In the summer the city filled with windless smoke from factories and burning taiga. Private car use was prohibited, windows closed. Children were sent out of town and whoever could leave did.

People boiled water for five minutes and let it settle before drinking it. "Raw water" was called a method of committing suicide. As purchased food might have been grown in toxic soil or be otherwise tainted, home-grown food was often announced to be "ecologically clean" because it had been grown upstream of the refinery or out in the country. The area was widely sprinkled with toxic dumps, however, and Omsk, in general, was downstream from the Kazakhstan testing grounds.[6] Vodka and certain mushrooms and berries were offered with the remark that they take radia-tion out of the system.

In May 1992 I wrote in my notes:

At 5:30 the other evening we all felt exhausted. My heart was pounding. Nadia and the kids came home, tired; there had been a tram accident with explosions, fallen lines, and fire. Grisha came and said that he had gotten tired and his heart pounded. He attributes it to an intuition of Nadia and the children's proximity to the accident. Others attribute it to sharp barometric and weather changes and to "pressure." Nosebleeds and headaches are often attributed to

---

[6] The theme of Soviet-era "experiments" often recurs in jokes like the one above: see Zi-noviev (1995), Banc and Dundes (1990:21).

"pressure" and "magnetic storms," though respiratory and throat problems are also always blamed on the factories and the powerful who abuse them. People tell me about vacations to beautiful barren places in Kazakhstan later found to be irradiated. Buildings built from stone quarried there reportedly stand deserted. Stories about children's blood, thyroid, and heart problems, coughs, nosebleeds and fainting, hair loss. Avoid getting rain on you. If you smoke, the air pollution bothers you less.

Once, driving by open land where the Soviet space shuttle had been tested, a man was telling me how secret that had all been. Now, on the contrary, details were being publicized "so people won't be afraid of what goes on out here. There are even mushrooms sometimes." I was so used to hearing about the "frighteningly" abundant mushroom harvest of the previous autumn that it took me a while to understand that he meant mushroom clouds.

I complained to Zhenia in the village about the city air. He said it was impossible to live in the city, but added that people had a hell of a lot more to think about than their health: "Keep going just one more year. Only," he said, "when the red rooster pecks do you think about it a little."[7]

Places That Should Warm Dusha

> People are saying dusha's been trivialized, cheapened. If a person grows up in a little room, and in our country it's good if he *has* a room, it's hard for his dusha to spread its wings, to grow them.
> Mila, Omsk, 1992

Some notes on dwellings. In central Omsk there were fine examples of nineteenth-century architecture and a few modern experiments, but apartment buildings were like Soviet apartment buildings everywhere. In 1990s Omsk they stood from three to twelve stories tall. Like houses, they were built or placed so as to create a yard (*dvor*). Yards contained benches, trees, cats, garbage, birds, grandmothers, children, and metal frames for beating rugs.

With the exception of communal apartments (where kitchen, bathroom, and toilet were shared by more than one family unit; see Boym 1994, Sinyavsky 1988:165–68), uncommon in Omsk, apartments of the wealthier and poorer, more and less powerful, even in 1994, still did not differ very much. Virtually all the buildings were deteriorating, with reeking, crumbling, filthy entryways. Many stairways in working-class neighborhoods had flat metal railings made lacy by negative spaces out of which parts for something or other had been stamped in a local factory. Elevators of most

---

[7] He mixed two expressions; when a *fried* chicken pecks, things have gotten bad; the *red* rooster pertained to arson perpetrated on the prerevolutionary landed gentry.

buildings were energetically broken and vandalized. Apartment interiors, on the contrary, were cozy, with a standard range of wardrobes, tables and chairs, beds, sofa beds, wall units, refrigerators, freezers, and TVs. High double windows with transoms were associated with both fresh air and deadly drafts. Most apartments had at least one balcony for drying clothing and plastic bags on lines and for storing food in winter. Wealthier individuals and the elite had more frozen food on the balcony and were beginning to have more appliances.

Water, particularly hot water (heated centrally, by district), was cut off for indeterminate periods. You might turn on the tap anytime and get only the hollow groan of Omsk's empty insides. Or something cool, cloudy, and rusty. When the water was off, there might be a pot for dipping water from a canister into the toilet to flush it.

Huge city neighborhoods of old wooden houses looked like villages, except for looming, not-so-far-off apartment blocks and tram lines running through unpaved streets. Their fenced yards contained sheds for animals, wood and coal for the stove, gardens, outhouses, bathhouses. Some houses had carved window frames and ornamental trim. One was carved with six-pointed stars, another with gargoyles, another with hammers and sickles. Many 1990s apartment dwellers had grown up in houses, and the parents of some still lived there.

"Private houses" in and out of the city had unheated entry rooms where shoes were removed and food stored. Zhenia's village house included a sitting (TV) room, two bedrooms, a kitchen, and a bathroom with hot but no cold water; the outhouse was in the yard. The family pumped water from a communal well into a canister. In summer water was pumped for the cows and pigs too; in winter the animals drank melted snow or water bled from house radiators with a hose run through a hole in the wall.

All kitchens featured a wall-mounted radio receiver. In one Omsk home there was also a plastic owl with the hour glowing digitally in one eye and the minutes in the other. I suspect it was not Soviet. An Omsk factory that during World War II had made tank clocks afterwards began encasing them in jewel-cut plastic; these were common. In kitchen cabinets were cotton sacks of flour and dried bread. During the winters of 1991 and 1992 there was rarely oil available and lines were common for black, "grey," sour, and white bread. Store-bought white dough, flour, and bread, often not as white as they could have been, were daily called disgraceful; drying bread in preparation for famine was discussed daily. A bowl sometimes collected bones for street dogs. Tiny scraps, dirt, and bits of toilet paper were thrown out during 1991–92, but nothing else.

Half-liter, liter, and three-liter clear and pale green glass jars, some with plastic lids, were visible through people's net and plastic shopping bags and in shops. The widespread use of small 100-ml jars was recent, indicative of the new value of such miserly quantities. The jars had come with food in them, but by 1991 they were brought to shops to receive food into. In homes jars held fermenting wine or liquor, jam or pickles, pickled tomatoes or mushrooms, leftovers of any kind, juice, milk, herring. Sometimes on a kitchen table there would be a big jar containing "mushroom" drink (*grib*), a layered, growing fungus into which sweet tea was poured, fermented, and enjoyed by children.

Living situations were seen as created or aggravated by "our System" (*nasha sistema*). In Soviet society residence was determined by kinship in conjunction with individual desires for privacy in interaction with "our System." Who lived where in a family depended to a large extent on where there was room. People got apartments from relatives, through work, by bribe, connections, or by waiting ten or fifteen years on a list. A waiting list is called an *ochered'*; *ochered'* is also a queue of people, "the living image of the Soviet way of life" (Sinyavsky 1988:153–89); one's *ochered'* is also one's turn in a game or an exchange circuit. Apartments were allotted according to a "norm" of nine square meters per person; families were entitled to an extra four, but apartment shortages led to epic machinations.

Legally exchanging apartments within or between cities was at fever pitch in the 1990s. Families often traded two apartments for one, one for two, and involved goods, services, or other aspects of their social persons. The issue of control of apartments had many implications. For example, persons without local residence permits and their "own" apartments did not, during perestroika's darkest days, receive ration coupons, and thus were multiply poorer.

Maria Fëdorovna, a retired seamstress, had an apartment near the petroleum refinery. In summer one didn't dare open the windows of these two tiny rooms with one bed and one sofa bed, a closetlike kitchen, a bathroom, no phone. When I visited, seven family members lived there, down from nine. Maria Fëdorovna lamented that her daughter, who lived there with her children, had to sleep on the floor. But, she added, there was always room for more.

Although rumors circulated that the system of residence permits (after 1932, one's passport had to be registered with the local police; see Corten 1992:118) had been outlawed, it was fully operational, and legal rights to the best possible fragment of apartment were still very important capital. A woman living with her parents and husband in a two-bedroom apartment registered with her husband's mother so the mother could obtain a larger one. Afraid that her daughter-in-law would steal her new apartment, the mother-in-law dropped her from the registration. My acquaintance described as terrifying and injurious to dusha, not her mother-in-law's betrayal, but the amputation of an official apartment in which she had never planned to live.

When one couple moved to an outlying town, they failed to retain control of their apartment. Their daughters later moved back to Omsk; one shared a small apartment with her husband, children, and an unpleasant stranger.

They hoped to eventually divorce this roommate by trading the four-room apartment for two smaller ones. The other daughter lived in a dormitory. The dorm administration had calculated that three beds would fit in the small room, so she had to pay three rents to have one room to herself. Rent was negligible until 1993, but then, suddenly, she was expected to pay her entire salary in rent.

Byt, everyday life, the topic of Chapter 2, was often considered dusha's arch enemy; apartments were one of everyday life's most painful aspects. "More often than not, *byt* means financial worries, lack of apartments." As apartments could be emblematic of what was wrong with Soviet life, it is not surprising that the powerful's apartments were the object of news and gossip. As his first example of injustices powerful people may commit, a public prosecutor described a manager taking a subordinate's good apartment. In 1994, an outraged friend told me about former Party functionaries who, after only a few months in jobs snatched from those who were more qualified but less well-connected, were wealthy enough to buy apartments.

Also in 1994, people told me that Zadornov had been their favorite comedian until he got an apartment in Yeltsin's building. At that point, many people told me, they "stopped liking him." Zadornov's apartment's clear message undermined his authority as one who lives like everyone else and can speak for them. As late as 1997, a pop star was accusingly asked in a TV interview if the rumor that he had moved out of his working-class apartment was true. He tried to defend his actions as not separating him from the *narod* (the people), but was embarrassed and did poorly.

The house of an Omsk artist had been made into a museum furnished in prerevolutionary splendor. Its curator told me that "Home is a place that should warm dusha," but that homes had become wretched and poverty-stricken. A woman who accompanied me there, however, later complained about the materialistic energy people put into making their apartments cozy and warm, and how soulless it all was nevertheless!

Another friend said that "people were promised that before the year 2000 there would be apartments . . . and now there are these fears of losing them to privatization. People worked for apartments . . . dreamed only about getting an apartment." The Soviet system was blamed for the apartment situation, in turn associated with dushevnyi deterioration: as Mila's words in the epigraph imply (I introduce Mila in the next chapter), "If a person grows up in a little room . . . it's hard for his dusha to spread its wings." It was axiomatic that friends could drop in anytime, but the hyperbolic lack of privacy complicated this almost as severely as it did sex lives. Cramped, deteriorating, and absent apartments injure dusha. A married woman in her thirties, referring to marriages entered into for the sake of a residence permit or access to an apartment, said: "Any marriage that isn't for love is prostitution. If you live with someone for an apartment, well, that's what you can be bought for."

A word about dachas, "summer homes." When many people built dachas they had seen them as places to rest. Now they only went there to garden. In Omsk, many families had acquired land (often more than one plot) in the last few years. Extra-light titanium shovels made from by-products of military plane production had been inexpensive, but in the late 1980s they disappeared, out of spite, just as people started having to relearn agriculture. Some city families kept poultry and other livestock in villages with relatives or friends. There was a lively exchange of knowledge and seeds. Almanacs, church calendars, informational booklets for sale at kiosks, and regular newspaper columns featured agriculture, herbal medicine, and gardening tips.

One friend's dacha was five minutes' drive from Omsk's center, on a hillside of muddy alleys and shacks near those built by ex-convicts who, when released, staked out land. Such neighborhoods were called Kopai-Gorod (literally, Dig-City), Port-Artur, and Sakhalin (far-eastern ports, referring to a place on the distant outskirts). Her parents had built the two small rooms, outhouse, and rain-tank shower on 600 square meters of land they claimed near a dump.

Evgeniia Pavlovna, a widow and grandmother, now retired, was spending more time at her dacha than in her Omsk apartment. Her daughter explained that Evgeniia Pavlovna had lived through the war, and like many of her generation, was a tireless worker who found an optimistic twist to everything and could not understand those who didn't share her enthusiasm. Her dacha had a porch, a kitchen, and two large rooms, and was surrounded by a garden, a separate summer kitchen, an outhouse and tank shower, sheds for chickens and pigs, and a cellar for potatoes.

Zina and Andrei Orlov had 600 square meters with dacha, bathhouse, outhouse, shed, compost heap, and troughs for rainwater and fertilizer fermentation and dilution (pigeon droppings). They were there almost every day after work in the summer. There were two trees in the yard: a little birch they hadn't had the heart to pull up—"We felt sorry for it. Let it grow"—and a little pine tree that Andrei had brought "for dusha" from his birthplace.

In 1992, Anna Viktorovna, her son Grisha, and his wife, Nadia, had temporary use of a tiny strip of garden land in the city. When I went there with them Grisha made a romantic fuss about growing one's own food, yanked a few weeds, and said it'd be easier when the weeds got taller. When he wandered away Anna Viktorovna bitterly commented on her son's character.

Grandmothers

As I introduce a number of grandmothers in this book, let me briefly focus on them. Age made one a grandmother, so any woman could be a grandmother for a large part of her life. During the Soviet era, the general use of familiar kin terms (e.g., *synok*, sonny) with strangers declined, but "Grand-mother" was hardier. On streets and in stores, when women were called by the impersonal *zhenshchina* (woman), young women *devushka* (girl), and men *muzhchina* (man), women over a certain age were *babushka*; "Grand-mother." All sisters of a grandparent might be *babushki*, as could any older woman if the relationship was intimate or much time was spent together.

If you were waiting in line for a bus, a scarved grandmother might come and make herself a place in front of you, pushing you from the curb with her back. On the bus, a younger person might get up: "Take a seat, Grand-mother." Or the younger person might not get up, a situation for which it seemed as if grandmothers sharpened their elbows. They had loud fights with people about respect. In 1992, I waited for a bus to the village next to a tiny babushka. She carried a tall branch as a walking stick and was trans-porting an enormous mesh bag of wooden crates. Wedged between net and crates was a worn copy of Esenin's poetry.

A college student described with great tenderness how his grandmother watched all three airings of every episode of the wildly popular Mexican soap opera *The Rich Also Cry*. For a long time, he said, Granny didn't un-derstand that the serial was not a documentary. She was "supernaturally so-ciable" and always got into conversations with strangers and brought home all the news, but she was so nervous about inflation that everyone was hid-ing prices from her.

When older people saw the new prices they stood in shock. Other times they loudly scolded the salesperson (who had nothing to do with the price) for being shameless. Babushki spent hours packed in line. "Babushki who never needed politics before are talking about it in food lines." "No money for a burial" and rumors about recycled coffins were big issues from the 1991 Pavlov currency reform through the following years' inflation.

At a school I saw an exhibit of paintings of grandmothers as witches, princesses, fashion models, and pirates. Some grandmothers knit socks and, at the market, told you how warm and well-made they were; if you bought them, they told you to wear them in good health; if you bought them easily, they kept persuading you after you had paid. What they and grandfathers sold at underpasses went from sunflower seeds by the glass and frozen car-nations to lilacs, to lilies of the valley, to peony buds that became huge white swans, and later, to roses, onions, and radishes.

A babushka's work included cooking, cleaning, shopping, and child care. During my retired friend Anna Viktorovna's terminal illness she secretly wept that she was unneeded and useless, and then proceeded to cook, clean, and care for the children. One whining babushka was brusquely shut up in the presence of guests by her daughter's husband. When Anna Viktorovna would try to explain something to me, her son Grisha might yell, "Shut up, Mama, you don't know what you're talking about." Some grandmothers were bitter and petty; many were hospitable, spirited, good-natured matriarchs. Most folk healers I heard of were village grandmothers. One in Omsk region reportedly healed by most obscenely cursing the illness.

Two Tours of Omsk, Winter 1992

Dasha and I started at what is called Kolchak's House, in reference to the Siberian commander of the White Army who briefly made Omsk his capital in 1918. It was really the merchant Batiushkin's House, but she calls it Kolchak's, as do most people, she said, because it's interesting. The steps on underpasses were atrocious, iced ramps; everyone was falling. We entered the park and headed toward the old fortress boundaries. The second fortress was built in 1768 where, in the early 1990s, the park, swimming pool, and abandoned heating plant stood. The fortress' Tara Gates (by the KGB building) were torn down in 1937 because "the elite who live there didn't like bums hanging out and swearing." They were rebuilt around 1990. Dasha showed me the Tobol'sk Gates through the park; on them were the dates they were built (1791–94) and a plaque to Dostoevsky.

Another time, Aleksei and I started at the shopping center and cut into uneven dirt roads with wood houses, some with beautifully carved ornament, some rotten or burnt out. A woman carrying buckets of water on a yoke was first, then others appeared with water canisters on sleds. Men with missing limbs. Children sledded down iced inclines in narrow passageways between houses. The colors were stunning; where there was still paint, houses were leaf and other greens, blues with white trim, with a few red, orange, or rust-colored roofs. Yards littered with horse skulls and rotting food had signs nailed to the gate calling them examples of sanitary excellence. The signs themselves were disintegrating, as were signs about small bad dogs that stuck their noses under fences lined with homemade barbed wire and bayed. Dilapidated mailboxes and shells of cars were covered with chalked comments. A fence of metal bedsteads had been erected around a tiny fir tree.

We walked into a yard for a panorama of the city. There, down through a dirty window sunk to ground level, was a pile of books. Deeper, darker, at a table with teacups, sat two women. One came out in a poor housedress and asked who had sent us; she had a sick son and lived in fear this place would be demolished.

We came to a Jewish graveyard whose decrepit gravestones were each fenced in with wood or metal factory by-products. Some markers were stone, some metal or wood from which the letters were gone; they had photos, five-pointed stars, six-pointed stars. One sheet-metal monument had rusted and become intertwined with a young tree of the same color. Stuck on fence posts were plastic flowers, glass jars, shoes. Roughly carved or painted Hebrew, Yiddish, and Russian inscriptions ranged from names and dates to heartfelt wishes, laments, and formulae.

PART II

AGAINST AND FOR DUSHA

CHAPTER TWO

In Public Transportation and in the Soul

You call this life?

"Daily life" and "being" are opposites, like little and big, trivial and sublime.

Sinyavsky 1988:159

Most everything now is with a minus sign. It seems like we're not *living* but *living through* something.

Lara, 1992

One 1992 day in an Omsk bus, a huge older woman in a tattered coat was yelling about how well *negri* dress in America. A woman's hip was cutting into me. A stranger with whom, despite ourselves, I was holding hands on the bar was grimacing from a position in which he was practically suspended. I was about to begin formulaically asking those near me if they were getting out soon (so as not to miss my stop near the food shops), when a reeling little man reeking of alcohol crammed himself in with a disintegrating bale of manure. The manure turned out to be only tobacco (stolen from the factory? received in lieu of salary?), but it still crumbled and stuck all over our boots. The young woman behind me started shaking with laughter and, though I was in pain, I did too. An old man shrieked that I should stand quietly and hold my jacket lower. His cry released a vicious argument somewhere in the mass of flesh and bones punctuated by discomforts. I smiled at him. Shock, exhaustion, and hurt floated up through his face's bitter meanness.

"You call this living?" Is this "life?" In this chapter I begin to examine what was "against" and "for" soul by looking at how the everyday world was discussed and treated as lousy, soulless, and murderous. I present these descriptions and their genres in detail. I touch on "Russian" suffering and habits of organizing what was seen as *this* world in opposition to various other worlds, and various meanings of the "real" world and of the world people "lived" for. This leads to descriptions of very specific kinds of life, soul, time, and space.

The few of my friends who had cars used them only to go to their gardens and potato fields and to visit village relatives. How awful public transportation was and how awful people were *in* it was remarkably often the first evidence people offered to illustrate the degradation, affront, and injury of their world. A writer, Lena, told me: "You get on the bus—negative energy—someone shoves you—'you damned communist!' Like that, to the point of utter idiocy." When the topic was offenses perpetrated by enemies such as "this life of ours," such recitals were impassioned, seemed inspiredly composed on the spot, and were remarkably uniform. Ries (1997:84) discusses passages in conversation when a speaker would "enunciate a series of complaints, grievances, or worries about problems, troubles, afflictions, tribulations, or losses, and then often comment . . . with a poignant rhetorical question . . . a sweeping, fatalistic lament about the hopelessness of the situation, or an expressive . . . sigh of disappointment and resignation." Suffering is the most immediate association to the notion and experience of Russian soul and has been discussed and written about extensively (see Ries 1997; Boym 1994:29–41). I will follow laments I heard in buses, food lines, and kitchens as a way to begin mapping out images, dimensions, and rules of the world in which 1990s "Russian" "souls" lived.

People told me that a soul enters a child's body, making it alive. This tenet pertaining to any soul was recited calmly, a bloodless anti-Party line, unlike passionate (but also dogmatic) accounts of Russian soul. In its own way, though, Russian dusha was exactly about specific kinds of *life* and *non-life*. These kinds of life and non-life related to opposition between the soul and various "enemies"; between soulful and routine, "this" and "other" worlds, Russia and the West, ascetic and bourgeois attitudes. This in turn relates to how dusha's enemies are felt to degrade, imprison, constrict, coerce, and crush, "killing" space and time. People attributed certain ways of feeling ill to a "pressure" that was not simply blood, barometric, or any other clearly defined pressure. This is all related to experiences of and talk about suffering. An interesting thing about pain—it is said to awaken, develop, *and* "murder" soul.

In suffering Russians are assumed to be similar. Complaining communally affirmed and reproduced that. Complaints were often about how *They* and *our life* force us to live, about what we have lost and are losing, about impotence and lack of control. Complaining becomes a way to invoke and appropriate that cruel, ruthless power in the form of depth and soul.[1]

---

[1] See Ries 1997 on these themes during perestroika and Steinberg (forthcoming) on them at the time of the revolution.

An acquaintance in his thirties grew up in a tiny village. He said, in defiant critique of the discourse of suffering, that people moan all season about how much work they have to do. Then they get it done in two days and start moaning about next season's work. "Complaining," he said to me, over tea he made in his attic workspace using a heating element and a series of glasses, "comes from a shortage of real interaction. It's a surrogate for communication. It's pouring out your soul like a child to its mother. Everyday life is a mess; people relate to it passively; they turn sour and hope they'll be pitied." Middle-aged women lamented "this System, where a person has no one to complain to." In other words, he implied, complaining is just complaining.

But complaining, rhapsodizing about soul, pondering the meaning of life and suffering were formally similar, shared certain implications, and were often conflated in everyday talk and understandings. Some friends claimed that when suffering unites people, as it is said to have done during World War II, souls opened. But 1990s stinginess, difficulty, disorder, and the new spirit of competition were said to preclude traditional, dushevnyi kindness. Sometimes a distinction was made between deep, great suffering, which, if it does not "kill" dusha, tempers and purifies it, and annoying, petty suffering that just dissipates and fouls. But these aren't objective categories. Much depends on the sufferer and the offense in question.

To return to my squashed crosstown bus trek, I did manage to get out and buy bread. At the dairy store I joined people who were being mean, complaining, and holding places in several lines at once. A stranger asked: "Bread—how much?" She expressed shock at my answer, then simultaneously bemoaned how low We'd been driven and cattily implied that perhaps *I* was not *We* if I could afford that kind of bread. Eventually, after futile attempts at other errands, I returned to Zina Orlova's apartment on foot rather than attempting to take another bus.

It was the season of the *ledokhod*—tinkling, crashing slabs of ice drifting north, at first white local icebergs, then worn-down, filthy Kazakhstan and "Chinese" slabs that boys tried to ride. Dogs jumped on too; Zina could recite the age and breed of each dog that had drowned this and last year. Another topic of outrage and rumor that April was a typed, anonymous order that had appeared on apartment building doors ingeniously hinged with tacked-down strips of tire that swung the door shut automatically. The notice said: "*We urge you* to spend Saturday cleaning up" filth exposed in the yard by the melting snow.

Unpaid working Saturdays, compulsory voluntary manifestations of enthusiasm, what Lenin called the "school of communist work relations," had formerly taken place this time of year in preparation for Lenin's birthday. Now that season was confused with Willow Sunday's swollen pussywillow branches and fumbling exchange of religious data, and with windowsills of baby tomato plants being nurtured from seeds. Some people replanted the seedlings at their dachas when they found time, but Zina, an engineer in her forties, had to be more careful:

> Formerly we planted only on "female" days—Friday, Saturday and Wednesday—but now we have to learn to pay attention to the lunar calendar too. We didn't know any better before. It's become much too complicated. You can't plant when the moon is in an inauspicious sign such as Aquarius.

She'd do it if she had to, but she tried to avoid doing anything to plants unless the moon was right.

A corpse killed by a car lay alone, dirty and blue, legs twisted and crossed. Police chatted nearby. I saw that a second anonymous notice scrawled on quadrille paper had appeared on the door: the water would be turned off in a few hours. Zina got home late from work because the body was blocking buses. The posted notices evoked for her the obscene degradation and affront, (*obida*) of "our life." "In this country it's impossible to make plans." She had to do laundry before Easter made washing a sin. "Is there filth like this in America?" "Would they shut off the water like this?" To top it off, she said, she had seen the neighbors' child on the balcony when she came in; "It's bad for children to watch the dying. All sorts of things are happening; dusha is separating from the body."

We filled pots and tubs with orange tap water until it abruptly stopped, while she complained, holding the thought of that bureaucratic "*we urge you*" in clenched teeth and shaking it ("... illegal! ... immoral!") like her stunning pedigreed dog shook rats.

Living Through Things, Emotion, Soul Pain, and Indifference

Russians have been said to have a "need to suffer," and Russia has been called a country of suffering (Dostoevsky 1980 [1873]:36; Ries 1997:83; Rancour-Laferriere 1995:2–3). Though the strong noun for suffering is *stradanie*, and to suffer is *stradat'*, in the 1990s I more often heard reference to *perezhivanie*. *Perezhivanie* is living *through* things, pouring your soul into them, suffering, caring, feeling. Though *perezhivat'/perezhivaniia* could mean, neutrally, to experience / experiences, my retired teacher friend Anna Viktorovna, who lived not far from Zina, told me that to live (*zhit'*) is to endure, suffer (*perezhivat'*), similar to *bolet ' dushoi*, to feel pain with dusha. I heard soul called *mesto perezhivaniia*, the place where emotions were experienced. "This" world, Russia, and Omsk were also discussed as places of living through, places where one goes through a lot.

An Omsk actor told me that Russian actors prefer their directors' cruel, dictatorial rudeness to foreign directors' politeness. When a person screams at you, he said, you can at least see that there's dusha, that he *cares*. Women whose husbands beat them may say: "If he beats me, it means he loves me." This is extreme, but not rare. It reflects a premise of Russian soul, that the West is cold, dispassionate, indifferent, *ravnodushnyi* (lit. even-souled, a synonym for "soulless").

Although use of *dusha* increased during glasnost, when issues it traditionally dealt with were forefronted, many younger people I interviewed initially claimed to find soul pain an old-fashioned, embarrassingly naive idea, passé, lacking in irony, something they'd transcended. But even people in that mode would confirm the justice of the proverb "To live [through] life is not to walk through a field." That is, not straight, simple, or painless. Words like *toska* (yearning and monotonous anguish; see Wierzbicka 1992) and *gore* (grief, sorrow), long used unself-consciously, now (as a result of increasing influence of non-Slavic categories, the idea that a market economy necessarily entails loss of dusha, and/or, perhaps, as a result of soul loss) were not used as freely by some.

Scathingly ironic and parodic uses of *dusha* could, however, become less ironic or parodic in a flash. It's so easy to mistake a feeling of ironic distance for the ability to create subversive parody! In such cases, the sense that one is safely outside the trite spirit of a word, song, or style ends up serving simply as license to engage in it. It's so easy to squander one's critical impulses like this, by not knowing what they are and are not capable of.

Lara, the teacher in her forties with whom I planted potatoes in the previous chapter, sat with me in her small living room over tea. Quietly and gently, she dismissed soul pain, *dushevnaia bol'*, as old-fashioned: "That *used* to be done. The eighteenth and nineteenth centuries are full of examples of people, usually women, dying of wounds to dusha." Then, without missing a beat or changing her tone, she launched into a discussion of her own and her friends' soul pain: "Dusha gets in the way of business. I feel it, yes . . . physical pain . . . It starts, unexpectedly, suddenly, and I can't get control of it; pain squeezes out all hope, dusha sinks into darkness . . . it passes, of course." Anna Viktorovna's son Grisha, a craftsman in his thirties and a central voice in this book, said on tape in their kitchen that "you sometimes can't say what's torturing you . . . dusha is an internal indicator. Something inside pinches, clenches, contracts. Dusha. It passes, naturally."[2]

In a story, *Pripadok*, "The Fit" or "An Attack," Chekhov (1985:80) describes a student's attack of soul pain:

All his attention was focused on the pain in his soul . . . blunt . . . undefined, like sad anguish, the most extreme fear, and despair. He could . . . show where it was: in his breast, under his heart; but it was impossible to compare it with

[2] I heard many references to inevitable passing of soul pain; the following excerpt from Chekhov is another. This characterizes particularly serious accounts of soul pain and implies that "soul pain" can be experienced either physically or *as* physical pain is experienced.

anything . . . Only two thoughts did not irritate him: one—that . . . he had the power to kill himself, the other—that the pain would not last longer than three days.

Soul pain was the legitimate, strong response of a "live" dusha to some stimulus. Chekhov's student's pain began when he noticed that prostitutes to whom he had spoken, though socially and morally fallen, were "*alive . . . they are alive.*" Often the first example people offered of soulful suffering was empathy. Empathy is a feeling that one allows to enter one even if that hurts.

Mila was in her thirties, unmarried, often depressed and often fantastically spirited and light. She earned a virtually nonexistent salary working in an office and lived in one room. Once I found her at her desk with a tired headache around her eyes. Her boss was out of town on one of his trips to China to buy "rags" to sell, such as down coats "probably with bugs inside."

When he was gone the office building seemed less brightly lit, calmer; things were not actually "better," but everyone had a little time for dusha, talking over tea or doing work on the side. Mila's talk that day was sprinkled with a full range of uses of *perezhivanie*:

> It seems to me as if dusha's here, and I show somewhere in the area of the heart. That means, it means that, on one hand . . . it exists independently of how your head works . . . And it characterizes you. That is, whatever condition it's in, that's some sort of human quality of you. If you look at the outer layer of things, at public transportation, it's as if the way we live today is absolutely counterindicated for dusha. Except for destruction it brings nothing to dusha. Our everyday life—I—in my youth—I suffered [*perezhivala*] greatly that I was born in this time. Seriously. Because it seems to me that by my bent, my temperament, by the way people suffered—lived through [*perezhivali— prozhivali*], rather, their lives, the nineteenth century is much closer to me. I somehow felt that . . . by my constitution—how I go through [*perezhivaiu*] various events, I was not contemporary, that is, I can't always do it all quickly. It demands inhuman efforts from humans. Everything connected with empathy [*soperezhivaniem*], with the pace of living through things [*temp prozhivaniia*], dusha can't *live* at such speeds. . . . This is not a normal life for dusha. It's every person's right to live, understanding that every moment is precious, even a moment of suffering [*stradanii*]. Although I do not love to suffer, and when I fall into a state of suffering [*perezhivaniia*] I find it destructive . . . I suffer [*perezhivaiu*] that I am living in this time. By the way I suffer, I am a nineteenth-century person. I read that today a person suffers in one day as much as a nineteenth-century person suffered in his whole life.

Mila is implying both that she feels too much and that people are going through both much more and much less than they used to (they *survive* more but don't *live* through it).

Pain and joy are both related to dusha, but differently. A college student

me as "the basis of a person, capable of suffering."
sha and suffering are the same sort of girlfriends as
get by without each other but for some reason they
ha is tempered and perfects itself through suffering,
gave us dusha for that alone."
description, most people I interviewed implied that
if it never suffered. I was even told that "It's easy
y life, routine), and dusha are incompatible, but
would hardly know that dusha exists. Only when
do we notice dusha alive in there. . . . They are
ngs out the other." Lara said (in her living room,
ere discussing soul pain) that "when dusha hurts,
hurts [pointing to her chest]; at that moment you
u acknowledge you have it." As the poet Marina
y Wierzbicka 1989:51): "To be pierced *means* to

The   Perpetual Loss

When time was scarce or stuffed full of what felt meaningless, people said soul was perishing. This is one of what I began to see as diseases of *time*. The more I looked at narratives about "this mess of ours" and "this life of ours," the more I saw them as descriptions of ravaged, perverted time and space. Like Venedikt Erofeev's (1990) Venichka, trapped on a train between Petushki, which he is repeatedly too unsober to catch, and Moscow, the center of which he also never manages to reach, much of the day people were nowhere nameable, moving from here to there, or stuck in a sort of nationwide gridlock if they found a line to stand in or if what they needed depended on someone else or on disintegrating infrastructure. People got salary raises, but the cash to pay them did not arrive, not even the initial paperwork required to request the cash had come, and the entity responsible for it all had become unclear. The friction on the path to even simple goals was greater than most people's power to overcome it.

Pride at making a fine meal or figuring out how to refill a disposable lighter was tempered by bitterness: "Look at what we have to spend our time on. *This* is the miserable level of our victories, when dusha craves something utterly different." "How degrading," Zina Orlova told me one day at dinner: "Educated people, professors, operetta singers, have no time to pursue their souls' interests because they have to garden and clean streets" splattered with, as Anna Viktorovna's son's coworker Masha, a craftswoman and mother of two, iambically burst out, *kharchki, smorchki / oplëvano, oblëvano*: "hawkers, snotters, spit up, barfed up."

The fallen, revolting *now* did not begin with perestroika. In 1914, a coal miner wrote that workers needed, more than anything, "more free time . . . for one's own intellectual development" (Steinberg, forthcoming). But many people in the 1990s told me that the past was better. For three years I heard that last year was paradise compared to this year. For three years I heard that "Even during the Stalin era and famine, people pulled together, helped. Now they push each other away." A current quip was *Zhili byly zhili*: Once upon a time, we lived.

Oleg was a businessman in his late twenties. I first interviewed him at his office the day after we were introduced. We sat by a low table and he offered me a Leningrad Porcelain Factory cup of a chemical luxury that was sold as Brazilian freeze-dried coffee and that nearly made me pass out whenever I drank it. He also offered me sugar, another luxury. Oleg had a very earnest look when he told me that the country and people were in a very, very big crisis. Not just in society but inside everyone. On the street, in public transportation, their eyes were empty. "I don't think anyone laughs anymore."

An apocalyptic 1991 complaint was exactly that things had become so bad that for the first time, including World War II and the Stalin era, there were no new jokes. I want to point out that whether or not perestroika actually cramped joke production and dissemination (Yurchak [1997:22–23] claims that it did), the *image* of jokes' absence was important. Joking was seen as laughter in the face of tragedy, and so, like complaining, it reinforced awareness of the present as spoiled. Alleging that even joking had died was one-upsmanship over all past simply formulable sufferings.

The future and/or the past, or neither, was bright. But talk about the present was dominated by a voice that, as Crone writes (1978:27), spoke of "the degradation of art, the dissolution of morality, patriotism, the Church, literature, and human sensitivity . . . [that] sounds [a] note of . . . inability to cope with [events'] incessant onslaught." This voice makes statements "sweeping, brash, apocalyptic, tragic" such as "The very soil of 'our time' is spoiled, poisoned . . . it grabs at every bad root and brings forth abundant fruits from it. But it kills the good roots." Crone (ibid.:12) also quotes the poet Aleksandr Blok on the "unremitting sense of catastrophe in the hearts of people of recent generations."

If the theme of a split between high spiritual and low practical concerns is ancient, so is that of impending apocalypse. A Soviet-era joke had it that "Lenin said Russia was at the edge of a precipice; now we have leapt forward." The peculiar eternal "recentness" or imminence of catastrophe and loss is striking. Descriptions of daily hardships sometimes targeted things people had only begun doing, but as often reformulated as fresh tragedies things people had always had to do. Much education and culture were said to have been lost during the Soviet era; but *now,* even kindness, social intercourse, and people's economic, temporal, and spiritual ability to offer hospitality, basic aspects of dusha, were finally being lost.

Dusha was portrayed as dying, deadened, disappearing, distanced, groggy, covered, encapsulated; and what was said about dusha was said about Russia.[3] In a proud, tragic image of continually losing but never giving up, Russia was portrayed in Govorukhin's 1991 film *The Russia We Lost* as never having been given a chance to blossom. As deterioration and loss were constant and there was always more to lose, any problem seemed to imply an infinite depth from which it had appeared.

A legend I heard repeatedly in the early 1990s explained why Americans were exporting "Bush's legs," chicken legs, the best part of the bird, to Russia. Apparently, a very harmful substance accumulates in chickens' legs, and Americans were keeping the nontoxic parts for themselves. Also, the sudden availability of bananas meant they had been treated with chemicals and/or were low-quality "feed bananas" for monkeys, which were starving somewhere. Like other kinds of conspiracy theories of the time, these rare indictments of non-Russians (indictments of one or another form of domestic elite were more common at the time) pertain to what Humphrey (1995) calls the post-Soviet "culture of suspicion." Even accounts of positive phenomena sounded menacing and eschatological; perestroika had disrupted nature itself: "This year was the hugest mushroom harvest" (since past social upheavals and catastrophes). "*Never before* was there so much condensation on the windows in winter." Waiting in lines for products out of which, undoubtedly, everything good had been stolen during manufacturing, people blamed perestroika not only for reeking, decaying stairwells with twisted mailboxes, broken tiles, and disembowelled lights, but for the unhealthily warm winter.

In the late Soviet Union, "tightly structured events of daily public life (the use of public transport, work at a Soviet enterprise where wages were centrally fixed, study in a Soviet school with a centrally adopted curriculum, and shopping in a Soviet store with ... centrally controlled prices and choices)" were felt to be immutable (Yurchak 1997:5–7). In contrast, in 1990–92, I often heard that Russia was on the brink of civil war, a prospect both terrible and alive; as Bakunin (1980:205) wrote, "Civil war breaks through the brutalizing monotony of man's daily existence, and arrests that mechanistic routine which robs them of creative thought." A common, competitive response was that some "war" had already been lost and we "normal people" had simply not yet witnessed the playing out of the tragedy. The senseless struggle had been resolved behind closed doors.

Time was characterized as not subject to individual control, fragmented, stolen, wasted. Loss was perpetual and eternally recent, but there was always more to lose; tragedy was that deep. A sense of stagnation coexisted with the imminence of a cataclysm that could represent failure, death, life, and/or hope.

---

[3] Much has been written about Russian "nihilism" and Nietzsche's influence on Russian thought.

Calculations and Opportunism: "Their size is in those bags"

> Reason . . . referred to articulation, precision, delimitation, and reserve—[Russian nationalists] opposed to it life so full of feeling that one could choke on it, the inexpressible, the unlimited, the hyperbolic. Reason had to do with calculation, reflection, predictability—they opposed to it spontaneity, the unexpectable, the unmeasurable . . . these qualities were vague, undefined. It was much clearer what they were not than what they were . . . perfect ingredients for the enigmatic Russian soul.
>
> Greenfeld 1992:255–56

> All these difficulties and contradictions . . . derive from the fact that this life has been upset to the point where one can hardly call it a life.
>
> Sinyavsky 1988:189

So what is life in the present, if it's "not life"? The word *byt* translates as "everyday mode of life," but attitudes toward the routine *byt* implies gave it a hellish nuance of rottenness. Roman Jakobson (1987:277) gives a passionate, representative example of this point of view. *Byt*, he writes, is "the stabilizing force of an immutable present, overlaid . . . by a stagnating slime which stifles life in its tight, hard mold," holding his own next to Blok's description of civilization as a cold dead crust congealing and stifling life and culture and Mayakovsky's *byt*—motionless, fat, coagulated "swamp . . . slime . . . moldy . . . crawling."

Not only poets hated "the evil continuum of specific tomorrows that only prolong today" and cherished "abstract faith in the coming transformation of the world" (ibid.:287). In Omsk, Aleksandr Ivanovich, a vital man in his late forties who worked in the middle management of a theater, graciously granted me an interview in his office and served coffee: "*Byt* is a burden," he said, "that doesn't let us fly away somewhere."

> Although that "somewhere" is pretty abstract. No one knows where to fly. And communism was . . . the same dream . . . They didn't know themselves what they wanted to build, but something like—not like *this*. Where there is no *byt*. . . . Let's have a common kitchen; let's have the children be raised in kindergartens, to not spend time on that; let's all dress the same . . . Eliminate *byt*! And occupy ourselves with something higher. Although there's this question of *what*; that's not so clear. . . . Our Siberian Old Believers were the same. It was all about freeing up time to do what was *real*.

Byt, one's everyday way of life, it's implied, damages soul through stinginess—in part by attacking time. A practical person could be seen as collaborating with this confining, diminishing force, as not only helping the spoiled present march into and befoul the future but as having no time to be pained about it. One night I had to leave a party early so I could get up to interview Kazannik, an Omsk law professor and nationally known politician. When I said I had to go, a drunk man stood up and condemned my desertion: "That's the difference," he said, "between 'you' and 'here.' What's a minute, between *people*? When people get together, everything else should fade. *Russians* don't *count* minutes when we sit. But *some* people have no soul. Exist exclusively by logic." The next morning, sitting with me in an empty classroom, Kazannik explained:

> If a person concerns himself only with *byt*, as you see among us now, deals only with surviving, it's hard for spirituality to appear. I'm not a proponent of Marxism-Leninism, but *byt* to a great extent does determine consciousness. A person goes off into his personal problems and doesn't concern himself with self-improvement.

Kazannik was referring to what is (very approximately) translated as "Life is not determined by consciousness, but consciousness by life" (Marx 1978:155).

In her living room, Lara, speaking slowly, mused on how routine, necessity, and materialism damage soul:

> Probably dusha gradually gives way [yields its seat] to practical considerations of the mind. People have to exploit their minds constantly, and constantly, and constantly, and everything concerning human relations and emotions isn't so important. Dusha can *move away*, maybe, somewhere in the shadows, get accustomed to not being listened to. That doesn't mean that it leaves a person, or maybe it depends on how intensively—maybe he's aiming for some sort of Napoleonic goals, trying to achieve them by any means possible. In that case he might certainly step over himself, his friends, over everything he held sacred . . . I have these acquaintances; in their home everything shines, but every day she goes out with the goal of buying something, it's not even important what. Some sort of huge knickknack. Dusha suffers from that sort of thing.

This is not new; "the given world of necessity," wrote Berdiaev (1955:11), in tropes similar to Blok's and Jakobson's, "is a prison in which the human soul is trapped."

In an old Siberian building on a back street, in a spacious office, I spoke with two writers in their forties. One, Lena, said, quietly and precisely, "It's thought that dusha, it's incompatible with *byt*. Dusha is always *above* everyday life, somewhere *there*. *Byt* brings it down. Makes it lower itself to some sort of pettiness." Her colleague Maxim added: "*Byt* constricts dusha if relations between people are based not on the spiritual but on the material." During our first interview, at his office, Oleg, the young businessman, said:

> *Byt* and dusha. Our classic immediately comes to mind: "Life determines consciousness." . . . It's probably hard for Americans to understand how dusha

and *byt* are interconnected for us. With our system it turns out like this: we live poorly, but at the same time, in dusha, or however you want to call it, spirituality or something, we're on a pretty high level. Maybe in terms of material goods we look like Africa or something, or there, somewhere in Asia, but I know that spiritually we're much richer, and maybe if we start to live much better materially, I'm afraid spirituality will get a little worse. Why? Well, when there's not enough to go around, you start thinking about human relations, but when everything is great, you start to notice some beautiful furniture, beautiful clothes . . . In our society . . . people who are . . . on a high rung socially . . . it's not so interesting to talk to them; that *effect* stands right in front of your eyes; but people like your average teacher, it can be pretty interesting to talk to them. . . . There aren't enough of those—those material valuables, so they want to supplement it with other valuables . . . deeper.

Dunham (1990:17–19) discusses how, by the late nineteenth century, the term *meshchanstvo* indicated petty-bourgeois lifestyle or personality. A looser, derogatory usage, she writes, indicating a vulgar, imitative, greedy, prejudice-ridden, spiritually deficient middle-class mentality, helped to stimulate the revolution. In an interview in her living room, Evgeniia Pavlovna, a staunchly optimistic retired teacher, used *byt* in its original sense, "mode of life," but indicted *meshchanstvo*:

A person's *byt*, way of life, as I see it, reflects his soul. It's not for nothing you came here; you needed to *see* that. Look: the blinds are worn. This woman is holding on to her old furniture. That's my *byt*. Could I have something better? I could. But that would be my dusha's top priority. We have a lot of petty-bourgeois types who have provided themselves with new wall units. A spiritual person is interested in understanding something general, in working in his field of interest. A practical person has a narrow dusha, is interested in kitchen appliances, cars. My students all had gold earrings . . . but my daughter . . . didn't need it. See what a spiritual world she turned out to have?

When I remember how dogmatically (if inspiredly) people preached about *byt*, I think of Masha, Grisha's blond, confident thirty-five-year-old coworker. Settling down with me in a cluttered corner of a communal workspace where we had both privacy and a potential audience, she said:

Russia is changing now . . . for the worse. People are trying to believe that one should snatch and grab as much as one can, and that the more you have—the more rags, the more of that same old sausage—that's prestigious. That you're living better than others, even. . . . They're not ashamed nowadays to talk about . . . how you ripped someone off, deceived someone, somewhere . . . that you have some sort of connections . . . that is, things that ought to be shameful. So this loss of conscience, and . . . it seems to me that they . . . some reordering, revaluing of values has appeared. But it's also Omsk . . . There were a lot of exiled people here, and whom did they exile? Kulaks, the best peasants, hard workers—and maybe that left its mark . . . People are more, it seems to me, suppressed, tight or something . . . not exactly suppressed, maybe I didn't express myself well—somehow overly concerned with taking *care* of things . . . I'm shocked all the time by these bags.[4] If people buy something, they buy a lot of it. That excessive hoarding makes my skin crawl. When I buy, it's as much as I need, and that's all. If everyone bought that way, there would be enough for others.

Masha's indictments of "kulak" and petty-bourgeois interests are reminiscent of Orthodox condemnations of the material trappings of this world, of nineteenth-century Russian soul seekers, and of early Soviet enthusiasts like Mayakovsky who saw canaries and palm plants as threats to communism (see Sinyavsky 1988, Dunham 1990, Boym 1994).

If growing and storing supplies was often listed as virtuous preparation for Siberian hospitality, it was also sometimes seen, as in Masha's words, as a sign of impoverished spirit. Socialist systems encouraged hoarding at all levels, paralyzing resources (see Verdery 1993:174, drawing on Hungarian theorist Janos Kornai's thesis of economy of shortage). The multiple importance of hoarding made statements like Masha's sound like bravado; as "sincere" as such statements could be, they had varying relations to the speaker's actual behavior. Another woman I knew, also in her thirties, proudly described behavior that she may have more admired than practiced: "I exercise my free will and not being a slave to this damned authoritarian system by not using ration coupons and by taking the same 300 grams of cheese I always did rather than the 500-gram limit; by taking not as much sugar as I *can*, but only as much as I *want*." Masha continued:

It's that excessive—they grab, grab, grab . . . a schoolgirl has to have gold earrings . . . When there's no flour anywhere, my own acquaintances say: "Oh, well, I have a 60-kilogram drum filled with it." I think: "Even if you did get your hands on that much, sit and be quiet!" It's shameful! But they aren't embarrassed, it's even pleasant to show that "I'm such a good homemaker, I have *everything*!" Aren't you afraid you'll get midges in those sacks of flour of yours? Or even—not long ago—also a coworker—We all cry that there's nothing for the children in the kasha—no butter. And this one says: "Oh, I have three packets of butter." That is, she knows someone who can get butter! Look at most people. They invest money how—on rags, jewelry—but that stuff is all *perishable*. People have shrunk somehow, lost their size. *Their size is in those bags*. These eternal conversations. I buy dough and do laundry too, but because I *have* to; I don't find it interesting to talk about. It's all repulsive.

Certain everyday objects recurred very regularly in such talk: food, clothes, gold earrings, and furniture, especially wall units and rugs. Rugs on

---

[4] Masha is referring both to the ubiquitous shopping bags people carried in the street and bags of hoarded commodities in apartments.

walls were nearly universal in apartments and houses. My friend Zhenia in the village called oriental-style rugs "the minimum" needed "for a home to feel like a home." When I was at Public Prosecutor Yurii Yur'evich's house for a meal, his daughter suddenly exuberantly thanked her parents for such a privileged childhood. When the embarrassed couple protested that they hadn't been privileged, she said they clearly had; her friends used to say they had more rugs than anyone. Anatolii, a sharp, thoughtful young friend of Oleg's in his early twenties, involved in contemporary music and computers, sat in his parents' apartment, on a sofa under a rug, across from a dark wood cabinet and display case, and also mentioned rugs and wall units critically, as what materialistic, practical people wanted. He said that "a *spiritual* person would use his land to plant an orchard, but a *practical* person would build a root cellar for hoarding supplies. And a bathhouse." Masha said "if I had extra money, I wouldn't be gobbling up those rugs . . . I'd put the money into my child's education."

Anna Viktorovna told me one afternoon, as we sat at an old round table in her bedroom,

> You know, civilization, it has a negative effect on our dusha. You understand? These days there's a lot to wear—people *dress*—and a variety of furniture—and their dusha, you know, is cooling off somehow. Furniture—obstructs, clogs. It's *meshchanstvo*; when a person eats, drinks, and everything is chic, shine, and beauty. But *there*, on the level of moral, so to speak, cultural, and spiritual, ethical development, it all passes them by.

A nineteen-year-old woman, though she had never read Berdiaev, claimed, as he did, that "Everyday life and dusha—it's the relationship of jailer and prisoner. Dusha should save us from *byt*, but *byt* is crushing, poisons dusha, strips it of its individuality, doesn't let it stop, rest, or calm down." Dusha was often nourished and undernourished with varying metaphorical food. And *byt* not only starves dusha but, as Boym (1994:29) notes, may "eat people up" altogether.

When Anna Viktorovna became ill, she would quietly cry in her room. She said she could not "open her dusha" to her son Grisha or his wife or even to a friend who, she whispered in a tone of moral judgment, had flat feet, no arch whatsoever. Her family depended greatly on her help and was not gracefully adjusting to losing it. "*Byt*," she said, "continuously destroys dusha; dusha *tears away* from your consciousness. It's not for nothing that they say 'dusha groans.' It's that *byt*; it's such a weight." Her son said: "I have kids, a sick mother, and no time to take care of them. I also have dusha, and it demands at least the littlest bit of food too. If I have to physically eat, dusha—it needs special nourishment . . . It's my dusha, I have to take care of it, or I'll lose it."

Everyday life was sometimes said to be killing dusha by killing (its) sensitivity. This relates to my earlier points about living or suffering through things. Insensitivity implied feeling less, needing more stimulus to respond, being more indifferent. Evgeniia Pavlovna, the teacher I interviewed in her, as she pointed out, *not* recently redecorated living room, called her dearest friend "Sensitive. For her dusha to ring, a very small push is necessary. Many of our people have gotten crude from this lifestyle."

I have mentioned that dusha was said to be destroyed but also to be developed (*razvivaetsia*), tempered (*zakaliaetsia*), ennobled (*oblagorazhyvaetsia*), and deepened (*uglubliaetsia*) by suffering. I never heard all four at once; they came in canonic groups of three or less. When life is "killing us" we notice dusha.

I sometimes suspected dusha of being complicit with *byt*, as if it depended on "superficial" things being dead to make its underground identity so alive by contrast. Might "our Soviet (or post-Soviet)[5] reality" be exaggeratedly superficial and insensitive to subsidize dusha's tenderness, interiority, and life? In any case, suffering entails depth, and *all* depth may be somehow painful. As a friend said, "one can feel too much to be happy."

Consciousness and Psychology

Feeling "deeply" is fundamentally valued, yet shades into something understood as "so deep" that nothing about it is felt. This brings me to an important aspect of dusha: psychology was a common Soviet educated synonym for it, as were "unconscious drives," "subcortex," psyche (*psikhika*), and mentality (*mentalitet*). *Dushevno bol'noi,* literally "soul-sick," means mentally ill, but mental illness is often seen as affliction of dusha, as in a 1996 New York Times story on the Russian revival of psychoanalysis in which a Dr. Aaron Belkin is quoted as wanting "to use psychoanalysis to explore the Russian soul."

Meanings of dusha and psychology resonate most when change is discussed. Zina's husband, Andrei Orlov, also an engineer, and passionately interested in horoscopes, fumbling with different images and theories of dusha, said: "My spiritual world has changed in the past couple of years—well, to be precise, dusha doesn't change once it's breathed into us; its condition changes, water changing states: same water, three states. Our psychology now is completely different."

Wierzbicka (1989:52) concludes that *dusha* "can refer to virtually all aspects of a person's personality . . . Given the richness and scope of this word it is not surprising that . . . *dusha* . . . tends to be identified with the person as a whole. For example . . . "I am my soul—my perception of it." (Tsve-

---

[5] *Sovkovaia. Sovki* (s., *sovok,* lit. dustpan) is derogatory for "late-Soviet-and-its-aftermath-person," implying jaded, hyperbolic crudeness and other faults of late Homo Sovieticus and no trace of "higher" ideals.

taeva 1972:124)."[6] I must stress, however, that there is a category of "experiences" *not* felt, a critical category for understanding how souls are "deep." Kazannik, the politician-law professor I cite above, defined dusha during his interview as "a complex of subconscious experiences (*perezhivanii*) that define one's internal world." As an example, he said that mutual attraction between people is "felt unconsciously; it's felt in dusha." I was very often told that people may not be aware that they are suffering or of how severe their pain is if it is "too deep" or their dusha is "closed."

This recalls nineteenth-century philosophy and psychology; Schelling's world soul (inspired by Plato) was the "most hidden part of nature . . . like the unconscious dreams of the sleeper" (Williams 1970:576). Romantic themes of split or dual selves abound in soul discourse: the Slavophile Grigor'ev, an influence on Dostoevsky in his literary development of Russian dusha, said Russia was like an individual with two selves, a conscious, "artificial," "surface" life of the ego, and a slumbering life of a truer, more perceptive, God-given self "hidden in us." In exile, Dostoevsky read Carl Gustav Carus' *Psyche: On the Developmental History of the Soul* (1846). Carus wrote that the key to conscious life lies in the "more healthy" unconscious (Williams 1970:583).

The "internal, deep" content of dusha was assumed to be more healthy, more alive, *more like a soul*. This is not tautological: as I will discuss, through practices of dusha, all sorts of rubbish get into the soul.

But How to Live? Growing Pains

"If man," Sinyavsky (1988:36) writes, "is inclined to ask himself about the meaning of life . . . a Russian is perhaps especially so." What Victor Turner (1969) called liminality—a transitional or marginal state of lowliness, poverty, and powerlessness that is also "alive" and hard to define, and represents "universal human values"—was valued as dushevno and characteristic of Russians. The "national pastime" of complaining can be seen as related to a sort of ritualized and/or degraded wondering at human helplessness in a time and place saturated in wrongness and evil, a way of asking / referring to the issue of *kak zhit'*, "how to live?"

The "meaning of life" issue, as much a romantic cliché as dusha, is evident in poetry (Pushkin's *Poet* or Lermontov's *Angel*) and in nineteenth-century social thought (in, among other forms, a sense of mission and potential; see Williams 1970). Sinyavsky (1988), like many others, claims that the Revolution was attractive to Russians as an attempt to introduce meaning to life. Berdiaev's (1947:30–31) vague rhapsodizing about illiterate Russians' love of posing questions about the meaning of life is not sociologi-

---

[6] *Osoznanie* is more awareness than perception.

cally authoritative, but Steinberg (forthcoming) has evidence that literate workers at the time of the revolution were "obsessed" with reflecting on individuals' nature, social place, and moral significance. The early Soviet goal of creating a "New Way of Life" (*novyi byt*), implied reengineering dusha, as Bukharin said in 1922, "people's actual psychology." In the 1960s, newspaper debates between *fiziki* and *liriki* had this as one of their orientations. In the early 1980s, Gorbachev repeatedly referred to spiritual, psychological, and social reconstruction (*perestroika*).

These are strong themes in 1990s media discussions framed as inquiries into what sense to make of (our chaotic) life, how to negotiate (our intolerable) life, where to find hope; newspaper headlines such as "In Search of Lost Humanity," "This Isn't Life," "I Don't Think We are the Land of the Absurd," "Perhaps We've Gone Insane?" and "So Who is to Blame for our Misfortunes?" were heirs to and often echoed such nineteenth-century titles as Hertzen's *Who Is to Blame?* and Chernyshevsky's *What Is to Be Done?*

Aleksandr Ivanovich, in the interview I cite above in his theater office, in which he described communists' attempts to figure out how to live, continued to discuss Russians' questioning, their searching. He began with suffering and dusha, which, he said, "are mystically linked . . . Suffering *facilitates* the birth or formation of dusha or its maturing." Then Aleksandr Ivanovich made a leap, implying that this soulful suffering may manifest itself as questioning, searching: "That strange, recurring question hypnotizes: for the sake of what do we live? What does this all mean? Why is it necessary?" Suffering was linked to a lack of resolution and to questioning. Denying (in pain) that this, the world we see, was the true or final form of things (and wondering what a better version would be) was often taken as a sign that a person was "still alive."

From there, Aleksandr Ivanovich's interview began drifting toward the topic of the vagueness of hope and the uncertain parameters of a better world:

Dusha is how you perceive the surrounding world. If you start to dig deeper into what dusha is, it turns out that in the center of that notion there is a system of values, a ruler you hold up in order to rank the whole world on a scale of important and unimportant. Serious or not serious. Essential, inessential. Of course dusha always had some strange, enormous, you might say, there, mystical, irrational . . . some sort of meaning in Russian culture. Why!! Our nation, it's as if every day it poses to itself the question of the meaning of its existence on earth. . . . As strange as it seems, that question is asked daily by everyone. From three alcoholics drinking under a fence all the way, say, to a university auditorium . . . whatever a group of Russians starts to discuss, the conversation always leads to that. It's as if the nation never definitively figured out why it came into this world. . . . Living to make money, love, to build a career, as if that's not enough. . . . From a materialist point of view, dusha, that enormous, warm, miraculous lump which never lets you live calmly, it shouldn't exist at all. It does not lead the organism to better adaptation; it only gives birth to dissatisfaction. But this enigma, the fact that dusha shouldn't be and yet is; the paradox of dusha is the best proof that a supreme, immaterial intelligence exists; we are its children, and it is leading us to a result which will make us happy.

At which point, with satisfied finesse, he ended our interview.

Suffering for and about Others

Suffering for others, compassion, empathy, were often mentioned as the essence of soul. Similarly, conscience (*sovest'*) was the epitome of suffering. Nadia said that "you understand what is happening to another person by letting something pass through you." Conscience, as a kind of centered moral evaluation aimed at self-improvement, could be synonymous with dusha. Like empathy, conscience is a "pain" that, flying in the face of self-interest, one does not avoid. Evidence of these emotions was seen as sufficient to prove a person's soul was alive. Raising her voice somewhat in our corner of the workshop, Masha went into detail:

> Logically you might think something is one way, but dusha hints at something completely different. If a person is a materialist, nothing torments him. "What I see is all there is, what I don't see can't exist." I'm not saying dusha comes only through pain—no. But you have to educate your conscience. . . . Some ask "why should I torture myself with a conscience?" Dusha is changing for the worse. People have hardened. If there's no conscience, there's nothing else left either, no self-analysis.[7]

Compassion is, I was told, "feeling others' pain as one's own." Pain can be proof of caring in a number of ways. The verb phrase *bolet' dushoi za* (not the same as the noun phrase "soul pain," *dushevnaia bol'*, I discussed above) is literally to be sick or pained in/with one's dusha about something, "sick at heart." It can be like "my heart goes out to" or may imply conscientious, passionate interest in or support of something, even a sports team. Anna Viktorovna, giving me examples from her life, described *bolet' dushoi* as "feeling a stab . . . deep . . . illogical . . . regarding a loved one or yourself." Public Prosecutor Yurii Yur'evich said:

---

[7] Although Soviet self-critique (*samokritika*) was encouraged, "self-analysis" was, from the Stalin era until the mid-seventies, officially discouraged as a morbid excess opposed to positive action. I never heard negative connotations from people I spoke to, though; in fact, some indicted Soviet discouragement of introspection as part of that time's "killing of dusha." Self-analysis (*samoanaliz*) was seen as a synonym of work on oneself (*rabota nad soboi*); examining dusha's cleanliness and depth was often seen as an important part of keeping it alive and developing it. A woman told me that an acquaintance had "a lazy dusha. Work on oneself is exactly the work of dusha."

A soulless person lives a vegetative life. If he's eaten, drunk, satisfied certain other needs, he needs nothing. If he hasn't, he doesn't *suffer*. He tries to find a way to satisfy them. At someone else's expense. A spiritual person suffers that despite his convictions he did something wrong to someone. A spiritual person *suffers*. Commiserates. Even in the thirties there were spiritual, moral people who didn't compromise their consciences. Raskolnikov had dusha; he killed and he was tormented. Many people . . . have no *suffering*.

This link to conscience shows that soul was not a matter of following rules; it most often appeared when a person had done something soulless. Then, pain at having done it appeared in their chest.

My first real talk with Zina and Andrei Orlov was a six-hour dinner in their big sitting room, during which Zina, in an initial presentation of herself (and of the state of her country / culture), distinguished between soulful people (who concern themselves with others) and animals or beasts who "just get off" (*kaifuiut*). She saw people engaged in moneymaking as concerned with themselves only. Their enjoyments were "soulless," somehow different from *soulfully* riotous drink, song, and dance (though the difference may have been empirically imperceptible). The distinction was not as much between exactly what was enjoyed as between the speaker's evaluation of the character of those engaging in it. In other words, what *sort* of dusha was fed by this pleasure? One like the speaker's?

Suffering could be for others even when not in the forms of empathy or conscience. Grisha said on tape, as we perched on tiny stools in his tiny kitchen by a cold, perspiring double window, "In our country there are practically no limits to dusha's suffering. Dusha can embrace it all. And suffer for everyone." This is the Dostoevskian compassionate soul, "yearning to suffer and at the same time to alleviate the suffering of others" (Cherniavsky 1969:202–3). In 1931, Valentin Tomberg (reprinted in *Gnosis;* 1994:44–45) wrote that the first thesis of Dostoevsky's conception of suffering is that it is never just a personal problem: "*Every sufferer suffers for all* . . . because of his crime or . . . through the greatness of what is passing through his soul . . . Dostoevsky shows how . . . every punishment can actually be transformed into the birth pangs of a higher life . . . such insights are only possible when one has an intense feeling for . . . the unity of mankind."

An aspect of revolution-era discourses, writes Steinberg (forthcoming), was linked to Nietzsche's ideal of a self that transcended narrow individualism. Marxists also advocated an individualism "in which the 'I' is 'identified with some broad and enduring "we." ' " Stalin-era diaries (Hellbeck 1998) show struggle as a central tool for transforming the self into something greater, "merging with the collective" as opposed to "remaining a half-animal."

I must stress that the range of ways in which these themes can be individually embodied, intended, and used is wide, from earnest transformative efforts (however defined) to rituals of community requiring mere reference to transformation, to habitual, mildly comforting touchstones, to cynical rhetoric in bad faith. The language was available; individuals used it and were used by it.

Context and Conclusions

> The world is a place where it is impossible to live, but not because of the price of sausage; departure from this world is a way of being in it.
>
> Mila, Omsk, 1992

> Dusha and everyday life depend on each other. What's more, not only dusha on everyday life, but everyday life on dusha. That says it all.
>
> College student, Omsk, 1992

Cherniavsky (1969:210–13) writes that Dostoevsky "formulated the greatest justification of the [Russian soul] myth by making Russian suffering . . . its main feature." But by doing so, Cherniavsky says, Dostoevsky revealed that myth's "human origin."[8] Despite this, he claims, the "myth" survived for a time, and the Revolution, rather than destroying it immediately, "provided an occasion for an outburst of mythologizing" (ibid.:223–24). Stites (1992:23) writes that the folkloric theme of the moral superiority of the poor was transformed into the Revolution's "central myth." I show here that the value of suffering for the Russian soul continued acquiring history and characteristics at least through perestroika.

One way aspects of "Russian soul" have survived is by repeated negation (see Lotman and Ouspensky 1984:3–35), including setting up "this" world in opposition to precious *other* ones. Two aspects of Eastern Orthodoxy are relevant to this. The first is the tenet that, by enduring suffering, one enacts one's belief that things of this world are "a shadow, a dream . . . nothing either in nature or duration" as opposed to virtues of the next world (Harakas 1990). Suffering is inevitable because this world is fallen; believers must shift value from this world to the other. But kenosis (Greek, "self-emptying;" Philippians 2:6–8 in Rancour-Laferriere 1995:28) is only a skeletal representation of the value of suffering in 1990s Russia. Drab, grueling everyday life was incoherent, unclear, fragmented, thus not the "real" world, not the one people *lived* for.

---

[8] One discussion about suffering's importance to Russian soul suggests that it represents secularization of soul. Philosopher poet Solov'ëv found that it verged on Russian self-deification (Cherniavsky 1969:211) and that suffering was inadequate to *truly* reject this reality. Dostoevsky was aware of this critique: in *The Possessed* Stavrogin accuses Shatov of reducing God to an attribute of nationality. Shatov responds that, no, he was rather "raising the people up to God."

A second relevant aspect of Orthodoxy (one that is quite vital today) is hesychasm, which emphasizes that, though God cannot be understood by the human mind, *irrational* experience of the Divine is possible. This emphasis on (experiences of) what cannot be understood prioritized the irrational over the rational.[9] By the mid-1800s the nationalist Russian dusha also implied Russian resistance and superiority to "the rationalist, materialist, work-oriented, and time-conscious world of industrial Europe" and its soul, seen as destroyed by materialism, mechanization, rationalization (Williams 1970:573). Solzhenitsyn said in 1978 (1980:12–13): "Through deep suffering, people in our country have now achieved a spiritual development of such intensity that the Western system in its present state of spiritual exhaustion does not look attractive . . . the complex and deadly crush of life has produced stronger, deeper and more interesting personalities than those generated by standardized Western well-being." And Natan Shcharansky, in a December 1989 interview (cited in Lapeyrouse 1990) for the American television program *Sixty Minutes*, said, on being shown a film of Perm 35 labor camp:

> An awful place, but . . . lots of good things were there . . . some of the most interesting . . . discussions. . . . And . . . to feel deeply, some of the fundamental things were there. . . . You learn about yourself . . . about how important are things like love, like moral values, like the feeling that you have your people, your country with you.

It is important to stress that if 1990s Russians labeled this world as bad and presented and saw themselves as like the Orthodox who called suffering "a sign of God's favor and trust" (Harakas 1990:54), it does not mean that they in any direct way rejected the material or practical. Bourgeois attitudes coexisted and interacted with the dusha worldview variously. What people usually bemoaned were, in fact, their truly difficult material and practical lives. If, in public "searches for solutions" to current sufferings, finding concrete answers was often utterly beside the point (Ries 1997), ritually paying homage to the lack of resolution could to some degree stand in for the experience of spiritual searching. This, again, is a matter of individual interpretation and embodiment of these discourses and traditions.

I have no relevant ethnography of nineteenth-century Russians, but I assume that there was always a significant range of variation in how individuals related to what they said and variation between how a given person related to it in different situations. This was certainly the case in the 1990s,

---

[9] Medieval Orthodox hesychasm held that aspects of the Divine that transcend understanding may nevertheless be directly *experienced* in the form of light. The light is the presence of God. The practice of the "Jesus prayer" to produce hesuchia, "quiet," was accompanied by Sufi-like breathing control and concentration on the place of the heart (Ware 1987:567). Hesychasm involved issues of (1) the person being an integrated whole of soul and body; and (2) the ability of humans to partake in the Divine by intuition, not understanding.

and was evident not only to me; it was an issue for Russians too, a criterion they sometimes saw as one of individual sincerity (*iskrennost'*) and often used in evaluating others' souls.

Gorbachev and other architects of perestroika were, in 1990–94, heartily, unequivocally despised by my interlocutors over the age of eighteen. Only one young woman (from the Urals) admitted being proud of Yeltsin (who is from there). A woman in her forties told me in all seriousness that glasnost had been a bad move; it would have been wiser to make everything OK first and then, when given freedom of speech, "*people would have had nothing to say!*" (see also Sinyavsky 1988:269). On one hand, this implies that speech itself was inherently oppositional; on the other, "everything being OK" probably indexed, for most of these speakers, Western-style comfort. Mocking, envious jokes that denied that foreigners who live and transport themselves differently could possibly understand asked: "What do Americans have to talk about? What they *bought*?" "What problems do Germans have? Where to park their *cars*?"

To sum up a few points, everyday life, *byt*, was portrayed as degrading and murderous in part because it was repetitive, seemingly could not change, did not allow people to develop. Neither deep nor internal, it was external, material. Everyday space and time were constricted, constricted spirit, resisted individual control. They were fragmented, stolen, corrupted, marshaled, scarce, wasted. A soiled present marches into the future, which provides more soul to be twisted. Dusha suffers, and in so doing, reproduces its "otherworldly" status and a demand for change. It was sometimes enough for an attitude or activity to seem to be in opposition to or violation of certain notions of practicality or superficial adequacy for it to be valued as dushevnyi, and for the person responsible to be classified as still alive and struggling with moral issues.

This is one of the points where, since context makes all the difference, I cannot give single definitions and opposites are often equally valid. Things get a little confusing. As often as soul was presented as an antipractical holdout for the "real" world, soul was connected to warmth, stability, support, and moral behavior. As such, it was *also* reportedly being "cooled off" and killed. "This" world separates people and weakens spirituality, yet only when it begins to crush do people join and feel dusha. Constriction and suffering were described as killing dusha, precluding internal vastness and meaning, and as giving it life, as significant. Dushevnyi joins contradictory meanings, sometimes espoused by different people, sometimes flashing in and out in the same person's words.

But if we see many of these different demands for dusha as essentially oppositional, as all saying "no" to something defined by a current context and by individuals, many of these demands can be seen to be artifacts of similar processes under different conditions.

"Russian soul" demands that the world be represented and valued in terms of a person's center. That is, the world must be *felt,* if possible, or thought or known, "as long as those other functions are somehow linked to values" (Wierzbicka 1989:52). And if the world thus represented or felt "inside" is not the hopeful "real" world but nasty everyday *byt,* that soul will be a problematic one that tries to squeeze life from representations of death, a soul that must represent itself as suffering. To the extent that an individual fails to focus fully on a "real" life and world, the story goes, "our Soviet reality" becomes her or his reality. The revolution brought about no new *byt,* Sinyavsky (1988:152–68) writes, but a world where light bulbs and garbage pails were vitally important and a "normal way of life" was nonexistent. As dusha suffered through bread lines, glass jars, and filthy buses, bread, glass, and filth became the stuff of dusha.

Dusha's status as an other world that miraculously survives despite crushing evils of society and fate is reproduced in part through images and practices of suffering. In the process, *byt* fills dusha. People ironically flaunt their genuine suffering. As the comedian Khazanov says, "you have to feel proud, even in public transportation during rush hour."

CHAPTER THREE

A Channel between Worlds

The person of Russia, the Russian person, would like to have
lived in some—not in the world of *byt* but in an over-*byt*
world . . . where it's more interesting and more important and
more meaningful . . . the everyday world, it's as if it prevents him
from living . . . doesn't let him escape into that real, genuine
world. This explains the endless searching in Russian history . . .
flights out to Siberia, searches for some sort of other, different
world. This one clearly is not suitable. This one is clearly bad.

Aleksandr Ivanovich, Omsk, 1992

Another world—an antipode, an anti-world to the one in which
we are living . . . dusha belongs much more to that world.

Lara, Omsk, 1992

So "this world" was often discussed and seen as constricting, destructive, as having neither time nor space for the really important things,
most of which were described with reference to dusha. As I began
showing in the previous chapter, as soon as I examined my data for evidence
of what was *for* dusha I ran into references to "other" times and spaces.
The term other world (*drugoi mir*) was most often used to describe good
things and objects of desire. Soul was often called internal world (*vnutrennyi mir*), soul world (*dushevnyi mir*), and spiritual world (*dukhovnyi mir*);
things were often described as "not from here" (*ne otsiuda*), and "from
there" (*ottuda*); distant otherworldliness was related to and often synonymous with dusha, the inner world.

Examining discourse of future, past, inner, and spatially distant "worlds"
led me to the issue of human powers to act with "soul." One man I cite in
this chapter calls art the only way "to bring out that strange notion of
dusha"; he calls artworks portraits of both the artist's dusha and dusha in
general. Creativity, hope, love, intuition, talent, and inspiration are usually
said to be directly related to soul, usually in a positive sense. Change and
development are also often said to be good for dusha and turn out to have

something to do with most if not all of these other things. This chapter investigates these and some other soul-related elements of human life.

What are other worlds like?

Material in the last chapter shows how hard it was to imagine a good future growing organically out of *this* present. Change turned out to be often understood in terms of movement between "worlds." Important imagined soulful other worlds predate the Russian soul that assimilated them into national imagery. Lotman and Ouspensky (1984:4–5) write that some Russian medieval texts indicated heaven and hell, but nothing between them. Change happened through radical rejection, turning the old inside out. Sinyavsky (1988:5–6) and others, discussing Russians' alleged fondness for images of radical transformation, cite the Apocalypse: everything will change and the entire social order be overturned in a single instant. Berdiaev (1947:13) notes that Peter the Great and Napoleon were seen as the Antichrist (I heard Lenin, Gorbachev and others called the Antichrist).[1] In the twentieth century, the Marxist image of a leap to a better society certainly won in Russian implementation over the equally Marxist image of a heavenly society's evolution from a hellish one. The Revolution, Sinyavsky (1988) writes, tried to fulfill "the soul's noblest aspiration": "to remake the world, having repudiated everything that went before as wrong." The Soviet Futurists were oriented, Kristeva (1980:33) writes, toward a future "in relation to which concrete history will always be wrong: murderous, limiting." These are similar to expressions of a hope "that meaning can *break through* meaninglessness" (Berdiaev 1955:30).

Negation and opposition were not just formal devices by which new and old, inner and outer worlds were imagined; they also seem to me to represent much of the imagined content of those "worlds." Close examination of images of "other" worlds and accounts of moving into them rarely show anything substantially different. As we see in many descriptions of dusha, other worlds are deeper, higher, *more* real and alive. They are more generative or as different as possible[2] from the everyday, all metaphors of scale. As Lara told me, "Only when we begin to relate to *byt* do we notice dusha alive inside there, interesting, like another world." The apocalyptic image of change is logical: if the other world is not this one, well, we don't have much information about what it *is*. What we *do* have plenty of are passionate demands for difference or hope for change. Sudden, disjunctive change stands for this hope, this lack of knowledge and for the brutal emptiness of opposition.

---

[1] See Lotman and Ouspensky 1984:53 on related imagery of the Petrine epoch; Timasheff 1946:38 on nineteenth-century intelligentsia and radical utopian reform; Bakhtin 1984:177 and 153 and Dostoevsky 1982 12:520–21 ("Dream of a Ridiculous Man") on imagery of "instantaneous transformation of life into paradise."

[2] Lotman (1984:189) observes that, in Gogol's writing, "the ideal other existence is seen in what is incomparably different . . . a highly rated other space."

So "what are other worlds like?" turns out to be the altogether wrong question. In fact, if I had asked it, I would have ended up with, rather than rich ethnographic material, the same romantic fantasizing I would have gotten in answer to "what is dusha?" Rather than, like Tiutchev, discussing the "entire world of mysterious and magical thoughts in your soul," I will side with Dostoevsky's Ivan Karamazov (1982 11:276) when he says: "I have a euclidian, earthly mind; how could we possibly make decisions about what is not of this world?" and start with what I could find out about "other worlds": how people already were experiencing them—how they hoped for, believed in, and communicated with them in "this" world.

Hope and Salvation

From the beginning the Russian soul was...a symbol of... hope for what [Russia] might yet become.

Williams 1970:581–82

Little country, where it's light and clear for dusha...who can give me a hint where it is?

Children's music video, mid-1990s

If a person's dusha is kind, he will always have hope...Unkind people—*expect,* but they don't hope.

Irina, Omsk, 1992

Figa is a thumb tip poking out between a fist's index and middle fingers; a child's gesture used by anyone to signify general, rebellious refusal, "You'll get nothing from *me.*" A friend and I were returning by bus from her dacha one hot day; a car peeled open like a sardine can roared by; two young men gestured *figa*: "Dale, *that's* a Russian person's dusha—he never loses optimism," beamed my rather refined friend, with no trace of irony or offense at what she saw as life-affirming obstinance, resistance to letting one's spirit be trampled. I heard optimism predicated of "simple Russians," and it had certainly been selected for the Soviet "proletarian mood."

Though, as I argue above, other worlds are negative by birth, they are usually hopeful. Aleksandr Ivanovich (the theater administrator in his late forties prone to eloquent speeches) said:

The only thing that gives a Russian hope is dusha. Hope for something completely different. Hope that...his stay in this completely enigmatic, hostile world is not for nothing, not by chance, has some greater sense...either some sort of paradise there, or that communism...Because if you want to talk about hope, the Russian, he lives not to be rich, have rank, be honored; he lives to be happy. And it's tragic: he can't even formulate what that would be. It swims murkily in his head.

Here again, hope, what Aleksandr Ivanovich calls sense, is unobtainable and oppositional. Politician Kazannik defined hope as "some very hard-to-reach ideal. If a person really achieved that goal, he'd be unhappy. People keep moving [those ideals] further and further away. And live by hope."

"Hope," it was said, "dies last." "If there's soul, there's hope." "Filled with dusha" means full of hope. Discussion of "where to find hope" related to that about where to find dusha. Lara, in the discussion of soul pain I cited in the last chapter, was explicit: "When dusha's in pain, pain displaces hope. Dusha heals itself with hope."

Veletskaia (1992:50–60) describes Russian religious "escapes" to the other world, but for most, long before the Revolution, the word *dushespasitel'nyi,* "soul-saving," began to be used rarely and/or facetiously. After the Revolution, at least in official language, images of salvation took other forms. During perestroika, however, as even the pretense of a dream of a bright communist future began to decompose, more literal uses of terms such as "soul-saving" began to reappear, and coexisted with burgeoning irony. Perestroika-era salvation came in many forms: Grisha used a tender diminutive for the creative "little world" he shared with his friend Kolia. "We have our *own* world," he repeated. A woman in her thirties described closing herself up in her own world-apartment to keep from drowning in the swamp of Omsk. The editors of an early 1990s newspaper for young people called it a *dushespasitel'nyi* "psychological shelter," a "space" where dusha could save itself (Rayport-Rabodzeenko 1998). One column was titled "A Different Reality."

Lipman (1998:106–9) writes, in the context of late and post-Soviet "yearning for radical change," that fashion appealed to some as "another world." Virtually anything could; it would be useless to try to list what represented hope in what circumstances to whom. I can, however, sketch a few categories of hopeful otherworldliness that were very often mentioned. These are assorted topics that popped up in conversation and seem primarily united by the kind of hope I have described.

America and Lies

In *Crime and Punishment*, a man about to commit suicide says he is preparing to go to America. In the 1990s, an American journalist (Kempe 1992:165) cites a Siberian woman asking him to take her to America and then saying no, "The cemetery will be my America." When, on an Omsk street, I bumped into a man whom I had helped in Russia and the United States in his dealings with Americans, he was visibly shocked: "You're like an apparition from *there*" (*ottuda*). I was often seen as "from there." This was aggravated by Omsk's former closedness. Some people hoped I would be their path to the world of business. Others just wanted, they said, to "talk to a live American." One of these, a dentist, said: "People from other countries are, for us, *all* more or less from America."[3]

"America" (meaning the United States) was a most popular other world during perestroika. Russians have, cyclically, admired aspects of the West and rejected them as soulless.[4] In addition, America's image included expansive, "wild," future-related and other *dushevnye* elements. During the Khrushchev era, writes Stites (1992:127), the writer Aksënov, inspired by the American beatnik aesthetic, "gazed out through a nocturnal urban frame as a 'starry ticket' into another world and another future." I heard American life imagined as brash, extreme, bright, yet, despite Soviet propaganda, a life in which people treat others "as human beings."

An other world America could evoke was what was sometimes, before the Revolution, called "for the soul": luxurious material possessions. The glasnost media at times created an ideal America, presenting video "documentaries" of the wealthiest American shops, homes, and schools as "typical." This was partially a crude flip-flop of Stalin-era imagery of an entirely bad America and a socialist "fairy tale" "reality" (see Stites 1992:66–67; and Ries 1997:42, 50). One woman scolded me: "Don't tell us bad things about America. We need hope right now more than anything." She said that the cult of America was not official policy, but that "for now, people need clear, bright goals." If, as Dunham (1990:27) notes, not all Soviets objected to socialist realism's glossy lies, "craving hope more than they craved truth," in a similar way 1990s images of an ideal America could be more valuable as hopeful than as true.

This is an appropriate moment to mention the values and practices of lying, a poignant aspect of dusha culture. A woman, talking with a friend in my presence, happily exclaimed "What Russian can help stretching the truth occasionally?" I have no statistics on Russian mendacity, but what matters is that talk about lying and fibbing enjoys an exuberant vocabulary[5] and corresponds lavishly to that of Russian soul. Dostoevsky (1980:117–25) relates fibbing to what he calls a Russian fear that the truth will be too prosaic and boring. He claims that among the intelligentsia there is no such thing as a person who does not fib; honest Russians lie, whereas only the "worst scoundrels" in other nations do. This practice, Dostoevsky

---

[3] See Bakhtin on how imagined social utopias can take the form of dreams or journeys to unknown lands (1984:115–18). Such realms can be "beyond the sea, on a high mountain or underneath the earth . . . a place of rebirth. . . . The 'other' values proper to this world . . . are simply other" (Vlasov 1992:28–29).

[4] Though, GoGwilt (1995:45–46) has pointed out, these rejections and acceptances have not always been polar.

[5] The noun *vran'ë* glosses both as fibbing and a fib; the verb is *vrat'* or to lie (*lgat'*). *Privrat'* is to embellish or stretch the truth, *sovrat'*, to come out with a lie, *navrat'*, to lie a certain amount, *zavrat'sia*, to have told so many lies that . . . ; *otvirat'sia* is to lie oneself out of something, and *perevrat'* to mistakenly give misinformation. *Skazat' nepravdu* is to tell an untruth, and *obmanyvat'* to deceive. "Hanging noodles [from a listener's ears]" is telling lies or tall tales.

suggests, has led to the result that in Russia the truth "has a completely fantastic character." The early twentieth-century writer Teffi, in an essay on fibbing (reprinted in 1991), calls whimsical fibs selfless, interesting, inspired, and from dusha. Only half-clowning, she presents fibbing as enigmatically senseless, awkward, and inspired.[6]

Student Days (The Past)

Utopias provide other worlds in the future and fibbing other versions of future, present, and past, but the past itself can be used as another world. Anna Viktorovna said, "Dusha can make one live in one's dreams or in the good past." Oleg often reminisced about the days when he and fellow students would sit for hours and discuss dusha and "how to live." Student days were when people said they had had the leisure to talk about dusha—a leisure, they said, that was tragically lost. Lara's student days, particularly precious now that she felt she was drowning in the grind of caring for a family and working, were both temporal and, like America, geographic: "In Leningrad, I won't say that I didn't eat, but I didn't pay any attention to it . . . spiritually I was overfull . . . I was a human being, a *person*, some sort of pure exposed material. And everything poured into me, with such speed and intensity. I consider the months spent in Leningrad the larger part of my life. I was dusha all the way through." Another day she said: "I didn't meet one bad person there. I bathed in communion with wonderful people. . . . I went in rose-colored glasses and left in those same glasses. Leningrad is the city of my dreams." Recent social upheaval distanced these already idealized days even further. The losses merged. "We've changed a lot," Oleg (the young businessman) commented, "and not for the better. . . . Something really has happened with that—that dusha of ours."

Religion and Mysticism

Mysticisms and religion in Russia in the 1990s were often embraced as part of an attempt at affirming that life is governed by systems, logics, and power hierarchies *other* than what are categorized as "worldly" ones. In Russian peasant culture, magic was very important. The introduction of Christianity transformed some of this into a lively interest in miracles (see Lewin 1990:166–67, passim, and Ivanits 1992:24–26 on Nicholas the Wonderworker). When Soviet attempts to transform life on the level of the social system failed, a special faith began to again be accorded imagery that offered hope from totally outside some legal or human system. Thus rumor

---

[6] There is a wonderful monologue on lies in Gorky's *Na Dne* (translated as *The Lower Depths*).

was the preferred way of dealing with authority and law, and religion, various types of mysticism, astrology, and faith healing became constant topics of discussion. Lara told me that all her friends had plunged headlong into religion: "It's the only thing anyone has to hold on to." Another woman said: "We were deceived. There is a dangerous dushevnyi vacuum forming in people. People are going through a great dushevnyi crisis. People of all ages are turning to religion for belief, salvation."

On TV the image of a vast, dark, starry sky was so common for a while that one could never tell if the upcoming "forecast" was weather or astrological. Astrological forecasts announced for which signs and for what the day was auspicious or inauspicious. English and slick graphics that indexed other worlds were liberally mixed in.

One afternoon Grisha's coworker Masha, whose scathing critiques of aquaintances' materialism I mentioned in the previous chapter, and another, much older woman discussed their mystical experiences at a long holiday meal at the older woman's home. For hours I listened as they categorized experiences and lore about healing, near-death, premonitions, and apparitions, all of which were woven into one category: "the true, spiritual world about which, for our entire lives, we have been systematically denied information." In a different tone, psychologically inclined law professor / politician Kazannik told me that

> Dusha is changing. A mania in a psychologically ill person, that's dusha, without a doubt. . . . Before, manias manifested themselves as burns, lesions. Suffering was visible on the body. Now, under the influence of science and technology, a change is taking place in dusha, how things appear is changing. In this crisis people are starting to believe in supernatural events. They're discussing nothing but whether they saw a UFO or didn't see one.[7] Mass psychosis. Psychics have appeared. This would have all been impossible if dusha hadn't changed.

These speakers have opposite opinions as to the nature of such experiences: what Masha and her friend take to be the true world they are only now able to perceive, Kazannik calls, in effect, recent onset mass hallucination. But there is no question for any of them that these are phenomena of dusha (a good example of how dusha differs from what in English is called psychology).

Expansiveness—For Dusha

> Gogol . . . suggested untapped potential in his famous image of Russia as a troika whipped into motion by its driver, "his soul

[7] See Platz 1996 and Stephens 1997.

yearning to be whirled away, to be plunged into reckless revelry,
and occasionally wanting to say, 'To hell with it all.' "

Williams 1970:582

Other worlds' otherness is often framed in terms of vastness and distances. Images of (opening or moving into) vast expanses, into physical, creative, and spiritual freedom, or into lostness, desolation, and barrenness, relate to dusha, often through the noun *prostor*. In her romantic 1916 book on Russian language, Jarintzov writes that *prostor* "bursts from Russian lips at the sight of space, far vistas, steppes . . . the longing for *prostor* is ingrained in the Russian heart." This great scale (*masshtab*) is linked in literature, philosophy, and speech to dusha, with its craving to open, expand. Various aspects of life could be evaluated in terms of expansiveness. Lotman and Ouspensky (1984:13) note that, in contrast to *prostor, tesnota* (lack of space, constriction) could be a metaphor for social evil. I often heard this sort of metaphor invoked (although *uiut*, the coziness of home, was usually an exception). Throughout this discourse about one or another kind of expansiveness, one encounters words with the prefix *raz*.

Raz- is a widely used Russian prefix that conveys dispersing, spreading, or annihilation by creating an expanse outward from some center. It has a nuance of "intensely," "suddenly" or "to a high degree;" it can also negate or unravel (as in *razliubit'*, to cease to love). *Raz-* appears so abundantly in discussions such as the above examples of what was *for* dusha, and is so linked to a sense of great scale and authentic impulse that it seems indispensable to a discussion of the metaphysical landcape.

Jarintzov offers *razdolie* as "almost a synonym for *prostor*. It . . . means one's part of . . . the world . . . lavishly . . . thrown out wide and far" (Jarintzov 1916:70–71). She calls *raz-* words "so essentially Russian that we simply could not live without them" (ibid.:69–71). *Raz-* and *razmakh* are always defined by a broad, energetic outward arm gesture. *Razmakh* is, I was told, when a person makes big, important, not small and petty, gestures. The most common images of hope were expansiveness, breadth, and an inner world identified or continuous with far off other worlds.

The impulsive breadth implied by *raz-* helps bring out a very important point: anything at all may be done in such a way as to be classifiable as "for dusha." Formal aspects of these modes may be energetic, reckless abandon, absurd, impassioned play, or self-indulgent expansiveness,[8] including fibbing. In addition, doing something for dusha is usually seen as not conservative: a craftswoman in her thirties described how, even if the crafts she made sold well, she still often had to start something new, for dusha. Lara mentioned "Creative *prostor* . . . *prostor* for fantasy . . . You can also say 'intellectual *prostor*,' meaning someone can think *broadly*." *Prostor* sug-

---

[8] An important aspect of expansiveness is treated in Lotman's (1984) discussion of riotous eighteenth-century drinking orgies (*razgul*, letting oneself go).

gests endless possibilities; "it is the seed-bed of creative impulse . . . Size and space impel a Russian to throw out his arms to embrace Nature, brothers, foes, friends . . . Prostor is a call for . . . mental receptivity. Why, even hopeless bureaucrats and police . . . love prostor" (Jarintzov ibid.:25–8).

Expansiveness, space, bigness are all facts of dusha, and are linked to creativity, the occult, receptivity, possibilities, interest, change, love, inclusiveness, and, again, reckless abandon that flies in the face of common sense. Stites (1992) cites popular culture heroes Stenka Razin, Esenin, Chapaev, and Vysotsky, whose "rash temperament . . . leads to impossible romance, hopeless battle, imprudent spending, or oceans of vodka." The value of riotous behavior, Lotman (1984:100) writes, "consists in crossing the limit that no one has yet crossed." In the 1990s such behavior was also often described, as Lotman (ibid.:98–101) found in nineteenth century texts, as significant, passionate, and meaningful, not routine and meaningless, as *chosen* rather than received, though the degree to which this affected people's actions varied. A doctor delightedly remarked that Russian dusha is when you don't know how to properly operate an expensive Western diagnostic machine but love to make the little lights blink.

Kazannik began his interview, in a dingy university classroom, rigidly and pedantically, defining dusha in terms of right and wrong. Soon, however, he loosened up and began to refer more to expansive, bold gestures. As a summary of Russian character and soul he described a prerevolutionary merchant who bought twelve expensive mirrors and let them lie in a shed "to show that [money is] nothing." The merchant went to an inn, drank, had a hole broken in a load-bearing wall of the inn, paid for it, and crawled in, "completely, completely content."

Later I return to such willful, clowning actions and images of them, actions seen as "so big" that practical and impractical fall away. I have mentioned a woman who, only sort of joking, insisted it was genetically ingrained in Siberians to lick metal outside in winter. As with lying, even telling such stories may "rest" dusha. "Bigness" can be identified with humanity as well as Russianness: in the eighteenth century Fonvizin claimed that Russians were "bigger people than the Germans." That is, writes Rogger, who cites him (1960:82–84), they are "more human, have more feeling, more heart, a greater capacity for love . . . Perhaps the 'broad Russian soul' here was first unveiled . . . In spite of his insistence on the full identity of the human situation everywhere . . . Fonvizin felt it easier to be . . . a human being in Russia."

What Berdiaev called the "correspondence of spiritual and physical geographies" was fodder for politicization of the expansive land. In the eighteenth century, pride in the vast land became a key symbol of Russian identity (Brooks 1984:241–42). With the Revolution, the alternate breadth and openness of internationalism coopted this nationalist imagery. Stalin later reinstated the primacy of the motherland (Sinyavsky 1988:250), using images such as that of the un-Russian "rootless cosmopolitan," a person,

Stites (1992:118) says, "devoid of mystical attachment to the land." This imagery continued through the cold war. Post-Soviet nationalism revived the same images.

Russia as Land of Miracles

In the early 1990s Russians' most popular nickname for Russia was *strana chudes*. This glosses as "land of miracles" or "wonderland," a bitter response to any evidence of what was considered the state of the nation. A variation was "land of fools" (*strana durakov*). *Pole chudes* (field of miracles), kept in consciousness by a popular game show by the same name,[9] was also common and, along with *strana durakov* and *strana chudes*, was used in countless 1990s newspaper headlines and cartoons on any number of topics. *Pole chudes* was the new name of the USSR on a cartoon map on the front page of *Komsomol'skaia Pravda* newspaper the day after the USSR disbanded. Russia was called a "special world" or not really "this" one; in a 1992 interview (*Moscow News* 42, 1992), former KGB chief Vadim Bakatin said that before glasnost "We all lived in a special world where there was one ruling party, one ideology, one punishing sword."

As I discuss in the previous chapter, Russians were seen as being open, wondering about the meaning of life. "For other nations," Aleksandr Ivanovich said earnestly, hands flat on the cool surface of his office table, "that question is important to philosophers, artists, people with particular psychological organizations. Here . . . it's asked daily by every person." Seriously questioning the status quo is, in turn, associated with obliviousness to its petty details. Svetlana, an institute student intensely interested in contemporary fashion and various types of mysticism, said that "When you're filled with creativity, you forget to eat. . . . When a person is creative, his *dusha* grows and feeds him." Berdiaev (1947:39) claims that "when a controversy was raging . . . and someone proposed they should have something to eat . . . [Belinsky] shouted out: 'We have not yet decided the question of the existence of God and you want to eat!!' "

My friend Mila, at her desk, squinted through her headache and said: "Bold gestures . . . expansiveness, . . . the unembraceability of it all . . . when you have too much of everything, you can't approach things rationally . . . unfinished projects and angles result." Svetlana, who had many friends trying to go into business, had a similar approach:

> Russian people are talented . . . entrepreneurship, that's purely Russian. People who spark, crackle with ideas. But let someone else actually *do* it. Russians are idea generators. Other nationalities are better at carrying it out. . . . With Rus-

---

[9] Modeled on an American game show, *Wheel of Fortune*, but named after a setting in the mythical geography of Aleksei Tolstoi's version of Pinocchio, *Buratino*.

sians everything's more towards God than earthbound. They aren't too tied to their duties so they're easily inspired. But carrying it out takes too long. Our people are in the clouds, don't keep everything under control.

Not from this World

Not measuring, not taking care of things, and failure in this world can be taken as symptoms of a soul trained on other things. "Not from this world" (*ne ot mira sego*) was originally used in religious contexts. It later acquired secular usages, overtones of which ranged from ironic to idolizing. When a person was called "not from this world" it could mean that he or she was dashingly or clumsily oblivious to petty, calculating, or self-interested detail. It could mean that a person's authority came from above and the focus of his or her soul was on another world. It could mean that a person was closer to [being a] soul. It could also derogatorily imply that a person was "not all there," unfit, or a combination of these, as in Kostylev's description of Luka in Gorky's *Lower Depths*, or in Dostoevsky's Prince Myshkin, and as when a Russian told a journalist that the popular phrase "land of fools" originated in a Gogol story about a man who starves trying to figure out how to break an egg (Kempe 1992:40).

When I asked people about "not from this world" I got this full range of answers. Lara, who loves literature and art, called "not of this world" people

"people with theories" who did not take the beaten path; or a noble person, serving higher goals. Or a sick person, a schizophrenic. A non-ordinary person who does not-customary things in not-customary ways, steps over thresholds, and people forgive him. Sometimes intellectuals or artists, difficult to communicate with, like Sasha [an acquaintance obsessed with his profession]. He can forget you, be insensitive. In times like ours, you might also call a good person "not from this world."

Student Svetlana said that a "not from this world" person was precisely

a *good* person, who does . . . what his conscience whispers, often . . . to his own detriment, which is why people consider him abnormal . . . It is not a compliment. It is said in an annoyed tone of voice because profit is more important to most people than conscience, and it's hard for them to see someone else being better than they are.

A young man described "not from this world" as people dedicated to some idea or occupation; " 'White crows,' people who don't fit stereotypes. Or unsociable people, locked up in themselves, with no friends, or who were betrayed and have withdrawn."

For the writer Lena (whom I interviewed together with her colleague Maxim), "it's a person whose dusha . . . is in contact with something far from the everyday, above *byt*, who lives not only for his family, work, daily tasks and problems, but who is looking over the edge, beyond." Evgeniia Pavlovna said the same:

> I have a friend who is "not from this world." She understands with her mind that right now you have to hoard supplies, stand in lines, wiggle your sharp elbows so you get some before it's gone. She can't do that. For her, "not from this world" is a compliment. . . . She puts her spirituality above things of the moment or the day or even on the scale of a year or two.

And Grisha said, concurring with Lena's image of "looking over the edge,"

> People "not from this world" are creative, animated (*odushe*vlënnye), inspired (*odukh*otvorënnye), have creative, tender internal dushevnyi worlds, are not always efficient and able to live in this world. A mentally ill person [lit. soul-ill] is someone standing on the edge of what we cannot understand, whose dusha is injured. . . . it's offensive that here, people who wanted to think in their own way, create something, were turned into abnormal people.

"Not from this world" could, in the 1990s, be used in these ways and then suddenly shift to being quite literal: as Lena discussed people "not from this world" Maxim suddenly interrupted with "I read a lot of science fiction." During our interview, Aleksandr Ivanovich repeatedly referred romantically to dusha as a world. Then he suddenly took the theme of not fitting in a different direction:

> We're like extraterrestrials. Russians, that is. We're thrown into this world. They explained how to behave, but we can't figure out why it has to be *this* way. In the depths of dusha, we *really* don't like it. . . . We'd like to behave differently. . . . But we have to live according to these . . . rules that . . . did not emerge from the people but were imposed. So we're extraterrestrials. Abandoned in a hostile world.

To return to the Land of Fools, "not from this world" partakes of the holy fool's obliviousness to practical detail. Rancour-Laferriere notes that the Russian Church canonized thirty-six fools, compared to the Greek Church's six, and illustrates continuing enthusiasm for foolishness by the 1991 formation of the Russian Fools' Party (1995:23, 122; see Ries 1997:65 on the fool). Vlasov relates fables involving Ivan the Fool to the notion of "another realm," the search for which begins with rejection of commonsense "wisdom of the world" and with a negative attitude to work confirmed by the New Testament's "Do not be concerned . . . what to eat and drink . . . Behold the birds of the sky: they sow not, neither do they reap" (Vlasov 1992:28–29). In short, a "not from this world" person is not subject to daily constraints, may simply have failed to adapt to the world of *byt*, or both.

Intuition, Hints, and the Inner Voice

Expanses and other worlds—within the person, mediated by art or nature, or outside the social world—are where things come from. In the last chapter I cited Lara on how people may not listen to dusha when it *speaks* or tries to speak. The modes in which some things "appear" into consciousness seem to imply that they are emerging from another space. Aleksandr Ivanovich told me, gesturing around his chest:

> I'm not sure, either intuition is a channel into that mystery called dusha, or the other way around, is a property of dusha that helps a person orient himself in the world. Either way the two are very closely related. Either it's the edge of dusha or the only fine channel that leads there, inside, across a barrier of some sort.

When one is neither in severe soul pain nor numbly deaf to dusha, other worlds speak to one in the mode of intuition or in what can be called hints, *podskazki. Podskazka* is a prompting, a suggesting, in a voice that one may heed or not. One is slipped one of these "hints" as a benevolent comrade might slip the answer to a test question to a floundering student. When not "overlooked" or "unheard," such hints may be described as blurred, as if by distance. Many people I interviewed chose this term, implying manifestations from "underground," as the best tactic to begin to discuss soul itself, and offered it as proof that dusha exists.

The verb *podskazat'* and noun *podskazka* were used primarily with two nouns, dusha and conscience (*sovest'*). Intellect is not usually said to "hint"; it speaks more clearly. Intuition (*intuitsiia*), which does hint or prompt, is not likely to be *said* to do so; that would be almost redundant: in fact, Grisha said "Dusha and intuition . . . I guess they're the same. When you say 'I feel it with dusha,' that *is* intuition." Something hints, prompts, affirms, or disagrees from a place described as so "deep" or "far" that the path is not logical or rational. It's *from there*. When Lara spoke, as when she discussed soul pain, her words often sounded meticulously descriptive of personal experience. "Intuition and dusha," she said in her living room, "that's pretty much the same thing. Dusha *hints*, gives you little shoves: do this, call that person, congratulate that one . . . warn that one . . . if I am in soulful relations with a person . . . I feel his condition. Intuition is dusha's little child."

Whether we understand those messages or not, whether or not we see why they are right, we are advised to listen. Jokes play on the assumption that any "inner voice" must be benevolent and/or wise and/or omnipotent. In one joke, the Inner Voice urges a man in the desert to a lone palm tree beneath which a nude woman is lying. As the man starts towards her, the Inner Voice stops him. In the canonical sentence structure of a benevolent old woman or animal in a fairy tale, the Inner Voice tells him what to do: he must not go straight to her but must climb the tree and jump down. As the obedient man is hurtling toward the ground, the Inner Voice remarks: "Boy, are *you* gonna get fucking hurt." Another joke tells how a merchant, having lost his fortune at roulette, is turning to leave the casino when the Inner Voice appears, telling him fairy-tale-formulaically to go to the third table, not the sixth, and to put his last ruble on red, not black. As he loses, the man hears, in the depths of his soul: "Oh, shit."

For those fluent in a culture, tradition may feel like and be called "intuition"; traditions can thus be revitalized, modified, and invented by apparent "intuition." Friends who did not know proper graveyard etiquette, for example, "intuited" approximations. "Intuition" and "dusha" were often used in contexts in which what others might label "culture" speaks to, through, or in a person. One might say that culture is understood as nature because it seems to speak from "inside." This is a meaning of dusha: "habitual Russian culture."

Though heart (*serdtse*) is not usually said to hint like dusha, it loves, hurts, and speaks. When Lara said, smiling, "If the heart hints then dusha *commands*," she gave dusha's voice to the heart in order to poke fun at dusha's more obnoxious authority. But premonitions, empathy, and knowing that someone dear is hurting are intercourse between a person and dusha, and often involve heart, as we see in a chain of associations Anna Viktorovna made: "Dusha reacts to all sorts of stimuli [irritants]. You're having a good time at a friend's. Suddenly you feel a stab at your heart. This sort of deep pain or worry is illogical: intuition. You're a healthy person but suddenly you feel some agitation. And far, far away someone close to you is going through something or something has happened to him." When I pressed her on the relation between dusha and heart, Anna Viktorovna began confusedly moving between physical and metaphorical hearts and pains, saying "physical, yet not physical." She tried out "biocurrents and magnetic storms" as possible bridges between body and intuition, then gave up: "Something influences dusha negatively."

Inspiration, Talent, Creativity

> The world of art—only there is the reflection of our soul (Michelangelo).
> Poster in a small Omsk region town, 1992

> "For the Soul, From the Entire Soul."
>> Article about a wood carver in *Sel'skaia nov'*, 1992

If talent is expansiveness and contact with expansive worlds, Russians must be talented. Crone (1978:40–41) describes one of Rozanov's literary voices speaking of "literature as a source of knowledge from another realm." Inspiration (*vdokhnovenie*) is something breathed into one; once in dusha, *like* dusha, it implies the pressure of something trying to emerge. One man told me that Russian dusha was good for poets and writers, but not so good for "the simple person." Simple people, according to this imagery, have few developed outlets. Dusha, full of huge, unformulated urges, just strangles people like that. "Dusha has to find a way to pour out its creativity," Svetlana said.

Anna Viktorovna, as did many people, used inspiration and the hinting voice as the best tactic for describing dusha:

> Sometimes Pushkin would write, he said, "with [or *as*] dusha." He wrote and everything poured from his dusha, out of dusha. . . . That means, well, look: a person falls in love. It even happened to me: I started writing poetry. What moved me to do it? I think it was dusha, with its poetry and its internal contents. "He wrote poetry from dusha," or "a letter written from dusha." He thought, and at the same time something hinted to him.

This can be an effortless stream through a wide channel. More often it is described as a painful birth: a musician told Kempe (1992:99) that "Siberian jazz was born in the prison camps . . . People don't write beautiful poetry if they have a good life. They write poetry if they are miserable." The writer Lena told me: "We have a tradition: there is no such thing as a happy poet, at least in our time" (see Dunham 1990:198).

Is dusha necessary for talent? Some believe so: "Talent," one woman said, "it's—probably—a little piece of dusha. Probably talent is a manifestation of dusha's possibilities . . . a way of developing dusha." Eleven-year-old Vitya played guitar and sang. When I interviewed him in his parents' apartment, he said that "When [Vladimir] Vysotskii played songs, he put dusha in them—that means he brings the song to life."

One would think the godlike power to breathe life into forms would require dusha. "But," Vitya continued, "a person can be talented and not have dusha." My businessman friend Oleg said: "Talent and dusha? I see no connection: dusha is always given to almost every person. But talent, excuse me, isn't. And besides, lots of talented people are cruel." Yurii Yur'evich said: "Pushkin called genius and villainy incompatible. I always think about that. Life shows that talented people and geniuses can be evil, if they don't have a spiritual core. A person must have faith in something. . . . Hitler loved music, he painted, but we know he had no dusha."

So if we assume everyone has dusha, what one "believes in" may determine whether it's a good soul. Talent, a mature pathway for dusha to express itself, can be a conduit for other things. People spoke, for example, of the "criminal world" as "another world" and the World of Roofs (*mir kryshi*, protection).

Effort, Education, and Love

I asked people to explain quotes from popular fiction. One, from a science-fiction novel by the popular Strugatskii brothers, was, literally, "Zakhar felt electronics with [his] dusha." A woman in her late twenties said: "Felt electronics with dusha . . . it was some sort of intuition, something internal hinted to him, let him know how it was built, how it worked." When I read the quote to Lara, she said: "Talent. Yes, a subject one didn't study . . . God-given."

Talent was rarely seen as the result of education alone. Kazannik described writer Leonid Andreev's movement "from one sphere of activity to another," in all of which he was brilliant, despite his lack of education, as a sign of his huge soul. Even those who most valued upbringing valued it as contact with others, a matter of dusha. Yurii Yur'evich continued interviewing himself: "Where does a person get dusha? From upbringing. From my atheist position . . . it all depends on the person and how he was raised. On his dusha, as we say." Note how Yurii Yur'evich compelled to add dusha to atheism and to add "it depends on the person" to "how he was raised."

Each individual's soul needs something specific. Pensioner Evgeniia Pavlovna said: "Our system, with its uniform plan for ten years of education, whittled dusha down. That's why it's unfair if they're saying our people are bad. Our government's educational politics had a hand in it. If they give the individual free rein for development, we'll have a different dusha." The day Mila talked to me in her office about how she had been born into the wrong century, one that cramps, crushes, and rushes, she told me that she was fortunate that at least her education "had coincided with" her dusha. Grisha presented it in a different order: "If I receive the education I want, dusha will be in normal, good condition."

Aleksandr Ivanovich, at his desk in the theater, stridently said that "Dusha and education have no link whatsoever. . . . Education . . . allows a person to express . . . some of the . . . movements he experiences in dusha . . . but if that isn't possible, it's not so bad. *If* there's dusha." Of Zakhar's talent, Anna Viktorovna said:

> It's handed down from ancestors, in your genes. When we say genes, genes, genes, that *is* that spiritual apparatus. It's all . . . programmed in. And if it's electronics, well, it's something God-given. And now they're saying that the cosmos affects us. Geniuses were born to simple people, under some star. My

grandmother told us that depending on who was born when, under what star, that's what would be given by God. That's exactly what he—those electronics. The same way my grandfather was born into a family of workers, and he could sketch. . . . Or my Grisha. Something appeared in him. . . . Barsova was this singer we had. . . . She began to sing at forty. A natural soprano. You see. It's built in.

Education's connection to dusha was particularly disputed in discussions of culture. Brought out by this gambit was a notion of innate culture (kul'tura) typically said to come to the uneducated, especially illiterate village grandmothers. In such cases kul'tura was sometimes called a "synonym" of dusha.

In the nineteenth century, dusha was seen as a natural link to the divine and a source of knowledge and perception deeper than anything reason could touch (Williams 1970:576). Andrei Orlov told me in 1992: "Talent and dusha are given at birth . . . that's all you get. . . . I got mathematical ability for free, it was God-given. I have a great memory for poetry. They blew it into me together with my dusha."

Even if "that's all you get," there is room for development. Andrei's wife, my friend Zina, said: "You can kill talent, develop it, but . . . in the beginning all people are talented." The same is often said about dusha: everyone is born with it, but upbringing determines its qualities. In the last chapter I mention "work on oneself." Irina used it to introduce a thoughtful refinement: "Talent is God-given. If we don't work on ourselves, that talent may not develop. Talent is given from above and dusha—that's what you can make of it." So, Irina indicates, dusha can be seen as giving life to talent.

Let's approach this from a different angle. Nadia (Anna Viktorovna's daughter-in-law), in response to my question about Zakhar's sense of electronics, said "He just has an ability, a facility that drew him to that thing; he *liked* it very much, that thing, and so he *felt* it. Everything you love you want to—take possession of, because it comes to you easily." This is different; Nadia is saying that facility makes you like or love a thing, "feel" it. One way or another, in all these different versions, facility, effort, and achievement have limited authority unless they are linked to something more mysterious, in this case, love.

Grisha's answer to this question went through a sea change that again demonstrates the power of love: he began by quoting "Talent is 99 percent labor." He paused, as if he assumed I would be shocked by him saying that, and then continued:

Talent is the final result of some kind of work. *And it is talent to the extent that dusha has been put into that work.* If not, you can tell immediately. Even if the work is done well externally, if the artist didn't put dusha in, there's no dusha there. Talent is when dusha *needs* something. Combine heart, hand, brain, and soul—they all pour into the work. . . . I never learned to draw, but where to put what color—I feel it with my dusha. Your Zakhar, he just *loved* it a lot. People made that electronic device, they put dusha into it, and with that dusha Zakhar found a common language. What kind we don't know, but if he felt it with his dusha, there's nothing you can say. He felt it, and had no education!

On one hand, in their answers these speakers all (except Andrei, who spoke out of his immersion in astrology) drew on some form of the Marxist principle that true value is created by work; but the opposite direction obtains as well: work and talent are created by what people value, and dusha is felt to be "where" people value things.

Through love for a medium and the resulting "natural" affinity for it, "alive" relationship with it, souls communicate. Intimacy with something's dusha lets one work well with it, and vice versa, if one's dusha is "not inclined towards" something. If a loved thing is inanimate, such intimacy may still be called love, communion of souls; a thing's or discipline's soul is its rules, conditions, principles. A talented person is one who is on familiar terms with a domain, which makes her or him like a creator of things of that world. As Bakhtin writes, "Indifference will never . . . generate sufficient power to slow down and linger intently" (Emerson 1996:112–13); "Only love," Emerson continues, "can 'see' the world with sufficient subtlety and focus to be aesthetically productive . . . It takes passionate energy and inner need."

The ideas that talent is God-given, that it is the result of effort, and that effort is the result of love, that dusha is given to everyone and that dusha is developed, are not simply opposing opinions of different people: they alternate, often in the same person's words, and define a repertoire. An individual may begin in an adamant voice suited to a specific context or project, and then shift to another version in a different spirit.

A note on Grisha's comment that it is immediately apparent if art has no soul: Mila also said that "A writer or composer must have what passes for dusha. Without it, he'd be a cripple . . . Just as a person with no arms is identifiable now, in the nineteenth century one could immediately identify a person without spiritual qualities." Masha, Grisha's coworker, said that from a person's art "you can understand what kind of dusha he has" and if he has one at all. Art was expected to have soul and foster it, and it is with dusha that one perceives art and identifies it as good or bad.

Williams (1970:580) finds the first full-blown use of *russkaia dusha* in a description of a writer who could "experience in his living soul the manifestations of the external world, and thereby . . . breathe a living soul into them."

A seraph in Pushkin's "Prophet" thrusts a live coal into the prophet's breast. God tells him to arise and set men's hearts on fire. What is put into one's breast can be used to create more of the same fire in others, whatever the nature of that fire.

Generativity

Art is supposed to reach and affect the soul. On the radio in December 1992 I heard: "If something good comes from dusha, from the heart, it will always find a path to people." Lara told me, gesturing at her glassed-in bookshelves: "In our society it's customary to follow ideals. . . . Literature offered us those ideals." But some art, Lara said, like Brodsky's poetry, does not reach the soul (*do dushi ne probiraet*, a transformation of an expression used when cold chills one to the bone). Lara is saying that Brodsky's work neither touches *her* deeply nor penetrates deeply into *things*.

"Good art" penetrates into the dusha of its subject matter. Prosecutor Yurii Yur'evich said of his favorite writer: "I'm attracted to the astounding penetration of his prose into Russian dusha [and] our nature. He was a . . . crystal-pure soul who helped those around him . . . he led such a *big* life." Aleksandr Ivanovich, in his theater office, made clear how these souls tend toward being one soul:

> Art is apparently the only means mankind has come up with . . . to bring out that strange notion of dusha . . . Any work of art is . . . a portrait of dusha, both of the artist and of dusha in general. When we paint a landscape, we paint ourselves. Our dusha. Not our exterior. Art is the only not-entirely-crooked mirror of dusha ever invented.

An aside: Aleksandr Ivanovich himself, under other circumstances, would certainly label different things "the only" and "the best" medium for dusha. Superlatives and exclusivity are an interesting rhetorical aspect of soul talk.

Writers, painters, and especially poets, musicians, and actors are described in terms of other worlds they interact with, represent, and help us enter. A toast at a theater's season-opening banquet said that we are all sleeping; actors awaken us "into a new, other world." An actor who "approaches his art," Anna Viktorovna said, "with dusha . . . lives his role *with all his entrails*. He gives himself with dusha. He doesn't just physically go through the motions; his whole dusha is *right here* . . . Strong!! The whole organism is aroused and works on it." She pointed at a place in her chest which is "where they say" dusha lives, continuing: "Heart pain and soul pain get mixed up."

Orthodox hesychastic techniques for experiencing divine light concentrated attention on the heart area. Aleksandr Ivanovich indicated this spot when he said "It's exactly with dusha that actors work. Russian actors know so well how to suffer, everything *inside* them works so well, suffers so deeply, dusha tears apart."[10] On TV in the mid-1990s I heard, in praise of

---

[10] This use of "work" and Anna Viktorovna's above, when I mentioned them to others, caused reactions ranging from agreement to objection to what was called "a crude choice of words." When "work" is seen as infected with everyday, mechanistic logic, it is of questionable accuracy or delicacy in discussions of spirit.

an actor, a fully serious use of the phrase "the full depth of the enigmatic Russian soul."

Actor / director Konstantin Raikin said, in a TV interview recorded at about the same time, that he dreamed of acting "so that something changed in nature, on earth, in the *system.*" He implies that if one approaches one's own "center," increases it through clearer or stronger perception or representation of it, one can affect the (center of the) world.

An artwork or performance may seem to open up a "world" with its own laws and terms. Those who create may seem to participate in such internal or external places, a relationship that, perhaps, anyone may have to something, but that not everyone is seen as being in a condition to have. Other worlds and soul were portrayed as necessary; their reign as one of need. Need from within, but need. Relating correctly to other worlds seemed to matter to people.

This apparent nervousness about accepting "this world" as definitive coexisted with intense late Soviet concerns with material goods and capitalist sensibilities, an issue to which I return. I also return throughout this book to the issue of "worlds" in which individuals operate more or less virtuously and between which people may or may not be able to build bridges. Love seems to indicate these places or be one way to contact them; and what is loved by an individual defines and is defined by the kind of dusha she/he has.

CHAPTER FOUR

The Language of Music and the Russian Language

[The voice] was slightly broken and rang as if cracked ... but it also contained unfeigned depth of passion, and youthfulness, and strength, and sweetness, and a kind of attractively careless, plaintive sorrow. The true, fiery soul of Russia resounded and breathed through it and quite simply seized you by the heart ... in every sound ... there wafted something native and vastly spacious, just as if the familiar steppe was spreading out before us, stretching off into the endless distance.

Turgenev, "The Singers," *Sketches from a Hunter's Album*

Maybe all our muteness comes from an inability to write music.

Erofeev

Music has long been associated with Russian dusha. It is seen as an integral part of national character. And many people love music. It seems to be a rich conduit for soul partially in that it can be rather independent of language. But although dusha-related things are almost always characterized as impossible to fully represent in words, the "great, powerful, splendid Russian language" indicates an equally important aspect of dusha.

Music

In the village, on Tamara's birthday, Zhenia kept trying to start playing guitar earlier than she wanted him to. He finally went to play for the children who, as usual, were having their party in a separate room. When he returned, before he began to play, he turned to me. Grinning, he announced that after I finished this book I had to start studying a mystery as profound as Russian dusha, one that deserves its own book: "Why, whenever these friends get together, is *this* always the first song we sing?" They sang that song, an obscure one, and then more, each significant to them for some idiosyncratic mixture of reasons. Zhenia switched to *baian*, a folk accordion with buttons; a guest accompanied him, rattling a fork in an empty vodka bottle. Her husband played spoons from the table, and concentrating hard, Tamara and Zhenia's son played a metal spoon against a wooden spoon against his thigh. Songs might be punctuated by discussion of them; which songs were discussed and which allowed to silently yield to subsequent songs, on which occasions, was itself an artfully manipulated medium. Zhenia and the neighbor alternated singing scores of chastushki.[1] In pauses between chastushki (often labeled "for dusha") people discussed more or less obscene versions, who had invented which and when, as well as comments to me about their ritual importance.[2] One woman said that it was hard to sing chastushki and dance at the same time, but that if you sat quietly you could remember a hundred at a time.

The next day I went to a tinier village with a group of musicians. Waiting for us was an audience of all ages. Men stood around the edges of the hall and outside, smoking. I was introduced from the stage; my hostess told the villagers to receive me "not with fear or alarm." They drank brown alcohol before performing and offered it to anyone who would sing, dance, or otherwise participate. After the performance, young people took off their coats and danced to loud recorded rock music. The babushki watched, then got up to dance in their wool scarves and coats.

When I returned to the city, Anna Viktorovna asked me if they had sung chastushki, stressing *they*; "*They* love to sing chastushki and *they* do it so well." She did not know Zhenia and Tamara; I had to assume *they* meant the "simple Russian folk." She tried to open a conversation about how *they* were so close to nature, but no one in the family took her up on it.

Music and song have long been associated with Russian dusha. In the eighteenth century, Herder (and Radishchev in Russia) wrote that a people's character was manifested in its songs:

> In Russia, national romanticism took the form of Slavophilism, and found in Konstantin Aksakov one of the most spirited spokesmen for the point of view which equated folk-lore with folk-soul, and folk-soul with the national character. . . . For Aksakov the folk-song became the national song and its study . . . would, he was convinced, reveal the national spirit. (Rogger 1960:156–61)

This opinion was informed by the fact that, Rogger continues, "the love for song seems to have been common to all parts of Russian society." The view of music and particularly folk song as an integral part capable of revealing national character persisted as the notion of Russian soul developed. In

---

[1] Four-line folk rhymes. See Chapter 11, Sinyavsky 1988:222–23, and Paxson 1999.
[2] One man told me about obscene chastushki sung at his daughter's wedding, saying that a wedding without "strong" chastushki (*krepkie,* as in "strong drink") just isn't complete.

1839, M. N. Katkov used the term "Russian soul" in his review of a book of Russian folk songs, what Williams (1970:577) considers to be a nearly mature reference to the Romantic Russian national soul. During the 1800s, Mussorgsky, Borodin, Rimsky-Korsakov and others were, independently and together, working on incorporating folk elements into a truly "Russian" high music. In 1992, a line from Mussorgsky was chosen as the post-Soviet central radio theme because, a person responsible said in a radio interview, his music embodies Russian expanse (*prostor*) and scale (*masshtabnost'*).

In December 1992, I watched a television show on Gypsies; the Russians I was watching with said that Gypsy entertainment helped Russians "rest with dusha," which explained why people used to pay so dearly for it. Gypsy choirs were, of course, associated with the legendary debauchery so often linked to dusha's willfulness and dashing, bold gestures. Lemon (1996:2) points out that although "most Russians do not acknowledge [Gypsies'] attachment and allegiance to places where they grew up," many "can hardly speak of Gypsies without reference to . . . Russian literature and national culture" and to "the vastness of Russian land" (ibid.:74–79). Gypsy wandering and willfulness are associated by Russian and Romani intellectuals with " 'longing for an unreachable ideal, a kind of nostalgia . . . directed not only backwards . . . but . . . forwards' . . . [linking] Gypsies and their songs to an image of the Russian soul as always in motion, 'constantly searching'." "Other discourses," Lemon says, "make a more direct connection, as if the Russian soul and Gypsy singing surge up from the same source." Thus "the melancholy and motion of the 'ever-searching Russian soul' . . . passes from Russian landscape . . . through the body of the Gypsy singer . . . a natural conduit for waves of national nostalgia" (ibid.:80–85). A woman watching the TV show with me said, by way of criticizing the TV Gypsy, that when you watch a Gypsy sing, "dusha should curl up, open, and curl up again. But nothing inside me is moving. Watching her, I feel no emotion at all. It's not the real thing." This "Russian" woman used her dusha to judge the Gypsy's authenticity *as a Gypsy*.

Of course, music was "selected" as a manifestation of and food for Russian dusha because of its qualities *as* music, as well as because music by Romantic definition expresses the souls of nations. I touch on this important topic only briefly and from a distance. In most of these chapters, discussion focuses on values and practices related to *wordlessness*, places where post-Soviet linguaculture (Attinasi and Friedrich 1995:34) gestured (or claimed to gesture) at what was seen and valued as "not linguistic," including aspects of what was categorized and constructed as transcendent, sublime, and extreme.

These "depths" that "could not be expressed" were skillfully gestured at and constructed, and jealously guarded as unfathomable and transformative. Fëdor Shaliapin, in an autobiographical work, recounts how, during a late-1800s performance of Mussorgsky's *Boris Godunov*,

When Varlaam began to sing his heavy, painful, and outwardly absurd song ... I felt something unusual was happening to me. I suddenly felt in that strange music something shockingly dear, familiar to me. It seemed that my entire tangled and difficult life was taking place exactly to this music, which always accompanied me, lives in me, in my soul, and moreover, that that music was everywhere in the world I knew. This is how I say it now, but then I simply felt some sort of reverential confluence of sadness and joy. I wanted to cry and laugh. For the first time I sensed, then, that music is the voice of the soul of the world, its wordless song. (Shaliapin 1960:109)[3]

One man described how he and trusted friends used to gather in secret to listen to the Beatles, how terrified they were, and how valuable the music was: "*Everything* was like that music."

Opposed to what was practical and "goes through the mind," music was popularly seen as falling soundly within the domain of emotions and the nonanalytic, and thus formally shared dusha's project. The privileged position of music was due partially to the sense that music could take up, as it were, where "language," tainted by its ability to express analytically, has to leave off. Music was felt to be a two-way channel of representation to and from dusha. I will give a few examples.

One is rather elementary: language can be "unsuited" for expressing certain things because of social sanctions against saying them or because of embarrassment or tact. I was often told about how during the Brezhnev years it was necessary to sing "cunningly" and "in code" to say things that could not be said directly. And Anna Viktorovna described how, in her youth, she used bits of arias to send her suitors messages about their relationship.

Music was very salient in speakers' descriptions of themselves and others. That a person was musically talented was an important biographical detail in descriptions of family members, acquaintances, and famous figures, particularly the conditions and qualities of those persons' souls. Mila, for example, mentioned her musical interests when she said that her dusha "coincided with" her education. She said that her brother was sensitive, but "now he has to toughen up to do his job—contract his dusha a little, a *lot*. He plays guitar and sings so beautifully." The first thing Anna Viktorovna said about her grandfather was that he loved music; "that was passed on to Mother and her sister. The most important thing was the guitar." Music was mentioned by Yurii Yur'evich, Anna Viktorovna, Mila, eleven-year old Vitya, and many others as an attribute of a cultured person, educated or not. A man in his thirties complimented Aleksandr Bashlachëv's music as being "from dusha, not from the mind," presenting me with a Bashlachëv album, "the most revealing thing about Russian dusha" he could think of.

---

[3] Victor Friedman pointed out to me the passage in the libretto to which Shaliapin is referring. It is an indictment of the love of money.

Artemy Troitsky, in a book on Soviet rock (Zaitsev 1990:47–55), writes that once, in 1985, Bashlachëv, "the only one who combined the whole wealth of the Russian soul with the raw nerve of rock culture," cut his fingers while playing. The guitar was splashed with blood;

> It's a banal metaphor, but he had really rent his entire soul. . . . "Vanyusha" is a song about the Russian spirit. . . . Unfortunately when talking about . . . Bashlachëv's songs . . . it is often necessary to resort to trite overused words, that is, to understandings that have depreciated almost to the level of kitsch such as the "Russian soul", "faith and hope", "love and death", or "spiritual strength." Of course, this is not Bashlachëv's fault.

In this book, participants in the Russian rock scene repeatedly use words the translators render as *soul* and *spirit* in reference to Russian rock.

I have discussed talent as a phenomenon of dusha; Zina said: "I've met many completely uneducated people who understand poetry, music, are painters." Everyday notions of culture could be quite different from official ones. Kul'tura could be dusha-like "inner" or natural culture. Anna Viktorovna said, for example, "Although Siberian aborigines were illiterate, those northerners naturally strived towards culture. When Russian exiles appeared here, they tried to imitate them. They were torn off from civilization, but strived towards it. Balalaika. Instruments. All those pipes, those rattles."

When Andrei described people he knew who were "not from this world," he defined them as having a "part of the intellect connected to the cosmos, or with some higher mind . . . [they] feel intuitively . . . even little things. A musician who just up and writes music." Again, this "deeper" representational ability is seen as two-way; music and poetry not only come from but speak to people who have not learned to experience them. This is possible because they "speak" *from* and *to* dusha. And implied by Russian dusha is "the cosmos," "a higher mind."

A third context, which vividly illustrates the soulful power of music, is the role singing and music play at gatherings. The same adjective, *zadushevnyi*, is used for soulful conversations and soulful songs. Jarintzov (1916:100–101) translates it revealingly literally as "behind-the-soul:"

> a quality which dwells in the deepest recesses of one's spirit. Thus, the man who is endowed with "behind the-soul"-ness is very deep and sympathetic . . . straightforward. . . . A conversation . . . can be a "behind-the-soul" one; also a voice, or a manner of reciting and of acting. The last two *must* be . . . "behind-the-soul" . . . to reach a Russian listener's heart.

Singing together, playing instruments, or listening to recorded music were important parts of rituals of sitting together, but a situation I experienced a number of times was especially revealing. Each occasion had this basic structure: subsequent to some social gaffe or mention of an uncomfortable topic, everyone at a formerly warm, comfortable table would fall silent, isolated by a lonely awkwardness. After a pause, someone would suggest singing, playing an instrument, putting on music, just mention some music-related topic, or simply begin singing or playing, heroically and abruptly pulling the company out of anomie by summoning music, dusha's agent, to reorient or purify the situation into comfortable dushevnost'.[4]

For example, I had been told a funny story about an Omsk boy whose mother spoke five languages and worked at the KGB: when asked at school what she did, he answered, "She listens." When I retold this at a dinner, rather than laughing (as had the woman who originally told it to me), everyone present fell silent, so unwelcome was the topic and so unmanageable. A woman sitting next to me became so uncomfortable that I felt my left side stiffening and numbing with her mistrust. This continued. Then she suddenly sang in a stunning, huge, powerful grandmother voice, with little sighs, twists, and ornaments, old, old Russian and Ukrainian folk songs.

Bakhtin writes that "the voice can *sing* only in a *warm* atmosphere . . . of possible choral support, where *solitariness* of sound is in principle excluded" (1990:170). By a common causal flip-flop, if one sings, the atmosphere must be warm; dusha, when it is happy, is said to sing. Mila needed to escape from the city for a few days, and a family birthday gave us a chance to do so. At her parents' house, in an outlying town, the next afternoon, a favorite family song was on the radio. "Sister, do you love me?" Mila's twenty-nine-year-old brother asked her. "The auntie on the radio sings so tenderly," remarked his five-year-old son. After a meal, Mila's father played accordion, his son guitar, and everyone sang. Mila's brother sang a romantic ballad, then satirical songs. Then he began a sad song. The lights were dim. His mother leaned over and asked in a whisper if I understood the songs' *sense*. When her son was a boy, he used to fall asleep at his father's feet while he sang; now it happens the other way around. We sat, affirming and creating community about "understanding" something, about certain emotions, a state of shared dusha.

These angles all imply that music partakes of another aspect of dusha—one that is totalizing, "strong." "To relate to something with one's dusha," as Mila said, "involves the entire essence of the person, emotions, feelings, thoughts, reflection—everything." Sinyavsky discusses what he calls the notion of a "primal, elemental force" in Blok's poetry about the Revolution, a force that, Sinyavsky says, shares a description with Russian dusha:

> that force is always a revitalizing, creative, musical principle, biding its time in nature's depths, in the popular and cosmic soul. It is the wild, unbridled spirit of music . . . where . . . culture blossoms and thrives. The elemental force is ir-

[4] Cf. Sugarman 1997 on Albanian weddings where singing avoids conversation that may lead to fights. See also Stewart 1994.

rational and organic. . . . To try to resist it is as senseless as trying to battle the
storm. (Sinyavsky 1988:15)

Professional woman singers (and amateurs who protected their voices) to
whom I spoke did not sing full voice while menstruating: they had been
taught that this could destroy the voice. If "sick days" were a time of
fragility, singing was a strong involvement of the "whole person."
Having feelings for music is a vital sign, sometimes literally. Oleg said
with delight that at a recent party his granny had been "dancing, rather
than dying!" In her room, at the round table, Anna Viktorovna said:

Before! You understand? Friends . . . we still sit, we fill up—spiritually—remembering student days. We're nondrinkers. It turned out that way. But when
I feel music and nature, I'm simply—*all* of me—here— . . . Either music, or
talking with a friend. I come to life. . . . There are young people with old dushi.
Yes. They're not so interested in music, in nature; they get sick often, and nothing—affects them, moves them. But a spiritually young person, every—string
moves him. He's all—you understand—here, *all*. I'm sick, but when music
starts I—my dusha—it's not that it's a good one, no, but it's *in* me. . . . People
who are missing vision, hearing, mute, they can't—but they're drawn—their
sense organs are—turned off, but with dusha they can represent correctly.
Beethoven. Deaf, he composed music. I think that was dusha working. My
grandfather subscribed to *Guitarist*. He had them bound, leather, and wrote
his name in there. . . . Those were *his* books. There, a fine dusha. Oh. Fine. Can
you—that—people with a fine dusha. Fine dusha. People keep it to old age.

The culture of poetry shares much with that of music (Friedrich 1997).
Poetry partakes of both language and music, bridging the wordless and the
expressible. As the writer Lena said: "a person who lives with an elevated
dusha . . . is in contact with something far from the everyday . . . poets and
writers are . . . not from this world. Why would a normal person need those
rhymes, rhythms?" Many people told me "Esenin *is* our Russian dusha."[5]
Lena said:

The most touching poetry is by criminals. They all love Esenin. Esenin is—you
understand, a poet in whom dusha is standing *right here,* and even criminals—
well, there probably are some in whom dusha will never wake up. But there are
moments—of awakening. For some reason I believe that. Dusha is sleeping.
Drowsy. Overgrown. Grown over with all sorts of bad—but one wants to believe that there are *moments*.

Feeling or loving music or poetry is proof that a person can be moved,
proof of "life," of dusha. Versions of dusha alternate here: one version

---

[5] The cult that arose after Esenin's 1925 suicide "included individualism, soulful verse, sexual machismo, heavy drinking and even suicide" (Stites 1992:62).

places dusha metaphysically above physical life; another only values it above physical life. Anna Viktorovna implies that lack of love for music can cause a tendency to illness or that at least the two share a cause. But she was ill and her continuing love proved that her dusha was more alive than her body. One toast at Mila's parents' house on the evening I discussed above was "dusha never grows old." But Anna Viktorovna invokes the not uncommon idea of an old dusha, a soul that something had managed to erode or shrink, making it less playful or responsive.

When I asked eleven-year-old Vitya what qualities would make him admire a person, make that person an authority for him personally, he said: "If he read a lot, played an instrument. Went to concerts, to the theater. When Vysotskii[6] sang, he put in dusha—that means he brought the song to life . . . music brings back dusha. When I listen to it." It was extremely common to hear in everyday speech and in the media that "songs warm dusha," in effect, bring dusha to consciousness, make it more alive. A segment of my interview with writers Maxim and Lena reflects this:

LENA: A soulful song is a warm song, a sad song—soulfulness presupposes suffering. . . . I saw this show on TV—they show peasants talking about Russian soul; they have a few shots, say that that dusha—you can't just step over it. And it continues: dusha, Russia. Then they cut to Buenos Aires and an orange tree, underneath it an armchair, clearly foreign-made, and there's this, excuse me, provincial mug from Riazan playing balalaika and singing "my fate is bitter, sent me to foreign lands." How many years have passed since he emigrated! And his dusha is alive! Written on the screen, former Argentine millionaire. He owned factories . . . but he just settled down in the middle class and sings under his tree.

MAXIM: I want to add, though, a dushevnyi song is not necessarily sad. "Dusha sings!" When we recently had that festival, *Soul of Russia* (Dusha Rossii), they had a Kuban choir, and tears sprang to my eyes, the sensation was so strong that you just start to *burst* with emotion.[7] There's suddenly a lot of air.

LENA: Well, everybody's entitled to his opinion.

The emigrant's sadness and his continued participation in Russia, represented and sustained by Russian music, which he is presented as preferring

---

[6] Vladimir Vysotsky (1938–1980) died of a heart attack. Like Esenin, and more recently, Venedikt Erofeev, soulful Russian writers who died tragically, singer/poets who became mythologized and represented the dusha of their time also included Viktor Tsoi (1962–1990, car accident) and Aleksandr Bashlachëv (1962–1988, threw himself from a Leningrad window).

[7] Burst: *raspirat'*. The verb *raspirat'* refers to a situation where something is propped up from inside, as a skeleton or frame supports a skin; in the context of feelings, it is when emotions fill one, push outwards, explode. A violin's "soul" (Chapter 10) is *dushka* (from dusha, a translation in this case from Fr. *âme*) or *rasporka*.

over wealth (the marked implied antagonism between these things is significant), proves that his dusha is alive.

Soul Death: Music

There were several ways in which present circumstances were said to be killing this particular aspect of dusha. One was the sense that national culture might be eclipsed and tainted by Western culture. But when my friend Grisha, Anna Viktorovna's craftsman son, said, apropos of a local school closing, "How can we have any hope now *at all*, how can the government say 'children are our future' if music schools are being closed?" he was not speaking of Russian music in particular; love of music of any kind indicated Russianness. Oleg said, after we listened to music with his friend Anatolii and I clearly enjoyed it, that I was "becoming completely Russian."

As I have mentioned, suffering, the epitome of soulful emotions, has (at least) a trinity of effects on dusha: developing, deepening, and tempering it. Yurii Yur'evich gave a similarly tripartite description of the effects of art on soul but included a paradox (resulting from both multiple definitions of dusha and multiple ways of seeing dusha):

> Why, if you come to a symphony concert, do you not see people sitting with their hats on and shelling sunflower seeds? And when you come out of the organ hall no one is suddenly struck with the desire, if you'll excuse me, to go bash someone's face in? . . . On the other hand, Hitler loved music . . . but he had no dusha. Taste was there, dusha was not. It depends on education and on spiritual upbringing. Literature, music, painting, theater, can resurrect dusha, raise [teach, give upbringing to] dusha, and kill it.

The socioeconomic situation was felt to be conspiring against song. A 1991 *Argumenty i fakty* (national newspaper) article, "Song Helps Us Survive" (a variation on a 1950s song line), began: "The last six years have given us much and taken away a lot . . . We have forgotten the main thing—dusha. Dusha is drawn to the land, to love, to song. And no piece of sausage . . . can touch dusha as can a quiet song on the accordion."[8] A thirty-year-old woman claimed that "Things have changed—to just embrace someone because your dusha is singing is not done anymore." Once, while I was interviewing Anna Viktorovna in the kitchen, her daughter-in-law Nadia, Grisha's wife, came in and joined us:

---

[8] A radio show on the 1992 Omsk *Russian Soul* cultural festival mentioned the secret of Russian dusha, and that, though the festival had not changed the city's appearance: "That's good; it has left another mark on the city's residents; something stirred in their dushi."

ANNA VIKTOROVNA: People are exhausted emotionally, psychologically. . . . In our youth, we loved dancing, and we loved singing. . . . Nadia's parents and I—

NADIA: My father's in a group.

ANNA VIKTOROVNA: And times were hard—

NADIA: Folk. There was this folk group. Young and old. And he danced great. When we'd get together on holidays he'd have such a good time—

ANNA VIKTOROVNA: You know, civilization sometimes has a negative effect on dusha—

Other times this effect was blamed on more concrete entities. One man in his twenties said: "True Russian culture, Russian dusha, for example, folklore, song—like they say, someone 'sang from dusha'; it means he *felt* it. Song was one of the useful fragments Soviet culture took from Russian. But then it exploited those things." Russian soul in the form of music was coopted by official Soviet kul'tura, as were other ethnic music and performance traditions. One May 10, during a Victory Day weekend, I followed four veterans, three grandmothers with shawls over their heads and one older man, as they crossed a city park loudly singing folk songs. Soviet patriotism could be continuous with Russian national pride, and song was part of that. A number of people bitterly cited Young Communist League songs they had, they said, sung proudly as children, and which in retrospect seemed to have been a cruel hoax and soul exploitation.

Music's soulful value persisted into the post-Soviet era, and interesting transformations happened to music in particular during the 1990s. Alongside Westernized rock and "punk" groups, some performers focused on variably parodic and ironic performances of folk music (the St. Petersburg-based Mitki are an example) as well as syntheses of Russian and Western music.

In Chapter 7 I cite Nadia characterizing the current loss of dusha as: "You can't make people sing or dance." In an essay, an eighteen-year-old student said the same:

We grew up in a different time. We're more open, less ideologized. We accept events more easily. Young people make money more quickly. . . . It's harder for our parents to get used to things. On the other hand, our parents are spiritually richer. At their birthday parties they dance, they sing. We don't do that, we aren't used to it.

When I say that music has privileged access to and power over dusha, that it can be a dominant of dusha and dusha of it, I mean that dusha was made, remade, and transformed in ritual contexts where music was important; that music, changing in meaning over time, fed into the meaning of dusha, and, vice versa, changing dusha fed the meaning of music.

The Russian Language

As much, however, as "wordlessness" and an alleged impossibility of full representation were characteristic of soul-related things, reference to the great, powerful, splendid Russian language (*velikii, moguchii, prekrasnyi russkii iazyk*, a phrase used by Turgenev, as much a cliché as "enigmatic, mysterious Russian soul")—pointed at an important aspect of dusha even in the late Soviet period, playing a central role in Gorbachev's description of perestroika.

Lomonosov (1711–1765) wrote that Roman Emperor Karl V said that one should use Spanish for speaking with God, French with friends, German with enemies, and Italian with women; but had he known Russian, he would have found in it magnificence, vivacity, power, tenderness, and the wealth and expressive precision of Greek and Latin (Rogger 1960:103; see also Ries 1997:30–32). Jarintzov (1916:xi) wrote that the aim of her book *The Russians and Their Language* "was to show that those who want to understand the *Russian national character* . . . should try and learn the original Russian speech" and that Russian reflects national character in its

> wealth . . . sparkling colouring . . . warmth, and . . . flexibility . . . due . . . to three factors: (1) The youthful vigour caused by the ever-present ingress of the child-young Old Slavonic and Old Russian elements; (2) the . . . influence of the 'syllables of nuances' and terminations, the scales of which allow boundless subtlety in the rendering of various . . . half-shades of thought; (3) the freedom of arranging the relative order of words. (ibid.:2)

Sinyavsky (1988:219) also takes as a given that "for its multiplicity of synonyms," Russian is the richest language in the world. Similarly, although the word for Germans is popularly believed to come from that for mute (those who could not speak Russian), the imprint of German philosophy on dusha is evident in the way native speakers of Russian talk about their language. They still very often discuss Russian as a microcosm of national culture, including " 'tradition, history, religion, and basis of life, all its heart and soul' " (Rogger 1960:86). In his February 1986 speech to the twenty-seventh Party Congress, Gorbachev (1987 3:273) repeatedly emphasized, using an unprecedented density of words based on *dukh*, that only literature was capable of enriching people's spiritual life, cultivating in them an honest, strong spirit.

Soul Death: Language

Beautiful and/or correct Russian was discussed surprisingly often. Opinions on details of Russian grammar were dispensed with an air of imparting esoteric knowledge that ennobled its possessor. Perhaps, as a Russian-speaking foreigner, I heard more of this, but it was a popular topic in the media in response to the recent influx of foreign lexical items, another front on which the times were said to be killing soul. A forty-year-old artist told me that only two kinds of people still spoke Russian well: descendants of emigrated aristocrats (most of whom, of course, had favored French over Russian) and the "real people." These are two versions of "good" Russian: one prerevolutionary high culture, one rural folk. Both, in this woman's view, imply purity and decency. I asked who exactly the "real people" were; she replied that they were people who work, and thus have access to the real, morality-bearing Russian. Oleg also spoke with respect of the few "cultured" people who still spoke beautiful Russian, citing it as a moral virtue as well as one continuous with ability to create in that language. In his accounts these people were first-emigration Russians, whose dushi, like that of the orange-treed Argentine millionaire, were "still alive."

Of course, writers have long enjoyed special respect in Russia, and not only among the intelligentsia. Steinberg (forthcoming) mentions that Revolution-era workers, in memoirs and letters, "repeatedly expressed a reverence for the printed word and for those who wrote." "Our leaders," wrote Nadezhda Mandelstam, have a "boundless, almost superstitious respect for poetry. There is no place where more people are killed for it" (cited in Dunham 1990:xxi).

The theme of the Jew, Russian-born yet speaking poor Russian, is one of many images that imply the Jew's questionable membership in the Russian-souled collective. Characteristic Jewish accent and grammar were assumed to stem from a lack of natural love of and talent for Russian (and thus dusha), in favor of alliance to other languages and cultures. The same Kuprin who claims (Lemon 1996:80) that the natural effect of the Gypsy voice intensifies Russian songs' emotional power maintains in regard to Jews, a people in legend as "homeless" as Gypsies, that in one domain "nationalism is forgivable:"

[Jews] are bringing into the splendid Russian language hundreds of German, French, merchant-conventional, telegraphically abbreviated, absurd and repulsive words. They have created an illegal literature and a social-democratic brochurese horrid to the tongue. . . . For God's sake, chosen people! Become generals, engineers, scholars, doctors, lawyers. . . . But do not touch our language, which is alien to you . . . you have pissed all over it . . . latched onto it . . . as sometimes a hysterical street whore latches onto a broad, wise, generous, tender, but too charitable soul.

I return to this 1909 letter by Kuprin, including its pissing reference, in a later chapter.

Language becomes a metonym for the larger principle that we can communicate with, be understood by, *ours* but not *not* ours. Love of and talent for interpreting and presenting Russian music redeems the Gypsy and identifies her wandering with dusha's wandering, making her, if not fully ensouled, at least a fitting conduit for dusha. The Jew's homelessness is unredeemed, thus soulless. Sinyavsky (1988:210), who in no way blames Jews, discusses Soviet projects of transforming Russian into a language for a new *byt*. He describes the Russian language's transformation into "Sovietese," dissembling and mystifying "incantations supposed to remake the world."

Sinyavsky also discusses how what had been seen as crude, cursing folk language entered wider use after the Revolution: "Metaphorically speaking, the Russian intelligentsia married a muzhik" (peasant) and was subsequently influenced by his vernacular (ibid.:199–200). Yet this muzhik, of course, had as much Russian soul as any writer. In Chapter 3 I mention the man telling me that Russian dusha was a good thing for poets and writers, but not so good for a simple person with few developed outlets. *Mat*, the rich, malleable Russian invective "language," was humorously called "folklore" with reason: it is the "simple" Russian soul's creativity flowing and bursting out.

For Dusha: Strong Language and Music

> Russian dusha—that's when a guy sits in a hut playing the balalaika, then he stops, gets up, goes outside, and yells: "Your mother!" It echoes through the frozen taiga, *mothermothermother*; then he goes back inside, and everything's OK. You understand?
>
> Maxim, Omsk, 1992

The verb *otvesti* usually occurs in two contexts: one is in rerouting a canal or other flowing water; the other is in conjunction with dusha; *otvesti dushu* is to get carried away, let oneself go, get it off one's chest, relieve one's dusha. It implies directing outward, expressing one's innermost impulse; one such context is in cursing outrage or frustration. Other contexts for *otvesti dushu* are unbridled revenge, resting, eating, drinking, or beating someone. Rough, blunt or obscene speech (called *mat, matershchina, fol'klor*, saying something "in Russian," and speaking in the "great, powerful, splendid Russian language")—like *razmakh* in gestures—can be seen as opposing some external constraint or in response to internal pressure, and are regularly associated with dusha. Such lexical art was commonly identified with Russian and Russianness in statements such as a friend's to me: "The trial of the CPUSSR was *purely Russian,* just insults and offense." *Moskva-Petushki* (Erofeev 1990:12) opens with a preface informing the reader that the chapter "Hammer and Sickle—Karacharovo" had been purged of offensive verbiage following the line "And I drank it straight down" because, in the previous edition (one copy), forewarned readers had skipped anxiously to the chapter in question and were overcome by its "pure obscenity." When we reach "Hammer and Sickle—Karacharovo" (ibid.:27), it is blank save for "And I drank it straight down," a charming illustration of the link between powerful language, silence, transcendence, and alcohol (see Dovlatov 1991:68 for a great example of cursing as an "art" and "literary Russian").

Revolution-era workers saw "culture" as "a key to recovering the self" and an exit from their "heavy nightmarish sleep" and animal-like life, targeting drunkenness, swearing, "savage manners" and crass taste (Steinberg, forthcoming). Seventy years later, searches for culture ranged from this sort to attempts at "Western" manneredness, to respect for "soulful" folk or "natural" culture in forms of blunt "sincerity" and even profanity.

I was often told that politeness was not dushevnyi. A genteel English teacher told me that swearing, as crude as it was, was more soulful; when someone's dusha was burning, it was better to express it than to keep it in. Once in the village I was sitting with two men who were discussing the problem of sharing cigarettes, which were in severe shortage. One said his neighbors came over to smoke too often and admitted that he once hid in the dark because he couldn't say no to a human being's face; "Dusha can't stand it! For fuck's sake! [lit., fuck your mother; *dusha ne terpit, ëb tvoiu mat'*]." The men apologized to me for the word, but as a formality. The words come together, they said; once you say "Dusha can't stand it," the rest just follows. "We're trained to that from childhood," one punned; "Russia, your mother."

When I told this to Mila, who spoke a certain delicate, refined Russian with relish, she laughed. Of course, she said, "If it's *dusha*, if it can't *stand* it, well, you just have to continue and let the rest out. That's the thing about Russian," she said; "you can do anything with the language, and perfectly new things are understandable to other Russians. That must be why emigrants feel such nostalgia; these things are impossible to explain."

In Dostoevsky's *Diary of a Writer*, an entire conversation between workers consists of repetition of one obscene syllable: "all thoughts, feelings, and even a whole chain of reasoning could be expressed by that one noun . . . without uttering a single other word, they repeated that one beloved word six times . . . and understood each other completely" (Vygotsky 1962:143).[9] And there is Maxim's wonderful story above, about the balalaika player's resounding "mother." Russian's "expressiveness" connects back to music: the consensus seems to be that there is little that cannot be put into Russian, with its richness, flexibility, openness to creation and poetic play. Then,

[9] Vygotsky (1962) calls this "abbreviation"; his theories on this topic are clearly related to meanings I describe here.

where normal language cannot flow, there is poetry, and then media that communicate only to the initiated or to those who have "natural" access to them: music, silence, intuition, the habits of Russian culture, bureaucratic Sovietese, and condensed, cursing *mat*, which so succinctly embodies the passionate suffering, unsettledness, and oppositional impulse of Russian soul.

CHAPTER FIVE

The Baths
A Celebration for Soul and Body

In prison Bumstein builds a world of his own. A clearly perceptible feature of this world is spirituality . . . but Isai Fomich does
not miss simpler pleasures either. In the bath scene,

Whenever steam was added, and thick, scalding clouds filled
the room, there were fresh shouts and laughter . . . There
was Isai Fomich howling with joy on the highest of the
shelves. He was steaming himself into insensibility . . . He
grudged no money on such an occasion . . . It occurred to
me that if ever we should meet in hell, we should find the
place exactly like this.

Dreizin 1990:88, citing Dostoevsky,
Notes from the Dead House

January 1991, Moscow

There is a shortage of places to meet. Restaurants admit whom they
wish, though most people would not want to be admitted to these
smoky places in which, seen through a crack, men in black fur and
black felt hats mill around, and then the doorman tells you to go away. The
only places to talk are kitchen tables and analogous ones in workplaces,
kurilki (where smokers smoke[1]), and the baths, where people steam, rest,
eat, and drink before reentering life.

Many of the "good" Moscow bathhouses have been closed "for repairs"
for years, the same sort of "eternal remodeling" that has riddled the streets
with unhealing wounds. My friend Inna can't go to the baths with me because, she told me, in an effort to get pregnant she has taped coins to her
belly. I go with a friend of hers. In a rubble- and stray animal-filled courtyard, a large sign on a door loose on its hinges says the baths are closed.

---

[1] In Omsk people rarely smoked in mixed company at the table. A long session at table
would be punctuated by trips by smaller groups to smoke. Originally a place for men, the
kurilka was increasingly for whomever smoked.

Opening it, we go through increasingly dark, filthy, cold, torn up rooms and knock. A door opens into a clean, brightly lit world of benches and clothes hooks. A naked woman in her good-natured fifties greets us. My acquaintance introduces me to her mother—"all of her at once." She and four other women come to this "closed" bania once a week.

We leave our clothes in the undressing room, (*razdevalka, predbannik*) and go to the next room, where a jovial red-faced attendant gives us towels, rubber thongs, and felt hats to protect our heads and hair from the intense heat. In most baths one brings these from home. The *parilka* (steam room), is, they say, a couple of hundred years old, with wooden steps up to benches opposite a brick wall with a deep, recessed, semicircular shelf oven framed in wrought iron. We sit on towels, hats on, small towels covering our breasts. Soon the attendant is "convinced" to join us. Putting herbs that smell of fir into a wooden bucket of water, she undresses and enters, ladling scented water onto the hot stones. We breathe deeply. Then each woman's back is whipped, by others or by the attendant, with an oak *venik*, a broom of leafy, bound branches soaked and softened. To whip oneself or be whipped with a venik is *parit'sia* (to steam). In a "christening" that they say is particularly auspicious on this day,[2] a day when one should go in water to release sins and impurities, we repeatedly leave the steam room and jump into the old, cool, dark tile pool—not city water, they say, but fed by an underground river.

Women of three generations are steaming. The elder women are boldest in dousing each other with ice-cold water and daring us to do the same. Alternation between cold and hot extremes is an integral part of what is considered the baths' healing power. These extremes are not good for everyone: some avoid cold water and some must, like my friend, avoid heat. I am perspiring but cold inside, especially a thin layer inside my feet. Everyone understands this: you have a cold still invisible inside; in the baths you feel it because it is *coming out*. I have to steam a long time until that cold core leaves. "You leave all of that at the baths. All of that has to be left here," one of the older women says.

We take a break. The middle-aged women, whose comportment is conservative and responsible in contrast to their mothers' exuberant relaxation and their daughters' self-absorbed distraction, set a table with a few thin slices of lemon and orange (a great rarity this winter), fresh parsley (for vitamins), herb tea, sliced sausage, bread, and a few hard candies that remind me of ones from Kiev my Omsk friends' Chernobyl humor had labeled *strontsy*, in reference to radioactive strontium.

The women talk politics naked, then have more rounds of steaming and cold water. Then we wash, scrub, shampoo, steam again, cool water, tea,

---

[2] Not only days on which it is best to bathe but other aspects of bania (such as cutting branches for brooms) may be tied to the church calendar. More and more people were more and more liable to appeal to Orthodox and astrological calendars, but the baths had continuously preserved Orthodox and pre-Christian elements.

talk. Spiraling complaining about how much food there used to be and what kinds, but we're not starving yet; about the Party closing TV shows, about money, clothing; the darkness of Russia's past, the shamefulness of her present, the absence of her future;[3] how Jews were responsible for the Revolution and all that followed; about a neighbor's dog that barks only at full-blooded Jews, how everything will continue to decline until the red star is removed from the Kremlin "and until Lenin is buried, because he is roaming the country." Amazing in this popular remark is how the spirit of communism roaming Europe has flipped over into an unquiet, haunting corpse. A rumor that Saddam Hussein (who "has gone totally insane") is Stalin's lost grandson is supported by evidence from the press, as were discussions of what a rich country Russia was, is, and could be, if she were not destroyed and betrayed at each step. If this was far from the first time I heard Gorbachev called a traitor, it was the first time I heard him associated with the *mafiia*.

All activities are in apparently spontaneous quantities. Unlike when one is a guest for dinner, individual needs and differences are important in the baths; there is an emphasis on "as much as *you* can take" and "until it feels right." Daring, commanding, and yelling for others to keep her company, each woman nevertheless goes in and out of the heat at precisely her own rate, uses the cold pool or not. Sitting and eating there is different than if I had been a guest, too. Food and drink are not urged on anyone. Clearly, each woman would do as she saw fit and could judge that. They all tell each other and me how "Russian" I look and act. It does not hurt that I perspire a lot. This is considered good and carefully gauged. I also manage to produce a coveted bright-red and snow-white spotted effect.

The older women shower first. Waiting, the younger ones discuss diets. One demonstrates something from a Jane Fonda exercise video. "Do all American women use these videos?"

Why am I so comfortable dancing around naked in a circle, singing in a freezing pool of water with women my mother's age? How like and unlike reeking doorless grey public toilets where everyone crouches blankly.[4]

Bawdy allegations that one older woman was a direct descendant of Catherine the Great, witness the equine curve of her back and rear as her back is scrubbed. My uselessly dainty washcloth is an object of general merriment and sexual jokes. I am ordered to let others scrub my back "with a *real loofah*."

We arrived at 2:30. At 5:00 a group of men is waiting. Fine, snowy, windy, clean, dark winter weather. Televisions show scenes from the night

[3] A line by Chaadaev often paraphrased and quoted during perestroika, and, I assume, long before.

[4] Condee writes that the public bathhouse "reconstitutes the communal privacy of the apartment in its naked bodies, washing 'unobserved' for all to see." Condee's article (1996:3–8) includes a bibliography and history of the baths. See also Gerhart 1974 and Minenko 1992.

of January 12th in Vilnius;[5] wounds, morgues, naked corpses. Worse than the holes in the bodies is their paleness.

December 1991, Omsk

Many city people who now had their own bathtubs still made use of bathhouses; many began using them more as water shutoffs at their apartment buildings increased. In many villages there was no other way to wash. The fact or idea of the baths was important even to people who refused to use it. Public prosecutor Yurii Yur'evich, telling me how he had "fulfilled his duty [to offer] hospitality" to recent visitors, mentioned first of all taking them to the baths and drinking vodka.

Omsk friends and bath attendants at an Omsk city public bathhouse were shocked at the oak venik broom I brought from Moscow—no oak trees in the steppes! Veniki here are birch. The best, I'm told, are fir. In the sauna women rub salt into their skin to cleanse the pores. It burns. Two sessions in dry heat, sauna, separated by a dip in a cold tiled pool under dim lights, then steaming in a separate steam room, a venik thrashing, and the slow, thorough scrubbing of hair and body with innumerable tubs of water and showers. One ruble, ninety kopecks, admission was charged to these baths near a prison and school, at a time when friends were earning between 400 and 1,000 rubles a month. Extra was charged for the use of a hair dryer that I used so my friends would respect me. As in most buildings, a mirror by the door was used for perfecting one's feminine allure before emerging to face the public. So my friends would respect me, I stood and pretended to add some final touches.

December 1991, Omsk

> When I come to the synagogue or the bathhouse (may they not be mentioned in the same breath)—
>
> Sholom Aleikhem

Lara said:

I went to Leningrad in rose-colored glasses and returned in those same glasses. That can happen. Yes. It's the city of my dreams, childhood dreams. Listen, we were going to the baths. Elementary. We had towels; we got lost or didn't find those baths right away. We ask this man, and he says, "Of course," turns around—180 degrees—and walks us there. Yes. I never met a uncultured per-

[5] Special troops, allegedly under orders from Gorbachev, occupied the Vilnius TV tower in an attempt to take over the Lithuanian government. Fourteen were killed and 110 wounded in the conflict. On January 20, five were killed in a similar incident in Riga (my thanks to Mr. Ints Calitis).

son there. It is a city of *kul'tura*. For example, once I was walking to the baths and I had to cross the square at St. Isaac's Cathedral and suddenly I felt how I was carrying my soap, my broom, and just couldn't walk like that across that magnificent place. I had to make a huge circle around it. Yes.

At this point Lara's son interrupted the interview by showing us a bunch of gas masks he had found on the way home from school.

January 28, 1992, Omsk

> They all, no matter what they did at work, they were all looking for some sort of dushevnost' on the side, all of them, government bureaucrats, all the same they loved to go to the baths to let loose [*dushu otvesti*].
>
> Oleg

Dmitri, a school principal, called and invited me to "rest." I resisted. "Rest" with new people in Omsk was no rest. He said we'd go to the baths. He was so insistent I agreed, a little ungraciously, to be picked up at a factory *Dom Kultury* ("house of culture," club) at 8 P.M. Uneasily. His firmness in offering relaxation, perhaps. A foreign jeep was waiting dashingly high up on the sidewalk, as cars are wont to do. I sat next to the young driver. We drove across town to pick up "just one other person" who turned out, after a long sidewalk wait in the car, to be two heavily made-up young women, introduced as teachers. Despite the anticipated trickiness of reverting back to *vy* the next day, the women immediately began an evening-long process of getting used to calling Dmitri the informal *ty*. We zoomed across town, turned, and there, in Omsk, near huge factories, we were in open fields with stands of trees. A guardhouse appeared. A drunk head opened a massive gate.

Inside a two-story home we were met by one man named Stas, a smaller man with a convict's wink, and a woman with a big curly hairdo. Stas said we'd met, which I did not remember. We'd talked about Chicago gangsters, he said; I said that's what people often ask me about. We'd talked in the office of the director of a certain company, he said. Suddenly, in this house being remodeled in light wood paneling, I remembered not him but my fear of his posture in the chair.

We sat down with apples, a chocolate bar, a bowl of candies, one of fresh, unsugared cranberries, a bottle of wine and tea. We drank and ate little and there was no formal toasting. There was no knife on the table, which they joked was for everyone's safety. Stas broke apples with his hands while the shorter man proudly described in a grinning, vicious, and tender way how he had gathered the berries himself on this land. There was a menacing party atmosphere, insinuations of great wealth. They invited me to come live here, to come pick berries, offers separated by an only marginally respectful conversational distance from Stas's suggestion that I invite them to see how an Omsk gangster would measure up in Chicago. The women seemed submissive.

On this land had been dachas of Party people, Stas told me, expressing distaste. They told stories about the cold and how much people drink in the far north. Stas let me carefully examine, under the new paneling, old wood brought and worked decades ago by convicts. Wood so hard you have to drill; you can't just come and drive a nail. Before we went into the baths Dmitri told Stas he wanted to talk to him in private, to settle something. Stas mocked his earnestness, saying they'd settle it naked in the baths.

In a dressing room adjoining the not yet very hot sauna, the women and I undressed, took sheets, and went in. Water was added, turning the sauna into a steamy parilka, often seen as an abomination. Saunas and steam rooms are built differently and are said to be for different ailments.

One woman wore her cosmetics into the sauna, saying she didn't want to be seen afterward without them. As the evening wore on, she gave that up. One reason Russians use so much makeup, the women confided, is that it is expensive; it is prestigious to obviously spend that much money on yourself (a typically exaggerated Dostoevskian "honest confession"). They told me that they "all" have a "women's illness," treated by injections of an antibiotic that works for a month. They say that with this "illness," even if you have a beloved man, you can't have a normal sex life. "It's all over for us." One woman wanted to run out into the snow between sessions in the steam room, but because of this she couldn't. The fact that I was unmarried but not living with my parents shocked them: "Living alone is looked upon as—" One had shaved legs and the other did not, and, unlike other women I saw naked at that time, both had shaved underarms. Both were bleached blond and full-figured, on which account they criticized themselves, though later the small man drunkenly remarked that Russian men love Russian women's figures. Both women regretted the absence of honey to use on their skin. As in Moscow, they discussed Jane Fonda and aerobics television shows and asked if American women are really all that slim.

Leaving, we dressed carefully and used a mirror. The littler man brought us cold white wine and the men got undressed. The women said that if an American had not been there, they'd have all been in the parilka together. "That's just the sort of people we Russians are"[6] implied that as uncivilized as such behavior must seem, *we* are resignedly proud of our "Russian character" that, against all common sense, thrusts itself towards even more wholehearted participation. Our Russian character which, the more they laughed at it, inched us more irresistibly toward the inevitable restripping and reentering the now much hotter steam room with the men, where we were whipped with veniki, professionally. I remembered how in the

---

[6] A version of a line often quoted, apparently from a film: "Strange nation we Russians are."

Moscow bania the attendant had been cajoled to undress and join us. It was important that bathing be done *right*.

The littler man, unexpectedly and apropos of nothing anyone had said, pronounced in the steam room that "According to Marxism-Leninism, dusha doesn't exist." I said that that's only in a religious sense; he pointed to his chest, announcing that dusha is what your mother makes for you, gives to you at birth, it's the thing in you that makes you good to others and kind. His squinting face distorted into glowing saintliness; stark naked on the wood planks, pointing at his mother's gift to him, his soul, he rhythmically intoned a list of Soviet-era abuse in the "high lamenting" tradition Ries (1997) notes in women's discourse about their befouled lives. The question of what it means that a certain genre of talk or kind of action was associated more with women or men is an interesting one, given that most such voices and behaviors were freely available to anyone.

I soon, under the guidance of the littler man, ran outside and rubbed myself with snow. Katya disappeared with Stas. When the rest of us were again dressed and groomed, drinking vodka and tasting cranberries from the lovingly cupped hands of their harvester, the remaining woman narrated wistfully but matter-of-factly: "Katya disappeared. All that is left is her dress. '*Rozhki da nozhki*,' " invoking the little horns and tiny hooves that were all that was left of grandmother's little grey goat after it was eaten up by the wolf in a children's song. "That's how it is," she said. Her understanding tone vanished into fake or superficial scorn when Katya reappeared in her sheet followed by nude Stas. Soon the cranberry man persuaded Katya's scornful friend to strip for a third time and go back into the parilka. "Russian nature," she shrugged, as if helpless. Later they smoked and told jokes about Jews in a calm patter that seemed to remark frankly and without malice on accepted ethnic traits. Each person carefully measured how well he or she had steamed. The search for red and white spots revealed scars on the two men.

Finally, around 1 A.M., I convinced Stas to drive me home. The girls, drunk and down, got into a fight with him. My hosts repeated offers to have me as their houseguest, ending each offer with "Agreed?" without waiting for a response. On the drive, I complimented Stas on his car. He asked if I wanted a car. At my door (I thought we were going to drive up the stairs) Stas instructed me to call if I wanted a car or anything else.

Bania and Sex

Men and women sometimes steamed together, so some comments on "uncivilized" Russians referred to the widespread association of "primitive" and sexuality and even to village life. Balzer (1992: note 140) notes that the bathhouse "was where licit and illicit lovemaking often took place." Traditionally, the bathhouse was used for male and female prenuptial rituals. During the Soviet era, bathhouses were allegedly used for orgies provided by members of the local elite to visiting inspectors, officials, and guests (Simis 1982:131; Corten 1992:128). Condee (1996:9, 12) examines the role of sexuality in bathing; some of her conclusions confirm my own sense of both single-sex and mixed bathing:

> While one of the traditional mythic allures of the male baths is the possibility of heterosexual sex, the [bathhouse's] wealth of pleasure . . . more often displaces the female sex. . . . This displacement has . . . to do with . . . an elusive state of consciousness attainable only under specific conditions . . . including the presence of good steam, good company, good beer, and good dried fish. . . . To speak about the *bania* at all is to simultaneously conjure up a cultural canon and to speak from the innermost place in the heart.[7]

Condee continues that in the baths people find escape from their burdensome and demanding day-to-day interaction. Sex, in other words, may be classified both with *byt* and its opposite. In the context of bania either association may prevail. During the above bania-centered evening, these possibilities alternated; but when we were in the steamroom with the men, it was simply not about sex. The issue of sex was much less in the foreground when we were in the parilka than when we sat and talked. Steaming was simply about doing it *right*.

February 1992, Omsk

At a bathhouse on the fenced-in grounds of a factory two women who write for a women's magazine were my hostesses. They had asked a common acquaintance to invite me to "finally get some rest." When I said that I would give no interview because all I was doing all day was answering questions and that is no rest, they solemnly agreed.

They tortured me for hours in the baths with their questions. Practically in tears at never, ever being able to escape the endless identical questions the First American was obliged to answer, even in the baths, where resting is almost a sacred duty, I eventually refused to speak. "What will we write?" they asked. Then, after a short silence: "It's too bad we didn't bring cards; we could have told fortunes." We had beer and herbal tea.

Months later, in America, a friend sent me a newspaper clipping of the in-

---

[7] A note about this "innermost place": Condee's uses of "heart" here and when she writes that "to speak from the innermost place of the heart . . . is to . . . make the journey to an inner place of mystic origins" (ibid.:10) seem to reflect (justified) squeamishness about using the English word "soul"; but "heart" (*serdtse*) has little connection with bania.

terview I allegedly gave. This was not the only case in which my name and a short discussion were used as an occasion to fabricate an interview. These "interviews," based on a short exchange, were a few of my words stuck in elaborate settings encrusted with the prevailing ideas about Americans (such as that American women are more "self-confident" and independent) and notions of "Russianness" (such as that I found Siberians to be more hospitable than any other people in the world).

June 1992, A Village in Omsk Region

Zhenia convinced me to use his friends' bathhouse minutes after the bus dropped me off on the village's dirt road. Later, at some drunken point of his wife Tamara's birthday party, stories were told about owning a bania. When neighbors and friends see by the smoke that you are heating the bania, you have to invite them or they will drop hints. Situations arise and are negotiated. You must earnestly persuade them that you really don't mind if they go before you do, demonstrating how much hot water is left, and so on. I'd never been to a private bathhouse in a village and was reluctant to go alone. Tamara wouldn't go because, she said, she had to cook. Plus, she said, she was used to the village's public bathhouse. Their own bathtub at home is for other things. It is where the clothes hang that Zhenia wears to tend to the livestock, and it smells like manure.

Tamara has long dreamed of a bathhouse and summer kitchen. Finally, bricks and cement clutter the yard. There is already a shed there, heated by a light bulb and two cows, each of which has one filthy side. There is a place for the pigs and white chickens covered in pig feces; an outhouse; and a house for a puppy whose job is to be chained there and bark too meanly and desperately for his age. Tamara, as if I needed company rather than guidance, shyly commanded me to take her six-year-old to the baths with me. When we got to the neighbors', someone was in the bania, so we watched a beautifully filmed science-fiction story for children on TV.

This is a two-room wood bathhouse, small and clean. After steaming you wash on the cooler side of the steam room and dump your water on the floor. It drains into the earth. Tamara's daughter either cannot wash her long thin hair and body herself or wanted me to do it for her. She has stuck to me like glue, watching me write, twining her skinny legs around me. When we reentered the house we were greeted with the customary "Light steam to you!" with which, when there was hot water, I was also greeted in Omsk apartments after I took a bath.[8]

[8] *S legkim parom* is also the name of perhaps the most beloved comedic film of the 1970s, by Riazanov. Subtitled *The Irony of Fate*, it was on TV every New Year. A group of Moscow

Every sign of my being or becoming "Russian" pleases ethnic Ukrainian Zhenia. He beamed to see me coming in flushed from the bania. Then he went to steam, and I sat with our hostess Tania and drank tea that smelled of sage, herbs she has gathered herself since two years ago, when "it started getting bad with medication" and people were told to turn to traditional remedies. We ate fried dough patties. There was no sugar for the tea; Tania put out a bowl of hard candies instead. She offered me homemade sour cream with the consistency of cream cheese and a vague smell of cow. She said her husband had been intending to go to a birch grove (these little groves are called forests (*les*) here, which sounds ridiculous to people from more forested places) to cut birch switches to make veniki but that they were told not to do that before Trinity Sunday (see story following this chapter).

That night, at the height of the party, I put on my boots to go to the outhouse. Remembering how last winter at an analogous moment dogs had howled over the black steppe, I looked up. The ground under my feet was stinky-slushy. It was already dark, after midnight. The fields glowed whitish, as if in mist or fog. A birch grove hovered above the white.

June 1992, A House in Omsk City

The sprawling working class neighborhood where Nadia's parents live is all old wooden houses with whimsically carved and colored shutters, but it is close to downtown Omsk, and decaying apartment blocks loom. Even without crowds of adolescent ducks many of these dirt roads would be impossible to drive on. Nadia's parents' courtyard is also full of poultry of all colors and ages in cages and pens made from wood and wire and plastic sheets. Deceptively curious-looking chickens peek in the window at your face. They didn't grow as big this year, probably the feed. The house, high front gate, coal shed, bathhouse, outhouse, garden and various storage and work sheds frame the yard.

The bania is not good-looking or new but when the chickens (who live there during the winter) were evicted, it was scrubbed and whitewashed. It has upper and lower benches, one deep trough for heating water built onto the side of the stove, one for cold water as far away as possible, by the door, so washing and steaming can happen in the same room. All water is drawn from a well on the street. The stove was built by Nadia's father.

From the outside, the bania is a tiny gray-brown shed, but inside it is roomy and spacious. I went in with Nadia, her daughter, and her niece. The picky older girl whined, so Nadia washed her while her silent cousin luxuri-

---

men meet on New Year's Eve, as they do every year, to steam. Drunk, they send the wrong man off to Leningrad, changing his life.

ated. When Nadia was little and the bania even more spacious, she and a friend used to love to steam and sing loudly. If traditionally, "loud talking, singing, and boisterous conduct of any kind were prohibited" in the bathhouse (Ivanits 1992:59), to my friends singing there seems more than appropriate.

Of course, when you come out the animal and outhouse smells are strong. While his wife bathed, Nadia's father served tea with mint and big stacks of blini she had baked.[9] He used to drive out to cut birch for veniki, but he doesn't have a motorcycle anymore. A man delivered oats. A clock chimed. There are photos of grandchildren and children on the wardrobes and the yellowed wallpaper, along with a calendar picture of the regional leader of the Orthodox church and one of a pretty model. Carved ornament frames the low doorways between parts of the house. My host hurriedly used his electric razor and a tiny mirror when I asked if I could take pictures.

June 1992, A Dacha on the Outskirts of Omsk

I had brought shoes back from the United States for Zina and Andrei Orlov. They had asked for them out of desperation and were uncomfortable about how to recompense me. I said they were a gift, but Andrei said we'd sit down soon and discuss it. I decided to ask to go to the dacha with them. They had been inviting me to come and steam anyway.

One must, Zina and Andrei instructed me, eat well, to have strength in the baths. This pleased us all as a pretext for making shashlik, a great luxury. Andrei roasted the skewered marinated pork, sprinkling it with wine vinegar to extinguish the flames. The meat should roast in hot smoke. Andrei, "Orlov the Georgian," as Zina calls him when he's making shashlik, said that "when everything was simpler" many dachas smelled like meat, but now it was rare. Pine and fir cannot be used for shashlik coals, only hardwood; we used birch. The best comes from fruit trees.

While the bania was heating, a birch venik soaked in a rusty tank. Earlier we had driven to two tiny birch stands to cut branches for these brooms. The steppes with rye, wheat, and steppe grass were as flat as Wisconsin lakes, and rare birch groves were tiny islands in the distance. But the scale was vaster than Wisconsin; you would have had to be a strong swimmer to go between islands, a frightening image of land become water. I lost a pen on one of those islands while we were cutting birch and looking for mush-

---

[9] Some women serve blini (crepes), flat in piles, others serve them folded in quarters for dipping in sour cream. Blini were sometimes folded around ground meat or sweetened farmer's cheese and sometimes fried. The first blin proverbially and in fact usually does not come out well. Most women could keep two or three pans going at once. Blini are traditional at any death-related event and some other holidays.

rooms. These were "mushroom woods," but no matter how hard my friends tried, it was just too early. At the next island I took my other pen from the car and lost that.

Andrei needs at least twenty birch veniki for a winter. A full Moskvich car trunk of male birch branches made eight (female branches sport painful little cones). I sat with him on the bathhouse porch while he made them. If Andrei steams alone, one broom lasts for three times, but with comrades a venik is only good for one time. Andrei is proud to have once steamed with a friend until five A.M. You go in and out of the heat as many times as you want, drink and eat as you desire. You talk, steam. It is like other moments in a person's life when he or she must try to get in touch with something fundamental. Andrei steams with cronies more rarely and uses fewer veniki since perestroika began. To do it right with friends, you need to take vodka, beer . . .

It's a beautiful bania Andrei built. He had to fight Zina to move some raspberry bushes to do it correctly—there had to be a chain of rooms of all possible temperatures. Andrei pays minute scientific attention to possible temperature needs. He brought wood for the bathhouse from his birthplace in the north of the region. People from work helped him build it. It's pleasant, Andrei said, that people help each other. He helped them later. "Just like the village." "And God forbid someone dies," Zina added, "everyone helps out." I did not see the interior of their tiny steam room because the electricity was out. The heat was thick and black. Coming back out onto the porch, I saw the meticulous woodpile and flock of upside-down drying brooms.

It is worth discussing feet, dirt, and shoes. Shoes were always, *always* removed on entering a home, even at a fancy birthday party. Often people wore socks, more often were offered or helped themselves to a pair of the worn slippers that lurk around entryways. Sometimes in summer, but far from always, a hostess would exclaim, in a burst of apparent generosity and self-denigration, that one should not take off one's shoes; "our" floor is dirty or drafty. Although later, in a few homes, keeping one's shoes on was instituted as a form of "Westernism," in mid-1990s Omsk under no circumstances were orders to leave one's shoes on to be obeyed; such protests stopped immediately, especially if one came up with a good excuse, such as that one's shoes were dusty from the street.

At an Omsk theater there was a subtle uproar when visiting American actors turned out to be insensitive to this dirt from below. An embarrassed official message from the managing director informed the Americans that "in Siberia, we do not put our feet on furniture, and we never enter the theater with our coats on, but check them in the coatroom." A rare joke at the time in which Russians were portrayed as more "cultured" than others deals with this subject:

A cowboy, a Turk and a Russian sit at a table. How many legs are there under the table?

Two: the Russian's (the Turk's are folded under him; the American's are on the table).

I participated in two sanctioned violations of this rule. One, late at night, was when a neighbor knocked and, weeping, told us of their "great misfortune;" their son had been beaten and lay in a coma. We went to sit with her near the phone; she ordered us not to take off our shoes and she meant it. As if we had to confirm how profoundly this tragedy had disordered everything by ourselves disregarding order. Taking the time to focus on feet and cleanliness would have been incredibly cold, petty, and probably bad luck. We would have looked and felt soulless. In Chapter 11 I describe the other time shoes were not removed.

At the dacha I was told to not go barefoot because my feet would catch cold, but there was also dirt; I had to make the transition from outside to inside by conspicuously changing something about my feet. When I first approached the bathhouse porch Andrei told me to wipe my feet. He then embarrassed me by washing my rubber thongs in a bucket. Then he wiped the floor with clean water and a rag "so it won't be disgusting to walk on."

Andrei and I sat on the porch while Zina steamed. This was nice not just because I enjoy his company, but because my attentive hostess's long absence spoke of her conscientious attention to her own "rest." Later we went into the house to eat and rest, leaving a hedgehog making funny noises in the raspberry bushes. Hedgehogs are apparently not indigenous to this part of Siberia.

They brought beer, mineral water, and flavored soda from the cellar. I later confided in a friend that I was afraid the Orlovs were incurring hardship because of me. "They're doing their best," she answered. In other words, I was probably right but she would do the same. Zina and Andrei didn't lie when they said that the weekend had been a rest for them, a rest for which they needed me as a pretext. They enjoyed it greatly, but it had not been optional.

Bania was a place for becoming clean, and its own cleanliness could be important. But traditionally the bathhouse (most often "black bania," sooty inside) was considered supremely *un*clean, "the home of the malicious *bannik* [spirit] and, sometimes, his wife . . . [as well as] a gathering place for various types of evil spirits, witches and the unclean dead" (Ivanits 1992:59). Russian ideas of impurity were linked explicitly to times of vulnerability and to the bania: "The belt . . . peasants wore . . . was . . . considered a talisman against the unclean force, and it, like the cross worn around the neck . . . was removed only in the bathhouse" (Ivanits 1992:42 and Balzer 1992: note 140). One man described bania to me as *moral'nyi dush,* a psychological shower.[10] But a man in his twenties told me that a spiritual person would plant an orchard, whereas a practical one would build a bath-house. The mention of bania in contexts of spirit, soul, purity, and impurity is both contemporary and traditional.

Above I mentioned the baths' "tempering" and healing effects, associated with extremes of heat and cold. Bania is transformational, involved in pu-rification rituals, prenuptial rituals (Pushkareva 1992:110), rituals associ-ated with childbirth and birth itself (Ivanits 1992:46), curing rituals, sor-cery, fortune-telling, and various other rites of passage (see Condee 1996:10, 11, 25 and Rancour-Laferriere 1995:191–200). Their bania cer-tainly mediated the economically delicate issue of the Orlovs' American shoes, as it had some issue between Stas and Dmitri in a preceding story. The following chapters contextualize this sort of mediation.

If bania was associated with rites of passage and forces that move be-tween worlds through holes in the earth and gather in bathhouses (Ivanits 1992:40), in the 1990s movement between hot and cold and the imagined opening and closing of the pores and blood vessels were linked to bania's role as a site for spiritual entities and substances to manifest themselves in-side the body or soul and continue that path outward.

December 1992, A Town in Omsk Region

Mila and I stood in a crowded train to the town where her parents live and walked up the icy main street. "Our house is wood—one breathes well inside it," said Mila's mother. They had moved there from an apartment. The backyard has a garden and a shed for two cows and a pig. They had killed the bull that day, "a lot of work"; there was meat all over the un-heated entry room and the yard was decorated with stumpy hooves, a long bloody bone, a piece of hide and tail, and more.

There are four bright rooms in the house. The floors are painted the usual glossy rust. The chalky walls[11] have a clock and pictures of an anonymous mother and child and of birch trees. A samovar stands on a dark wood table covered by an embroidered tablecloth older than Mila is. The house is "fully equipped" with a one-spigot sink, bathtub (in which were buckets of farmer's cheese and jars of solidifying sour cream), water heater, and seat-less toilet. On the floor were fresh *khonorka* skins (a polecat/mink hybrid), part of an "experiment" by Mila's brother. Due to the state of the economy

---

[10] "*Moral'no*" is strongly connected to dusha but not only as what would in English be translated as "moral." When in Russian something is said to be "*moral'no ochen' tiazhelo*" it is not "morally" difficult, though it may be "demoralizing"; the translation "psychologically" can be more accurate. This sense of "*moral'no*" corresponds to the English "morale" and "moral support."

[11] This chalkiness is endemic in hallways. A woman with a chalky coat back might be as-sumed to have been kissing in the hallway of the apartment building.

most people had something they were trying to make or do for the first time and about which they gathered information from the radio, pamphlets, books, and by talking to other people.

In the morning Mila's mother called from her room that she had entertainment (lit., a cultural program "*kul'turnaia programma*") planned: going to the baths after "tea," which turned out to be a huge meat-and-potatoes breakfast. She repeated this "funny" statement many times and was amused each time. Equating the baths, culture, and entertainment was charged: it's not going to a concert, but it's more than just washing. It's related to dusha as much as or more than a concert. She added that in the baths "stresses" (a popular term) are shaken off, erased.

Mila's father agreed by noting that in the baths people don't talk about sausage. The baths are subject to conventions that pertain to spiritual situations. Then, as I was a foreigner and he knew I was interested in dusha, he associated a chain of comments. *Dusha—chelovek* (The soul is the person), he said. The association that followed was just to another two words connected by a hyphen, and he laughed: *rubakha-paren'*, literally a "shirt-guy": open, outgoing, one of us. Then his wife volunteered that good dishes are "prepared with dusha."

We watched anxiously off the porch of the house before we saw, halfway across the little town, smoke beginning to rise out of the bathhouse chimney. Mila's mother said, "The baths are a holiday (celebration) for soul and body." She immediately followed with the saying that "everyone is equal in the baths; naked with tubs," referring to the metal tubs people use to wash with. Power relations (symbolized by clothing, something superficial masking dusha) are supposedly set aside,[12] as they supposedly are by people who drink together. I thought of the Omsk woman who only reluctantly, finally, removed her cosmetics.

As "rest" related to dusha, as something done "for" dusha, bania is like drinking. The two are sometimes, but far from always, used together. But the simultaneity obligatory to drinking together is less important in the baths. The baths are a holiday and for dusha because, Mila's mother said, each in his or her way "gives him or herself utterly, completely," to this long, leisurely process. As many ritual aspects as there are, as stridently as people disagree on what is good and bad, only by attentively looking inside you can you achieve that red, relaxed glow.

Saturday, *subbota*, the day of rest, is "bath day" (Condee 1996:5). The writer Shukshin (1992, 5:156) describes one Saturday of Alësha, a man whose Saturdays were devoted to the baths: "he woke up . . . and a quiet joy spread in his soul." Bania was sacred. When his wife wanted him to do something else one Saturday, he exploded: "What do you want, should I cut

[12] Chekhov has a story about a man who unknowingly interacts with a priest in the bania. Condee (1996:12) lists proverbs in which the venik broom reigns supreme, "senior even to the tsar."

my dusha into pieces?" (ibid.:160). The story is a detailed description of bathing, both materially and in terms of the dusha and sense of time involved.[13] After elaborate preparation, Alësha enters the steamroom, "and life began there—entirely concrete and entirely inexplicable, dear and familiar . . . all harmful pressure emptied out of Alësha completely, petty thoughts left his head, and a kind of wholeness, bigness, and clarity settled into his dusha" (ibid.:164).

The expression "a holiday for dusha," which Mila's mother used to refer to the baths, occurs in Gogol's *Dead Souls* as an exclamation by a flowery-speaking landowner. Dovlatov (1991:250) shows spirits in which a late Soviet transformation of this was offered and received: a character's lover has him read a passage about himself in her journal: "He was a celebration for my body," it read, "and a guest of my soul." The character "shuddered. The room filled with intolerable heat. The light blue walls crawled upwards." An asphyxiating attack hurled him into the bathroom, where hangover had its way with him. Although the maudlin phrase was long used ironically and considered to be in poor taste or adolescent, I often heard it used in only slight quotation marks.

In Shukshin's screenplay *Kalina Krasnaia* (Red Guelder Rose), a character nicknamed Gore (Grief) leaves prison. Asked what he wants, he answers: "Maybe to arrange some sort of rest for my dusha." At the village home of a woman, Liuba, he is still trying to find that "rest." In a pivotal scene, Gore invites Liuba's brother out to the cold, dark bania to sit, talk, drink, and sing. They discuss how cognac smells of crushed bedbugs. The next day Gore is finally calm. Liuba says she'd have been afraid of the bathhouse at night: "There are devils there! . . . that's just where they live!"

We arrived at the public bania in Mila's parents' town and paid five rubles. Herbs steeped in a tub of the hottest water, and women sanded their softened heels on the rough, wet concrete floor of the washing-room. Mila's mother said they wanted to build their own bathhouse but there was no room and "the fuel situation is bad." While her mother beat Mila with a venik, she ordered sickness and evil things out; Mila laughingly told me to write this down, but we both knew she was doing a good thing, like spitting to ward off the evil eye. You are at the mercy of a lot in "our life."

In a conversation later that day about a current scandal—malfunctioning, dated American equipment received as "humanitarian aid"—Mila's mother said it was a bad reflection on the donors, and so degrading. Donated feed grain was being used to bake "inedible" bread while local farms' bumper crops either could not be harvested due to systemic disorder or were being exported for hard currency; "dusha weeps." On the way back in the train I thought people were going to kill each other shoving, and drunk men were

---

[13] In this story (Shukshin 1992: vol. 5, 164, passim), as often happens, people formulate their preferences as "correct," saying that others do it "wrong."

sleeping with their faces in the laps of strange women, their cheap fur hats, worn bare in places, still on their heads or in their hands.

April 1994, Omsk

The former Pioneer Palace has a pool and sauna in theory public, but in fact accessible only to elite like the young toughs outside next to a foreign car, sharing a facial expression and style of leather jacket. Friends who work there let us in. The steamroom was hot; men and women in bathing suits sat on little boards. Never, in all the years the young man who brought me there had been swimming, he said, grinning and amazed, had he seen a woman hoist herself out of the pool as I did. It's considered uncultured, he said; girls use ladders, majestically.

Conclusions

What does bania show about dusha? What kind of soul is it, in bania? One could say that the steam bath is *kul'turnyi* and dushevnyi insofar as many elements associated to dusha appear there, dragging contexts along with them. One might reverse this: the baths invite other elements as part of their own dushevnyi, historically "Russian" role. In either case, the fact that baths are a locus for meeting and promiscuity, dirt and purity, power and equality, heat and cold, sobriety and drunkenness, health and illness, communion with others and contact with one's own "deepest" needs, as well as drink, song, and healing, makes them dushevnyi—*anything* that unites things is. These elements and contexts, especially when they meet, are "Russian."

I disagree with Rancour-Laferriere's (1995:181) claim that bania is evidence of cultural "masochism." I was told that bania, with its extreme cold and heat, tempers the body, just as suffering tempers dusha. But these temperings are primarily transformative—dirty to clean, sick to well, from this world to the world of dusha, from one time of life to another. These transformations are often imagined as occurring across the boundary of the skin, as bad things come out through pores. There can also be the aspect of, in this isolated world of the parilka, taking stock of things—hitting the bottom, so to speak—so as to rise again renewed and different. Like dusha, bania is a separate "place" where you become aware of things and of oppositions (like inner or hidden cold, illness, and impurity, emotional pain, and various truths) as part of the process of them either leaving you or emerging into the light.

In narratives, the baths are a place of change: Riazanov's 1975 film *S lëgkim parom* (Light Steam to You) centers around life change begun in a steamroom, and the bania scene in the screenplay *Kalina Krasnaia* (Red Guelder Rose) has an equally transformative role; it was there that Gore finally (if temporarily) found the "rest" his dusha craved; it was there he bonded with Liuba's brother. Things "of dusha" in literature and thought are also present in interpretations of (and living of) perestroika life; Yeltsin publicly told how "in a Moscow bathhouse in 1989, he [realized] that he [was] no longer a communist. . . . Yeltsin's conversion in the bathhouse assures the implied reader of its authenticity, its native legitimacy within the historical development of Mother Russia" (Condee 1996:13).

Bathhouses can be both locations for discussing details of everyday life and places where "one doesn't talk about sausage." They can be both "a moral shower" and so impure that a man likened them to places for hoarding food and Lara could not bring herself to cross St. Isaac's with her birch broom. Bania is caught in the same opposition between pure and impure, cultured and primitive, as other things I describe.[14] A partial but too simple explanation is that opposites coexist at liminal times and places (Turner 1969), when people are undergoing transformation, developing, temporarily stripped of social status.

But experientially, this coexistence of opposites is not always momentary and not always directional. The baths and dusha are not only rites of passage; they are also valued as images of *static* loci of impossibly coexisting opposites that may never resolve anything and may not, in good faith, want to.

[14] Condee (1996:3, 12, 26) describes the baths as loci of contradiction, like "the railway carriage of Russian culture . . . a mise en scène for self-revelation and self-deception" where holy and carnal are juxtaposed.

Story

For Anna Viktorovna

Anna Viktorovna had been sent home to die of cancer in 1991, without being told what was happening to her. In June 1994 we had a grave to tend.

Rancour-Laferriere (1995:185–86), citing Paul Friedrich on the birch as a five-thousand-year-old symbol of young femininity, notes that slogans such as "the birch is the symbol of the Russian land" accompanied a late-Soviet rise in national awareness. Traditionally, birches were associated with women's suffering in lyric songs, and on Trinity Sunday (the fifty-sixth day after Orthodox Easter; see Dal' 1882, Propp 1995, Minenko 1992, Ivanits 1992, Paxson 1998) girls used to dance around birches, cut them down, twist and rip branches and bark, address wishes to them, and offer them food. In the 1990s, Trinity was observed in villages with fishing and picnics. The village woman who told me that it was forbidden to cut birch switches for veniki before Trinity had no idea why; "People must know." Most city friends to whom I mentioned Trinity knew it only as the most important "parents' day," a day to go to the graveyard and tend to one's graves.

Not on, but close to Trinity Sunday (close was often good enough) Zina and Andrei Orlov drove Grisha, Nadia, and me to a cemetery to tidy things up for Anna Viktorovna and to visit her. Nadia and Grisha had grown up in the city and observed ceremonies idiosyncratically. Here, as in many situations, they only knew / felt / "intuited" some of the "right things to do." In the cemetery, women were supposed to cover their heads, but Nadia did not; nor had she had time to make blini. They didn't bring a shovel. They had a hoe and rake. Zina objected: a rake had no business in a graveyard, and neither did children or dogs, because souls of the murdered get into them (the children and dogs, not the rakes). Grisha and Nadia had also forgotten water for the obligatory hand washing after tidying the grave. They did bring a candle stub left from Willow (Palm) Sunday. Zina made up for their lacks, and when she and Andrei got back from their relatives' graves, she interpreted how the candles had burned in terms of the "rest" or "peace" of the deceased. Her father's had burned steadily down, her recently deceased younger brother's sputtered and refused to stay lit, Anna Viktorovna's father's burned deep into the dirt. Anna Viktorovna's burned brightly halfway and then went out.

Nadia had brought stewed fruit in a plastic bottle I had left there months before, a smaller bottle of spirit-based infusion of herbs, a piece of Easter bread, red-brown Easter eggs, and a piece of sausage. We tended to the grave; melting snow had revealed a messy mound and had deposited faded wreaths on it. Months before, a friend of Grisha's had built a fire to soften the frozen earth and had dug the grave alone; children cannot dig parents' graves. Grisha gave him a gift. We prettied things up for Anna Viktorovna by salvaging paper flowers and other wreath parts. After rinsing our hands we put a cup of water, an egg, and a chunk of Easter bread on the grave and drank a toast: May the earth be like down (soft, that is) to you, Annushka Viktorovna. Guided by known necessary elements and "intuition," the deceased's character, life story, and relations to those present dictated what was left, said, and what might be planted if they got around to it. We poured our remaining "vodka" on the earth, mostly on Anna Viktorovna's father's grave.

Nadia talked to Anna Viktorovna as if to a simple-minded person—no, as if to someone who just couldn't *see* what was happening: Look, Dale came from America, you wanted so badly for her to come, we'll try to come more often, your grandchildren too, we'll come and light candles, don't be sad, don't be lonely; rest, here's some water, you were so thirsty those last days. While addressing the dead Anna Viktorovna (by first name and patronymic, as always), Nadia referred to her "grandchildren" rather than mentioning their names.

While we were away tending to an aunt's grave, drunks ate the egg. When we returned and found it gone, Nadia broke up sausage and bread and scattered it: "Let the birds eat." Nadia claimed to know nothing about rural Trinity celebrations, which, in a melding of spring agricultural rites with rites for the dead, included scattering grain for birds to spread its fertility. She seemed to want first and foremost to render the food inedible to graveyard drunks. Her way of doing this included an inspired act of generosity to the birds.

PART III

Everyone Wants Something, but Only through Someone

Two Stories

Decency (Oleg)

Oleg was neat and nervous about gifts. He tucked chocolates for his daughter in his briefcase, wryly accusing me of bribery. What he saw as Russians' slavish readiness to sell themselves to America was an affront in the depth of dusha he said he felt on behalf of his country.

Once we sat in a cafeteria and watched a craftsman smilingly deliver goods ordered by Americans for whom I was interpreting. Oleg described the man's falseness. "He has no respect for others or himself. If it's an honest business transaction, *do* it that way; if it's a present, and there *is* such a thing as hospitality, deliver it as a present. It's a matter of cleanliness." The artist's grin and "the look of hospitality, especially while taking dollars," sickened Oleg.

I knew that craftsman. I had once complained to him about a family that made me feel exploited. He said it was just a low level of culture on their part that called attention to utility in human relations. "Everyone needs things," he said. "It's a pleasure to help those who make it pleasant to help." But then he suddenly fiercely defended "pure friendship," giving as an example a friend from student days: "All he wanted from me was company and conversation." I told Oleg that maybe the smiling artist was just embarrassed or being pleasant. "No," he said, "later he'll kick back and smile again, at how much he made off the stupid Americans."

Oleg was "working on a deal with pens" in Moscow. After a while, he stopped mentioning pens and came back from Moscow with different plans and a wounded look, describing *how* big bribes had become and *how* expensive things had gotten "for us."

Once, staying at Oleg's family's apartment, I said I felt awkward that I was given the only real bed. Oleg interrupted: "Dale! Have you forgotten where you are? In Russia the guest always gets the best." Another time, on the phone, his wife Oksana said the same thing: to her standard "When are you coming over?" I had stupidly answered: "Whenever you say." "For God's sake, Dale!" she exploded, "We're *Russian*! Come anytime! Just come over!"

Oleg interspersed thoughtful considerations about what he felt in his dusha and how dusha had changed and was changing with caustic teasing. He found my project naive: "You must be hanging around with literary people to talk like that. We, to tell you the truth, don't talk like that anymore." A day later he admitted that he had not realized how much, after all, "we *do* use *dusha*." He said he understood what had brought me to Russia. I think he assumed it was nineteenth-century high "culture." Unfortunately, he said, people had lost that during the Soviet era. He had lost it. Plus, though he came from and had sympathy for the working class, he couldn't stand the crudeness of their relationships.

One day I asked an acquaintance to intervene for me in a practical matter. She made a phone call, wishing I'd leave, but I stayed. The conversation had an oblique quality, an etiquette according to which everything meant more and referred to other things. She requested nothing, prefacing descriptions of what needed "help" with sentences such as "We are relying on your continuing good will towards us." Her closing phrase before goodbye was the ritually worded, "We will not remain in debt before you" (more direct and vulgar would have been "We won't offend you").

I asked Oleg about these formulae. He said they emphasized official relations by explicitly stating that one was indebted and by pretending to look up to that person. He went on a tirade about how distasteful it all was, though I had heard him boast about his own brilliance at polite manipulation. He ranted, listing intricate layers of insincerity and calculation, and culminated by blaming traditional Russian power relations, saying that nothing had changed since feudalism, that the Revolution had aggravated already foul worker/boss relations: common decency had been replaced by devotion to ideals, an isomorphism that didn't fool him. He recalled the honor of moving up in the Young Communist League, stressing what many did: it had not been about communism, but about being kind, good, decent people.

Oleg said he had to go into business to support his family, despite his distaste for business people. He tried to drum up some enthusiasm for it: "I'm purely *interested* to see what I can do." He mentioned an impending birthday with apprehension, threatened by the idea of a biological end to a set of youthful characteristics. For a while Oleg claimed to be reading German philosophy, doubting his past goals. Then he claimed to be reading Agatha Christie. He talked about how much more interesting "decent people," scientists and teachers, were than were dissidents, how their sense of humor and distance from politics made them better company. When I told him about a fascinating formerly fervent communist I had interviewed, he agreed: "A lot of those people really took the idea of doing things for others very seriously, but all the crap that has floated to the surface now, presenting themselves as lifelong fighters against the regime . . ." He made a loose gesture to illustrate their rubbery moral fiber.

He complained about lack of dusha in the economy and the city and about how insincerity crept into relations. He talked about how, before, "if you wanted to go to a restaurant, you *knew* someone there; to the baths, you *knew* someone. More and more these days, you have to pay. It *feels* different, less *human.*" He said he missed relationships in small towns like the one where he was born, where after ten years of school he entered a technical institute, but soon "got the feeling it wasn't my thing and, you know, if I feel something isn't my thing, that's it." Eventually he entered, as he put it, "an institution connected with our Security Committee, the central institution." On tape, he caught his breath, then reassured us both: "It's fine, it's all fine." He said that his decision to work for the KGB had been based on romanticism, but that later, during perestroika, he had again begun to feel that *"Dusha uzhe ne lezhit k etomu vsemu"*—literally, that his dusha was no longer lying or leaning toward all that.

He said that this training had made him able to predict people's moves, see through bluffs, and that it would surely help him and other KGB-trained men succeed in business. He said they had been taught topics the mention of which made members of various ethnic groups open up and start talking; he complimented me on my interview questions, which very precisely, he said, spoke to Russian national character. His former profession and mine, he said, involved "the same questions, different goals." As backhanded as this construction of our similarity was, and as disgusting its implications, it was interesting to hear in so many words that the KGB used the same categories and practices I had identified as those of "Russian soul."

And agents have souls too: months later Oleg told me in the course of conversation that a KGB employee must put dusha, *all* of himself (*vlozhit' dushu*), into conversations with people in order to extract what he needs.

When I joked about hospitality, Oleg's eyes blazed and his lips tightened. He both took hospitality dead seriously and teased me and his friend Anatolii about it. Anatolii was in his twenties, neat, with bright eyes. When he had a party, he served caviar, dumplings, and chocolate. Oleg teasingly demanded he bring out more. A few days later, Anatolii brought me a gift: a cassette of music we had listened to. He would not take in exchange a blank cassette he admired on my desk: I didn't understand that *"here, now,"* that was not a possibility. He did offer to either trade another tape for it or buy it. He accepted a Chicago postcard. During an interview he explained:

Politeness can seem insincere. It's been bred out of people. If you are well received in a home and give a small gift, 99 percent of the time they'll think you're trying to enter into an exchange-type relationship. Probably you'll want something from him in the future, since you're being so polite. Before the Revolution, you only found this sort of thing in boss-worker relations. In the rest of society there was less ass-kissing. It was more honest.

Oleg joked about the remarkably small microphones they make these days and about how well or poorly I was hiding that I was a spy, making simple words like "coworker" and "connection" into tiresome, smirking double entendres. He commented on my caginess in not telling where I'd gotten a bottle of wine, saying that maybe when I left I'd hand my connection over to him. I said that no one else told where they got things; why should I be different? He agreed: "Yeah, no one knows where things come from. Land of Miracles."

Eventually he began making fewer spy jokes and acted hurt when I made one. When he spoke about his (former?) profession or from its point of view, it was swift, quiet, and in convoluted Russian. When I mentioned this, he attributed it to his devious nature, in Dostoevskian fashion calling himself *prokhindei*, a shameless crook who can wriggle his way around, a Soviet word he often used to condemn businessmen with no scruples.

For Oleg's birthday I brought him a gift of American typing paper. "What a scam!" he marveled. "If I forged something on this I could get loans for millions!" Western respect for contracts amazed him: it won't fly here, he said, no one takes what's written seriously. A breach of trust is dealt with by taking a gun and friends and paying a visit. One theme at his birthday dinner was the often-cited quip about what's going on in Russia: "They're stealing." Oleg and Anatolii argued about who had said it; Anatolii said that it was Belinskii. Oleg said no: "*I* have a humanitarian education. . . . Gogol said the thing about the troika and that 'They're stealing.'" He muttered about how after the party I would probably go home and say "What a bunch of idiots." His wife Oksana apologized oddly for this and that, saying fondly that they as a culture had lagged behind and were, of course, monkeys from an American point of view.

Once I complained about how people were never on time. Oleg took me as meaning that Russia was a primitive nation of uncultured slobs and launched on a stream of doubly and triply ironic expositions. Then, as he understood that I had not been speaking in that voice, the bitter stream sputtered out, and he advanced a theory that in bureaucracies such as this, where people always had to sit and wait to talk to bosses, this attitude filtered down, resulting through the generations in generalized tardiness. And then, of course, in this System of ours, this *mess* of ours, there are always glitches. His final summary of the situation was "marazm" (senility), a popular one-word summary for quirkily less-than-ideal situations.

In the cafeteria, as Oleg finished criticizing the poor craftsman's smile, someone came to say the boss was looking for me. I jumped up. Oleg laughed: "Don't forget you're in Russia. Bosses give orders and immediately forget them," he said. "They just need to satisfy the impulse to tell others what to do." I should go when *I* felt like it, he advised, because the director had already forgotten he'd asked for me and in general couldn't care less. As an example of soulful people who did care, Oleg spoke gratefully of his KGB education: "The instructors were really good, *perezhivali* [tried, cared, were concerned]."

Generosity (Grisha)

Grisha, Anna Viktorovna's son, was generous and energetic, in his thirties, small and dark. He could give a souvenir from his collection or a toy he made to someone he had just met. His wife, Nadia, and mother loved his dushevnost', but it made them nervous. He complained that no one understood what was important to him. One afternoon he told me he would not live long; people like him were not long for this world. Setting himself up as "not from this world" was one way Grisha used to steer conversations towards dusha. In various ways he would abruptly challenge interlocutors to acknowledge dusha and engage in it.

His mother's family had come to Siberia from Russia. "Smart people," Anna Viktorovna said. "Apparently they exiled them. I don't know why. Papa came from a cultured family and met a girl. But she died. There was typhus here. And civil war. Then Papa met Mama." She described her forebears: how honest and good-natured they were, how spontaneous and responsive, if they had musical or multiple talents or easily acquired new skills. She noted what trees they planted and if they were physically large or typically Siberian, hard-working. Anna Viktorovna stored away what supplies she could and spoke well of this virtue.

Grisha's hearing was bad. His squinting concentration was hard to distinguish from strong emotion and had made him uninteresting to the army. He said that at seventeen, after graduating, he had traveled and saw everything. Then Omsk friends got him a job with them where they could enjoy his company. Grisha was utterly committed to friendship, and was always organizing things. Over tea he entertained us with physical humor and scatology, often featuring himself in absurd roles. On walks, his profanity-sprinkled ramblings targeted improprieties in an election or how a "communist" former schoolmate had asphyxiated in a car with a secretary: "They thought their heads were spinning from sexual excitement." Another former schoolmate had fattened repulsively at his privilege-encrusted job and reportedly offered to get Grisha food, a string Grisha confidently, defiantly, said he had not pulled.

One evening I went to a show with Grisha's family. At one point, children in the audience were invited to come out and dance, but everyone was shy.

Then Grisha leapt on stage, prancing, overjoyed, preaching with his actions an ideal soulful lack of false shame and inhibition, a model of expansive abandon. The children joined him.

He had other ways of bringing people together: he made a gift for me by asking one friend for materials, taking them to another who began the job, asking a third to finish, and going mad with rage when coworkers told me all about it. Grisha announced plans for gifts long before he gave them. One plan was to send me home with gifts for every possible relative and friend. "With my maximalist character, I could never find the golden mean," he said, but he got angry when I suggested that this plan was extreme. Once he spontaneously announced a gift "from all of us" and only then turned to the others to ask what they thought. He was brilliant at getting people to joyfully work together and morosely shaken by misunderstanding. He said he'd "stop being able to talk, and would think and think."

Once, before I learned to not tell such stories, I complained that I had missed an opportunity to buy a nice dictionary. Months later, in Chicago, I got a message from Grisha. He had found a copy and sent it. In subsequent communications together we imagined the dictionary's trajectory, moving, sitting in dank warehouses, moving. Then it stopped. When I returned to Omsk Grisha offhandedly mentioned that he had tried but never found a copy. If the scale of his generosity was unreasonable, he could create alternate worlds where generosity was omnipotent and togetherness primary.

When, during that time of extreme shortages, mutual friends opened a rare box of chocolates in my honor, Grisha bolted down a long series of them, apologizing rhythmically, parodying his own lack of culture, defying etiquette and poverty. Unlike his mother, Grisha found accumulating supplies soulless: "Siberians pride themselves on how much they manage to store up. People probably think we're lazy: we don't jar things, have no dacha, and don't keep a lot of food." In Chapter 1 I mention how when, for one season, they did have garden land, Grisha made a romantic fuss about growing one's own food but did not help much, leaving his mother to remark bitterly on his character. He subsidized his spontaneity by taking for granted that friends, neighbors, wife, and mother would have what he needed. He did not reflect on the fact that they had stood in line, pulled strings, or weeded. He took with the half-naivete of a guest and gave with the splendid fervor and flourish he expected of others.

He was expert at sharing playful alternations between strict rules of creating soulfulness and soulful violation of the same rules. Parties at his house were great fun, and though he did not begrudge others vodka, he was an erratic host. Grisha had a cycle of myths pertaining to his refusal to drink, but, as friends said, he didn't need vodka anyway.

Grisha protected me. Two acquaintances had intended to invite me to daughters' weddings, but Grisha had told them I was too busy.

Just before leaving Omsk for a trip to the United States, I offered to try to sell crafts for Grisha and a friend of his, Igor, in America. Grisha, as always, intoned: "I cannot sell my work, only give it away," but as soon as we were out of Igor's earshot, he shrieked that *he* had invented these techniques and I had no business making offers to Igor. I then did the bad thing all his friends eventually did. I accused him of inconsistency.

We did not speak until I stopped in Moscow months later on my way back to Omsk. He was there with the blond, silent-eyed son who loved watching ants on the windowsill and tirelessly trotted along as Grisha roamed Moscow, buying ice cream with dollars I had left in case Anna Viktorovna needed medication, which she hadn't. We arranged to meet. He embraced me, weeping with joy at the post office, surrounded by mumbling hard-currency dealers. Later, in Omsk, out of the same tenderness, thanking me, he made off with a calendar I had brought for his mother.

Grisha's actions and ideas were bursts, grabs in defiance of what he thought was the status quo or prevailing opinion. This lost him friends. In confrontational moods or pain, he artfully distorted people's words into examples of unjust, hypocritical, fawning, cowardly, or selfish behavior, treating himself to an opportunity to preach dusha. Some began to indict Grisha not so much for his "fantasizing," on which they relied heavily for making their workdays interesting, but for lying to serve himself, for "exploiting others in his own interest."

Until Anna Viktorovna died and he had to stay with the children, Grisha spent his free time "somewhere." He returned from those amorphous parts of Omsk with objects and stories of how he made them. The toys he eventually began making visibly were in a different style.

He spread rumors. Friends compared them. A museum in another city had offered him a job, and though his soul was drawing him there (*dusha tianet*), in his soul he knew (*v dushe ia zhaiu*) that he belonged in Omsk. He had even more souls than these two. How clear it was becoming that everyone has more!

People began asking me about some Australian sister of Grisha's who had emerged from the sea foam of his dusha complete with an invitation to emigrate. Neighbors nervously prepared to ask him to trade apartments before he left. Gingerly, I told him I had heard he was planning to emigrate. He changed the subject but soon started discussing his character as a "fantasizer" and how he used to invent life stories to entertain strangers on trains.

For a time Grisha was, in the strong opinions of his coworker Masha, an intolerably dishonest individual. But when they were not feuding, Masha and Grisha were a dushevnyi pair, sharing dirty jokes, expansive pranks, flaring temperaments, and exhibitionistic virtuosities. His playful gregariousness brought out people's best. They loved him for challenging boring *byt*. Nadia, Grisha's wife, groping for a way to describe the relationship between character and dusha, said: "A person may, by his character, be one way, but in dusha—His character may be happy, and in dusha he may be sad—for example, our Grisha. I know his dusha is very pure, but once in a while he blazes up,[1] starts to swear. Then it passes. That's character, well, temperament. Dusha, that's everything inside, what a person goes through inside."

Not only his wife and mother, but all his acquaintances whom I interviewed spontaneously chose Grisha to illustrate dusha and *kharakter*. As did Grisha himself: "What's character? I'll tell you honestly, I have a lousy one."

Friedrich (1986:46–47, 59) describes certain people as "virtuosos," referring to their relationships to specific parts of the culture: language, ceramics, guitar. I think an individual can be a virtuoso of less circumscribed phenomena, too; even phenomena like a range of meanings of "soul." Grisha was a virtuoso of perestroika-era dusha culture. In a sense, his virtuosity consisted in his sacrifice of his daily life to both succeeding in realizing and failing momentously to realize and embody certain images of the romantic Russian national character.

Grisha and Russian soul, as Paul Muldoon (1973:3) says in a poem about tree branches grinding together in the wind, were breaking each other.

Grisha's dearest beliefs were embodied in the most delightful friendship I had the honor to see in Russia. Kolia and Grisha knew the value of what they had: "The Strugatskii brothers, Il'f and Petrov, they wrote *together*. That's very rare. And here we are, Kol'ka and me. We're sometimes amazed at how we, with our different characters, can work together. We're connected by an invisible thread."

As 1992 wore on, the national obsession with "business" gave some people a breath of fresh air, suffocated others, and made Grisha bleed. He had a lot to say about it:

> The market sounded great, but you know how it is, Chukcha[2] sees long underwear and asks what it's for. The clerk says it's clean and warm. Chukcha buys it. When he goes to the john he forgets to pull it down. Afterward he looks in the toilet: nothing. "Hey, they *are* clean!" Then he puts his hand in his pants: "and *warm*, too!" We're like Chukcha with our market.

When Kolia tried a few doomed plans to make money, "business" became Grisha's archenemy: "I said "Kol'ka, go do business. . . . But the next day he came and said 'No, let my family live on bread—this is all I have, the only place where I'm open.' Everything is flying apart. We have to join forces." When Kolia eventually did get a higher-ranking job, Grisha bitterly

---

[1] The word *most* commonly used to describe the character trait *most* often mentioned was *vspyl'chivost'*, explosive temper(ament). Andrei said: "Dusha and character—are closely connected, but . . . character can be *vspyl'chivyi*. . . . When those explosions pass quickly . . . that means dusha is telling him what to do."

[2] In Russian jokes, Chukchi are portrayed as stupid.

noted that "Bosses don't drink with subordinates." He said Kolia needed to move up and their friendship had been holding him down. He started mentioning Kolia's name only with a pained pause, the same pause Kolia made.

At this point, a fleck of primordial economic ooze, a "privatization voucher" representing a tiny citizen's share in Soviet government-owned enterprise and an order to invest it wisely, fell into each person's hands; people waved them in verbal fists, held them up to the light, tied them to moral strings to bait each other, multiply inventing themselves as individuals, families, and collectives in terms of vouchers. The notion of vouchers' value was initially skimpy and inchoate. Over months, at kitchen tables, in the media, at coercive meetings in workplaces, and at the stock exchange, voucher-related discourses and tactics were developed that directly and indirectly determined vouchers' value. Both market prices for vouchers and theories as to whether one should save them, invest them, or get rid of them fast fluctuated and went through fashions, though many also saw it all as a scheme aimed at enriching a few, which it ultimately became, more or less. Grisha said he was saving his family's vouchers to use as toilet paper, but that if he could get a few more, he could paper the walls (these jokes had also been told during the 1991 currency reform).

If I didn't sit and drink liters of tea with him, it seemed to be more painful to Grisha than if we hadn't seen each other at all. During one wonderful liquidation of time, as he was musing boldly that he'd just trade his voucher for a coat, "a present from the government," because to invest it you "had to be a businessman in your soul," probably because of the light from his kitchen windows, I saw not the soft face of my playful, generous friend but a mask of ruthless readiness to be soulfully flexible.

CHAPTER SIX

Do Not Have a Hundred Rubles, Have Instead a Hundred Friends

Dostoevsky's Mitya Karamazov's interrogation and conviction center on his most shameful secret, a secret he kept hidden "here"—the center of his chest. Eventually we learn that the object of this gesture, which we have long assumed is Mitya's dusha, is a rag pouch under his shirt. The ultimate shame was not that he stole money, but that he calculatedly hid it for the future.

A quality of what became understood as Russian soul was opposition to the allegedly rational, work-oriented world of "the West." During the last decades of the tsarist regime, though Russia's social structure and popular culture were becoming more like Western ones, Russia was distinguished from them, Brooks (1984:355) writes, by "a widely held antipathy to the functioning of the market economy." "Money . . . although clearly sought after . . . was regarded with ambivalence or hostility. . . . Commerce and industry were associated with the exploitation of others. . . . In a village economy . . . anyone who got rich seemed to do so at the expense of some other person" (ibid.:278, 285–86).

If, before the Revolution, a clear distinction could be made between peasants, among whom talk about money and money itself were hardly ethical, and other classes for whom the market and money were accepted (Ostrovskii's plays show these attitudes), the subsequent standard communist education evened out this distinction somewhat. Then, Dunham (1990:19) suggests, during the Stalin era, a petty-bourgeois mentality spread throughout Soviet society. The transformation Dunham documents from Orthodox combat against acquisitiveness to postwar middle-class mentality was followed during perestroika by a situation in which money became an even more touchy theme.[1] I found that not only communists, members of the in-

---

[1] Dreizin (1990:5) lists words referring to trade, property, and possession that had "acquired a derogatory flavor." Many of these began to lose their negative connotations as the market gained acceptance.

tellectual elite, and village dwellers pleaded uneasiness about middle class values—much of the population, even though very "embourgeoised," still treated material success with ambivalence or surrounded elements of it by ritual behavior. In 1992, after several deaths at an Omsk school, rumors circulated among teachers that the school was cursed because the new principal was involved in business. This man, assumed to be Jewish and soul-impaired because of his direct involvement with money, became somewhat suspect of being related to the misfortunes.

One thing I do in this chapter is examine late to post-Soviet aesthetics of money as related to dusha. Treatment of and attitudes to money suggest that the Soviet economic "system" was a collage of systems; I discuss forms that sneakily and conveniently united them, many of which have to do with the aspect of dusha that is related to community. The majority of my urban Siberian acquaintances in the early 1990s claimed that market relations, even if a necessary evil, led to opposition between people. Stories such as Kazannik's (Chapter 3) of the romantic merchant throwing his money away could be quite meaningful for people. Perhaps in the capitals people became accustomed to private enterprise earlier, and "underground" moneymaking had certainly existed in Soviet Omsk, but attitudes in this closed city altered slowly and later.

In 1994–95, "business" still meant, essentially, buying and reselling imported goods. Profitable resale to one's "brother" or "neighbor" (in any of a great number of senses which could, if poetically or politically opportune, include anyone) was still widely seen as speculation even as more and more people, especially young people, enthusiastically engaged in it. Families were torn by arguments over whether or not a teenager should drop out of school to do "business." One man, hearing that I was a foreigner, the first he had met, quietly complained about socioeconomic change, then suddenly burst out that "This is from *you*, from *there*, this 'business.' "

Village values of generosity and mutual help informed the Soviet system, which transformed and appropriated their ideology and etiquette in the name of a bright communist future. It featured what Grossman (1986:49) calls "low moneyness of money," an attenuation of money's importance (Rose and McAllister 1993). Ideologically, money's moneyness was attenuated under socialism in the interest of reducing exploitation. Instead, the value of community was exploited and riddled with broken promises. However, though it ended up "corrupt" and exploited by the elite, the Soviet system did *not* work exclusively in their interest. If individuals used to "village economies" tend to prefer a moral code and state of consciousness that include sentiment over market imagery, the Soviet system shared enough aspects of village aesthetics that people's opportunities to choose that version were somewhat protected. As the writer Maxim told me: "When perestroika began, I condemned the System, but what we're seeing now is worse; it's no system at all. With all its problems, that [hypocritical, corrupt Soviet] System had more soul."

Although in village and kinship contexts mutual hand washing and back-scratching were usually not felt to be unsanitary, many complained that in the Soviet system, "It's all on the principle of *kumovstvo*: I [give to] you and you [give to] me; one hand washes the other." *Kumovstvo*, which in Soviet Russia indicated cronyism and/or nepotism, was derived from a kinship context: *kum* is a ritual parent, a "godfather."

In these chapters on exchange I show how the economy was inseparable from a folk aesthetic of consciousness and sentiment that was labeled and experienced as morality, humanity, and soul. I offer a different image of the manipulable relationship between the consciousness of economics and sentiment than we find in Marcel Mauss's summary of the gift, "in theory voluntary, disinterested, and spontaneous but . . . in fact obligatory and interested" (1967:1). In this statement alone, Mauss prioritizes (in terms of reality or primacy) "fact" over "theory," implying a notion of a unitary system and consciousness. That was not what I found.

People in Zhenia's State-farm village often traveled to Omsk city markets to sell food they produced. Yet when he told me about a man in their village who planned to buy commodities elsewhere and bring them home to sell, he asked: "Is that considered business where you come from? Here it's called profiteering." In the early 1990s, traditional and Soviet discourses about exchange coexisted with increasing acceptance of capitalism, often in complex, shifty incarnations. Even when "fictions," and/or in poor faith, discourses that emphasized "helping" were not only revealing as to a kind of hope many Russians were choosing over some hypothetical "truth," they were identity- and action-shaping narratives. From a 1992 interview with writers Maxim and Lena:

MAXIM: Russian dusha, you won't change it. Russians will never work for Western motivations. The *idea* of money, of getting rich, never shone in the Russian soul. Until we find a new ideology, dusha will go into hiding. [Prerevolutionary] millionaires first of all built churches, places to pray before God and society for forgiveness for the sin of avarice.[2]

LENA: I can't speak for the Russian people, but I do represent part of it—total rejection of what's going on. The idea of getting rich is *in principle* impossible, even if we all start watching those commercials that remind me of a women's bathhouse. In Russia we always pitied the poor, the downtrodden—now . . . I will *never* buy that brand of soap. Never. *Complete nonacceptance.*

MAXIM: Our politicians with American bents are going to break their heads on this one. Russia will not. To force her to live according to the idea of the

---

[2] Brooks (1984:276–88) finds a tendency in prerevolutionary popular literature for success and wealth to need justification.

market is impossible. *Give her a worthy idea! The market cannot be a goal!* "Get rich!" you say to the people. The people will answer you: "Go screw yourself!" That never was the basis of life.

When I told Zina and Andrei Orlov that I had been told that Russians would only work for a great idea, not money, they objected: that was over-simplifying. "There are infinitely complex invisible threads connecting things, but everything is interwoven with the material." In 1992, Andrei and Zina said:

ZINA: We can't afford anything right now. We'll wear out our clothes and that's it. We don't know how to make money.

ANDREI: Even 10 kopecks over our state salary was considered speculation.

ZINA: We're expected to do favors for superiors. My tongue would never turn to say, "Pay me"—how much? If I ask for money, attitudes toward me will be different, as though I were a thief. I'm not prepared. If I'm supposed to enter a market economy—our psychology is completely different. I can't even sell berries from my tree. If I don't have the sugar to preserve it, let it rot, but *no selling*. Only bad people, we thought, do that. In school in the sixties we tormented one girl. She ended up in a psychiatric hospital. Her parents sold radishes and onions. They were considered profiteers, thieves. My mother was a saleswoman, a profession considered disgraceful; I was ashamed to tell my friends. "He who sells does something dishonest." . . . I'd feel as if I was standing there naked; that's how we were raised. Andrei sold for the first time at the market not long ago.

ANDREI: I stood there, my face burning.

ZINA: That's our upbringing, way of life, psychology. You can't overstep it.[3] I . . . understand I'm not doing anything bad, but to go out there and stand, I can't. People would see, judge me; I'm ashamed. I'm not ready for business at all, I live according to a different moral code. Money *itself* was immoral, and now they're telling us to make more!

Tension between the ideology of gratuitous giving and market pressures resulted in people pedantically ranting about selling's immorality and then quietly doing what they had to. This was rarely as simple as hypocrisy, and I find it fruitful to interpret it in a different spirit than what has been called misrecognition (Bourdieu 1990:105, Yurchak 1997, Ledeneva 1998:59–72). I elaborate on this below. Although most people I talked to said they couldn't sell, Nadia told me Grisha had sold items they no longer needed. Even shy Anna Viktorovna admitted that she once sold a night-gown she didn't need at the market. While she stood there, however, she be-

---

[3] "Impossible to overstep" appears in many interviews. *Perestupit'* is to step over, trans-gress, and is related to the word for crime.

came warm and took off her good sweater. Someone thought it was for sale and asked her the price. She got flustered and sold it cheaply.

I should mention the importance of shame, *styd* (see Friedrich 1996). Shame seems to be a fundamental "content" of the depths, of dusha, and being shameless (*besstydnyi*) indicates a sick dusha. Shame appeared in my interviews on virtually all topics.

Accounts by those (Ledeneva 1998, Simis 1982) who grew up in "the System" document Soviet everyday economy better than I ever could. I point at dusha in this part of "the System" by beginning with attitudes toward money, as Zina said, "*itself* immoral," during a period when money's importance was rapidly growing. Then I discuss the *blat* system of informal networking and various values of its "infinitely complex invisible threads."

Rubles have been increasingly important and involved in bribery since the 1960s (Simis 1982:209, passim). Money could make things appear, but gift and hospitality bribes were preferred; cash bribes "spelled things out too clearly" (ibid.:130). Alongside their increasingly open interest in exchange, commodities, and a more comfortable life, many people, when possible, avoided the *open* image of money and treated it ambivalently. I start by looking at a late to post-Soviet aesthetics of treatment of money according to which, as Zina said, "*My tongue would never turn* to say 'Pay me.'"

Money Avoidance

Speaking of money was often avoided. In 1992, a young Omsk woman wrote, by way of thanks, to an American friend: "Talk about money is embarrassing, complicated, you know what I mean? That's why I won't say many words of thanks for the envelope." Many acquaintances complained that *speaking* of money, as of the quotidian, spoke of a person's pettiness and low spiritual and/or cultural level. Discussions about money, "getting things," and comparisons of prices and wages could be accompanied by self-conscious asides that talk like this signaled the death of culture, or that "The conditions of our present life have made it necessary to talk openly about such things."[4] "If you're interested in dusha," a woman said, "such talk about money and pay was not done, not acceptable, nekul'turno. And now it's the first thing people discuss." During TV coverage of the 1992 St. Petersburg marathon, a sportscaster awkwardly apologized for an impending commercial: "These days, even in the context of *pure* athletics we're

[4] The fairly new expression *shkurnye voprosy* (from an older expression for a self-interested person, *shkurnik*) was sometimes used as an apology or frame before broaching such subjects. The word "money" itself (*den'gi*) was often replaced by "means" (*sredstva*). Of course, delicacy about cash is not limited to Russia (see Epilogue).

obliged to mention our sponsors; without them there would have been no marathon."

Though interaction with medical professionals was a common context for monetary "gifts," tradition has it that one ought not say thank you on receiving a gift of medicine. This was usually observed in the form of the recipient thanking the donor, who in turn reminded him or her not to; or in the form of the recipient reciting, "One doesn't say 'thank you' for medicine." Such a gift is indeed help, for which one may certainly show "appreciation," but health was often distanced from *reference* to exchange. Babushki who healed rarely accepted money, calling it a sin. It would have been, as was resale, profiting from others' misfortune—their neediness, in particular. But most babushki accepted gifts.

When possible, exchange was not only discussed but *experienced* in terms of friendship and help. I noticed that if I gave several gifts to one person, the least commercially valuable (and often the most easily classified as "spiritual") was often the most explicitly lauded. I once thanked a young woman for a great favor with an assortment of gifts: cosmetics, a thank-you note, a pen, and a cassette I made for her to study English with. She silently accepted my gifts. The next time we met she twice elliptically thanked me: the cassette was [thumb up, the gesture for "great"] and "Especially, especially, for the note." She did not mention the other gifts, though it was clear that they had not offended her. It was uncultured (*nekul'turno*), or uncomfortable (*neudobno*), to thank me for the rare cosmetics. Many people would have thanked me for all parts of the gift (open admission of neediness could be a sign of trust), but this woman's omissions were not unusual. An American presented an Omsk friend with a gift-wrapped paperback containing an envelope of cash. He opened the wrap, opened the book, saw the envelope, saw her see him see it, and thanked her for the book.

The sight of money and physical contact with it were also attenuated. I received lecture fees camouflaged in decorative envelopes. Once, a man responsible for giving me this envelope opened my purse, which lay across the room, and placed it inside. Clearly opening my purse was less of a violation than handing me an envelope. When I bought earrings from a craftswoman, she wouldn't touch my money but opened the corner of her bag and silently indicated to put the cash in there. A former Muscovite living in Chicago once folded a check and handed me the folded edge, sparing me both physical contact with the meaningful side of the check and being observed seeing it. When friends repaid debts, money did not usually pass from hand to hand without "cooling off." Money was often placed, folded or otherwise diminished, on a table; only after the friend had left would it be approached. Likewise, discussion or transfer of money often took place out of sight of third parties.

As a friend and I waited for a bus on a deserted village street, I took out my bus fare. She, as if scolding me for doing something unpleasant or embarrassing, said "Put *that* away," pointing at my three exposed bills. I hid them, assuming she wanted to pay. In the bus, with a punitive air, she bought tickets, but then unhesitatingly took the rubles I offered her. She had not been trying to be hospitable; I had been behaving indecently in public.

These issues were aggravated when foreigners appeared. Americans were guests. Guests must be gratuitously given what was referred to as "everything" (*vsë*). When a Western journalist tried to pay a local interpreter I had provided, she refused, telling him to give me what he felt proper and I'd get it to her. She repeatedly used both me and the time it would take money to circulate back around to mediate the transformation from "helping" to doing a job for money and vice versa. At the sight or mention of cash she'd back off, gasp, shield her body by waving "No" with out-turned hands (a gesture I saw often), though she both needed and expected compensation. I, a Russian-speaking foreign friend, positioned between her and the market, could help.

Americans were not only guests. They were thresholds to the world of the market. Out of embarrassment, lack of skill in evaluating their work's monetary value, and fear of under- or overcharging, craftspeople often asked what one wanted to pay. If in many cases this was awkwardness about money, there could also be, *simultaneously*, a nuance of wanting to see how much would be offered, to get at least as much as was fair from these people who, it was assumed, had money in abundance, and to have one's work informatively "priced" by American "experts."

The Weakness of Money and the *Blat* System

> I can't start this project without you, and for you to do it without
> me is much, much harder than with me.
> An Omsk bureaucrat to a man in her office, 1992

Money avoidances were supplemented by money's economic weakness ("Money won't do it; only bottles will"). If money was, until the late to post-Soviet rise in its importance, weaker than commodities in proportion to their demand, money was also less important than acquaintances. Since the 1960s, monthly salaries were an absurd, joking curse: "May you live on your salary alone." During the 1990s, salaries became so relatively minuscule that they lost what reality they had had.

During the Soviet era, Omsk had relatively low food prices; in late 1991 this changed. Sour cream was, at the time, the popular indicator of inflation. "You used to buy a glass of it for lunch. What does that glass cost *now*?" "People used to buy three liters at a time. *Now* you see people with half-liter and even smaller jars." "Children need sour cream." In January

1992, the price of sour cream ranged from 6 to 76 rubles in the same store, depending on the day. At 50 rubles a kilo salesgirls said people were stupid to buy it, but there were lines. A March 1992 newspaper claimed farmers were feeding pigs sour cream while city people lived on potatoes and bread because city markets had been taken over by "leather-clad bruisers" charging protection money. Thus, the article raged, the "normal" resident was paying the farmer *and* the middleman and racketeer: "The pensioner, like an old regiment horse, bolts from prices uttered by strapping young bruisers. Has the miracle of Omsk grocery prices disappeared?"

Around this time, as the highest inflation began and the street exchange rate for the dollar was around 125 rubles, Zina's monthly salary was 500 rubles. Members of the ballet earned 350; a seamstress was making 1,000 at home. A year later, a man who had an administrative job with the police was making 3,500 a month, a teacher 3,000. A former partocrat claimed to make under 4,000. By 1993, according to *Argumenty i fakty* (cited in Humphrey 1995:3), over 30 percent of Russia's population had an income below the survival threshold.

Although markets carried fruit, vegetables, meats, and dairy products, these were too expensive for everyday use. State stores charged less, but they were empty. When one discovered inexpensive food, one had to wait in line for it, so when they found something, people bought in the largest quantities possible. Supplies were hoarded, traded, shared. A joke, actually a common occurrence, describes a person getting in line before asking what exactly he is waiting for. Bribes worked, but were swelling. The "back door" of restaurants, stores, and factories was a source of goods contingent on one's talent and luck. Friends and relatives lent money. Grandparents and parents usually helped whenever possible (typical were a woman in her thirties who got money for boots from her mother and a father of teenagers whose mother paid for his driving lessons).

As one man explained, "If you spend your entire [monthly] salary on boots, you still have to eat." Given prices, salaries, and spending behaviors,[5] it is clear that people were obtaining commodities without paying for them out of their salaries. Other sources made shortage of cash in hand somewhat less of a "curse." In warmer months many families spent their "free time" at dacha gardens and potato fields and gathering and preserving wild produce. During the early 1990s, to compensate for or subsidize inadequate or delinquent pay, workers sometimes (thanks to the director's connections) could buy hard-to-get commodities on site at subsidized prices, received coupons redeemable at on-site cafeterias, or were paid in commodities of some sort. The latter created problems for those like Zina, who received exotic-sized shoes in lieu of her salary and was mortified at the thought of selling anything.

---

[5] In Pesmen 1998 I list some of these. Humphrey (1995:16) gives statistics on how incomes were spent in 1991–93 (from *Argumenty i fakty*, no. 12 [649], 1993 and Hansen 1993:99).

Stealing from the workplace or other accessible institution had long been easy to rationalize, as there was no visible owner. During perestroika this was snidely called privatization, or, in a pun on *privat-* (private) and *prikhvat* (grabbing), *prikhvatizatsiia* (something like "piratization"). Handelman 1995:104 notes this as well). Others' jobs also gave one access to commodities and services, and one might spend the better part of a day finding someone to talk to about getting something to trade with a third person for what one needed.

In other words, every person had a repertoire of ways to help others, make money, provide for the family, and be a good host, much of which created good feelings and a desire to reciprocate.[6] This repertoire's variety and its social importance show why the word meaning "to get," *dostat'*, was so charged.

Simis (1982:253–54, 298) calls it an ethical paradox that most people did not see theft from the state as real theft, stole food and alcohol from enterprises that produced, processed, or stored it, did not think twice about lifting nails, light bulbs, and equipment, bribed with no burden on their conscience, but would not steal a penny from another person: "*Homo Sovieticus* is not immoral, he simply has two separate systems of morality." People just wanted to thank those who helped out in moments of need. Simis claims that in such cases there was no sense of corruption or wrongdoing, but then he tells how a friend, showing him a list of chores annotated with names of those who could help, "was horrified" to realize that in every case he would be behaving dishonestly (ibid.:111, 205–6). "*No* sense of wrongdoing" alternated with a sense of wrongdoing. The Soviet whose conscience was not bothered and the one whose was, the same person at different moments, both tended to blame the state and/or System for their moral duplicity.

The notion of misrecognition (as in Ledeneva 1998), as appropriate as it may seem when Russian speakers, in certain moods and positions, accuse themselves of dual morality, is inadequate in this case. Misrecognition, like Mauss's classification of certain giving behaviors as "in fact" self-interested and gratuitous only "in theory"—like other writers' descriptions in terms of "false consciousness" and "lying to oneself"—chooses an "underlying," often "hard" truth—self-interest, for example—and assumes that if *that* is present, other kinds of things— less calculated gestures, for example—must be either absent, ideology, or masks. What assumptions lead people thinking about everyday life to feel such choices are necessary? "Blat" and "helping" are different explanations for the same action, but is there only one truth about an event, so that all others must be opposite, mutually exclusive, fight it out or be hierarchically ranked in terms of their "reality"? This fails to take into account the roles time (successive moments), sentiment,

---

[6] On the "underground" economy and blat system, see Simis 1982 and Ledeneva 1998. See also Verdery 1993. For statistical studies, see the Berkeley-Duke Occasional Papers on the Second Economy in the USSR series edited by G. Grossman and V. G. Treml.

and the failure to logically analyze all their actions play in allowing people to be and do more than one thing. Some of what have been conceptualized as economically and sociologically incommensurable structures are just different moments of consciousness.

Explanations in terms of misrecognition rely on imagining in people and situations a sort of single, internal, underlying space the logical hygiene of which is protected, a locus of one reigning fact (or struggling others). Assuming this cramped and coherent interiority stems from and leads to inaccurate, diminished, and uncharitable senses of what human beings can do.

Blat—"credit" or "pull" with or through friends, relatives, and acquaintances—was a powerful economic tool. The *blat* system rested on individual repertoires built up over lifetimes. One's present and past jobs, those of friends, relatives, and others with whom one had blat, and all *those* people's social and kin relations gave one access to commodities and services. That repertoire was an attribute of one for others who might hope to get something through one. A job was more valuable for the people, places, supplies, equipment, and services it gave access to than as a source of a salary. For example, one man's job provided him with unlimited free supplies, but he preferred, he explained, to use almost his entire tiny monthly salary (about the price of a carton of Marlboro) to buy higher-quality supplies stolen from a factory for his use both off the job and on, because if done well, his job brought him more valuable work on the side.

American businessmen I worked for were only half right when they accused potential Russian partners of talking big and promiscuously hatching off-the-wall schemes. A Russian might be creatively scanning the landscape for possible connections between people, interests, debts, and favors. As he couldn't know what "possibilities" the American had, each of his own represented a possible discovery. "Shifty" behavior and shameless name-dropping were, in part, also the Russian exposing some of the special capital he commanded in his "system."

Mauss familiarizes the strangeness of potlatch and related "total social phenomena" by characterizing them as "in theory voluntary, disinterested, and spontaneous but . . . in fact obligatory and interested" (1967:1), ultimately prioritizing economic aspects of exchange over sentimental ones. Tania, an Omsk woman, in a letter to an American, briefly alienates the familiar by presenting American economics in her terms: indebtedness, power, support, *help*. "Maybe in America," she writes, "unemployment is high because you can't make other people indebted to you until you have a high position, and you can't get the support to get that high position without help." I was with a former partocrat, Petrov, in a car when we ran out of gas. He emptied a plastic bucket of tomatoes and flagged down a truck driver who siphoned off some gas for us. Nothing changed hands but the business card that Petrov handed to our smiling savior.

Though some blat was earned by concrete favors, the claim on "help" activated by mentioning the name of powerful kin or acquaintances was perhaps the most potent. It was a half-joke that the powerful, unlike other Soviets, had actually lived to see communism: "Money didn't exist for them," they could live in the System without it. During the Soviet era, the elite's apartments cost no more than others', and *no* amount of money could obtain such an apartment. This does not mean that the elite had less money than others: another joke has it that after the Revolution there was discussion as to whether money would exist. A compromise was reached: some people would have money, others wouldn't. If Party members had formerly lived better without relying on money, during perestroika they were among the only ones in positions to "restructure" toward a market system and were soon among the few *with* money.

Shifty Transformations

Money avoidances led a double life. Any pause in accepting money could be opportunistically parlayed into a more open situation and even into more inclusive notions of exchange. Sometimes people took the approach of "getting these issues out of the way" before proceeding to other topics, but more often "such issues" were put off or saved until "later" or "some other time," if the favor-doer wanted to keep the recipient indebted against future need or felt like stalling until drinks had been shared, that is, until the issue of exchange had been humanized, socialized, by a ritual "washing." Talking to a woman who had enabled him to buy circus tickets, an acquaintance began: "If you need anything related to sewing or electrical supplies—." She waved: "We'll talk about it another time." When a powerful woman tried to reimburse a man for a purchase he had made for her, he resisted, saying that it had been very inexpensive. She took out money; he claimed to have forgotten the price, and that was that. She would repay him or already had. Refusing a gift was offensive. Refusing money affirmed one's commitment to helping from the heart. But rubles were also simply worth less.

Certain words were full, active members of these contexts. I asked a man I knew only superficially how I could repay a friend of his for his help. He laughed nervously and denied that the friend would take anything. I reformulated, asking him to please give me a clue (*podskazat'*) as to how to do it properly. He agreed willingly, telling me what I could do to help his friend's family.

When money had been involved in a favor, its timely transformation into a form other than direct repayment was usually desirable. Among aesthetic reasons for this, both exchange and friendship relations were developed by keeping debts and favors amorphous, uncalculated, moving. This is, as Mauss (1967:36) writes, "characterized by etiquette and generosity.... When it is carried out in a different spirit, for immediate gain, it is viewed with the greatest disdain." People sometimes used the word "independence" as a sort of insult when I insisted on reimbursing them. This was quite succinct: deferment of repayment, conversion of creditor's and debtor's positions into a vaguer sense of helping, confirmed people's mutual *dependence*.

Friendship included this dependence. Expecting help didn't make relationships manipulative, parasitic, or exploitative unless the "using" aspect became too visible, obscuring the "spiritual" or its superficial sister, tact. If it did, people were called calculating. What's more, through spirited chains of "help," one might occasionally lose track of for what one owed whom and what one was owed. New friendships were born.

Jowitt (1983:275) writes that "Soviet social organization resembled primitive economies" in Polanyi's (1957:73) sense of "reciprocity demanding adequacy of response, not mathematical equality." "Adequacy of response" was in this case a flexible enough criterion to allow for extremely subtle sorts of values and signs to partake actively in sociocultural and economic processes. Commodities in shortage were worth more than their store price (see Humphrey 1992). By keeping debts unresolved, incalculable "human" values (a combination of use value and those of warm, concrete individuals) were *included* in debts, modifying them in the form of feelings of connectedness, willingness, even warmth. Sometimes this grew and gave rise to both more "human" and more economic value, rather than stopping dead at what Mauss would have identified as "a refusal of friendship and intercourse" (1967:11). It depended on situations and individuals, but as a rule, repayment in kind was refusing to play the game. Of course, there were jokes: I gave Zhenia a pack of Marlboros. He laughed and threw me his rough tobacco wrapped in newsprint.

"Help" could be transformed into its ideological opposite, "economic" exchange, even business, and vice versa, business transformed into community, by means of formal similarities including sharing meals, tea, talk, alcohol, and the use of certain highly valued words. Explicit money talk was a short circuit that violated community and the continuum of selflessness and interest. The formal similarity of and behaviors associated with semantically broad and flexible words like "friendship," "help," and "culture" were taken advantage of to purify, mask, exploit, and to allow people to act in ways that allowed for more than one interpretation. During and after the Soviet era, the word kul'tura was used to create noble-sounding official auspices for vast moneymaking schemes. Two actors, discussing how their theater had signed a "declaration of friendship" with a factory, explained, "friendship meant we did free performances for them, and they came to all our openings." As Handelman's (1995:63) informant said, "It's all based on personal sympathy." This sentence pertains to the most and the least ironic performances. "Interest" was another shifty term. Just as exchange can be of potatoes, as Grisha said, or of warmth, interest had a range of meanings of which Mauss's "*in theory* disinterested and *in fact* interested" is just one.

Interest

If all parties were in one way or another *interested,* it facilitated transactions. Interest has the same range of meanings in Russian as in English (except that in Russian it is not used in reference to percentage return, and an attractive woman or man is often called "interesting"). The word interest has its origin in the Latin *inter*—between, among, in the midst of, mutually, reciprocally, together, during. In American dictionaries, the first entries under "interest" indicate feelings or attitudes of concern, involvement, curiosity. Subsequent entries narrow this down to advantage, profit, and, ultimately, *self*-interest.

In my interviews, interest and interesting were emphatically opposed to self-interest. They implied passionate, lively curiosity divorced from notions of material gain, though not divorced from spiritual gain. This opposition, however, was easily and often finessed or destroyed under the auspices of the word "interest." Spiritual development is certainly "bettering one's condition," to use Adam Smith's (1976) term, but how could one possibly better one's spiritual condition at others' expense? *Nezainteresovanno* (disinterested, impartial), could deny selfishness. In fact, shifts in meanings of interest can be seen to parallel shifts in criteria used to define welfare.

Hirschman (1977:32) writes that in late sixteenth-century Western Europe, interest implied concerns, aspirations, and advantage not limited to material welfare; "It comprised the totality of human aspirations, but denoted an element of reflection and calculation with respect to the manner in which these aspirations were to be pursued." Interest came to partake of a distinction that has "dominated the analysis of human motivation since Plato, namely, the passions on the one hand, and reason on the other" (ibid.:43). Increasingly associated with reason, interest was increasingly linked to calculation, and further, to self-interest, narrowing "to the pursuit of material, economic advantage" (ibid. 38; see Mauss 1967:75–83 on interest).

Interest could be associated with reason in Russia, and could imply a cosmology of shortage in which it would take an invisible hand to reconcile individuals. Though raw ambition or desire for personal profit were anathema to soul ideology, if a person was interested enough in wealth, his craving became "deep" and was treated like other deep things. Even before the Revolution, material luxuries might be called "something for the soul." This version of "what dusha really wants" reappeared in a September 1997 Russian *Cosmopolitan* advertisement touting Triumph brassieres: "Perfection of the body. Triumph of dusha."

"Interest" was semantically shifty, spanning a range from pure to impure. It could associate virtually *any* object, event, or sentiment to dusha, overriding a simplistic definition of dusha as where the purest lives. In short, interest was an emotion indexing value *of any sort,* and where value was discovered was highly individual.

Saying and Seeing the Unmentionable and Invisible

Late 1980s political economy and ideology resonated with and coopted ready cultural meanings, as had Soviet ones. Unlike Soviet ideology, however, perestroika propaganda fit traditional categories of the profane more than those of the sacred. Blat, a word that acknowledges the existence of unfair advantage and corruption, was part of a system of exchange woven through with an ideology condemning exchange of anything except human warmth (and occasional "constructive" criticism). Talk about "getting things" was often open, and the blat that was being used was often specified when asking a favor, but I also often heard people intone before mentioning blat the precautionary phrase "as they say in Russian . . ." used before profanity. Variously constructed intimacy and a "crude" or familiar manner were other ways of obtaining or claiming the right to speak in economic terms. Jokes attributing a stroke of pure luck to "blat" or "a bribe" implied that the blat was with, or the bribe to, God or some higher power.

Some people accustomed to overpaying under the table were offended at similar prices charged openly. At the other extreme were "businessmen" with their obscenely naked cash. Many "New Russians" initially took the Stalinist image of the calculating, ruthless capitalist shark as a model, inverting only the value. The shadow economy floated to the surface and demanded insane prices, like an open black hole. Money came *out* of hiding and, as one student said to me and others also claimed, "Dusha went *into* hiding to protect itself." The student continued: "I hope that's what's happened, and not that it's gone away so we can throw ourselves fully into business."

What had formerly been done in a closed manner was now to be done openly. This left, some complained, only "animal" self-interest. But a verdict that someone had entirely lost dusha was problematic for the one judging as well—compassion is part of soul. Thus it was usually to everyone's advantage that a bad person's dusha be seen as only slumbering or mutely suffering rather than dead. I return to this in subsequent chapters.

On the morning after the announcement of the January 1991 currency reform, the proverb "Don't have a hundred rubles, have a hundred friends" (*Ne imei sto rublei, a imei sto druzei*), appeared as the headline of a national newspaper. During the reform, 50- and 100-ruble bills, which could be exchanged for new currency only in limited quantities and for a few days, burned their owners so badly they were called "mustard plasters." Each person dealt with them as best as he or she could. The issue of money could no longer be finessed; everyone needed help, advice, information, from anyone at all, and spent days sharing information and strategies. Cash was suddenly the most critical commodity.

Banc and Dundes (1990:119) cite a joke about how the ways Soviets made ends meet, given their inadequate salaries, was "none of your business." Even in the midst of the currency crisis, discretion did not totally disappear: where this cash had come from, even after people had, under threat of losing it, admitted its existence, was rarely asked except, perhaps, behind a person's back, with the resulting implication that that person was somehow worse for having so much. On the second day of the crisis, when a young man sitting at a makeshift table drinking tea with coworkers mentioned the amount he needed to exchange, a coworker ingenuously asked where he had *gotten* that kind of money. Everyone laughed. Someone said to me "Pay no attention to him, he's crazy." Discussing where a person had obtained money could have the quality of nasty gossip, a reproach or even a threat.

Only when, for one reason or another, the awareness of economics was crudely forefronted did an opposition have to appear between spiritual and self-interested people. That opposition appeared constantly; people waited for it to appear, *caused* it to, so as to have opportunities to argue in a discourse that examined and performed the tension, not only of constantly alternating systems but of alternating passions.

Restructuring, Change, and Invisible Hands

During perestroika blat's webs were reorganized and dissolved by an importance of money less temporary than that of the currency reform (see Ledeneva 1998). Yurii Yur'evich said:

> For seventy years people were raised in a spirit of collectivism. In the idea of communism there is much that resonates with Christianity: man being a friend to man, and a comrade, and a brother; "Help those close to you." These ideas, they're useful. People are simply not morally ready for business. Everything is moving farther from the good. Because market relations inevitably lead, it seems to me, to opposition of man to man. And family relations are changing. The reason is the same—the need to make money. Lately an enormous warp [or skew; *perekos*] has happened in our propaganda. Everything is measured by the ruble. The ruble. Less is said about the spiritual.

This "skew" was coined or generously used by Stalin to euphemistically say that something had gone off track and needed to be rectified at all costs. In 1992, Yurii Yur'evich is describing current events with a hint of Stalin's voice.

In a 1992 TV interview a man said he could not tolerate betrayal in friends, but that, tragically, "*All* our present life is tuned to that note." A prevalent kind of complaint about perestroika killing Russian soul indicated that evidence of soul illness (such as desertion by friends) had a great deal to do with economics and the growing explicitness of exchange.

If the blat system and associated cronyism, stealing, and so on were seen as "corrupt," they were also seen as *necessary* corruption of the official system. They were formally similar to folk values of helping relatives or neighbors. Requests for "help" of all kinds tended to obey the same etiquette. In addition, both village economies and the "corrupt" Soviet economy were sometimes said to "work out" all right. This invisible hand (Smith 1976:477–78; 1982:184–85), however, was both moved and bitten by the question "What's in it for me?" "Theft," I was told, "became a virtue: bosses stole but everyone had access to something, so things worked out. Every family in that System somehow got approximately what it needed." Nearly everyone was "corrupt"—those who were not, due to honesty or lack of access, were de facto penalized. In other words, corruption was also solidarity-forming and definitive of community. Solidarity in these cases was against the powers that be, whether powerful humans or "fate" (*sud'ba*).

The System had some divinity to it. When parts of the "old system" were supposed to have died, as much as the System was hated, people explicitly said that life and soul were disappearing. If a person comes to love material possessions, he builds his identity by consuming (see Verdery in Humphrey 1995:20). If a person loves maneuvering around in the System or getting rich, he seems to take social roles to heart, and his heart seems to become of "this" world.

Money's growing moneyness was said to spoil something the System had preserved. On one hand, when Oleg described how, before, he had "known" someone wherever he went, he described corruption. On the other hand, his landscape had been literally alive with acquaintances. People and association with people could purify things. Now "It feels . . . less human. . . . You look at a thing and that *thought* creeps in, 'How much does it *cost?*' " Grisha told me:

> Our dushi are cooling off. . . . That's when I stop feeling others' misfortunes and joys . . . start to think like a consumer. . . . When people exchange not sugar, not oil, not potatoes, when they give each other warmth and kindness, then we can fend off what's happening now. . . . The more money gets involved, the less friendship can exist. During *the famine* people were kind, but with this idea that people have to get rich, relations deteriorate, dusha cools off. I stop taking others' pain into dusha.

When money, self-interest, or suspicion of them affected friendships it was called soul loss. I was told: "Those people selling, they've gone crazy about money, they forget that the one who pays is a *person*, too." The Orlovs called "soul loss" the way their neighbors became wealthy, went into business, and stopped socializing with them. Most "New Russians" at that time would probably claim that they had Russian soul, but Andrei saw this as a degraded parody:

Friendship, that's to drink tea, communicate. That's necessary and sufficient. Similar views on life. But recently a parallel to this real process is developing. . . . The *kommersanty*, they've become spiritually impoverished. They look down on people of the same intellectual level. But they share an *interest* in money; they have a material basis to their relations.

In the late 1980s power began changing hands often, so blat didn't "keep" well. With inflation, money became more necessary even as it developed a tendency to spoil. In these circumstances, friends started having to repay small loans; people couldn't help gratuitously; and shamefully, some became creditors. All this made for increased consciousness of calculable exchange value rather than engagement in incalculable yet specific, concretely contextualized helping. When, as Oleg said, "that thought creeps in," a lot changes.

Living Better than Others

There is a strong tendency, perhaps pan-Slavic, toward negative attitudes about some people living better than others. Russian proverbs include "It's not offensive that the wine is expensive; it's offensive that the innkeeper is getting rich," and "Beat to death the one who lives better than we do." Hedrick Smith writes that Russians can "bear the pain" as long as they see that others are sharing it. "The collective jealousy can be fierce against those who rise above the crowd" (in Rancour-Laferriere 1995:207–9). I heard and read in the press many stories about attacks on privately owned businesses. The future ought to be brighter, but people should not live better than their contemporaries. Zhenia told me that in the village until recently, no one had raised extra cattle for meat to sell and had had no interest in extra money, because "having extra" meant having more than others (see Dunham 1990:92).

Money *itself* also implied living better than others and it implied power; if not present power, then future power. A man in his thirties explained: if you make money, you also need "the power to do in those who would do you in." The desire to destroy anyone with money and the inevitability of exploitation by anyone wealthier were often taken as givens.

The Jew

Earlier in this chapter, I mention a businessman-school principal people assumed was Jewish. I would like to return to the issue. It was partially in the terms I have been discussing that Jews were portrayed as not part of the Russian community and in images used to negatively define that community. A joke asks what each of various ethnic groups brings to a party and with what each leaves. The Frenchman comes with his wife and leaves with someone else's. A Russian comes with a bottle and leaves with a fight. The Jew comes with his family and a small cake and leaves with his family and a small cake, wondering where else he can go (alternately, he comes with his family and leaves with a piece of cake). Only the Jew is not transformed by the social experience, only he has another tidy social unit to which he has greater affinity. He takes care of his family and only appears to contribute to the feast.

Dreizin (1990:3, 5) notes that "The 'shortest anecdote' of Russian anti-Semitic folklore is 'The peasant Jew' " (I heard "the Jewish janitor"). He describes the image of the Jew in Russian culture as that of a philistine whose social obligations stop at his family, which is served at the expense of society; his interests are petty; he avoids hard work, speaks unattractive Russian, is ugly, greedy, cunning, and related to petty and dishonest business, trade, and possessions.[7] The author Kuprin, in a 1909 letter, writes:

> A barber is cutting a gentleman's hair and suddenly . . . says "Excuse me," runs into a corner of his shop and begins pissing on the wallpaper. As his client becomes numb with shock, Figaro calmly explains: "It's all right. We're moving tomorrow anyway." . . . The kike is just such a barber with his approaching Zion. . . . This is why he . . . is indifferent to nature, history, others' language. . . . This is why, in his limited indifference to the fates of other peoples, the Jew has so often been a pimp, . . . a thief, a cheat, an instigator, a spy, all the while remaining a clean and honest Jew.

Dreizin (1990:107) notes that Fëdor Karamazov is a sort of fictive Jew, having been apprenticed to Odessa Jews. Jews (and often Caucasians and Asians) were accused of calculating hypocrisy, lack of respect and conscience, and ruthless interest in self-enrichment. Jews in positions of power were often despised. Russian imagery of "The Jew" constructs dusha by opposition in other ways, such as "The Jew's" alleged ties to Israel and other Jews and his "rootless cosmopolitanism." After all, a proud element of "Russianness" is: "we're stuck with it, it's our fate." I mentioned being told in a Moscow bathhouse about a dog that barked only at Jews. That woman also repeated the indictment that Jews were responsible for the Revolution. It followed, as I heard several times, that Soviet era "corruption" of Russian national character into a hybrid Homo Sovieticus was due to an injection of Jewish culture into Russian. Economic changes during perestroika saw a repeat of this: I heard a man who was opening a cooperative called a "cooperativist mug" (*kooperatorskaia morda*), a transformation of an insult usually applied to Jews.

[7] Cf. Dreizin (1990:xv–xvi) and Sinyavsky (1990) on late Soviet antisemitism.

Concluding Thoughts

A conclusion to this chapter, and an introduction to this section, which deals with various relations of dusha to various kinds of exchange, was revealed to me at table, in an intense, drunk voice, by Grisha's friend Igor, who wanted to explain to me the secret heart of the situation: "Everyone wants to have something, but only through someone."

The path "through people" runs between and confuses holy and profane. Details of the System are downplayed out of decency (they partake of the practical innards of things), out of jealousy (to protect information and power), because of the value of images of "magic," and, I suggest, in order to take advantage of and tap into people's powerful ability to be flexible, many-souled, and logically incoherent. What was seen as vile and practical exploited what was seen as gratuitous and pure and was itself purified in consciousness by time, by a shared desire for it to be purified, by the unthinkably eclectic nature of some exchanges, and by the often urgent way in which needs arose and acquaintances were called on. Or it was not purified completely, fueling endless moral judgement and negotiation.

Maxim said, "That System had more dusha." Earlier I cited a student saying that "Young people make money more freely . . . they don't have those complexes. . . . On the other hand . . . our parents are spiritually richer." Grisha was speaking in the same voice when he said:

> Dusha right now is locked up with a key because a person has to . . . meet people there, come to some agreement here . . . You don't always remember there's a key. . . . You don't always remember . . . about "nonconsumer relations." A person who has acquaintances not to fill his needs, but because they *interest* each other . . . [and] who spends time with people close in spirit, he loses on the material end, pays more, has to buy at the market.

Comedians, at least since the 1960s, have "tried to persuade the audience how inhumanly boring life would be without bureaucratic obstructionism and theft of state property" (Stites 1992:167). Anna Viktorovna claimed that when Grisha was a boy he told her "Mama, it's good that you owe someone. Those rich people, they have no interests at all. It's uninteresting to live." "He was still little," Anna Viktorovna said, "and that's how he had it figured out."

If something comes "through someone," people could, given the impulse to do such a kind thing, prioritize their consciousness of community over their consciousness of economics. Dusha, in this sense, is simply emphasized consciousness of community, with all the changes in the world that result from this interpretation. At the same time, economic and ethical systems and explanations rapidly alternated or coexisted by virtue of people's lack of logical coherence. Noticing this at seconds, especially when engaged in stressing someone's genuine warmth or indicting someone's manipulative dishonesty, people formulated an explanatory image of infinitely complex invisible threads spatially interweaving everything with the material, a complexity that became part of Russian dusha. The Soviet and early post-Soviet souls, as the following story illustrates, were like the rag pouch under Mitya Karamazov's shirt—the sacred and the profane in significant cohabitation, the consciousness of which was necessarily and opportunistically controlled.

Story
Pulling Something Out of a Hat

Her duty was to help, and she was anxious to, though she was weary when the plane of drunk *biznesmeny* landed in Omsk at 0600. We had worked together and had had stiff chats. She got me passes to plays. I was good for small gifts. But I had been traveling for two days, and the theater had sent her to meet me at the airport. We waited for my luggage, shivered, dazed, gossiping, too tired to stop tossing around the decision to wait in the van, out of the cold air, which I later noticed smelled not only of toxins from factories but of apple blossoms. In a week this was replaced by a lilac smell dangerous to sleep in and a lily-of-the-valley scent between bits of newspaper proffered by downy-haired old men and downy-chinned women, advance scouts of the airborne poplar fuzz that cruelly transforms a sticky honey cake on the windowsill into an uneven adolescent duck and that layered streets and parks with drifts and films that a lit match makes into a flashing, running sheet of flame. A friend almost started a fire that way "across from the KGB building, near the public prosecutor's office."

The woman standing with me, for me, was around forty, well-dressed and tinted, and exhausted and dutiful in a way I understood: tatters of anxiousness to help flapped from some arbitrary part of her. I left Vera a sincere note of thanks and a fancy umbrella (that had been given to my grandmother) in her office two days later, when she had gone to meet the Americans for whom we would work.

A day later, Vera dashed in, grasped my arm, made eye contact, gushed, not thank you, but markedly, that she was *very grateful,* and vanished. A few days after that, she said she had a present for me. We left the office so a coworker wouldn't see what was in the plastic bag whose naked woman was faded from repeated washing (nudes had replaced churches, flags, and eagles). Gifts were often given in word and only later in deed. The announcement of a gift weeks before it was acquired afforded an initial moment of pleasure to all. Surprise on receipt of a gift was often not preferred to such multiple pleasures. Vera did not prepare me, though she did say "*What a present* I have for you." In the corner, next to the manager's "American" toilet, Vera drew from a torn box (thin, speckled Soviet cardboard with everything stolen out of its very substance!) a sleek dark mink, of hats the most surely about status, tidy uniform splendor. It was like ones the *Mafiia* wore, and young saleswomen at the market; but it was also the unmarked hat for respectable people. It had false earflaps, sewn up. Real earflaps, though never brought down by such people, indicated a better hat: all that fur had been splurged on the intimate, never-seen side of the ears. In cold weather women often wore intricately knit Orenburg goat down scarves with scalloped blocked edges (they fit through a wedding ring) or print wool shawls under their hats to cover their ears, deftly wound around to the back of the neck and tied. Older women had round minks or sables. The mink Vera handed me was a little too small, but I demonstrated its fit. She might be pleased to know that I later gave it to my mother.

I myself am indifferent to fur, which was found at the market in tight passages made of people who, their sides touching, clutched a bottle of shampoo relatives had brought from Germany, stolen salami, nylon Chinese panties. As we chugged sluggishly between these shores in 1990 Grisha and Kolia had persuaded me to buy a huge fox hat for the equivalent of $20 (twice their monthly salaries) and jubilantly brought me and my stupid bushy tail to Olga, who caustically scolded them for having dushi too Russian to know well-tanned from rotting fur. In a room that smelled like bread (skins were covered with dough-like stuff as part of tanning), Olga fixed the hat, gave me a jar of peas, and offered to introduce me to useful people in exchange for baby clothes from the United States.

I found myself lusting after a rough sort of water rat, shortish reddish fur with dark tones, not the airy, pale red fox that flamboyant or perhaps lightly spiritual young women preferred. I had only seen men's hats from this *ondatra* fur, but they were the traditional shape, with tied-up ears, that both men and women wore. When I mentioned to woman friends that I was thinking of buying a hat they assumed I meant the fashionable light mink or sable, which, at $30 or so in rubles, were out of most people's range. When I revealed my preference, I was treated like a not particularly intelligent child. As if I nursed a passion for the dog fur some men wore, as much a sign of poverty in an adult male as were child-related hats of leather, sheepskin, or rabbit, or extremely worn mink. Just this side, that is, of the economic abyss of wool or acrylic knit. An otherwise decently dressed woman in a knit cap could mean only fear of the violent crime increasingly committed against the well-furred.

Sheepskin was not expensive, but could be crafted into original shapes and styles. Foxes bloomed above females in their twenties and thirties.

Some younger men were also spikily framed in fox. Middle-aged to older women, those dressed village-style, and Gypsy women had heavily furry goat down shawls, medium gray to charcoal to browns. Nutria was striking. Black or brown baby lambfur was in revival; new shapes were being explored. People were raising a cross of polecat and mink (*khonorka*). Hats were about economic reach, taste, character, aspirations, class, fashion, individuality. I was not a drunk peasant. I was an American and was aided in the purchase of an interesting light brown sable. Everyone calmed down.

Vera's gift shocked me. This was no umbrella. Even an imported umbrella, even during an umbrella shortage. True, the umbrella was from China. Some people classified electronic and other commodities as post-Soviet bloc "red," Asian "yellow," and German, American, and European "white." The Chinese sent Russia the lousiest stuff, but this yellow umbrella had come through white. Vera's gift outclassed mine, though, even after she told me she knew someone at the fur factory and asked me to find out if visiting Americans wanted fur coats. They shunned fur. I apologized. My failure to sell fur, one of a species of swarming possibilities that don't pan out, crawled back through Vera to her fur-factory friends, and her hat kept on outclassing my umbrella.

Casually, Vera said she wanted a jeans jacket. Any *Sovok* would have seen, hovering over us, the spirit of Vera's possible jacket. She distractedly complimented the one I was wearing, briefly mistaking it for hers.

We shared increasingly sympathetic, weary discussions of what might please and interest our guests. We shared an ordeal, a dance with a moment's economy. A kind of soul that is promiscuous, all volatile flash. It's not resilient or durable. Nice, though.

When the Americans wanted to buy Vera something to show their appreciation, they asked my advice. What happened then? Something switched into gear, approximately. A funny inspired feeling of a moment of structural significance, possibility. I told them the truth. Nothing they could buy in Russia could compare to something American. For example, I said, Vera had said she wanted a jeans jacket. They had one they'd love to give.

Later I gossiped to Vera, who was chatting with our boss, that I had been consulted on her gift. As she slowly, rapidly, began to begin the insincere, excited, obligatory "Nothing's necessary, don't be silly," I said I'd told them she'd love a jacket. I then did a strange, rather self-serving performance of a kind of "Russian," buffooning my own allegedly inspired calculations when I was asked. Perhaps I *did* think those things; perhaps I made them up later. Vera and the boss shook their heads, pleased with my accented performance of the familiar gambling daring (*azart*). Vera, by way of complimenting my luck and alertness, rhetorically asked the boss if I had Russian blood. "She does, she does," he said, acknowledging not only this but my intermediary role with the Americans.

About Russian blood. What I did to Vera by giving her an umbrella was a heartfelt gesture of gratitude for how she stood with me at 6. That's how it felt. At the same time, the Orlovs, my warm and generous family, had lamented, and lamented to me, and perhaps, who knows, lamented suggestively (though who cares), that they used to see every play and couldn't afford to anymore. I'd thought how much I'd love to get them tickets. Did I think when I gave it that my umbrella might indebt Vera? I'm not sure. A lot happens on the edge, a nuance easily forgotten and as easily exaggerated by others to forefront mercenary or calculated aspects of one's actions.

Vera conjured up a magnificent response, after which giving her a jacket would have only tediously indexed me as a wealthy American or America as a place out of which things could be screwed. Better, I pulled something out of a hat, proving myself a "Russian magician." And no one had had to touch money.

Are Vera and I, "Russians," forgiven for wanting things from each other? We forgave each other. We made a little soul together, some would say degraded, by moves *in theory* soulless, shot through with self-interest, but that *in fact* created a story of the kind you have to live, Russians say, to understand anything.

CHAPTER SEVEN

Like the Trojan Horse's Gut: Hospitality and Nationalism

If we give something, it's from dusha.
                                    Grisha and others, Omsk, 1992

Forty to fifty percent of the population did little reading of books
or moviegoing . . . leisure culture was still dominated by visiting
(or entertaining) friends.
                                                    Stites 1992:174

In late 1990, I waited through a long line before being rudely told I
needed Omsk identification to buy cheese. Recognizing me from TV coverage of "the first Americans," a stranger approached, said, "welcome to
Omsk," stuck her own ration of cheese into my hands, and vanished. I don't
want to seem to be anything but in awe of such gestures.

In the Decency story, I mentioned Oleg's and his wife's exclamations
about being "Russians" in "Russia." In context it was clear that they
meant hospitable. When I sent a telegram to the village asking if I could
come visit, Zhenia called, hollering, only partially because of the terrible
connection, that I'd better go study Russian for fifteen more years if I
hadn't understood I could come *anytime*. Another time, drinking, feeling
the weight of his culture's "complexity," he muttered to me that I'd have
to sit seven hours at table (gesturing at the bottle of yellow moonshine)
to start to understand Russian life, then fifteen more years to understand
anything.

Often the first question I was asked by Russians looking for a clear contrast, a sense of what the difference was between Russia and the West, was
"What do Americans do when they sit together *like this*?" They chose the
table as a starting point from which to generalize about the importance in
Russia of others and of dusha. They contrasted Russian-style communal sitting, "resting," with an image of bleak Westerners impaled on barstools. In
a fabricated newspaper interview, the first question I was asked was what I

thought of Siberians; my fabricated answer was a canonized remark on hospitality and warmth. Anna Viktorovna said:

> Siberians are hospitable. Whatever they have they put out for a guest. That is a trait of dushevnost' . . . of Northerners. And they love to store up supplies. They work hard. And they're big. Now Muscovites, they buy just a little bit. And they cut it up and offer you a little. Apparently that life of theirs, it built that into their characters. They seem to be hospitable, but it's all constricted. You can *feel* that tightness. And here in Omsk we have [whispers] *khokhly* [Ukrainians]. . . . They're completely different.

Conscience, hospitality, and altruism (a trait exploited in Soviet culture and thereby partially thrown into disrepute), have in common that a person tries to act in such a way that things are good for someone else. Andrei Orlov told me: "The most noble person I know is Zina's aunt. She's capable of self-sacrifice, tries to do whatever's necessary for other people to feel good. Gives her last. Shares." Though some maintained that nobility (*blagorodstvo*) referred only to bloodline, others redefined nobility as altruism. "Cultured" was similar in that it could imply acquired social skills, good or aristocratic breeding, but was often emphatically redefined as dushevnyi and as gotten by growing up among good people or from an inner source of kindness. These democratic criteria for culture and nobility were historically part of dusha: in the eighteenth century Fonvizin wrote that "A man of low estate may have the noblest soul" (in Williams 1970:575).

My friends said you had to understand hospitality, generosity's performance, to understand dusha. They certainly were related economically, culturally, philosophically, psychologically. A generous (*shchedryi*) person is "wide-souled," (*shirokodushnyi*) or "great-souled" (*velikodushnyi*), magnanimous. In this chapter I examine some meanings that relate to the equation of hospitality to Russian soul, as well as how such soul is made.

Urging, Offering: Making Others into Guests

When I came to stay with Anna Viktorovna, I told her that in the morning I only drank coffee (I brought it with me, as it was unavailable in Omsk). For weeks, however, she forced food on me, mistaking my obstinance for the obligatory polite first refusals. Then we entered a stage where she commanded me to eat, I laughed, then we laughed together. Despite this, she concluded the interview I cite above by saying: "Grisha says 'Don't tell her twice to eat!' But that's how we *do* things! If a person visits us, we must *give ourselves* to him, as they say, with all our dusha." The word *otdat'sia,* to give oneself, is used in sexual contexts and when one abandons oneself to music, work, etc. I cited it in reference to the baths.

Anna Viktorovna eventually stopped urging me to eat in the morning. Then one day when I got up she was the only one home. Shy Anna Viktorovna greeted me with, "I'm making pirozhki. You're going nowhere. Rest." She ordered me to eat a pile of meat pies, our individual history eradicated by the Hostess's mission. As much as I remained a guest, however, it was taken for granted that food was by definition communal. Children and guests were fed my espresso.

Many months after a stranger handed me her cheese ration and vanished, I was introduced to Lara by an acquaintance and we became good friends. She eventually identified herself as that stranger. That's what she was like. I left Omsk for several months, and on my return I called her to see if I could drop by. I had just eaten and said that she was not to feed me. When I arrived she had fish cutlets, buckwheat kasha, tomatoes, cucumbers, strawberries, coffee, stewed fruit, and wine on the table. I brought her a blouse as a gift; she formulaically accused me of having dreamt up some sort of foolishness, but then refused to take it. I explained that I hadn't bought it, it had been given to me. She accepted then, remarking that the giver's dushevnost' stayed in a gift.

Noticing a banana, I mentioned how strange they looked in Omsk (they had appeared in my absence). Lara grabbed it, washed it, and put it on the table. I sat twitching in fear that she would make me eat this precious thing. When her son came in and asked for it, she said, "of course."

Later I told Nadia that Lara had fed me again. She said it was ancient tradition to feed guests. Her children were so used to being fed that if they stopped by someone's house with their parents for a minute and were not offered food, they would ask their parents what was wrong. When I visited friends, it was always time to eat, often for the whole family.

Ugoshchenie is food offered a guest. As a verb, it is to treat someone, offer hospitality. This offering included saying "take some," "come on," "help yourself," "be my guest." *Ugoshchenie* was directed against an assumption of "shyness"; "Don't be shy!" A guest often did not accept the first time something was offered. Dishes were named, proffered, ladled from, or a guest might be asked what he or she could be served. Sometimes the hostess touched an item with a utensil. Touching a dish or serving utensil was a sort of threat. She might recommend a dish as ecologically clean, or might complain that guests weren't eating enough, "did not respect the hostess's labor," referring to herself in the third person, a kind of ritual speech similar to how Nadia spoke to Anna Viktorovna in the graveyard.

I might eat more than anyone present, but hostesses would catch me pausing and, in a surprised voice with no laughter, say, "You're not eating anything at all!" "Take it while they're giving" expressed the Soviet certainty that whatever it is, it won't be there tomorrow. It was also a joke made in hospitality situations. On leaving a dinner, paralyzed with food, I heard another guest sigh: "only in *Russia* do you get this full."

Offering "Everything"

> You arrive, tired, with suitcases. I open the door and say "Well, come in." Do you feel that I'm glad? That voice is indifferent. The voice speaks and thinks something else. I put no dusha in. My dusha is not *all* here.
>
> Grisha, Omsk, 1992

The word "everything" (*vsë*) appeared constantly, as when Anna Viktorovna said "That's how we do things ... we must give *everything* ... as they say, from dusha." Andrei said: "Hospitality is strong in Russians. If a hostess makes blini and a guest compliments them, that's the greatest reward. That's already, as they say, everything ... We put everything into it, try to show our best side." The host or hostess' job consisted in guessing the presumedly "shy" guest's needs and desires and remembering to *ukhazhivat'* ("take care of") him or her. *Ukhazhivat'* is also a term used when a man courts a woman.

Offering displayed that one was willing to give "anything." I described earlier how a hostess might order a guest not to remove his shoes, an excessive offer that indicated the essence of hospitality. Even during sugar shortages some hostesses put a battery of spoons in the sugar bowl to create a "hedgehog," a vivid image of *ugoshchenie*. A guest might be shown a bowl of salad and told, "We have to finish all of this." Often that was impossible, but the pronouncement instituted a pressure to "Take more." Even when everyone was full, a hostess might open more food. Cookies might peek out of a package, indicating that "nothing" had been held back. At one home in 1992 I drank tea next to a full kilo of butter. There was nothing to butter, but I got the message.

The Orlovs and I sat at a holiday table laden with cheese, bread, butter, meat, dill, green onions, cake, strawberries, smoked salmon, potatoes with wild mushrooms, and an always-full plate of fresh tomatoes. Andrei asked Zina why she hadn't opened a jar of marinated tomatoes. She said "Because we don't need them," but glanced at me for a clue that they were, on the contrary, needed. Oleg's wife's mother, a delightful hostess, showed me a jar of honey she got from relatives and put a small crystal dish of it in front of me, telling me to eat it with a spoon. As I was leaving, she wrapped meat pies for me and asked if she should give me some honey. I saw that she loved that honey and was offering because dusha gave her no choice. I gladly declined.

Geographical Axes of Hospitality and Embedded, Alternating Ethnicities

> Siberians are more open than Russians. And infinitely kind. Ready to give *everything*. Not thinking, is it your last, not your last ... And forget about it immediately, never remind someone.
>
> Dasha, 1992, Omsk

> In Moscow a new type of person has formed . . . they cut sausage in tiny slices. It's offensive. Here we do it differently. If a person comes over, everything there is goes on the table. In the army the only thing that united Russians with Central Asians was hatred of Muscovites, who say "an uninvited guest is worse than a Tatar."[1]
>
> Oleg, Omsk, 1992

> The object . . . was to produce a friendly feeling.
> Radcliffe-Brown in Mauss 1967:18

Friendly feelings could be created through cruelty. Among my south-central Siberian acquaintances, hospitality was imagined to increase as one traveled farther from the center of "civilization," particularly north and east, to a legendary critical level. Friends said that in the north of Omsk region guests were received *ten* times more warmly. When Zina complained about the cruelty of hospitality in Andrei's village, he explained: "They *offer*, they *force* you." He himself scolded Zina for asking if I wanted something rather than just giving me some. You're giving her a chance to say no. In my village you'd be a terrible hostess.[2]

Slicing cheese or sausage made tempting, available pieces. Like opening packages, like potlatch, it destroyed the supply in honor of a guest. Sausage slicing was often taken as indicative of how well-developed an individual's hospitality was or, as in Anna Viktorovna's and Oleg's statements, as evidence of an ethnic group or regional population's stinginess. Muscovites, city dwellers, and Ukrainians reportedly sliced sausage thinly.

Allegations of Ukrainian greediness and stinginess were common. Current jokes included:

A Georgian, a Russian, and a *Khokhol* are each given an apple. Each eats it. Each is then given a kilogram of apples. The Georgian eats one and sells the rest, the Russian eats one and gives the rest away to friends. The Ukrainian eats them all. Given 100 kilos of apples, the Georgian eats one and sells the rest, the Russian eats one and gives the rest to friends. The Ukrainian takes a bite out of each one.

A *Khokhol* finds himself in a train compartment (where soulful interactions happen) with an African, who takes bananas out of his suitcase. The Ukrainian asks what they are. The African gives him one to try. Later, the Ukrainian takes out *salo* (salted or smoked pork fat, called, in another joke, Ukrainian aphro-

---

[1] A reference to what is commonly called the "three hundred years" of Mongol rule (c.1240–c.1480); Russians may refer to all Mongols as Tatars, because Tatars made up the shock troops that reached Russia first.

[2] Hingley's (1977:49) idea that hospitality is "competition in national prestige whereby 'the honest, hearty, all embracing Russian stomach' " challenges its non-Russian counterpart may have been the case when a foreigner was guest, but similar behavior obtained between Russians.

disiac). The African asks if he can try it. The Ukrainian says "What's there to try? Fat's fat."

A *Khokhol* on a plane takes out *salo* and begins slicing it. The pilot finds out and has a stewardess ask for a slice. The Ukrainian responds "Oh, he won't eat it." After several rebuffs, the stewardess tells the man that the pilot is himself Ukrainian and will eat it. "He won't eat it," repeats the *Khokhol*, "because I won't give him any."

Ukrainian ethnics told *Khokhol* jokes, remarking that Russians really *were* more generous. Ethnicities were nested; people felt local, Siberian, Ukrainian, Soviet, and Russian. The "Russian" category became evident and was invoked in situations of expansiveness and generosity. Telling stingy *Khokhol* jokes, ethnic Ukrainians had recourse to their Siberian "Russianness."

People sometimes made gifts of their possessions; I had to be moderately careful about complimenting things. Central Asians, though often depicted as disrespectful and thieving, were also seen as supremely hospitable. Tatar and Kazakh women were said to make the smallest (most time-consuming) pelmeni.[3] Lara said: "In Central Asia if you admire something they give it to you. We don't do that but we might apologize for not being able to." Some Russian and Ukrainian ethnic Omsk residents saw this practice of Asians more or less as "law," whereas, when Russians did it, it was seen as soulful impulse.

On entering the home of a couple I had never met, I was ordered to help make pelmeni. My hostess rolled out a sausage of dough and started handing me slices. I was immediately put at ease. She said her grandmother had told her about Uighurs who, "before the 'Tatar yoke,' " would feed a guest until he vomited, give him a horse, and send him off. If he looked back, they caught up and killed him. She herself was Belorussian, Polish, and God knows what else, she said. Her husband said he himself was fully Russian. Only his "exterior" (pointing at his face) was ethnic Korean, he repeated during the toasts to Russian soul, people, and culture that followed.

"Ours" and "not ours" was fluid and rigid.[4] When people brought out photo albums to show which family friend was a "spy," how Omsk used to be a "garden city," and which uncle had "disappeared," ethnicity came up. While Evgeniia Pavlovna was using her album this way, the sight of a beloved individual from her past shifted her meaning of dusha. I had asked if an Eastern person's dusha was different from a Russian's. She answered: "No, an Eastern one won't do. Won't do. Different traditions of sitting at

---

[3] Pelmeni (dumplings with ground beef, pork, lamb, a mixture of them, or cubed meat) are the quintessential Siberian food. They are frozen, then boiled and eaten with butter, broth, vinegar, pepper, or sour cream.

[4] Zinoviev (1982) indicates complexities of such alliances. These groupings included what Friedrich (1979) calls *ty* and *vy* universes, but was far from limited to them.

table. But wait, no, *that* doesn't affect dusha . . . the essence is the same. Look, a full-blooded Tatar girl. See what a princess?"

Although soul's nationalism is evident when one hears unaccustomed pairings such as "Tatar dusha," *any* person may be deemed ensouled. In contexts such as this interview question, terms such as Tatar dusha are legitimate. Evgeniia Pavlovna shifts from her nationalist meaning of dusha to a religious or psychological one. Even then, she facilitates the use of dusha in reference to a Tatar woman by emphasizing her love for her. Another time I heard dusha extended to Tatars was when Anna Viktorovna could hardly force out "natio—natio—nalism" (Chapter 1) and then continued: "There were a lot of Tatars here. A lot. But they and Russians lived in harmony (*dusha v dushu*)."

Including non-Russians in the community of Russian-souled is not always possible. Failures to do so happen in all sorts of hybrid and ambiguous situations. In another interview a woman who called herself "pure-Russian-blooded" and who spoke romantically of ethnic Russians' unique creativity said that several years earlier she had almost gotten married, but hadn't because her mother had said, "We don't need any Jews." Then the woman added that she suspected her mother was at least partly Jewish herself.

Children and Animals as Guests and Hosts

> Any peasant would say his dog is a living dusha.
> Aleksandr Ivanovich, Omsk, 1992

As an example of the difficulties implied by offering everything, here's a joke: guests and hostess are sitting around a table. There is only one meat patty left. Everyone looks at it, is "shy." Suddenly the electricity goes out. A shriek is heard. When the lights go on, the hostess's fork is stuck in the patty and everyone else's forks are stuck in her hand. At a poor meal at which no one filled up, just stopped eating out of modesty, Anna Viktorovna would catch my eyes being drawn toward the last two blini and push the plate at me. I'd refuse; the plate drifted away. She once or twice furtively tore off a corner "to try." She asked Nadia what to do with these leftovers, then told her to eat them. Nadia said she would, but didn't touch them. Soon her daughter came in and grabbed both, glancing at Nadia, who said "eat, eat."

In city and village I saw children crudely yelled at when there was even a suspicion they might have been *considering* misbehaving. Despite this, I never saw a child chastised for eating. Treatment of children differed, but I often saw children and animals unquestioningly given rare, expensive food. If a little boy wanted to eat all the chocolate I brought my hostess, that might be allowed. By the same token, children were taught to share and be hosts. Once Zhenia and Tamara were at work when I arrived in the village. Their eleven-year-old served me a meal, formulaically urging me to eat. He was later grilled on how he had fed me. Actually, he was scolded in case he hadn't taken care of me well. I defended him, complimenting his performance. Whenever even selfish children had candy they offered me one. A little girl ordered by her grandmother to give a piece of rare "bird's milk" candy to a mongrel laboriously tore off a piece so as to include a sample of every delicious layer, laying it on the filthy stairs.

Dogs were treated to slices of cheese even when it was in shortage. A puppy stole two pieces of chicken and was not reprimanded. Cats ate meat and sour cream. Once, over tea, Grisha, grasping for some interesting detail to treat me to, announced that he had evidence that despite perestroika, some people still have dusha. His proof was a pensioner who had paid a veterinarian a quarter of her miserable monthly pension to treat a stray cat.

From the Breadth of Your Nature, and According to Your Means

When, during the interview in her living room (aspects of which she constantly used to illustrate what she had to say), I asked Evgeniia Pavlovna, my optimistic retired teacher acquaintance, about hospitality, she pointed at my lone glass of juice:

> I'm receiving you European style. Russian style, that's with national dishes, the apartment should shine, the hostess should look good, and—well, whatever each can manage. *From the breadth of your nature. And according to your means.*[5] Where the spiritual world of a person is narrow, hospitality is limited. Where a person's spiritual world is wider—of course, our hospitality in a material sense is inadequate, but what we have, you know it's from dusha, and we're glad when people are pleased with it.

There was often a conflict of opinions—contingent on class, location, age, and education but also on the individual, topic of conversation, and so on—regarding the morality of hoarding supplies. Hospitality was a primary way of creating dusha. It was said to be difficult to impossible without a minimum of food and drink. A view regularly voiced by some intelligentsia, fanatical others, and few in the village, but by anyone, given a conducive context, considered hoarding to be too stingy, calculating, and materialistic to be soulful. Yet hoarding was the heart, if not the soul, of the shortage economy. These conflicting voices focused on different moments of dushevnost' and dusha ideology.

[5] Evgeniia Pavlovna's statement resonates with a slogan paraphrased in the *Communist Manifesto*: Socialism was "from each according to his ability, to each according to his labor." Communism would be "from each according to his ability, to each according to his needs."

The supplies people were accumulating often shocked them. Every apartment, Grisha's friend Pasha (the one who dug Anna Viktorovna's grave) said, was a warehouse and a factory. When he opened a cabinet to get a jar of wine, he exposed floor-to-ceiling jars of vegetables, fruit, and jam.[6] Potatoes, beets, onions, carrots, sugar and flour filled cloth or paper sacks. Vodka and condensed milk were all over the place. "People have gone crazy with this supplies thing," Pasha said. "It used to be we'd buy a bucket of potatoes. Now we have thirty-five bags." He joked about how it would look all spread out on the floor; then laughed, musing on the size of the mountain if all Omsk's stored-up supplies were thrown in one public pile.

Possibilities and Magic

Dunham (1990:57) describes a skilled hostess as one who directs a supper's progress, assists shy guests, and accepts compliments as if this meal had not taken planning, effort, and two weeks of saving money. The hostess's skills also include timing. During shortages, meals where guests were present might consist of a large appetizer/salad course and tea. If this was abundant and lasted hours, guests started to think that that was it. And then Ukrainian stuffed cabbage, roast chicken, and pelmeni, candies, lemon, cakes, and dark-capped meringue mushrooms would appear. Despite courses' formulaic order, it was still often surprising when the next one appeared.

I have already listed ways of creating a generous table out of economic incoherence. All "possibilities" were vital to the ability to offer hospitality. Russian women were still, however, called "magicians." Their "sorcery" made possible what was jokingly called the "magic" of a meal when stores stood empty. Calling a hostess a magician complimented her skills while avoiding mention of the gray, degrading process of getting things. When Zina appeared in the kitchen and gave me a calendar, Nadia blurted out, "Where did you get it?" Zina got a coy look and delayed her answer: "I just came by it." On the same day, Nadia had come in brandishing boxes of matches. Anna Viktorovna asked if she had bought them or got them from her mother. Nadia answered reluctantly, after a pause. Another time she materialized fresh *balyk* (cold smoked back portions of sturgeon or salmon) and refused to say how much it had cost or anything about its provenance.

Magicians worked the System, pulling rabbits out of hats and smoked fish out of another world. Again, there is an important continuity between

---

[6] Women made jam from wild or dacha-grown cherries, strawberries (many varieties), raspberries, currants (red, white, black), honeysuckle berries, blackberries, lingonberries, cranberries, gooseberries, pumpkin, apples, quince, apricots, and rarely, black ashberries. In 1995 friends made dandelion jam, a dark brown-yellow mass of furry hairy flowers pressed against the glass, bright little lemon peel cubes shining when you opened the refrigerator.

this and other aspects of the economy: a master of *blat* whom Ledeneva (1998:105) discusses was known as the one who "can do everything." *Blat* was magic (ibid.:15). I will look at other ways in which important images of magic and mystery were constructed and subsidized.

From Christ—and Our Economic Conditions

Some people were good at getting others to accept things. Once, when I dropped in at her workplace, Dasha, the friend who gave me tours around Omsk, produced two lemons, a rare and expensive "source of vitamins." One she sliced thinly so we could all have some with tea. The other she heartbreakingly slipped in my bag as I was leaving. I objected, thinking how dearly it had cost her. She asked if she accepted things from me. I said that she did. In that case, she answered, I should do the same.

A poor relative of this gambit backfired on a Moscow friend. When I objected to his doing things for me, he coyly asked if I'd let him do this for himself if he were my guest, inadvertently reducing his gesture to an investment. The same dizzyingly ambiguous juncture of calculation and generosity is apparent in the words of Svetlana, the institute student in her mid-20s: "Hospitality," she said, laughing and gesturing at the tiny dorm room she shared with another woman,

> is a tragedy. Home is where you open up most. . . . When a guest comes, that's your opportunity to show yourself, to let someone understand you. It's like letting a person inside you. . . . When you receive a person and treat him to things, that's the main thing, among us the most important. You somehow start feeling better yourself. . . . Communal taking of food is sacred. It comes from Christ—and our economic conditions. If you're hungry, you go visiting. When they invite you to eat you think, "Wow, there are still human beings left!" When they come over you remember how they received you.

Vitya, eleven, offered as rather economic proof of God's existence that "If you lie or steal, it'll come back to you; if you do a kind deed, they'll thank you later. See, we have icons hanging."

In the Decency story I mentioned Alexei's statement that uncultured people simply "don't know how to make it pleasant to help." Kul'tura, like hospitality and dusha, can be "what makes it pleasant;" the ability to keep hospitality feeling gratuitous was a kind of kul'tura. These efforts were evaluated in terms of the giver's apparent practicality or apparent gratuitousness. This was a serious challenge to people disposed to putting effort into "sincere" introspection. As Dasha said, "To put dusha into something is to give yourself completely . . . But how can you know you've put *all* of you in? You just have to try, try for . . . your dusha . . . at that moment, to bring something, to be of use" (see Hellbeck 1998 for examples of such earnest introspective work in Stalin-era diaries).

When desired, in problematic situations and regarding problematic and marginal others, people not only distinguished exploitation from hospitality; they made fine distinctions between hospitality ritual and soulful goodness. As we left the home of acquaintances of Grisha's whom I had just met, I said they seemed like good people. He fine-tuned my compliment: "Yes, very hospitable." It was, again, the consciousness or explicitness of exchange as separate, analyzed out from the fullness of emotional and social life, that was problematic. Exchange's existence was not denied, but wouldn't it have been nice, it is wistfully implied, if it hadn't had to be so explicit? Time and space, others, etiquette, sentiment, and deviousness militated against the perceived coherence of exchange, smearing it out into a time of help, friendship, and "humanity."

Gifts and hospitality could also be used as bribes. Words like "interest" mediated this psychologically shifty area. Words based on *otklik* (a response, an answer) also could mediate. Vitya, eleven, continued:

> If you go to see an important person, you have to bring a gift and not be stingy, not hold out, spend a lot of money. And you have to give from your whole heart, from dusha—"To give is more pleasant than to receive." I like to give. We were giving cedar cones as gifts to the Americans, with nuts in them. Two were left. Who could I give them to? I already gave to everyone! These cones won't get an answer! But I *want* to give them . . . I forgot Susan! I went, I gave them! [*Poshël, podaril!*].

Simis (ibid.:136–8) discusses the gifts and bribes necessary for various Soviet officials. Vitya has a solid introduction to this aspect of the System. Yet his "I went, I gave," has the unquestioning impulse of flamboyant generosity. His discussion of kindness that followed embodied the same tension:

> Giving your seat in the bus to an older person, helping a grandmother carry a bag, helping someone at their dacha; later they'll answer you, it'll come back. And "don't be stingy": when the Americans were here, we gave them gifts—It all came back. We didn't lose anything, we even got back more—gifts and money, about 40,000 rubles! And we spent, maybe, 10,000! A friend is someone who will help you, get money for you, lend it.

What "responds" is dusha. Lara said: "You have to exercise dusha. It develops. A dushevnyi person helps though he doesn't need to. He responds when you need to approach him." Dasha said: "To be pained with dusha, that's to let something pass through dusha. That is, to pay attention to others' misfortunes. Or *just come in contact with them. Dusha will respond.*" Dusha automatically responds when it witnesses need.

People implied in many ways that gifts remained associated with the giver. Either, as Yurii Yur'evich said, "When a person gives a gift, under-neath he's thinking about how there will be this thing, a person will think about me," or in the sense that details of the donor's spiritual or physical condition are accessible through a gift. Svetlana, who, as I mentioned ear-lier, was fascinated with various new religions and mysticisms, said, as we sat in her dorm room, "A gift is a small battery; it accumulates energy. You can feel what the person came to you with, a sort of energetical envelope around it."

As a rule, however, I got answers that implied spirit embodied in given objects only when I asked a dumb question like "How do gifts work?" and someone tried to answer it. Food cooked in a good spirit and alcohol im-bibed together may be an exception—these situations were somewhat more likely to be felt to involve direct spiritual exchange. Although I did hear about malicious people cursing objects and inflicting them on others and about secondhand objects (especially metal jewelry) infected with previous owners' bad energy, statements about spirits inhering in gifts rarely ap-peared spontaneously in hospitality situations. In everyday life, spirituality in the context of exchange had more to do with the opposition between ma-terial and spiritual wealth than with the actual spirit of a gift. Giving de-pended both on the value of the objects and on them being not valued, "just objects." Treating objects as not spirited augmented the spirit of the giver. In his interview, Aleksandr Ivanovich even applied this logic to the extreme case of monetary bribes: "Unfortunately," he said,

> word's going around that Russia's a country where they take bribes. . . . That is, well, it seems to speak of a love for money. But look—it actually speaks of contempt for it . . . Money isn't seen as anything substantial. If you come to me with some request, aren't you willing to give a trifle like money? It's exactly be-cause nobody takes it seriously that they end up selling their honor, their worth, exactly because of that.

A "Home" Away from Home

A common description of hospitality implied that a host or hostess's job was to create a substitute home: Irina said, "You can find yourself with a very simple family, grandmothers with no education, but they are so rich *in-side*—with dusha—that you feel as if you're in your own home." Grisha's coworker Masha said that a man she knew rested his dusha when he visited mutual friends because they are "simple in the best sense of the word." When I asked her about this simplicity, she said: "when you say village people are simpler, it means that the way they are makes others feel at home." For example, once when I bought mittens and socks from a babushka at the market, in addition to the usual "Wear them in good health," she added that I could tell people that my own grandmother had made them. I was often asked to pass on greetings, even from people I myself had just met, to my mother, and to answer questions about her health. Related was "Your mother will think we didn't feed you here if you don't eat more."

My interviews with Yurii Yur'evich are dotted with his urges that I drink my coffee:

> We love to entertain. Hospitality is exactly the sort of dushevnyi things we started out discussing. Striving to do something kind or helpful. Someone comes to a place, he is torn off from his . . . family—when he encounters warmth on the part of another person, he's invited to dinner, they have a drink, they get to talking, he feels at home.

On the other hand, the home one was made to feel at by hospitality was not *home*, but a home for dusha, an other, better world. I asked several people if a houseguest might hear: "There's the refrigerator. Help yourself to anything!" One woman responded: "It's not your home and it's not your refrigerator. That would be like taking something that belongs to someone else. If they say that the food in a bowl in the refrigerator is for you, then it's all right." Those who had been to America told me they went hungry because Americans didn't urge and offer.

The hostess's right and duty is to make magic. Eating without being persistently "taken care of" in a certain style was inadequate. Nadia said: "Hospitality, if it's . . . sincere, a quality of dusha—a person, at those moments, makes his guest feel comfortable, warm, taken care of." Andrei was more explicit: "Gesturing at the refrigerator, that's too little for us. We need to talk, spend time, *see* that process." Hospitality was a "process" to be seen. I was told, when I insisted that I had just been fed, "maybe you were, but *I* didn't see it."

Moments: Creating an Ideal World for the Guest

> The life of the feast is . . . compared to the life of toil and responsibility . . . the opposition between the world of work and another world of . . . merrymaking . . . had a place in Russia's cultural past.
>
> Brooks 1984:184–86

The "process" of hospitality ideally created what I came to think of as *moments*.

Speeches of welcome, at a banquet or at lunch with an extended family, were usually made at the first toast and shared a fairly set series of elements: a welcome to Siberia, to Omsk, to our home; the word "guest"; and, nearly always, "I/we hope this is not the last time we'll sit together like this." At one semi-official meal a government official complained during a toast about how, these days, everyone had to hustle and bustle, wheel and deal. "I don't know," he said, raising his glass four inches, signaling the end of the preamble and the beginning of the actual toast, "if I'll ever be in this house again. But what's important is not how often, but *the one time,* how you felt, that time—*one* time is something you never forget." Hospitality implied, as I mentioned, repetitions and performances of "everything." The imagined everything included the apocalyptic aspect I have discussed—everything changes in a single instant.

Focusing on the value of moments helped me understand something about the way people tended to treat promises and plans. When, during a chance meeting on the street, I was asked "When are you coming to dinner?" or told "Come visit us," naming a date or time was usually inappropriate. *Dogovorilis'* (agreed, OK), and *Sozvonimsia* (we'll phone each other), were more apt. I would have been welcome, as people said, "anytime," but that was a separate issue and distinct act of hospitality from the moment of warmth and contact created by the offer. Moments were "simple."

Often, plans were made, agreed upon, and not executed. The unclear connection between promises and what came to pass could result from the fact that people were very busy or be a product of insincerity, but it could be something more as well. Gifts might be given inspiredly, but, as I mentioned in the previous story, they were also often announced in advance. By announcing a gift beforehand, the giver got and gave pleasure twice: from the announcement and from the giving. The announcement manifested the impulse. It was a gesture of willingness to engage; the gift itself might be secondary. Expressing this willingness, one implied that one's plans and possessions were subordinated to others, available. Statements of intention themselves gave off sparks of the relation so valued, made moments of dushevnost'.

This brings me back to how mystery and magic depend on point of view. For an "outside" observer, a guest, the hostess was miraculously generative. For an "insider," consensual opacity provided privacy, the internal freedom, so to speak, to do what was necessary to make magic. Once, when she was out of sugar, Anna Viktorovna produced a tiny jar of honey, complaining: "55 rubles!" Nadia snapped that when one treats a guest to something one doesn't say such things. "She's not a guest," Anna Viktorovna retorted, hurt, "she's one of us." Above I described Nadia's and Zina's cryptic behaviors when asked where they got things. By quarantining information about where things come from, miraculous abundance becomes part of the gift. Everybody knew and discussed what it took to make a meal, but a particular meal's secrets might be esoteric.

Hospitality allowed for treatment of a guest in such a way that she or he spent time in a different world than the one he suffered every day. I mentioned showing what was called one's best. Evgeniia Pavlovna called "not touring your guest past a garbage dump" part of hospitality, part of creating an effortless world of abundance, warmth, care, *everything*. Only another person could offer that exit from one's own resources. For this a guest was grateful.

Once, when the water was shut off, Lara apologized for not offering to take me to their dacha to steam in the bathhouse, but they didn't have a bathhouse. Grisha, with his dushevnyi fantasies, was an extreme version of this. In Chapter 3 I discussed how talk about fibbing invokes the otherworldly, inspiration, mystery, enigma, and dusha. This is the case here. Dostoevsky, in "A Word on Fibbing" (1980 [1873]:117–25), says Russians lie out of altruistic hospitality, to give others pleasure, and whimsically continues that, having been indulged in his or her own fibbing, a Russian cannot deny others the pleasure, so that "the delicate reciprocity of fibbing" becomes "the first condition of Russian society." Teffi (early 1900s—reprinted in 1991) also portrays fibbing as selfless. Her hyperbolic equivalent to Dostoevsky's basing all Russian society on fibbing is to suggest that this boundless, gratuitous, natural force could be harnessed to fuel abundantly, generously all the nation's electrical, heating, and transportation needs. Hingley (1977:90–104) cites Andreev's claim that Russians feel utmost love and tenderness for fibbing because before you're caught, "you come to life for a moment."

Sitting together made *time*. "Time out" was one of the gifts.[7] Sitting together made *space*: When another chair was added to a crowded table or when a fork or knife dropped, indicating that a man or a woman was about to arrive, someone might remark *V tesnote da no ne v obide,* meaning "Cramped, but no one's hurting." A space or time filled with friends was a spiritual expanse (*prostor*), the only place or time with room for "anything."

Generous impulses also had power over fate. Andrei said that he once "simply, with a gesture, treated a Gypsy to a beer." She was pleased with his generosity, he says, and told his fortune well. The refrain of *everything* in reference to hospitality is a village ethos and a faintly potlatch-like tradition enforced, coopted, and remolded by German romantic holism and communism. These all help formulate Russian dusha's alleged revulsion at doing things halfway.

The "Feeling of Elbow": *Obshchenie*

> Our feasts are the movement of the needle which sews together . . . our reed roofs, making of them a single roof.
>
> Mauss 1967:19

---

[7] Attinasi and Friedrich refer to Turner (1967) in pointing out interpersonal dialogue as liminal, and add a second sort of liminality of dialogue: time shared by interlocutors to the partial exclusion of the rest of the world.

It was common to spend an entire evening at table, no step anywhere else but to the kitchen, toilet, or smoking area (*kurilka*). "At table" (*zastolie*) was food, drink, and their rituals, and, perhaps primarily, *obshchenie,* communion with others. This intercourse was associated with the table, the kitchen, at a party, the living room, and the smoking area. "Kitchen talk" and "what's said in the smoking area" was (supposed to be) candid. Aleksandr Ivanovich said:

> Our system of values, what we call dusha, is so different from that in any other part of the world. For example, friends. Life, success, money, even success with women, as shocking as it sounds, none of these are the main thing. The main thing in this system of values is "the feeling of *elbows*." The feeling that people will . . . come to your aid. . . . In a close circle of friends that feeling appears, that impression of oneness, unity of dusha.

Obshchenie is communion, but, unlike the English word communion, *obshchat'sia* had become as easy to say as "socializing" (though different in spirit). One could *obshchat'sia* with art, books, people, one's dusha or conscience, anything with a "voice." I have discussed the importance to many people of memories of student days. People characterized such times, as did Lara, as connected with a circle of friends, *obshchenie* with whom you value more than anything.

Earlier I mentioned how a man announced that Russians "don't count minutes when they sit together." On emigration, he said bluntly that he'd stick with Russia. When I had to go, he was cruel and adamant. Inadmissible. It meant I "wasn't Russian," which he translated as having no dusha (not the common *bezdushnaia*, which can mean heartless, but *net dushi*). I was refusing the effortless world made for me. I was refusing *obshchenie,* refusing to exchange human warmth, refusing to "open," "enter into partnership" (Mauss 1967:25).

A joke describes a guest who, urged to help himself to all sorts of delicacies, refuses: he isn't hungry, he says. The host says to the hostess in an undertone, "Hungry, not hungry, just like an animal!" "Your soul knows how much is enough" (*Dusha meru znaet*), a proverb says. Consuming and offering were foci of dusha-governed rituals that defined humanity.

I was told that when people received me in the kitchen I had become "*svoia,*" one of their own. *Svoi chelovek* (one of ours) was used in many closed groups, such as the *Mafiia,* and in economic and power-related contexts. "One of ours" was a person with whom one could speak openly without fearing that what one said would be used against one.

But it is important to see that the volatile, flexible way in which groups of "ours" were constructed and remade left the possibility for anyone either raised in Soviet or dusha culture or engaging in it, *even briefly or ephemerally,* to have Russian soul. This was a competing theme to those of dusha as encoded in "blood" or "genes," but these themes were mediated by the way the experience of Soviet or Russian life was felt to leave an exceptionally "deep" mark on the soul.

One way "to warm the soul" was to sit with friends. "Warmth" was an authoritative kind of dushevnost'; if a person was warm, he or she was human, and it wasn't nice or tactful to point out other sides of him or her. Although women's "soulfulness" was often associated to food and "warmth" and men's to bold gestures and drinking, both included generosity and openness.

The absence of communion was not only un-Russian and dehumanizing, it was lifeless. Although train cars had the reputation of an ultimate site for *obshchenie*, late one night, when three people entered my compartment, I heard one of them, a drunk older man, say in the dark: "I don't like these little cars." A woman's voice said that she didn't either. He continued: "It's better where people talk and you can *obshchat'sia*. Here it's closed up. Like a tomb."

Loss: "The Mood Changed Too Fast. Like in the Cartoons"

> Dusha—it's become harder. And relations between friends. I felt [with dusha]—a little black circle separate me from them . . . the mood changed too fast. Like in the cartoons.
> Grisha, Omsk, 1992

During a weekend organized by a business for American guests, at the end of a meal, two Americans got up, taking a bottle of vodka and one of mineral water. A waitress asked me to translate her request that they bring back the empty bottles. An Omsk couple was scandalized. The woman said they would pay for the bottles. The waitress apologetically said she was responsible for the actual bottles, which were at that time worth more than the contents. The wife said to her husband that they should go find some empty bottles to turn in so the guests could do what they wanted. The women began to lament how low they and the country had fallen, expressing dismay at the limits to hospitality perestroika had brought. They summed it all up: the System.

A friend who had left the Soviet Union in the early 1970s said, after increased contact with post-Soviets in the early 1990s, that he found usage and frequency of *obshchenie* and *obshchat'sia* to have changed. These had been, he said, fairly elevated words for spiritual communion. Now they were being used constantly to refer to "communication." When I asked them, my Omsk friends agreed that the word had changed, that it hadn't always been so often mentioned. But *obshchat'sia* had not simply become devalued. True, it was being used in business contexts and as a euphemism for discussions involving bribes, but I heard it many times a day in wistful, marked expressions such as "normal human *obshchenie*," the alleged increasing absence of which was lamented. *Obshchenie* was a dushevnyi word, and dusha was irritated by the social changes.

I heard that "Having guests come, sit, *obshchat'sia*, is done less because people can't set the table properly" ("set" here means providing food and drink). In late 1992, Zhenia said there could no longer be any question of real *hospitality*. Without the means to cover a table with food and vodka, the old traditions "could not go on." "The only thing that keeps people going is the collective spirit, and—well, we haven't *completely* stopped visiting each other."

Increasingly, if one failed to produce a lavish meal, it could be an occasion for solidarity, inspired by how bad things had become. By late 1992, I heard less often than a year before the proud Soviet-era claim that Russian women were magicians, and more often (and, interestingly, from men) that "I'm not a magician—I'm just in training." Children were said to be "forgetting what candy is."

In 1993, I heard on the radio that "The hardest thing now is the loss of the spirit of collectivism, the development of entrepreneurial relations. But we will learn." As hospitality and help were considered primary to dusha and humanity, life seemed to be providing concrete "proofs" that perestroika was killing soul and humanity. Money was blamed. Other murder weapons were shortages of affordable food, shortages caused by Gorbachev's war against alcohol, and time hemorrhaged on tasks. Crime and irregular transportation made it hard to visit.

Increasingly clearly, some people were living better than others. In 1994, there was still not much differentiation between products people had, but these products were valued differently depending on the ease with which they were obtained. One family, going from kiosk to kiosk to find a better price, might buy one carton of imported juice for a party. Another family drank it daily.

In 1995, my friends had lost weight and said they were always hungry. Milk was too pricy for indiscriminate use. Grisha said some days he and Nadia ate less so that the children would have enough. Lara said they hadn't seen meat for months.

Lack of "human contact" was said to affect one's psychological state. A male friend in his thirties asked: "Why are we suffering so much? Why is there so much stress? It's all due to a shortage of *obshchenie* and a shortage of faith." Nadia saw the inverse; it was people's psychological states that were affecting their ability to *commune*: "Everyone's so gloomy. Not many people have fun anymore. You get together and everyone is closed, guarded. They just sit and sit. You can't make them sing or dance, they just want to stuff their faces and crash. Big fun. People have become like that. Our whole life has gotten like that."

Nesting Hospitalities and the Inclusive Russian Soul

> To be . . . entirely Russian means ultimately to be the brother of
> all men, to be *pan-human*.
> > Dostoevsky, 1880; the so-called "Pushkin" speech

A man entered the office of his boss, a bureaucrat, to give her a calendar
as a gift; she accepted it and then told him to give me one too, shifting roles
on the hoof, from guest to generous co-host. A good friend gave me an object he had made himself, a thing he loved and of which he had every reason
to be proud. When I asked him to sign it, he wrote "To Dale from the
people of Omsk." "Showing one's best side" may be showing the best side
of one's family, workplace, city, country, or of humanity. The issue of who
could be a host, when and where, was also fluid. And as I have shown, even
non-Russians could see themselves and be seen as having Russian soul. I
was often in situations where someone would be both guest to a "primary"
hostess and host, and hostess to me as representative of a group of friends,
city, village, ethnic group, Soviets, Russians, or those with dusha.

When I left after staying at friends' houses, I heard the solemn pronouncement "Forgive us if something was not right." To *provozhat'* someone was to see them off, waiting until the bus came and went, or waiting
and waving until a plane or train was out of sight.[8] If the guest had come on
foot, one might see her to the corner or the host, hostess, and often the
whole family might extend their territory to the guest's own door, expanding the power and moment of hospitality and their identity, becoming representatives of Omsk as they walked, talking, through the dark, iced streets
or balmy spring ones, tenderly depositing the guest at her home.

The entity that offered dusha was flexible. To whom dusha was offered
was flexible as well. I have discussed Russian soul's suffering "for everyone," what Tomberg (1994:44–45) calls an intense feeling for the unity of
mankind. Sinyavsky (1988:260–61), discussing the importance to "Russians" of defining who is and is not "ours," asks how this exclusivity could
possibly be reconciled with Russian soul's universal compassion. "It does-
n't . . . of course . . . Russian national consciousness oscillates." This oscilla-
tion can be seen as between tactics and criteria for defining highly contingent *ours* and *not ours*. A remarkable characteristic of dusha is that its
narrowly exclusive, nationalist component "shared space" with a broad,
expansive, generous, open soul, skills for discovering soul in anyone.

While Erofeev's *Moskva-Petushki* hero is away from his train seat, someone empties his bottle of alcohol. Identifying the perpetrators, he invites
them over, demonstrating how what is called "understanding" is the

---

[8] The New Year's celebration (before midnight) was also *provozhat'* (to see out) the old year,
the same expression used in seeing off the dead. It included approaching the coffin, touching
the deceased's hand, and asking him or her to "Forgive us if something was not right."

medium of solidarity: "I understand you, yes," he says. "I can understand everything if I want to forgive . . . I have a soul like the Trojan horse's gut. A *lot* fits in there. I'll forgive everything if I want to understand" (1990:44). He then drinks with them, proving that his dusha is "big enough" to see theirs, trying to see more of them.

But if some people regularly used dusha's rituals and conventions to draw strangers into rites of soul, even using their option as Russians to adjust dusha's criteria to suit a stranger who "turns out to be the same after all," other people, or the same people at other times, don't. I began this chapter with a wonderful example of generosity, a stranger giving me her ration of cheese and disappearing. Sometimes, however, proverbial Russian "respect for elemental humanity," "readiness to ignore institutional barriers which separate man from man" (Sapir 1960:88), deep sentiment of equality (Friedrich 1979:81), the fascinating ability to share one's national soul with strangers, is, perversely, invoked to be inverted:

> One cannot blame the Jew . . . for the smell of his dusha. . . . If the Jew wants rights of citizenship, freedom of residence, of education, profession, and faith . . . to not give him these things would be the foulest of deeds. Violence against the Jew is violence against me, because with all my heart I forbid such violence, I forbid it in the name of love for all living things, for trees, dogs, water, earth, man, sky . . . because my pantheistic love is more ancient by a thousand years, and more wise and genuine than the Jew's exclusive love for the Jewish people (Kuprin 1909).

As Russians say, *etim vsë skazano,* that says it all.

CHAPTER EIGHT

Standing Bottles, Washing Deals, and Drinking for the Soul

Love for the motherland: sensory confusion, deteriorating coordination, hand tremors, ache in the temples.
                                                        Erofeev 1995:324

When a Russian has a good drink, you won't find anyone more soulful.
                                Nineteen-year old male student, Omsk, 1992

And for the Soul, a "Raiska!"
        Headline of a 1992 *Argumenty i fakty* article about liquor
    bottles; a new small size was nicknamed for Raisa Gorbacheva

Not realizing that drinkers are the one solid Soviet pressure group" (Wilson and Bachkatov 1992:9–10), in 1985 Gorbachev launched a vigorous campaign against alcoholism, featuring heavy-handed sobriety campaigns and vicious cuts in beverage production. The campaign resulted in revenue losses for the government and great progress for the illegal *samogon* (moonshine) industry, with associated poisonings. The campaign lasted until 1988 and had tragic personal, economic and social repercussions for years afterwards.

A 1992 television program on "society's alcoholization" estimated 42,000 alcoholics in Omsk region and reported a 240-percent increase in alcohol psychosis over the past year. But alcoholization was more ancient and comprehensive. The practice of setting bottles in front of people to gain access to goods, services, or a desired position is a well-known feature of Soviet culture, but its treatment as a bribe or even as simply economic tears it from its wider context, a wider sense of exchange, and a wider sense of value without which neither the economic situation nor dusha up to and into the post-Soviet era can be understood. Bottles were not only indicative of social and individual disease and economically meaningful; bribery with bottles (*postavit' butylku* is to "stand someone a bottle," stand one in front of him) could result in hours of *sitting* together and the shifty transformation of a deal into an intimacy and a genre of communication felt to be central to Russianness. Even when the bottle was not emptied together, the gift might point at and invoke a ritual that claimed to deny the ascendancy of calculated exchange and offer another route than the usual image of a market economy.

Rituals including alcohol were the epitome of hospitality, condensing economic, sociocultural, philosophical, and psychological dusha. Before the 1861 emancipation of the serfs, vodka was indispensable at *"rites de passage* such as weddings, births, deaths, fights and reconciliations, funerals, . . . when things are bought or sold, when one peasant helped another, and various moments of village politics" (Christian 1987:67–68). It continued to be important at many such events, as well as at birthdays and sometimes at the baths, in the 1990s. Drinking situations, including situations where tea was drunk, were also privileged contexts for other dusha-related activities, such as playing music, singing, cursing, and reciting poetry. This chapter explores drinking ritual, the upward direction of bottles, how it also could be bottles all the way down, and ways in which this slide occurred.

Time and Space

> "We . . . have come together in infinity . . . Drop your tone, and
> speak like a human being!"
>   Bakhtin 1984:177, citing Dostoevsky (Shatov to Stavrogin)

An often-cited absurdity of life was the garage. Due to shortage of space in city centers and increasing numbers of cars, rows of tiny metal or brick and metal sheds, the roofs of which boys tended to run across, were built, often on the city's outskirts. One evening in April 1994, Andrei came home, across town, drunk from garaging his car. When his garage neighbors begged him to "sit," there was simply nothing he could do. If you didn't want to drink you still had to find it in your heart to keep your friends company for half an hour, by which time more time and more bottles had appeared. And then there was the drink for the road (*pososhok*, from *posokh*, walking-staff), and many joyfully labeled drinks beyond the *pososhok*. Drinking time was different from other time. It created or defied or claimed to negate time, as could drinking tea, a related ritual and common euphemism for drinking "something stronger." Besides drinking tea or alcohol, "drinking tea" could refer to eating, having dessert, or to chatting or having an intimate conversation. "Sitting" also referred to any or all of this. *Povod dlia vypivki* was a humorous phrase that suggested any possible excuse to sit and drink. But, as much as drink, it was the dusha that drew people together to create a specific kind of communion that, my friend Lara said, "you value more than anything else in the world." Coworkers would use any excuse to rinse the cups out and put on the teapot. Even my shortest encounters, especially with new people, were marked by minimal sitting, for which ingestion of any liquid and an exchange of even rushed, token confidences were necessary and sufficient.

As I have discussed, hospitality created "different worlds." Conspicuous consumption or theft of time spent sitting created a world of "us" where one could discuss what was called "anything." A young man told me: "You know, we only value conversations we have in the kitchen or smoking area. Only away from *any* time and place can we talk openly." These events were liminal; what Victor Turner (1969:96–97) calls lowly and sacred "moments in and out of time and . . . social structure." If the Soviet proletariat had failed to dissipate the world of false consciousness, sitting in the kitchen could hold that world at bay and bind people together.

Ritual Sitting

The first two shots usually came in quick succession. Drinking a shot was often announced: "let's drink up" (*davaite vyp'em*). A rhyme might be quoted to justify how soon a second shot appeared: *Mezhdu pervoi i vtoroi / Promezhutok ne bol'shoi* ("Between the first and second, the interval is short"). After this initiation into ritual space and time, subsequent drinks were usually administered by a man at whatever rate he deemed necessary, though women seemed to be always welcome to make toasts. Some men were sought out to perform this function of master of ceremonies[1] at childhood friends' and army buddies' weddings.

The first toast or two, as a rule, consecrate the event to something. At a birthday, for example, they may be to the birthday man or woman, then one to his or her mother or parents, for which people may stand. A parent toasted might with good-humored severity object that "it's not acceptable to drink to parents with half-full glasses." And so on, with increasing creativity (and perhaps, depending on the individuals drinking, vulgarity; see Erofeev 1990, Ries 1997:66–67). Toasts in verse, original or not, were appreciated.

Conversation may be interrupted by someone announcing that a toast has "ripened," but even a ripe toast might keep growing, stretching, becoming conversation, while raised glasses droop awkwardly above the table, as

---

[1] *Tamada*, master of ceremonies, is a Georgian word. People cited Georgian celebrations where the *tamada* made perfect toasts, where drinking, dancing, eating were balanced, and it was a shame to appear drunk. Russians did not aspire to this, but it occupied a respected place in their mental geography. Cf. Holisky 1989 and Gromyko 1992:230.

once a toast is begun, under no circumstances may glasses touch the table again before drinking. If a toast changes or evolves as a result of such talk, someone may reformulate it; if conversation after clinking and before drinking gets long, a second clink may be necessary before drinking. It is all governed by the freshness of the toast's image and by participants' sense of unity in it. A toast to acquaintance might be first in my presence; then to the hosts, to health (everything else we can buy), facetious toasts to politicians, one to women, when men stand, or, even more gallantly, elbow higher than imaginary epaulet, to splendid ladies, or, rudely, joking, to broads. A toast may be to this "not being our last meeting, I hope."

Sitting was an elaborate, malleable language. Dimly remembered or new traditions were often labeled and treated as "the right way." On the first officially recognized Orthodox Christmas (January 1991), at exactly midnight, my friends rose haltingly, crossed themselves and others with raised shot glasses, toasted Jesus' birth (pinpointed, on the model of New Year, at that second), and then stood, bricolage (Levi-Strauss 1962) having run dry, unsure of how to proceed. A year later I drank to toasts such as "Attaboy Christ!" and

—Are there tigers in America?
—In zoos.
—Here's to tigers!

The prototype and reference of the common form of this toast is in the film *Svad'ba* (The Wedding), based on a Chekhov story. The bride's father keeps asking a Greek guest if one or another natural or social phenomenon (whales, generals, etc.) exists in Greece. It does, of course, and each discovery of commonality is the occasion for a soulful drink, resulting in the drunk middle-aged heterocultural men kissing, dancing, and sleeping together at table.

At a chicken dinner, Zhenia, smiling, raised his glass "To the rooster. Rest in peace. You sang well and were a sexual giant." This was in response to me having taken photos of the bird mounting a hen, wiping his filthy feet on her white feathers, then of Zhenia chopping off his head.

In late 1990, everyone who drank drank vodka, samogon, or a *nastoika*.[2] Only in 1992, after long, hard, shortages, did young entrepreneurs appear on the street with a local alternative, beer. Milwaukee's Best was sold at kiosks by the tasteless can for fantastic sums. People occasionally obtained Armenian or Georgian "cognac" or sweet port. By 1994, wines, liqueurs,

[2] Home brew in the Omsk area was sometimes made with by-products of sugar-beet processing. *Samogon* could be clear and delicious or cloudy and noxious, depending on the skill of the man or woman making it. It often sat in large glass jars under a sink or in a cabinet. *Nastoiki* are infusions made by steeping berries, herbs, or nuts for a number of weeks in 40 percent (or stronger) alcohol.

and imported and new local beers were available. Many women chose to drink what was sold as Sangria and German wine, but vodka was still chosen by most men and many women.[3]

A bottle opened usually had to be finished "to the bottom" (*do dna*), and once empty it had to leave the table (it was often set on the floor). As in emptying one's glass to the first and all significant toasts, performing *completely* corresponded to the sense of "everything" I have discussed. It added to a sense that the prayerlike toasts might be efficacious in fact. Yet, despite certain rigid exigencies, the range of ways of being effectively dushevnyi flirted with an opposition between obeying "traditional" rules and markedly, "anarchically," breaking them within a certain range. This range was used by individuals to define themselves. At some gatherings everyone was obliged to drink up at all toasts; in lenient company each paced himself with partial shots. Some groups held to allegedly rigid canons of drinking, which were, after all, designed to create and facilitate dushevnost', but Grisha had even to be reminded to toast the mother who gave birth to him, and somehow he was no less dushevnyi for it.

In the 1990s, to clink glasses was attenuated in some circles by a belief that this "very Russian" thing was not done in the West and was thus "primitive," though after a few restrained drinks someone often said "Let's do it Russian style," and led a hearty toast. At a banquet for regional government figures, attenuated toasting contributed to a sense that *we* the powerful had transcended common relations. The few toasts at that banquet to which glasses were raised were scarily vague: to success of implied financial or political projects, but no hint as to their nature: something elliptical was said, received truncated reactions, the topic was dropped.

People who defined themselves as more "cultured," gathered to discuss literature, also might not clink glasses or propose toasts, but would still drink together. Where toasting was minimized, people might catch each other's attention across the table or room, their eyes would meet, clasp, a pause, a nod, a gesture of glasses "to" each other, and drink. Drinking was explicitly with others: I was told that even the worst alcoholics don't drink alone, perfectly untrue, but far from absurd. Many ritual elements can be easily manipulated, but simultaneity was hardier. Nondrinking Grisha tended to his guests inaccurately, or rather, he and Nadia found their dushevnost' in looseness rather than strictness of the rules of sitting, invoking breaking them as dushevno. There, however, as always, everyone drank simultaneously.

The usual technique was to exhale, drink, and then, before one could smell the alcohol, wash it down with a sip of brine from pickle or tomato jars, fruit juice, or diluted jam; or snack on appetizers,[4] "whatever God

---

[3] See Christian (1987:66) on how, in the 1850s, "Grain vodka replaced everything."

[4] Zakuski, some rare due to shortages and cost, were: marinated and salted mushrooms, pickles, and tomatoes; herring; cheese; liver in cream; salami or bologna; tongue; caviar; fermented cabbage (sometimes with carrot, cranberries, or lingonberries); red sweet pepper salad;

sent" that season, including just sniffing a piece of bread or, in parody of one's poverty, sniffing one's own forearm ("snacking on fabric"). After-drinking grimaces and remarks included "foooo—disgusting!", or, as Tamara inspiredly labeled Zhenia's moonshine, "stinky dog!" Erofeev's (1990:12) "deletion" of obscenities following the line "And I drank it straight down," leaves, of course, nothing in the chapter but that line.

For the Russian Soul

> I'm ready. I'm meek. / Look at this troop of bottles! I'm collecting corks / To plug up my soul.
>
> Esenin

> Drinking was ... perhaps the most important of all forms of recreation.
>
> Christian 1987:66

I told Andrei and Zina Orlov how my village friend Zhenia had bellowed over a terrible connection from a friend's phone that I should bring a *spirtomer*, a device to measure the percentage of alcohol in the "stinky dog"; they laughed, commenting on how cruelly villagers drank. People expressed derision for a drunk or pitied him. He may be out of control because, as Oleg claimed, "Russians' soul lives through everything (*perezhivaet*) so intensely, it gets overheated and leads to depression and drinking." The man who told me Russian soul may be all right for intellectuals but not for simple people added that simple people "become alcoholics from it." Alcohol and its rituals are privileged in relation to dusha: it is directly on dusha that alcohol and its rituals act. After deciding that the Japanese live like "normal human beings" in part because they don't spend their time getting drunk, Victor Pelevin's (1998:57–58) fictional hero Serdyuk's soul immediately fills with "the fixed desire to have a drink." Drinking always meant something about a person's soul, often his or her explicitly Russian soul, and it acted on that soul, though what it meant and what it did ran from one extreme to the other.

Sitting was linked to feeling human. Public Prosecutor Yurii Yur'evich said, "Many people drink because of their inner character. A shy person still needs to talk to people (*obshchatsia*), and there are traditions for that: he drinks, opens up, can start talking, and feels like a *person*." Oleg said: "Drink has taken over one sense of dushevnyi, especially among men. Most

---

dill, parsley, or cilantro; canned fish; hard-boiled eggs; radishes; eggplant or squash salad; tomatoes with onion and sour cream; cucumber; grated beet, garlic, cheese, and mayonnaise salad; spicy grated carrots; herring "under a fur coat" of beet and potato salads; *vinegret*, shredded salad; canned shrimp, calamari, or crabmeat salad; grated cheese, garlic, and mayonnaise; *Salat Olivie* (chopped potatoes, pickles, bologna or other meat, peas, mayonnaise, fresh dill, and other available vegetables).

often, a zadushevnyi conversation is when you talk from the soul and drink." The ritual is humanizing: "Only animals," I heard in an expression ascribed to Georgians, "drink silently" (that is, without toasts).

Drinking could also indicate absence of essential humanity. Several people mentioned as examples of soulless people those they saw in lines for beer. Director V. Kristofovich (1987, *Lonely Woman Seeks Life Companion*) shows these filthy, slow-motion queues, as does S. Govorukhin (1991, *The Russia We Lost*), who calls them "the degradation of the country, the spiritual death of a people . . . not one bit less tragic than physical death." Anna Viktorovna, quickly turning a loaf of bread in the gas flame, explained: "The alcoholics who unload bread from trucks have dirty hands." She then stridently added: "Drunks are dead already. Live corpses. But wait," she added, pausing, getting confused; "Mussorgsky was a drunk and then went insane, but that dusha of his, it stayed as it was." In any case, drinking had to do with humanity. In the opening pages of *Moskva-Petushki* (1990), Erofeev's hero gets repeatedly tangled up in and tumbles and wrestles with fine points of humanity, inhumanity, various beverages and stages of inebriation and illness and dusha.

Culture (*kul'tura*) also had a privileged relation to drink. Culture was often mentioned as an alternative or cure for drinking, as if they occupied the same place. And interest reappears: Yurii Yur'evich said "When a person is not spiritual (*bezdukhovnyi*), when he has no other interests, to get together with cronies, get drunk, that's his interest. His spiritual need." A 1992 television show described a plan to "foster cultural needs in children of alcoholics" to keep them from going the same way as their parents. Both drinking and culture (in the sense of appreciation for the arts and humanities) were seen as leading to opening (or heightened awareness) of dusha. If nineteenth-century "educated contemporaries saw vodka as a working class equivalent to the high culture of Russia's educated elite" (Christian 1987:66), in 1992, Grisha said: "We Russians need to rest our souls and we are not developed enough anymore, not kul'turnyi enough, to use museums for that. But with vodka or tea we can sit and talk about anything."

The links between alcohol, soul, and culture relate to how "fundamental kindness" was usually seen as a much more necessary component of kul'tura than manners or education. Oleg said: "A soulful person can be a drunk and a bum, but soulful—that means he just, well, it's good to sit with him, you can talk without any of that meanness." So when Lara called drunks soulless and soon afterward told how a drunk once bought her a train ticket, admitting that "In that state they're all soulful and kind," she was shifting between definitions of dusha, not contradicting herself.

In a list of delicacies on a table, liquor was called "something for the soul" (*dlia dushi*). I have mentioned drinking revelry as for dusha, for "letting go," "attempting to eliminate all restraints." This does not apply only to the riotous eighteenth-century aristocratic uses of alcohol Lotman (1984) describes; Christian (1987:65–67, passim) describes prolonged prerevolutionary village drinking binges as a "release from the rigid constraints of . . . rural life. The aim was to lose control." This was also relevant to 1990s drinking. On one hand, vodka was said to calm dusha, a medicine indicated for dusha pain.[5] On the other hand, Anna Viktorovna once pronounced (despite the fact that she very rarely touched alcohol herself and tended to see drunks as "corpses") that "indifference is the greatest sin and drinking talk is not indifferent." Drinking helps some people experience what they conceive of as their soul's restless, passionate life.

This brings me back to the many meanings of *dlia dushi*. In earlier chapters I show that things "for" dusha, that fed it or helped it "rest," usually in some way included expanses, elements associated with other worlds, or had to do with impulses of something of great "size" "emerging." Any action at all could be for dusha, if done to satisfy an "internal" need, invoked the importance of (coming into) experience or (shifts of) awareness, was done with energetic abandon, performed as absurd play, or related to allegedly Russian things such as inclusiveness and generosity. Psychological, physiological, and sociocultural aspects of alcohol speak to all these parameters.

"Getting Drunk is Not the Goal": Drinking as a Path

"Drunkenness is so well-developed in Russia because we think about the meaning of life too much," Aleksandr Ivanovich rhapsodized:

Our nation daily questions the meaning of its existence . . . from three drunks gathered behind a fence, to a university auditorium. . . . It's like in Gorky's story: the unneeded man drinks money he was given to buy trousers with. Why does he need trousers when his dusha wants vodka? We even get drunk differently: it's only in order to open up and feel like brothers. . . . But if you want to know about that we'll have to *sit down* sometime.

During a lunch at Oleg's home he explained that the goal "is not to get drunk but to communicate," indicating with a hand that the clear bottle was a gently winding path.

In times of alcohol shortage, including perestroika's catastrophic drought, spirit-based products were imbibed by the desperate. Tragicomic narratives about aspects of drinking culture, including fine points of innovations beginning with cologne and toothpaste and ending with brake fluid, ornament the genre of wallowing in Russian dusha immortalized by Erofeev (1990; see also Vitaliev 1998). On train trips across Russia, a man told me, "you're with the same person for days: *there's no way out*, so zadu-

---

[5] See Vitaliev 1998:189; Hivon (1994) mentions vodka's role as medicine for other illnesses.

shevnye conversations happen; there's time to drink, tell jokes, complain." Inability to leave, shared fate, and proximity to others are presented as a microcosm of Russianness; and if there is no community before such conversations, there may be afterwards.

As Andrei Orlov said, to drink tea together, to talk, *obshchat'sia,* is necessary and sufficient. Drinking together, in the same way, may become synonymous with *being similar,* on the same side, and conversation may center on finding commonalities, as in a film I mention above ("Are there whales in Greece?"). A friend said he once shared a train compartment with Ethiopians who mixed vodka with cola and sipped it. "And you know how *we* drink—you down half a glass together, dusha warms up, and you start talking."

It follows that familiarity with the state of alcohol and alcohol lore could earn one more general trust. In a hospital I sat with doctors, respectfully toasting our acquaintance and playfully toasting friendship between nations with shots of "vodka" until I tactfully called their bluff by discussing samogon; relaxing, they announced that what we were drinking was not vodka but diluted medical alcohol (*spirt*), and added a few drops from a Latin-labeled bottle.

In pre-emancipation villages, drinking included women and children (Christian 1987). In Omsk, I met critical wives, wives who joined in, and wives who did both; and women did drink together, often not so differently from men. Zina with almost completely false severity scolded Andrei for "making" me sit and drink, but she did drink with us. Other wives would *really,* disdainfully, yell in big voices like grandmothers sang in. In return, these women, like those who discussed mundane details at a festive gathering, might be accused of hindering dusha's unfolding and stretching out. As women could sometimes get away with just "doing their best" rather than drinking "to the bottom," I could have invoked my gender, but drinking with the men was more interesting and proved that I did not want to hold back. An option I did choose, and which many men chose (though some sometimes markedly did not choose it), was to eat something very oily, such as a slice of smoked pork fat, before drinking, to slow the absorption of alcohol.

I cited Oleg above saying that "Drink has taken over one sense of dushevnyi, especially among men." Ries (1997:65–70) discusses drinking ritual as male. I want to emphasize that this in no way means that only men engage in it. The fact that it is statistically "male" is much less important than that it is in or informed by a voice (Bakhtin 1981) labeled "male," a voice fully available to be fluently spoken in by others. "Bakhtinian voices represent . . . points of view or philosophical positions . . . such that any concrete individual speaks in and through sets of social voices" (Coleman 1999). It is important to separate labels such as "male" and "Russian" from concrete groups of people; these are voices, available, understood, and performed, in communities with amorphous boundaries that broaden as parts of the world come to know more about each other and have access to fragments of each other's cultural repertoires.

Tamara told me to not bring bottles to the village; "Men don't know how to drink; as long as there's something in a bottle they have to finish it." When I returned to Omsk after an absence, Anna Viktorovna whispered to Nadia and me when Grisha left the room that we would have a drink in honor of my return. The three of us (the canonical number a bottle services) did not finish "*our* bottle," which Anna Viktorovna corked and refrigerated. After her death her wardrobe was found lined with bottles of vodka of the most varied vintages, hoarded not for drinking but against economic need (see Riordan and Bridger 1992:183). When, after a later return to Omsk, Nadia suggested the two of us drink to Anna Viktorovna's memory, we drank not wardrobe vodka but an infusion they had made "so as not to poison anyone at the wake."

A friend's mother, still a party member and, she confessed in a slightly accelerated, quieter tone, retired military factory worker, was, rightly, proud of her samogon. Her daughter made ashberry and currant wines (grapes were too expensive). Many people who rarely drank prepared their own alcohol because it was inexpensive and to avoid serving or giving as gifts toxic industrial alcohol sold, often as imported vodka, in kiosks, where what looked like cognac might well be tea. This homemade alcohol sometimes went to the village to pay acquaintances for raising fowl and sometimes was transformed into goods or services in the city.

When Andrei told Zina in a persecuted, loving tone to either sit down and keep us company or leave us to commune in peace, he invoked the popular association of drink to Russia herself: "Dale is an anthropologist; she should know *everything,* the most important things, about Russia," he said, gesturing at the bottle. When, in the course of conversation, he mentioned that vodka with beer gives one a headache, I agreed. He laughed: "And they say there's a difference between Americans and Russians!"

This *everything* about Russia in which alcohol figured so prominently was both more and less than kitchen-table communions. In the village, Zhenia was always pleased when I drank with him in his kitchen, and, as Tamara cooked and sulked (with reason; alcohol did seem to be "burning" her husband), he would announce, pouring me another shot, that it was only "50 grams—for company" or "for the smell." At a party one night Zhenia gestured, as Andrei had, at his shot glass and a roast chicken, saying in an undertone: "Understand—*everything* comes from and everything depends on these little things; everything comes from *this*." Ideally, sitting was a "total social phenomenon," as Mauss (1967:35–36) wrote, religious, mythological, economic; "a phenomenon of social morphology." Dusha and drink again illustrate the power of interest. Drinking was an occasion for individuals to define their interests against those of others.

The Power to Make Things Appear and Disappear

> Sitting . . . bind[s] the guest to the house in which he was sitting.
> Cajkanovic 1985

Above I mention the garage shortage. Another shortage, of places outside the home to meet, transformed one cluster of garages into "kitchens." The men would drink a shot of samogon in one garage, vodka or an infusion in another. While mixing amaretto with a cedarnut infusion Andrei described his dependence on his garage neighbors' help and vigilance. Alienating oneself socially endangered one's property. Friends protect friends.

Bottles were called hard currency, they worked so much better than rubles (see Riordan and Bridger 1992:185 for a joke about "freely convertible" bottles). Gorbachev's anti-alcohol campaign further increased their value. During 1991–92, locally registered adults received ration coupons with which they could buy certain goods, most importantly vodka, at a very low state price. Even with this discount people spent 8-10 percent of their incomes on bottles of hard alcohol (Humphrey 1995:16). Those who did not have their "own" apartments, due to their monthly inability to obtain two cheap bottles of vodka, were much poorer. As I have discussed, shortages of alcohol and food were blamed for the death of traditional relations. Gorbachev was cursed in toasts, jokes, and chastushki. Perestroika was said to be doing to dusha "exactly what Gorbachev did to vodka."[6]

If the mechanic didn't get a bottle, the elevator stayed broken; and "if someone wants to become a boss," Zina said, "and can set bottles in front of people, bottles, bottles, up he rides into management on bottles." But if it was bottles all the way up, it was bottles all the way down. Vodka and its hours spent creating the intimacy or pseudo-intimacy necessary for business were transformational. Cross-culturally, alcoholic drink is widely seen as having magic powers and providing spiritual experiences, usually sought collectively and associated with community (see Leake 1963, Christian 1987). And "magic" can be of many sorts. Alcohol's effects on consciousness were not separate from the social and economic transformations it could effect. When, on the TV game show *Field of Miracles*, a contestant had to think of "a magic word," the answer was not the predictable "thank you" but "bottle." "When the head of the dorm came to tell me to move," I was told, "I had a bottle ready. We drank and he forgot why he came; *Russia: Land of Miracles*." Bottles greased the winding paths of exchange and partook multiply in Christian and pre-Christian things for the soul. On

---

[6] In Pelevin's (1998:58–59) story, the hero finds a bottle of the same port he drank as a youth; only by drinking this bottle does he find "proof that reform had not really touched the basic foundations of Russian life, but merely swept like a hurricane across its surface."

Nicholas the Wonderworker's feast days "it was considered shameful *not* to get drunk" (Ivanits 1992:24–25).

As I have discussed (and will discuss much more), when people indicated that something was *inexpressibly* something, whatever else was implied, dusha was. The *depths* were often referred to by gestures: "much, much further there . . ." People gestured at bottles; drinking was too profound, familiar, and many-faceted for mere words. The information that someone was drinking or under the influence (if not indicated by one of myriad expressions such as *pod gazom*, gassed) was more often than not communicated entirely by a gesture, a flick of the fingers to the throat that replaced "drinking" or "under the influence" even when performed in ephemeral and stylized ways.

In the village, I was sitting in a yard with two men. One mentioned that he was trying to sell some sable pelts; his neighbor implied he might be interested. The topic was dropped. They began smoking, one sharing the Marlboro I had given him with the other. Then we slowly made our way to the other man's house "for *one* drink." We drank, ate a full meal, drank; the sables reappeared out from under several drinks. As I have discussed, work was transformed into rest, business into community, exchange into help, and vice versa through fluidity, leakage, and formal similarities between economic and emotional solidarities.

Terms like "friends" and "one of us" labeled both transient business partners and lifelong acquaintances as belonging in some community. Both business and leisure might involve sitting, talking, drinking; and drinking could, as Pelevin (1998:59) writes, transform people (in the drinker's eyes) from "disciples of global evil into its victims," victims like oneself. The "we" established or assumed while sitting could be exclusive and lasting, or as fleeting as the high from one shot of vodka. Drinking together could "wash" a deal between friends of its defiling consciousness. It could label as friendship a deal between strangers. It could help friendships begin. At a central Omsk afternoon intersection, to men holding each other up or having a nose to nose talk, arms around each other's wrinkled suits, the criteria of purity, sincerity, corruption, or manipulation were pretty irrelevant.

Communion and Expansiveness

Sitting was a priority; all else was expected to fade. A person who allowed everyday time, matters, or, increasingly, diets, to affect his or her sitting might be challenged: "It's like you're not Russian!" The association of Russia to drinking was clear in the question "What do Americans do when they sit like this?" Other ways of making communion were *truly* foreign.

In the Primary Chronicle, tenth-century Prince Vladimir is said to have chosen a religion for Russia. Among his arguments against Islam was that "Drinking is a joy to the Russians, we cannot do without it."[7] Pelevin's (1998) "Moscow Dynamo" is a tale explicitly about a post-Soviet soul destroyed when it trustingly, in despair over social conditions and hungry for comradeship and community, allows its Achilles' heel, its drinking traditions, to be infiltrated and coopted by foreigners.

But this sort of injury from without is rarely possible, because Russians' relationship to drink is seen as transcending others'. A 1990s joke tells how a woman, in despair about her husband's drinking, consults a doctor, who says that a new, "Western" approach was to associate alcohol with something extremely unpleasant. The woman brings a dead cat home, drops it in a bowl of vodka on the kitchen table, and leaves. When she returns, she hears her husband's weeping, pathetic voice: "Kitty, please kitty, please!" It worked, she thinks. She enters the kitchen to find him trying to wring one last drop out of the dead cat. Another joke, gesturing at the practice of "wanting something, but only through someone" asks:

—What is Soviet business?
—Soviet business is when you steal a wagonload of vodka, sell it, and spend the money on vodka.

This joke is reminiscent of Taussig's (1980) stories of money being socialized, purified, moved into another economic system, fertilized. Furthermore, as in this joke, not only money but exchange itself was often hidden between subtle acquisition and gratuitous splurging for dusha. Jokes about Russians as moronically generous drunks suggest that by sitting, they boldly, dashingly challenge the hegemony of a world that coerces people into living by mundane laws:

A Frenchman, an Englishman, and a Russian are stranded on an island with a case of vodka. After they sit and drink for a week, an angel appears, offering each a wish. The Frenchman wants to be in a Paris cafe; the Englishman, in his garden. They vanish. The Russian thinks, thinks, and finally says, "We were sitting so well; bring the guys back!"

Apropos of coerced sitting, the actor Leonov's character in Daneliya's 1979 film *Autumn Marathon* enters an apartment and cruelly railroads two busy writers, one a foreigner, into drinking with him, which they do under duress, Theseus and Pirithous bound to their chairs in Hades, "deceived into sitting" (Cajkanovic:1985). The newcomer, having become host in their apartment, breaks the miserable silence with the customary "We're sitting well" (*Khorosho sidim*). To sit includes doing "nothing;" if doing noth-

---

[7] Twentieth-century Soviet scholars contextualize this in Kievan Russian pagan feasts and the "magic origin of the . . . ceremonial common meal" (Froianov et al. 1992:6 and note 17).

ing *well* sounds irrational, that only increases its "Russian" value. This comic attempt to breathe life into what had been roughly sewn together is only a slightly exaggerated version of what often happens. The damn thing is that, after a few drinks, it *can* come to life. Soon the *Autumn Marathon* intruder is asking the foreigner if mushrooms grow where he is from and will not take no for an answer.

A hostess I had just met told me about the mushroom harvest, about Siberian hospitality, how vodka counteracts the effects of radiation. She started picking out strings of dried mushrooms to give me, one of tops, one of legs, rattling off all the sorts that grew locally. We sat down to dinner, toasts were offered to acquaintance and to Russian soul, though neither she nor her husband had any "Russian blood." Soon she jumped up and gave me more mushrooms and a cloth bag to store them in. She said, laughing: "I *knew* when I'd had a drink I'd think of more things to give! I admit it, I was being stingy! I knew it but I couldn't *help* it!" Drink helps one be one's "true," dushevnyi self. After another drink she leapt up and gave me a carved wooden cup; and later, "because God loves threes," a jar of jam. As Andrei said, "Sitting at table is a process."

The Power of Alcohol

Later we all went on to another home. My first host (the above hostess's husband) said that, as he was older than the rest and their boss, he could propose a toast even though we were not at his table. He at first used this appropriated power as a supervisor, coopting the ritual, proposing a toast heavy with implicit context, that we must "be kind, not let circumstances separate us." With the obligatory simultaneous drink he exacted forced consensus on his agenda in the very moment of dusha. Then, shifting from a "work" intonation to a resting, kitchen-talk one, he comically concluded (with a toast that would have been an utter non sequitur if it had not been aimed at one of the only conceivable entities in opposition to which everyone present was on the same side): "And here's to the complete absence of communists!"

The process of sitting rarely extends to the fellowship of higher- and lower-stationed members of a hierarchy; as the saying goes, "Bosses don't drink tea with subordinates." This instance was due to my presence, a commodity to be shared. At home, at their respective tables, bosses and workers complained about each other, but the rituals and results were similar.

In drinking, as in other activities, dusha and its declared enemies were tangled. Zina claimed that "We drop our duplicitous Soviet masks in the kitchen." Part of sitting and resting was feeling united against the boss, the System, Fate. Sitting claims to defy power relations. Most bosses' presence would have infected a gathering with the quotidian: bad for the subordinates trying to rest, bad for the boss; for, I was told, if a boss sees the other side, shows interest, does not maintain indifference, he won't be able to play his part. A woman told me: "Sitting together happens according to spirituality. It's unpleasant for me to drink tea with my director. Because his methods of doing things, his views, are foreign to me. I'm comfortable drinking tea with those under me, we can talk on any topic at all, openly." I could not interview this woman's subordinates for their point of view, but anything is possible.

Drink was multiply linked to power. First, drinking could help establish friendships one needed to move up in life. Then there is soulful authority a drunk's outspokenness commands. In a January 1991 performance at Moscow's Sovremennik Theater, a drunk character said to a bureaucrat that he and his like should be "exterminated as a class." This coopting of a Marxist slogan was wildly cheered by an otherwise quiet audience which heard its "inner" feelings of communal betrayal blurted out by someone "more in touch" with them. "What a sober man has on his mind" (or in his dusha), it is said, "a drunk has on his tongue." Another angle of the soul—drinking—power relation is evident in the fact that if you refuse to drink with someone, they can hurl the sarcastic or joking challenge: "Too squeamish?" This implies that the elitist, reluctant one is repelled by the thought of drinking with a "normal" person. Refusal to engage can be taken as lack of respect.[8]

Respect and Openness

> People . . . must enter into contact, come together face to face, and *begin to talk*.
>
> Bakhtin 1984:177

As Grisha, Masha, a few other friends, and I sat and drank in their workshop, Masha was joking about how drunks ask: "Do you love me? Do you respect me?" I asked her to discuss it seriously. She thought, then startled me with her answer's Dostoevskian Christianity: "He wants to hear that you respect him, and he wants proof of it, because, look, he's drunk, but he's respected anyway. Even in *that* state he's still a human being!" To the same end, the comedian Raikin parodied an exchange between drunks (Stites 1992:138):

—Do you respect me?
—Yes. Do you respect me?
—I respect you.
—Then we're both respectable people.

[8] In the village, however, I was taught the word *storonik* (from side, *storona*), a person who tends to sit "on the sidelines" but does not necessarily invite judgement of being too proud (a problem of dusha), just, perhaps, of having a certain temperament or character, lesser flaws.

"Although we laugh at ourselves," Aleksandr Ivanovich said, "what question do we hear when men are a little drunk?: 'Do you respect me?' it's like: 'Do you feel that I'm an absolutely related, dear person?' " A thirty-year old woman said: "Respect is awareness of others. Dushevnyi contact is focusing on others. Soullessness is thinking only of yourself."

When a man "stood" another vodka, it was a sign of respect to drink. At a theatrical tribute to a designer I saw a distilled version of this. In a parody of Revolution-era mock trials staged by actors and aimed at political and moral targets (Stites 1992:50), "witnesses" came on stage to pay tribute to the guest of honor's career and character. The choice of this genre in Omsk explicitly played on the still-shocking presence of Americans. As each witness finished speaking, still on stage, he or she had to drink a shot of vodka, validating the good wishes, earning the right to wish them, proving respect. Only then did the audience applaud. Respect was empowered similarly to interest; both derived power from their mandate to make contact.

Much of what was indexed during so-called open talk was the value of openness. Drink increases candidness, but in Russia, drink(ing) was such a central trope for soul's other aspects that the effects of alcohol were often implied when alcohol itself was absent and unmentioned. Hospitality and soul in general were informed by the experience of "sitting" and drinking together.

As conversation becomes more intimate and sloppy, rarely formulated things may be said, and participants may have a satisfying sense of mutual understanding. Once a host offered tea after supper. A jar of instant coffee, a rarity, was ostentatiously opened. We refused coffee, but thanks to the vodka, more than usual was made explicit. One guest mentioned the price of coffee too soon after declining it. Another joked: "We refused coffee because we want sugar with our tea," a version of a joke about having to choose between sugar for one's tea and soap for one's hands.

Shiftiness

The art of dealing out thoughts and stories, of reaching a sense of communion and consensus, would flicker, alternating with the skills of teasing out and revealing gossip and of clamming up and backing off while maintaining a sense of gratuitous warmth. Sitting was a dance governed partially by the mysterious power that "candid, open" revelations (statements in the style of openness) had of making one's companion want to reciprocate in kind. Or in *some* kind. Boundaries between "gratuitous" help and an economy of favors were blurred by emotions' shiftiness, fleeting impulses of warmth, by the way one is never aware of all one's motives. Bottles and shot glasses facilitated such transformations.

David Christian (1987:62–63) writes that Russian drinking culture had, by the nineteenth century, become "two distinct drinking cultures: an older . . . derived from the traditional life of the rural working class community; and a newer . . . associated with modernisation and . . . a cash economy." In rural Russia, Christian argues, drinking had been social and ceremonial, but, as rural communities were undermined, a drinking culture emerged in which "the crucial decisions were those of individuals." Christian quotes a Yaroslavl priest writing in the 1840s:

> the Siskarets will try not to miss an opportunity of getting drunk. If he has contracted to build a boat . . . or chop wood, he has to drink . . . if someone is hired, again a drink . . . or bought logs to start building, or sold something . . . and so on . . . on Sundays after service the people drink, as they say, "to extinction."

A peasant said in 1882 that the Mother of God commanded them to drink for three days on a church festival (ibid.:64–66). But if such drinking was an obligation as much as a pleasure (ibid.:70), 1990s drinking was also a physical and economic burden. Difficulty did not make it less for the soul; we need not go as far as Venichka's (Erofeev 1990) hungover torment to see that.

Christian argues that serfs saw vodka as a highly inelastic necessity on which most of their budget was rationally, calculatedly spent. Later, he says, men began to drink "individualistically," without special reasons (ibid.:71–76). In my experience, however, even when individuals found "excuses to get drunk," drinking was sacred. Stites (1992:6) notes that urban rituals of sitting at table attempt to reproduce village life. In the 1990s, claims that dusha was being killed by inadequate access to vodka imply that the soul's demands for communion were in fact fairly *inelastic*. Christian (ibid.:84) writes that studies of alcohol produced in societies where drinking is governed by individual decision exaggerate drinking's individual psychology; but one must also be careful, I insist, not to exaggerate the power of "individual choice" and thereby exaggerate differences between behavior apparently dictated by calendar, by soul, and by "choice."

The appearance of drinking to drown one's sorrows, as carousing, decreased connections between drinking and rural life, and increasing formulations of need as individual inclination or habit do not imply that sacred aspects vanish. Venedikt Erofeev, a poet of solitary alcoholism, calls it a monk's labor, obligation, and feat (1990). There are differences between drinking to fog personal grief, to celebrate new shoes, and drinking at a wedding. But in many ways, urban drinking is often not *experienced* as a result of some idealized free choice, but as adamant demands of one's dusha, a fellow human being's dusha, or the social context. Some people sometimes feel a need to drink in their souls and pressure others to join them in this purposive ritual. Festivals dictated by the church calendar were replaced by Soviet holidays, birthdays, and economic exchanges dictated by inelastic, socially respected, communitas-producing demands of individual dushi.

To return to Zina and Andrei's kitchen table, I had been trying to explain to Zina why I had recently declined to meet her coworkers "for tea." I understood that she was under pressure to produce me there, but I was so tired. Zina got excited; although I had described my dilemma in terms of exchange (my presence as a commodity), Zina rephrased it: all Soviets, including her, had been spoiled by power and felt they could simply tell one where to be. It was at that moment that Andrei entered, explaining how he had had no choice but to keep his garage friends company. I found myself holding two versions of the harsh, obligatory aspect of keeping company. Zina presented them as coercive power (opposed to what one would do for dusha). Andrei showed how dusha demands that people participate, sacrifice themselves to others, as in drinking "for the company" and the way, as I describe in Chapter 5, a young woman's "Russian nature" forced her back into the baths.

In conclusion, alcohol was regularly mentioned in reference to positive contexts of dusha, to funny ones, and to degraded soullessness. Drinking made it possible for those with "less developed channels" for dusha to "rest"; helped them express something of great "natural" "size," (re)gain their animation, passion, generosity, emerge from under masks, speak truth, see the big picture, as well as be cruel and hopeless. Drink and dusha were often set up in tropic parallel, but that is not all. Drinking, as the epitome of hospitality and communion, related to exchange of all sorts of substances, physical and spiritual. Drinking, like dusha, united people and domains felt to be fractured by life. It seized and transformed "this" world's time into time governed by dusha. Drink was a focus of performance and a drug whose effects were culturally informed and appropriated. Spirit and soul have not come away untouched from their ancient relationship with alcohol, and vice versa. If dusha was a master trope for many values in Russian life, drinking was a master trope for aspects of dusha, and soul informed by the experience of drinking alcohol.

In the morning, after a first or second soulful interaction and zadushevnyi talk, after sharing one's "deepest" thoughts, after constructing a community of dusha and using it to more or less creatively indict selected others, after sharing stories of degradation at the hands of superiors or even ritually rebelling against that degradation, after sharing a drink or two or three for the road, did new acquaintances wake up as real friends? Not necessarily, of course; shared moments of soul often sink back into a realm opened up by kitchen, night, and alcohol. They may or may not color everyday relations with a distant knowledge that with this person one can sit, that is, that *somewhere* he has a soul.

The art and science of sitting, creating dushevnost', depend on selectively laying cards on the table; if it works, masks seem to fall, apparently revealing your similarity to each other, perhaps to "all humans;" if it fails, you lose power, privacy, safety, and face. In conversations that toy with dushevnost' information not usually available is timidly or brazenly advanced. Under the sign of supposedly gratuitous drinking, these morsels are thrown down as teasing bait, as stakes and challenges in dances of shiftily constructed and easily dissolving power, exchange, friendship, and other things felt to be too deep or complex to formulate, only to share. How a person does this dance depends on his character, skill, morals, goals, beliefs, his context for such soul gambling. Sitting implies a vast range of possible meanings of elements, on the surface ritually similar, a limited palette that can reduce a drinking interaction to earning a favor or, conversely, sketch a future friendship or other alliance.

CHAPTER NINE

If You Want to Live, You've Got to Krutit'sia: *Crooked and Straight*

> Continually, along a mysterious thread, everything draws to a
> single theme ... Russia, marvelous mother. ... Could there be
> any path more difficult or twisted?
>
> Yulii Kim 1990:234

> Each person tried to screw out of the system as much as he could.
> Taken together, the aggregate of these "screwings out" consti-
> tuted the course of Soviet life.
>
> Zinoviev 1990:64

Sharp Turn, Steep Path, Winding Road

As I mentioned, one key to how the enigmatic Russian soul related to various kinds of exchange was revealed to me at table, in an intense voice, by a drunk guy who had just figured out the secret heart of the situation: "Everyone wants to have something," he said, "but only through someone." He was touching on a kind of indirection in the "Soviet system." Shortages had put a premium on what Omsk friends presented as skills of wriggling one's way through the System (see Verdery 1993:174). Oleg made a snaky hand gesture while saying "by dishonest or some other means"; Masha referred to these sneaky skills when she complained in the corner of her workshop about how Soviets "got something somewhere there ... have some sort of blat." In the course of creative, grueling Soviet winding around, "mere things" took on unholy importance. Indirection in the System melded with what was visualized as dusha's winding complexity.

In Chapter 3 I explore the implication that there are mysterious channels between worlds, access individuals had to highly valued, unseen, essential domains. Most of these chapters have touched on the value of gestures pointing at such ineffabilities. And when people indicated something inexpressible, dusha's depths were implied. In the money chapter I discuss how people formulated an explanatory image of infinitely complex invisible threads spatially interweaving everything with the material, a tangle that had become part of Russian dusha. In the "Hat" story, I show roles exchange played in the "soul" Vera and I developed, a soul that some, under some circumstances, would call degraded. But dusha is usually, as I have shown, quite inseparable from images it supposedly opposes.

In this chapter I examine a cluster of salient, vivid mechanisms and tropes relating to creative practices of survival, achievement of goals, and interconnection of people and things. These issues were spectacularly critical in 1990s Russia, and I was fortunate enough to stumble in everyday speech onto a current poetic process intimately related to them. As related to survival, goals, and all sorts of interconnection, this linguistic phenomenon is clearly linked to aspects of morality, hospitality, drinking, and dusha as I have discussed them so far.

Beginning in 1991, I documented a burst of perestroika-related linguistic activity surrounding words based on the Russian root *krut-*. In the Russian language, a root is the common element in often extensive families of nouns and verbs. A word's root may be framed by one or more prefixes or suffixes that modify its meaning in a rich variety of ways. What I call *krut-* words are words containing what most people had always taken to be two separate roots, one in the adjective *krutoi* (steep, hard, abrupt) and one in words based on the verb *krutit'*, which relates to bringing something into a state of rotating, turning, winding motion. For the convenience of non-Russian-speakers I have underlined the embedded *krut-* root in some examples. In this chapter I follow these two *krut-s* to explore changing late and post-Soviet attitudes to straightness and indirectness and related implications about dusha.

Despite the fact that *krutoi* and *krutit'* are based on one proto-Indo-European root, *kert-*, to turn or twist, most speakers had no sense of this connection. In the 1970s *krutoi* could be used in reference to "tough," "cool" people, but was not associated to the verb *krutit'*'s wheeling and dealing. A link between *krutoi*'s blunt, abrupt, steep, and *krutit'*'s twisty indirection (and even, occasionally, *krug-*, linked to circularity) was poetically imagined[1] and "selected" by speakers beginning in the late 1980s. This was widespread by the early 1990s. When a person noticed the similarity, by punning or as a result of my queries, they often said, as did Zina Orlova: "Look, I just realized—There are opposite meanings there! On one hand, *krut-* is 'not yes, not no; around and near, sort of, approximately. On the other hand, it's strict, straight.' " Zina and Andrei claimed that everything is connected to "the material" by infinitely complex invisible threads. I found that descriptions in terms of unseen complexity, tangles and links

---

[1] Friedrich (1979:13, 446) writes that imagination uses language creatively, including "the emotions, sensuous image use, aesthetic appreciations, and mythic forms of imagining," moving "between relatively linguistic meanings . . . and . . . the system of cultural values."

characterized both what was seen as the worst in situations and people and what was seen as the best. Grisha, for example, said that he and his best friend Kolia were connected by invisible threads. But so were the government and the Mafiia, for example.

The conflation of *krut-* words and changes in what they could mean reflect changing values and consciousness of values and how imagery condensed by *krut-* related to moral paradoxes and "inchoate" phenomena (Fernandez 1986) of perestroika, a confusing moment called by Gorbachev (1987 3:203) and many people a *krutoi povorot*, sharp turn. In the early 1990s, current *krut-* words and expressions were of various styles and levels of language and dating from many eras. *Krutoi* was the most predictable entry in popular media glossaries of current jargon, for example, this from the magazine *Znanie-Sila* (Knowledge is Strength) in March 1992:

krutoi:
1. good, excellent;
2. Strongly expressed: e.g. "*krutoi* avant-garde"
3. *Sistemnyi*—recognized in a certain circle of people, *svoi* (ours).

I will show these new definitions to be interrelated and to be related to older colloquial and dictionary definitions.

Krut- words replaced vast numbers of words along certain dimensions. There were also hand gestures that augmented or replaced words, snaky winding or spiraling motions from close to the chest outward or at an angle. A word often tended to be replaced by a gesture or silence when it seemed so "overcharged" with connotations as to seem internally vast and paradoxical. As one can see in much of the speech I quote here, talk about "deep" or "complicated" things also often took the form of broken, halting sentences, floundering around, saying "how can I explain," reaching "inside" ostensibly to express what was there, relying on knowledge shared with the listener. Words, ideas, and experiences called "impossible to express" were particularly valued. Terms tended to seem simultaneously "obvious" and "very hard to express" when their meaning varied so greatly with context that it could not be summarized.[2]

Sometimes these comments and speech patterns gestured at "things working in mysterious ways," the way things were assumed to get done when *we* couldn't see them getting done. The word *provernut'*, though based not on *krut-* but on another root for turning, came to share some of *krutit's* temporary vitality: *provernut'* can mean both to run something through a meat-grinder and to "fix things" so everything winds up OK. Once Nadia, Grisha's wife, haltingly described how "The ones who are liv-

---

[2] For example, a woman Ledeneva (1998:33) cites calls the meaning of blat "obvious," yet cannot explain it; Ledeneva notes that *blat's* meaning differs contextually.

ing well here now, *krutye*, business people, can fix things (*provernut'*), that is, somehow do something somewhere there [*gde-to tam, chto-to kak-to*], get things done without being open, get money." While listening to a man explain over tea about how he had managed to get a TV set, just as he was winding a *krut-* gesture to accompany his words "by a left-handed path," I happened to choke a little on a piece of bread. He smirked, saying "Yeah, like that," seeming to imply that what I choked on had been the indirection I had glimpsed in his gesture.

Screwing Things Out of the System

One set of *krut-* words relates to situations of twisting, screwing, wringing things, money, satisfaction, or information out of people or a situation. Wrangling money or a bottle of vodka "somewhere" out of "someone" was vy*krut*it' or ras*krut*it'. Anatolii, Oleg's friend in his early twenties, into music and computers, during an interview in his parents' apartment, told me a great deal about *krut-*. He started: "A lot of it has to do with money: za*krut*ka is starting some enterprise, usually a moneymaker. And when people call some enterprise or action na*krut*ka, it can imply that it's just to make a buck."

Krut- terms were not only themselves fashionable, they referred to most currently fashionable phenomena. *Krutit'sia* had long meant to engage in business, people told me, from petty speculation to buying and selling large lots of goods and "something serious in the shadow economy," a darkness that, like "underground," refers to "visual" inaccessibility. An eleven-year-old boy told me that "ras*krut*it' business is finding out where things are and where you can resell them." Already in the 1970s "He ras*krut*ilsia well" could mean "He made a lot of money"; this economic *krut-* got a new lease on life when moneymaking became openly fashionable. While Anatolii was telling me how *krutoi* referred to a cool, fashionable type of person, he suddenly said "Hey! *Krutoi* now means a person *krutitsia*! *Krutoi* and *krutit'* go together! A *krutoi* person *krutit*, engages in resale, makes money somehow."

A saying constantly cited and played on during the 1990s was "If you want to live (or, alternately, survive), be able to *krutit'sia*." Once when Grisha quoted this, he added: "You know, blat and *krutit'sia* are the same thing. A *normal* person comes to the store and can buy only what he *sees*. Blat is completely different." Another reference to visibility.

Lara said that one might say that a boss is "*krut* with people; severe, uncharitable . . . He risks accidents trying to reach his goals. A *krutoi* conversation is cruel. *Straight* talk. Frank. And *krutoe slovtso*, a sharp or harsh word from a lower lexicon or designed to cut a person to the quick, a word with a *purpose*." In Anatolii's opposition of *krut-* to normal we again see an interesting union of straight and emphatically not-straight, and how "straight," practical people may be seen as "not straight," insincere:

A person who has something wrong with his spirituality, well, he starts to *kru-tit'sia,* that is, make a living like this [winding gesture]. This gesture, it's doing *anything,* not directly, not straight, not right out in the open. "I get what I want, my way." To get rich at the expense of someone else's grief, of shortages. To be practical, that's an aspect of a *krutoi* or businesslike person. He tries to accumulate material goods rather than spiritual things. *Krutit'* is *to do,* but some*how,* not normally.

I return to the opposition of normalcy to not normal.

It was usually assumed that part of a *krutoi* person's abnormality is that he or she could not feel for others: a teacher complained about cruelly steep prices; taxes made them *krut-*er, and then merchants with no compassion, with "some problem with their *dushi,*" were cranking up the prices (*kru-tiat*), *krut-*ing on their own. But if self-centered moneymakers were killing dusha, they might also display respected "Russian" qualities. If *krut-* talents were used for the good of a collective that included the speaker, the *krutoi* might be seen as dushevnyi. Public Prosecutor Yurii Yur'evich, after describing the depravity of *krutoi* crooks, told of good *krutoi* factory heads who *krut-*ed, "somehow" arranging to support their workers.

In 1992, a young man told me: "You could go into stores for years and never be able to buy cabinets for your apartment unless you were the grand-son of a veteran and could wait for years. *Or something.* You couldn't get them whatever you tried [*kak ne vykruchivaisia*]." But his *krutoi* uncle had that something, a telephone number, and the young man went and bought his furniture. "No problem! Our Soviet System," he said, winding his hand in space.

Grisha gave a variation: "If you want to live, be an entrepreneur." This demand, suddenly made on each individual, was sharp, harsh, abrupt (*kru-toi*). The brutal, complex System, steep, sudden, and harsh inflation, the way entrepreneurs seemed to wind through tangled networks, their cutting edge fashion, and their brutal, blunt characters, all touched on *krut-.* And over all of it was the restless urgency of activities called *krutit'sia,* all char-acterized by trying to impose one's will on things. *Krutit'sia* is running around in control, hustling, or out of control, "like a squirrel in a wheel" or "like in a meat grinder." A door attendant said that the boss *zakrutilsia,* had gotten out of control rushing around doing things. To run oneself ragged was also *zamotat'sia,* an image of winding string around a spool.

The Simple Person

All of this alleged complexity and *krutizna* was meaningful in the context of a cluster of understandings of simplicity, including eighteenth and nine-teenth-century intelligentsia notions of "simple" village folk with innate *kul'tura* ("culture"), sympathy, tact, and hospitality that were supposed to result in community and "everything" being simple. Village "backwardness," writes Rogger (1960:126–27), seemed to insure the survival of virtues coming to be considered Russian: spontaneity, artless honesty, generosity, humanity, the soulful Russian peasant contrasted with the petty, accumulative Western man (ibid.:173).

These continued to be professed virtues for many post-Soviets too. People who presented themselves as spontaneous and/or uninhibited, whose impulses seemed to come directly from dusha and protest the miserly calculation that separates people were called "without complexes." From dusha (*ot dushi*) means, in a sense, "simply"; not *for* anything, a readiness to drop everything and enter into a relationship not based on utility. "It means we're more accessible, make contact more easily than Westerners," I was told. But people were becoming beasts during perestroika, a man told me; "All that's left of the mysterious Russian soul is that people can still take joy from little things, from little, and can still sympathize."

Simplicity, linked to imagery of the village, could also entail notions of "primitive" and "uncivilized." Post-Soviets of all classes could be playfully delighted to crown themselves (in Rousseau's voice) superior, natural savages, and to claim (in Herder's voice) to be naturally creative and in contact with national feeling, to be folk, the people (*narod*); in short, "normal." Alongside the revaluation of simplicity Dunham (1990:95) describes, "simple" seems to have retained much traditional value and was even used alongside the supremely valuable "real," *nastoiashchii*.

Another attribute implied of soulful simplicity was that it was a special form of depth. When Grisha said, equating simplicity and superficiality, that "If you call someone 'as simple as Siberian felt boots,' you're just not interested in that person's depth," he meant to be shocking. "Profound" simplicity may include the philosophizing I discuss in Chapter 2, as when Berdiaev (1947:30–31) romantically wrote that "The illiterate Russian loves to pose questions . . . about the meaning of life . . . about evil and injustice, about how the Kingdom of God is to be realized."

A group of Soviet researchers (Levada et al. 1993:9) published a study of the USSR's "basic social, demographic and ethnic groups" entitled *The Simple Soviet Person*, intended as a portrait of an "historical, sociocultural, anthropological type: the Soviet person, Homo Sovieticus . . . the product and focus of an unstable sociopolitical system." In this text, Homo Sovieticus is both a complex product of a complex System and, whatever his/her demographic and ethnic particulars, "simple." The authors (ibid.:6–8) explain "simple person" as having "a complicated set of interconnected meanings: related to the masses ("like everyone"), deindividualized, opposed to everything elite and idiosyncratic, "transparent" . . . primitive in his/her needs (survival level), created once and for all and immutable, and easily controlled." When respondents were asked to attribute personal qualities to Soviet ethnic groups, Russians ranked as being the most hospitable, open and simple, peace-loving, and tolerant (ibid.:282).

The image of Siberians includes positively and negatively valued simplicities. "Siberian" could be a distilled version of "Russian." An actress accused an Omsk translator of doing a "Siberian" translation of her lines from an English she did not understand but assumed was refined and cultured; "You know," she explained to me, "Siberian—in felt boots, crude, done with an axe." But just as "Russian-style" could imply uncultured but open, undiluted, inspired, capable of pointing at the Emperor's nudity, candid, humorous, or obscene generalizations from dusha were felt to point at Russian or Soviet experience.

I was watching an American video with two men in their thirties. When the film's hero risked everything, jumping out of a plane with no parachute, one man commented: "Very Russian." The other answered: "Americans are *krutye* too. Who went to America? Daring, active, curious people. And criminals" (notice that *krutoi* is briefly a synonym for Russian). Straightforward impulsiveness, one aspect of self-attributed national character (see Stites 1992:5–6), was *krutoi* when combined with another "Russian" quality, a clever quick imagination (see Brooks 1984:282–83), forging a "simple" for a System that demanded complexity.

Complications, Enigma, Evasiveness

> A "twist" [za*krut*ka, zavertka, zavintok, a tangled bunch of stalks] in a grain field was perceived as a type of sorcery that could bring sickness or death . . . and ruin to the entire harvest.
> Ivanits 1992:109–10

A woman mentioned something about "our System," adding "Well, it's already not our *Soviet* system, but *that* [she gestured twistiness] is still with us." Grisha said: "Blat has taken on such broad, extended, circular, winding forms, you'll never figure out what's going on." "You can't go into business here," Mila said to me in her office one day, "*simply*, with funds, a plan, and honest business qualities. You need something else. There's already a system. A field already exists [she gestured the field's knottedness]. You have to join in and make a place for yourself or be crushed." Even when her words had passed this "field," her fingers kept distractedly describing its tangled, devious furrows. After a silence, she summed up with a pun on *krutoi* and on a System that made opposites coexist: "Our situation is *krutoe*, hard-boiled, and soft-boiled at the same time!"

The words meaning "complicated" and "complications" were heavy, overused, as if every moment in the dying state was itself mortally ill. As a man said to his American partners, "You can't possibly be aware of *how* complicated everything here is." I asked Lara about complications. "Well," she said,

> lately you hear more about complications after the flu, something undesirable, unforeseen, some misfortune. And complications in the country now, yes, internally. Here, with us, it's solid complications. . . . The main thing is, it's *all* complications: something . . . unexpectedly turns, shows another side, and you call it a complication. Complication, also, it's an increase, a deepening, more complexities appear in a complicated situation.

The ambivalent *krut-* was continuous with the dilemma of "our life." When I remarked on what interesting answers I was getting to my questions about *krut-*, Lara sighed: "That's just the kind of life we're leading now." A pervasive theme was "You have to live in Russia to understand—it's all too complex." An actor confirmed that a key to insight into "us" Russians was suffering the same way of life: "If you immerse American actors in our Russian life, they'll start to know a little better how to act Dostoevsky." But even then you won't understand: a director told of a Frenchman who came to Russia, as foreign romantics do, to try to figure out "dark spots" in the Dostoevskian soul. Amused at the guy's clichéd quest, the Russian reported saying: "Give up—we don't understand it either." In other words, this theme goes, as in the poet Fëdor Tiutchev's denial that Russia can be understood with the mind or measured using any ordinary stick, we can understand neither Russia nor the System with reason, but only if we have crawled through their winding pathways, and can to some extent operate or be operated by them. Again, cultural fluency was taken as soulful intuition.

In the village, Zhenia was rolling a cigarette in newspaper, tearing along the print lines. "It rolls well," he said. I said that it was probably because the print ran perpendicular to his rolling. Startled, he looked at me with momentary respect, but then, elliptically, said no, I wouldn't really understand Russian life until I had to feed a family on rubles. When I displayed some quality Americans were assumed to lack, I was often challenged: "But would you come here altogether, to *live*?" This was a particularly serious question I heard often, a probe for the point at which I would back down from Russianness. Once, a friendly person who overheard me being rather aggressively asked this question interjected that "one's motherland is where one's dusha is," allowing me to rhetorically keep both my motherland and my soul.

People and news reports used *krut-* imagery in splendid metaphors to describe "infinitely" complicated machinations. An Omsk TV program was called *Reform: A Krutoi Route*. This is a pun: a *krutoi* road is steep, and new meanings of *krut-* gestured at the devious, crooked pathways of what was in rather bad faith called reform. One show described the Department of Municipal Property as the site of complicated, tangled intrigue and fishing in murky water (profiting from disorder). At the same time, a documentary on how Russia's diamonds had slipped into *krutye* pockets called this process "ras*krut*ka" and "dark and complicated music." *Krut-* words described foreign soap operas the country was obsessed with (*The Rich Also Cry* [Mexico] and *Santa Barbara* [United States]) and the devious behavior of writers and producers in designing the twisty plots that spin on (ras*krut*-iatsia), leading one on (za*kruch*ivaiutsia). A film critic might use *krut*-based terms to call a plot "tightly wound" like a spring or convoluted. A man told me that a *likho zakruchennyi* plot has both spring and convolution, which he equated with unpredictability. "Something like 'Indiana Jones.' Someone who just saw a film like that might say 'Look at how (or what) those Americans *nakrutili*!' " This implies both that the plot had suddenly turned in some weird, surprising direction, and that the American scriptwriters were cunning bastards, weren't they. So *krut-* is used for sudden, unexpected, and ingenious twists.

Everyday situations were seen as just as complex. An Omsk friend and I were standing in a small town school auditorium talking to a teacher. My friend, who worked in a big Omsk theater, giggled at the tiny stage; the teacher said yes, in your theater everything's big. He answered, "Well, not so *big* as [snaking hand gesture]" diverting the discussion to the "main" difference, the complexity of big-city relationships.

Cleverness, muddledness, capriciousness, or dishonesty all make mystery. Lies, inspired invention, gratuitous complexity, obfuscation, were all *krut-*. Though a *krutoi* person may be brutally straight in going after what he wants, he can also be devious or crooked. A fifty-year-old man, when I mentioned "*krut* guys" (*krutye rebiata*), said simply: "I dislike insincerity." Curved- or crooked-souledness (*krivodushie*), is insincerity or dishonesty. In the Stalin era people went to jail for deforming, damaging, or polluting the Party line by curving it, as a spine is damaged by curves.

With my dear friend Lara, a married teacher in her forties, I planted potatoes, dug up radishes, and looked at paintings; mostly, in her little living room over tea, we talked. Once I raised the subject of what I had begun to notice about *krut-*, she often returned to it. One day she mentioned that a babushka might say "I'm sick and tired of your vy*krut*asy, your tricks," defining *vykrutasy* just as she did complications: when people act *like this* [hand gesture]; unexpected, inexplicable behavior. Expressions for turning someone against someone and twisting facts are based on *krut-*. Adolescents' brains were za*kruch*eny, wound up, around sex. *Krutit'* could be to present plain things indirectly, be evasive; *krutit'sia* included "lying to get your way." Deliberate lying was one extreme of a continuum that included being confused and making confusion.

In criminal slang (Baldaev et al. 1992), there are *krut-* words for to arrest, to start criminal proceedings, *and* to steal or deceive; for a criminal investigation and the criminals. Lara called a restless boy *krucheny*. "A synonym," she added, "is *krut-vert*." *Krut* and *vert* were also names of cartoon characters of the recent past, and recall a prerevolutionary song that refers to a ball that turns and rolls (*krutitsia, vertitsia*) above our heads. *Krutit'sia vertet'sia* was abundantly coopted and varied in the 1990s. From simple restlessness, Lara continued:

> *Krutit'-vertet'* [to twist and turn] became to sweep away your tracks in some unclean business. He's *krut*-ing something means "he's keeping you in the dark, hiding the essence, he's up to something." O*kruch*ivat' is to go further and further from the truth to achieve some goal, one lie builds on others, maybe he gets lost in there—then he winds himself up, gets all wound up, and might attack.

By the 1970s, the use of vy*kruch*ivat' for wringing out laundry or unscrewing light bulbs had been augmented by more morally charged "twistings." Asking someone to stop wasting one's time, confusing one with superfluous details or lies, one says to not twist one's head or brains. Like expressions where arms, ears, tails, and testicles are twisted and screws tightened, imagery of evasive wriggling merged with brutal, coercive twisting. Worming out of things was a common *krut*-. For example, if you lived in a village and offered a neighbor a ride to town but later changed the subject and got out of it, you vy*kruti*lsia. Slithering out of things could be seen as more deeply rooted. Jews were widely seen as hypocritical, cunning, diametrically opposed to open, simple Russians (see Levada et al. 1993:282), as in this joke I heard in 1992:

> —Doctor, I'm afraid my baby's not positioned correctly in the womb.
> —What's your ethnic group?
> —Jewish.
> —It's OK. He'll worm his way out of it.

Kolobok, a doughball, a sort of muffin, rolls away into the world in a Russian fairy tale; every time he escapes from someone, his refrain is: "I got away from grandmother, I got away from grandfather, and I will get away from *you*!" A businessman, coercing subordinates to buy tours to Turkey so he could charter a plane for his business, in Nadia's words, "wiggled out of it, wiggled out of it, wiggled out of it everywhere." But ultimately, he "twisted, twisted, but couldn't close it."

Once, after discussing how bad wriggling out of things was, Lara suddenly said, sadly and sympathetically: "In our life, everyone *krutitsia* as best as he can, is always busy with something, gets something here, makes money there somehow . . . People are using all possible paths to make ends meet." Everyone, in other words, was trapped in a "brutal, *krutaia* reality"; *krut*- was part of the post-Soviet condition of Russian dusha.

Working: Enforced, Inspired, and With Eels

Krut- often turned up in notions of work, both as a "way out" and as finding ways "in." A businessman's rushing, wheeling, and dealing were derogatorily seen by some as not real work; middlemen and retailers created, according to their Marxism, no true value, just profited from others' labor. Others admired the same *krut-* as "not real work" that magically spun or whipped up something from nothing. In criminal jargon, both a lucky crook and a proven businessperson were *kruchenyi. Trudoliubie,* being a diligent worker, may seem *opposite* to many uses of *krut-*, but, as Mila's mother said as she finished milking her recently acquired cow and scraped cow shit off the path to her house, "To survive, you've got to *krutit'sia*. Work, that is."

So many points on a moral continuum were tapping the same imagery. Though in Mila's mother's and Lara's statements *krut-* referred to good people and their honest, hard work, this work was, I believe, seen as framed in a wrong world, a wrong System—brutal, uncompromising, *krutoi*. Returning to Anatolii's statement that when you have something wrong with your spirituality, you start to *krutit'sia*, it works the other way, too: people seen as simple, as not "by nature" *krut-*, had to chemically soak the month out of their bus passes, update them, hustle, work much too hard. Which harmed or corrupted their souls.

Mark Steinberg (forthcoming) notes that socialism emphasized the relationship between work and selfhood. Revolution-era workers, he says, dwelled quite earnestly on how their labor injured their selves, as opposed to how "normal" labor, according to Marx, should develop one's slumbering powers, humanize. A 1990s form of this was to blame *krutye*, who did no "real" work, for turning the world into one where so-called normal people had to be abnormal, exploit their alleged natural creativity, lose their humanity at work tainted by having been wrung out of them. *Krut-* was an epidemic infection.

Another way of being *krutoi* is being able to handle incomprehensible or chaotic situations in a chaotic, incomprehensible system. One evening I met a man I knew in an Omsk underpass. He told me his boss was about to return from a business trip—meaning the end of sitting over tea, the beginning of work. He quoted the old, romantic song: everything will start spinning and rolling; the shit will hit the fan.

Being krutoi was being able to handle chaotic situations, thus *krut-* was associated with management styles. Pensioner Evgeniia Pavlovna, optimist that she was, described qualities she saw as necessary for the new Russia. She had read, she said, that the Japanese used to choose directors of firms using a basket of eels;

The committee sits here and over there sit candidates for director. An eel. Live. Have you seen live eels? Well they crawl out, and what'll you do? . . . What'll you do? Here you have respectable people. And this thing is crawling—here, and here! And here! Not just anyone can hold that eel.

We laughed as she acted wriggling eels and squirming candidate. "People who can by any means control eels," she said, "are developing. With businesslike qualities." But in the same breath she indicted the bad system that made flexible eel-catching adaptation necessary. She had one dear friend, she said, "who will not bow down. Her organism repels evil. She can't [winding gesture] maneuver. She can't adapt." But another woman said, at first proudly, that her husband could adapt, adjust, *krutit'* well. Then she quickly added, "To survive."

There was not only a new emphasis on adapting; there was an equally ambivalent one on taking initiative. As Lara said, " 'He's so *krutoi*' can be positive or negative: *oborotistyi, delovoi*." *Delovoi* is businesslike.[3] *Oborotistyi* is yet another term based on *turning*—someone who can "buy something here and *turn around* and sell it there," or turn capital over quickly. This turning had only recently started being openly represented as a virtue, and was still very easily recast as bad in other moral speech contexts.

Some formulated the new mode as working hard, being practical, going straight. In a 1994 interview, theater director Yurii Liubimov was asked what he would wish for Russia. He answered provocatively: "Wish for Russia? Well, stop messing around and use your head! . . . It's time to forget Tiutchev's poetry and switch to chastushki:

Davno pora (da *da* da) *mat'*
Umom Rossiiu ponimat'!

[It's high time . . . la la la . . . your mother / To understand Russia with your mind!]. Liubimov metrically, "da *da* da," omits *ebёna*, fucked. "And as for the enigmatic Russian soul," he continued, "it's enigmatic all right, but now it's time to *work*!" Although his parody of a parody of Tiutchev expresses a view sometimes seen as "less Russian," here its Russianness is redeemed by flamboyant, rebellious coarseness and rejection of high culture.

Male and Female *Krutye* in a *Krut-* Time: Authority and Fashion

The world was splitting into *krutye* business people and those unable to be *krutye*, unable to operate or pull things off but only to spin their wheels, a schism with some roots in class structure. Zina, Andrei, and others said

[3] The term *delovoi* was often used by Gorbachev (e.g., 1987 2:5) in a classical communist sense of taking a businesslike approach to social transformation. *Del'tsy,* a prerevolutionary term for business people, gathered negative connotations during the Soviet era. During perestroika, it was revalorized, though a new term, *biznesmeny*, became more popular.

they were not prepared for the market. But, they said, former partocrats and others involved in the "shadow economy" had "floated to the surface and adapted." Links between *krutye* were twisty: "The layers of power," Zina said, "unite somehow, invisibly; it's something everyone understands, but only on the level of intuition." Many people lumped former black marketeers, "reconstructed" communists, mafiosi, New Russians, and the *krutoi* guy together in one negatively appreciated group of those who, Lara said, "adjusted, went into business and za*kruti*li there, somewhere, za*kruti*li a car for themselves."

Though there were many ways of being *krutoi*, there was a group called "the *krutye*." Lara described it as being "on the crest of the wave . . . independent, self-sufficient, those for whom external authority does not exist." Anatolii said that during the Brezhnev era, the *krutye* were kids whose parents' positions afforded them "things no one else had. 'Rags' from abroad . . . girls, jeans, dollars . . . Things were *krutye* if they were hard to get, cost insane amounts of money, or were good quality. Not necessarily imported; some girls sew cleverly."[4] "The *krutoi* part of the population determines fashion, not Pierre Cardin," Anatolii said.

What was deemed *krutoi* in 1992 Omsk? Graffito on the new Casino labeled it very *krutoi*. When she saw the shoes I had brought for a friend's baby, Svetlana shrieked, "Even *krut*-er!" *Krutoi* appeared relentlessly in reference to contemporary music. In the paper *Argumenty i Fakty*, a band's lead singer called techno "more *complicated* than hip-hop, the most fashionable style in the world. There's nothing *krut*-er. Americans *krutiat* [spin] only techno."

As Western was fashionable, fashion-related "*Kruto!*" was often replaced by words linked to other "cool" things. *Valiutnyi* (from the word for hard currency), for example, meaning first-rate, "the real thing." A *Montana* brand cigarette ad asserted: "This is America!" and for a time "*Montana!*" meant *kruto*. A man lovingly called his toddler daughter's antics *toyotovskie*.[5]

If mentioning money directly had widely been considered uncultured during the Soviet era, hard-boiled *krutye* did it *kruto,* bluntly, and in cruel situations. In 1992 Omsk they were identified by their uniform clothing, muscles, and brown mink hats. Of course, fashion indexes "original and creative" long after it becomes a uniform; as Lara said, "A *krutoi,* . . . everything's this standard, this stereotype." An October 1992 *Omskii vestnik* article, "Our Life," described them as "brightly painted, lazily smoking

---

[4] Clever, cunning (*khitro*) is a traditionally negative description coopted as positive in late Soviet contexts. Anatolii once mentioned that in the 1970s, when censorship was *krutoi*, "you had to sing cunningly," winding with his hand outward from his middle—regular, measured, sneaky. Western songs, he said, were more superficial.

[5] Toyota was associated with American life. Humphrey (1995:20–22) observes that toward the end of perestroika, Western goods became less able to constitute Russian social identity. And, as Ries has pointed out (personal communication, 1998), people did begin selecting favorite brands rather than generally fetishizing Western commodities.

maidens and huge '*krutye*' guys dressed in the latest squeal of fashion (all in exactly the same thing, new and shining)." Also in 1992, a man wound up a televised discussion of that day in the Orthodox calendar by saying that "Our dushi and the Russian spirit will survive the politics led by people in black leather jackets with kitchen knives in their pockets." By 1994 the fashions had spread to other parts of the population, and young *krutye* were identified more by their defiant, sometimes scarred or bruised stone faces (Zina called them spade-faces, and one nineteen-year-old man called them "The Mug You Need" [*rozhe, kak nado*], their imported cars, and their uniform stance, feet placed wide, loose knees, a "ready" slouch from the hips.

In 1992, two floors of an Omsk hotel were being used as offices by smoking men. On a Saturday evening its restaurant was in full swing, in contrast to dark neighborhoods of carved shutters, birdhouses on poles, kids in felt boots with sleds, outhouses, animals, and so-called "normal," that is, impoverished, families who had not been to restaurants for years. Here, long tables of done-up women and men in parachute-material warmups and leather feasted on rare food, cognac, champagne, and fashionable two-liter plastic bottles of forged Coke and something called Orange Go-Go. The *krutye* squeezed them manfully when they poured, conspicuously consuming not just the soda but the coveted light bottles their mothers would have given their eye teeth to have to take water or tea to the dacha in.

Although they were often called heartless (bezdushnye), monsters, *krutye* could be highly skilled eel-handling professionals. Andrei Orlov told of a garage near his that had been broken into through a brick wall; the thieves saw that the Mercedes was not there and left (in pride and anger, Andrei imagined) without touching four brand new tires. "A million or nothing!" he exclaimed; "*Krutye*. Even in the world of crime there's an elite whose methods are beautiful rather than straight and crude." *Krut-*'s possible nuance of charisma, professionalism, and/or technical brilliance appeared in phrases such as "the most *krutoi* photographer in Omsk." A businessman writing promotional material was said to have v*krut*il (spun) a clever sentence. Anatolii said:

> Each current of youth culture has its own *krutoi;* if a guy does well with girls, plays guitar, he's *krutoi*. It's authority in something. You feel spiritual closeness, you want to be like him, you respect him because he's a professional, a master in fixing primus stoves or writing music. Or because of his connections. He's achieved something. *Krutoi* implies a large scale, the best, ties to the criminal world. . . . And good material circumstances.

I was initially reluctant to interview Svetlana, but she, as she later coyly told me, managed nevertheless to wring an interview out of me: "I'm a devious woman," she joked. As the term *krutoi* guy did not have as popular a parallel for girls, I asked people about the difference. Lara's answer spiraled round and round. First, gesturing at the notion that women have more sensitive souls, she said categorically that "*Krutoi* sounds derogatory for a girl, as if she's proud or maybe loose. Women aren't capable of *krutoi* business." Then, as an afterthought, she said: "No, actually, *krutaia devchonka*, chick, is rare, but it can be said. And o*krutit*' a guy, that's to make him marry you," Lara said. "A girl, no. Only a guy. It's a feminine quality. Only women are capable of that! And when a woman's husband does anything she wants they say she twists (*krutit*) ropes out of him. But wait, men do that too, to get a bottle of vodka from their wives."

Anatolii mentioned a parallel to Lara's o*krutit*' a guy to get him to marry you: the phrase "ras*krutit*' a chick" in the sense of convincing her to become sexually involved. So it may look different when women and men are *krutoi* or *krut*-ed, but it is unclear that one gender is more often *krutoi* than the other.

The Great Operator

If a *krutoi* is dodgy in wriggling out of things, he can be just as resourceful at snaking in and starting the wheels turning. *Krutoi's* ancestors meant "shift" or "move." Ras*krutit*' and za*krutit*' could mean, besides "moving" goods, unleashing something, as in (from a 1992 TV show) "Stalin ras*krutil* an antisemitic campaign." Of an enterprising friend, twenty-three-year-old Svetlana said "She *krutitsia*"; she works, *takes the initiative,* and may even succeed. A woman in her late forties said that after her husband died, "The situation po*krutila* me." Then one day, she said, she got up and asked herself what she could do. "I can sew," she answered, and started to *krutit'sia*. One might say she reappropriated the *krut-*.

Krutit' could imply originality, as when that *krutoi* photographer used Svetlana as a model "but *krutit* (does) whatever he wants with the photos when he develops them," she said, winding a gesture. It could be cunning invention or manipulation: newspaper editors "re-*krut*" words to express what they want. A dishonest fabrication or gambit in poor judgement could be na*krutka*, as Mila called a project a coworker had initiated. "But it's too late;" she said, "work is already za*kruchena*, begun." An impulse *krut*-ed may be silly or idiosyncratic: Dasha and I walked right by a gate we were looking for because, she exclaimed, she hadn't expected "they'd *krut*-ed them green." Her *krut*- word for this fickleness implied not just "paint," but "took it into their heads, *God knows why*, to paint." An impulse *krut*-ed may be passionately clumsy, with surprising results: a teacher told a repairman that the photocopy machine's problem began after she impulsively "*krut*-ed" a whole ream of paper in there at once.

Krut- relates to what Humphrey (1995:14) has called the Soviet culture of suspicion and cheating; owners underpaid sellers, purchasers stole, buyers were given defective goods, and sellers hid the takings. This was still jokingly labeled "magic:" during the 1991 currency reform I was sitting in a workshop with acquaintances. A young guy was pensively transferring sugar cubes from a box to a tin. His friend told me: "This is a favorite Russian game: take the sugar out, put it back. If some is missing, you win." This game was not newly Soviet; as I mentioned in the Decency story, the classic answer to "What's going on in Russia?" was "They're stealing."

Reading Il'f and Petrov's *The Twelve Chairs* and *The Golden Calf,* the adventures of Ostap Bender were, as I have mentioned, what many people told me was *the* prerequisite for understanding Soviet life or, ironically, "our Russian *dusha.*" Ostap, called "The Great Operator" (*velikii kombinator*), proclaims a "selfless love for banknotes," effortlessly squeezes information out of people, slips in and out of roles, and penetrates through situations. The *Kombinator* in Ostap's nickname comes from *kombinatsiia,* a chess term implying a planned sequence of moves that bring unexpectedly great profit. *Kombinatsiia* also refers to underwear, hence the riddle: "What does a Jew have in his head and a woman under her dress?"

Ostap claims that life is "a complicated thing, but . . . that complicated thing opens simply, like a box" (Il'f and Petrov 1984:81). I saw a certain admiration for people who could open that Soviet box; their calculated, worldly virtuosity transformed into a sort of second order soulfulness by virtue of standing in opposition to a grueling *byt* imposed by soulless bureaucrats.

Sinyavsky (1988:174–181), echoing what I heard said daily, writes that "the Soviet way of life is a class by itself when it comes to the great resourcefulness with which it stamps a person's psyche . . . the lives of those who contrive to find something 'for themselves' [can be] . . . interesting." Sinyavsky describes the Great *Kombinator*'s brilliant twistiness in the aesthetic of other worlds; Ostap is "luminous against the dreary background" of socialism. The Great Operator, Sinyavsky continues, appears "not in certain people but in certain tendencies that permeate Soviet society."[6]

More than once I heard that the Revolution, having been "made by Jews," had spawned a "Jewified" Soviet culture. Some radical Russian ethnonationalists go farther, classifying even Christianity as a disruptive ideology imposed by Jews (Schnirelman and Komarova 1997:215). Such theories were, of course, too extreme for most Russian ethnics who nevertheless constructed some of the image of their own "Russian" souls in opposition to images of the souls (or absence thereof) of Jews and Asians. Yet in the case of the Great Operator, what would otherwise be seen as soulless worming in and out of things is aestheticized, epic, oddly transformed into "Rus-

---

[6] Sinyavsky (ibid.:182) tells of a money-making scheme "interesting" "for its being concocted out of nothing except shrewdness and an uncanny sense of the Soviet system."

sian" creative resistance. Ostap Bender is the *form* of romantic Russian dusha with the *content* of its imagined nemeses. In 1990s lore, images of the New Russian sport a related mixture. How inseparable is dusha from images it opposes!

Talking to Oleg on the phone, I used a metaphor. He teased me about using excessive imagery. He used three verbal forms of *krut-*, meaning to express oneself in a complex, obtuse manner, with ulterior motives. Joking, he claimed: "We Russians aren't so *krutoi*," "Americans think they're the most *krutoi.*" He then launched a lament about the *krutoi* ties some men had begun wearing and how unfair it was that *that* sort of person was on top now. This ran into a description of New Russians in which *krut-* s were so dense there seemed to be no room for other words. More sarcastic *krut-* s described the blustering bravado of a firm that was carrying on about how international it was. In this run of *krut-* based words, poetic play of repeating, varying forms, Oleg would use several *krut*-s, play with them, and then *jump*, striking out a new form or usage. He described how the "crap" (new business people) *krut*-ed, *krut*-ed; *krut*-ed an idea, *krut*-ed themselves into some state . . . "It would all dissolve into groveling," he said, "if someone *krut*-er, dressed well and speaking with a fashionable accent, walked in." Most of Oleg's *krut-* s parodied the authority of individuals or nations that show off but would "sell everything in the world for $150."

Conclusions

> Complication can be a signal that—well, so much has been done
> and is . . . bad . . . that perhaps it is already possible to undertake
> something to turn that direction around.
> Lara, Omsk, 1992

I mentioned the proverb "To live life is not to walk through a field." Unlike an open field, that one needs no paths to cross, life has narrownesses, restrictions, complications and opacities, and, as in Lara's definition of complications, things may unexpectedly take a turn. Impulsive, changeable aspects of *krut-* relate to dusha's generativity and intolerance of routine, as when a woman said "I have to change jobs every few years. Dusha demands a change."

To sum up, *krut-* words could mean "to do," in a clever, devious, hidden, twisty, harried, cold-blooded, strong, blatant, direct, silly, unexpected, original, eccentric, or fashionable way, pulling it off or *not* pulling it off. As an adjective, *krutoi* could add an *intensifying* nuance of extreme, better, bigger, denser, newer, unexpected and unpredictable, more, or very; it may be used to describe a bitter offense, a rolling boil, dense forest, or strong tea. Both *krutoi* and *krutit'* could refer to types or fashions and be dushevnyi or soulless.

Common to most of these aspects, I want to stress, is an issue of *differing relative points of view* on some social/cultural domain. The difference in points of view takes the form of reference to things as enigmatic, hidden, and deep to one group of people, and thus as having some sort of authority or power over them. *Krut-* relates to whether an individual is in the know or out, in or out of control. In the 1990s, life was a struggle for individual control of *krut-*; *krutoi* and *krutit'*, as infused with the presupposition of different relative social and economic points of view, threatened to separate people. Individuals referred to as *krutoi* or as able to *krutit'* could seem less tied by laws that bound others; their twistiness represented what was assumed to go on where normal humans could not see. Those who had different ways of operating, within the System (inside or outside relative to the speaker) or outside of it (foreigners) were suspected of being twisted, distorted, bent; of having lost soul or of having it deeply hidden. As Alan Cienki put it (1997, personal communication), "*Krutoi* as 'steep' seems, as you suggest, to have to do with the divergence of a straight ('upright') form from its norm." Both *krut-*'s "goodness" and its "badness" also derive in part from the sense that *the explanation* is "inside" or in some domain to which *normal* people have no access. Public Prosecutor Yurii Yur'evich, describing the transcendent landscape of the spiritual world, fell silent, winding his hand through space. In a minute he made the same exact gesture to show how "frightful and zigzagging" Russian history was.

Twistiness was always seen from some point of view, but separation into *krutye* and non-*krutye* wounded everyone spiritually. Everyone had to *krut-*. In the summer of 1996 a successful St. Petersburg woman offered a toast, saying that for the past five years: "All we have done is business, all we have thought about is money, *krut*-ing, in short, solid System. Here's to just sitting like this and drinking with friends." Krut- was, on one hand, how people had "always" had to work. On the other it was acutely 1990s, a *krutoi* social turn that *krutye* could negotiate. A person forced to do something absurdly clever was often discussed with resigned laughter and reference to "this reality of ours." All "our present difficulties" were implied by *krut-* words; *krut-* was the urgent forward edge of the ancient evil *byt*. Having used one's "Russian" creativity in a Soviet *byt* that forced both "cool," fashionable "operators" and everyone else to muddle and hustle helplessly through their days, having used and developed "genuine" abilities and interests in "this" world, it is implied that dusha was affected and reproduced accordingly. This creativity usurped the place of soulful creativity, this interest usurped interest's soulful locus and role. Interest became materially oriented self-interest.

In the face of coexisting systems and notions of complexity, people found themselves with a representation of invisible threads interweaving good with evil, ideal with actual, everything "with the material." The complexity of Dostoevskian wrestling with internal good and evil was recreated from "outside," "twisting" dusha and anima-ting *krut-*. Dusha was seen as poisoned and Soviet, but the anguished consciousness of that poisoning affirmed it as a dusha. The image of the System, in turn, became isomorphic with the depth and complexity of soul. Together dusha and the System defined an overdetermined *krut-* space open to poetic play.

"So you see," Lara concluded a recital of *krut*'s context-dependent richnesses, recontextualizing them in terms of her sense of the tragedy of that time and place: "the root *krut-* has lost its meaning, is losing it."

PART IV

AUTHORITY

CHAPTER TEN

Depth, Openings, and Closings

Pick your nose, pick it and stick
Your whole finger into the hole,
But with the same force to pick
Don't climb into your soul.

Esenin; tr. by Michael Wasserman

Just as Democritos applied the concepts of above and below to infinite space ... philosophers ... apply ... "inside and outside" to ... the world. They think that with deep feelings man penetrates deep into the inside, approaches the heart of nature.

Nietzsche

Depth

The poet Blok (1880–1921) called Russia the triumph of inner man, a reproach to outer man (Cherniavsky 1969:216). Eighteenth- and nineteenth-century imagery of Russianness referred to hollow, full, deep, or shallow insides, expanses, and surfaces. The West was said to be dying of an empty soul, Russians said to have more *in* their soul, to understand more deeply (see Williams 1970:577). Everyday life in the 1990s was densely populated with insides, outsides, and expanses of many kinds and provenances, promiscuously, opportunistically combined. The opening phrase of remarkably many documentary radio programs and newspaper articles was "Deep down, everyone ..." [lit. Each person, in his/her dusha ...]. Dusha was the "other" self imprisoned inside, crushed by life. "The outer layer of things," said Mila, "is counterindicated for dusha." Soul was deeper. Depth was always proliferating. Anything can be felt in dusha, I was told, as long as that feeling is inward, secret, deep down. Wierzbicka links "the hidden nature of feelings associated with dusha" to "their 'deeper' nature" (1989:51). But what do hiddenness and depth imply? Dusha is an issue of depth and of hiddenness; this chapter explores that depth in the context of a closed city deep in the heartland during a time when some of glasnost's opennesses were said to be damaging dusha. I examine this damage. I look at how 1990s Omsk spaces—private, public, imagined and metaphorical—were manipulated, shifty, and hybrid. I also examine depth's ascendancy, its centrality, its *authority*.

Depth is a master organizing principle in discourse and in the understanding and use of space (see Whorf 1956:145). It is related to what, in his novel *Friday*, Michel Tournier (1969:67–68) calls it a prejudice to take superficial to mean "of little depth," whereas deep does not mean "of small surface." My goal here isn't to analyze what was uniquely Russian. Depth is a widespread trope.[1] I begin by presenting a range of sometimes conflicting ways in which depth and models of many kinds of insides and outsides were creatively used in discourse about everyday life in Omsk, Russia, and soul; I move to examining what can result from such creative activity over time.

Radiating, Crushing, Absorbing, and Taking Things In

Mila called herself a lemon squeezed out by life. She said that expansive, voluminous dusha is always being forced into some little hole where it can't spread its wings, grow them. Dusha, a dominant story goes—crushed and denied its true scale by Them (the powerful), by *byt*, by cramped dwellings—retreats, surviving within an insensitive shell as a tender center.

But it was surviving there: some people stressed the preciousness of life and internal vastness in confinement. Examples were prison, the soul, the kitchen, the bathhouse. Mila said:

Expansiveness (*prostor*) is a rare feeling which appears even when size is not large. Internal freedom . . . Expansiveness is whatever coincides with dusha, is where dusha feels in its element. A clear horizon, fields, wheat—it's a lyrical landscape, but a typical Siberian one. These fields aren't themselves comfortable. They coincide with my internal condition, which I try to name using the word dusha.

Grisha said that, although expansiveness is when he can throw his glance out to the horizon, it may also be felt with the soul: "When you want to embrace it all, like the sea. Expansiveness of thought, of action. You can yell: [yells, loud]. Lock me in a toilet, but give me a book, and I have open space." I cited Kazannik's tale of a drunk merchant demanding a hole be made in a wall and then, oddly, as the soul supposedly wants to stretch out, crawling into it. Such stories and actions parody and dramatize dusha's mythical and structural origins. Oleg told me that "Sakharov did his best

---

[1] Antitheses between depth and superficiality and inside and outside are part of *Kultur* as discussed by Elias, who follows the eighteenth-century contrast between "external" manners, "*superficiality* . . . and *inwardness, depth* of feeling, *immersion* in books" (1994:16, emphases mine).

work in confinement," also indicating (though in the context of a rather repulsive justification of the values of political repression) that formal constraints may unlock rather than kill generativity. Then there was a toast: "Here's to the open soul in the closed city of Omsk!"

The vitality of the "center" could be described and related to as surrounded by diluted, deceptive, less essential aspects such as character or "masks." Kozlov (1995) suggests the nesting doll as "the perfect symbol of the Russian character." The tiny central doll, he says, is "the all-important Russian *dusha*, or soul hidden deep inside, like a person's honesty with him- or herself" (Russian soul and human psychology are one here). Kozlov defines the doll's concentric shells in terms of openness and communication, implying that dusha and masks are less things than modes of interaction.

Similarly, culture and soul could be seen as decaying entropically away from a metropolitan center. When eleven-year-old Vitya, who lived in central Omsk, associated living on the city's edge with soullessness, I was shocked at his association of soul with a concentrically organized map and of "uncultured" village lifestyles with soullessness. But a flippant Muscovite told me that interesting, intelligent people live in central Moscow; the suburbs are increasingly cultureless. Amazed that I had survived in Omsk, he repeated his thought on a national level, calling the capitals and Sverdlovsk cultured and the provinces a "hopeless" wasteland with no "real people."

The center might be generous: Mila described dusha as a sun emanating rays of kindness. Moscow emanated plans, funds, standards, approval (see Polanyi et al. 1957 cited in Verdery 1993:173). The poet Mayakovsky wrote "The Earth begins from the Kremlin" (Sinyavsky 1988:249); it emanated virtues that populated USSR rivers with excursion boats named *Moskva* and, through Pioneer songs and school curricula, made Leninist Muscovites of children.

Most things were valued in terms of either conformity to socially standardized norms or in terms of their interaction with a person's moral, emotional center. When I told Zina there were no universal American curricula, she quietly concluded that what was going on in America was sheer amateurism. Uncentered decisions had no authority or truth, seemed fragmented and made-up.

Grisha began one discussion with the sort of models I mention above; "everything gets to Omsk as echoes." Provinciality is one result of the center's authority. But then Grisha suddenly switched to an equally popular inversely valued model that romantically associated the nourishing soul to the profundity of village life. The provinces were called *glubinka* (the depths), a vast heartland that Western values and manneredness had not penetrated, poisoned, or shrunk. Grisha said, "Omsk is the depths, but the best is always inside, like the pearl in an oyster." The national scandal surrounding Mendeleev's theoretical location of Russia's true "center of gravity" at Omsk shows a struggle between these different locations and meanings of the center.

Dusha is called one's internal world (*vnutrennyi mir*). Wierzbicka (1989:51–52) says dusha suggests "a dynamic internal spiritual theater." But performances there did not just go on *in* it. They constituted dusha as a meaningful space related to others.[2] Cities, countries, rooms, artworks, and other domains seen as framed or bounded, including circles of friends, family, and acquaintances, were all sometimes called and treated as "worlds," often "internal" ones.

As I have shown (Jarintzov 1916:25–27, Berdiaev 1947:2, 1960:9), people untiringly drew parallels between spiritual and physical geographies, material spaces and soulful values. Shifting families of tropes of expanse, constriction, depth, and height related features of space to various determinisms and human attributes. *Prostor* (vast, expansive space) properly refers to landscape, but *everyone* I asked about it responded in terms of *prostor* as a trope for soul. Then, through the dusha connection, they would shift to specific local landscapes. Sometimes very small local landscapes.

Almost universal in Omsk dwellings were "wall units" (*stenki*) with glass display cases, cabinets, drawers, and shelves. I return to these cases as an example of a very telling small local landscape. Evgeniia Pavlovna, discussing people's hypertrophied interest in material accumulation, their soul distortion, mentioned "contemporary wall units" first of all. A case might display crystal; porcelain; worthless, smelly one-ruble bills received at work; scribbled notes; cigarette boxes; Coke cans; starfish; Asian girls; photographs; books; a MacDonald's styrofoam box; or, if one was born in the Year of the Boar, pigs.

The contained areas of various "displays" in living and work spaces expressed relations, as Boym (1994:145–59) argues, to the "outer world." A wall in one Omsk workplace had long been used as a forum for humorous collages, ironically intended Soviet banners, and labels from foreign products. Then, during a bitter war with the directorate, the wall was progressively stripped to a bare expanse in the center of which a little crippled fascist eagle looked in the direction of what was missing.

But displays did much more than "express." Omsk cafeterias that did not sell imported beer, coffee, chocolate, or cigarettes had elaborate displays of empty packages from them not only to "attest to the forces of the dynamic universe that by definition lies outside the . . . heartland" (Helms 1988:16); the packages' saturated color and crisp detail were a relief, brilliant, alive, shining out against the grey world. In many apartments, neatly arranged displays of empty red and white imported cigarette boxes were growing in lavatories and glass cases.

Wall units were symbolically constituted foci of practices (Munn 1986:7–11). Most urban glass cases held more imported commodities than

---

[2] See Munn 1986:11, Helms 1988:4.

those in Zhenia and Tamara's village living room, with its few paperbacks, crystal glasses, and one cheap lipstick. But the trick is that no one inventory could reveal how things went in and came out of these cases. More than expressions, these cases actively contained and coopted things "charged [like their sources] with . . . supernatural, sacred, or mystical connotations" (Helms 1988:114). If these display cases survived campaigns against bourgeois domestic trash (Boym 1994:29–40; 150–56), it seems to me that it was partially because they offered spaces and possibilities (different in different families and rooms) for working with the opposition of superficial to spiritual treasures. My watch, camera, and gifts from me were immediately placed in Zhenia and Tamara's village living-room case. Their eleven-year-old once *ran* there to put an American chocolate bar next to a dead Polish watch.

Let me return for a moment to the "contained space" of dusha. If suffering deepens the soul, the notion of empathy paints a similar picture: taking things in, making them of the soul, is considered life-giving. Aleksandr Ivanovich said that dusha is how you perceive the surrounding world. That is, *soul is practices of internally representing the world to give it life and depth.* The "outer" world pierces you, you take it to heart. Once in there, it is subject and object of typical experiences, like feeling. Emotion and the center are mutually defined and determined.

The morning after one of our talks, Grisha was waiting for me in a robe and tattered house shoes. Rather than "good morning" he blurted out: "Dusha and suffering are closer than dusha and joy because suffering is deeper; it's not visible on the surface, it's *harder to understand.*" Pain seems to challenge us to penetrate some surface and find meaning.

Closedness as Invisibility: Omsk

> What's *really* going on in Russia you won't see on BBC.
>
> Newspaper headline, 1992

> I love my city. As every Omsk resident loves it—with an inexplicable love . . . Not everything in that feeling can be expressed in words.
>
> Sergeev 1981

A Russian proverb says that to others, a person's dusha is the dark, *unfathomable* part.[3] Secrecy or hiddenness is an important part of depth. One afternoon in his kitchen, Grisha discussed the soul's tuning, disposition, condition:

---

[3] Wierzbicka (1992:50–1) cites this proverb, describing dusha as an internal place unknowable to outsiders.

In different situations a violin sounds differently. One of the most enigmatic instruments. Inside there's a *dushka*. A little stick. No one sees it. The violin's character, its sound, depends on it, and only the violin master feels where to place that dusha. The one who made us placed that in each of us. A violin without a *dushka* isn't a violin.

"How much did the enigmatic Slavic soul store within itself!" Greenfeld (1992:256) writes. "Nobody could see it . . . [yet] nobody could deny the Russian nation superiority which expressed itself in the world beyond the apparent." But one must remember that deep things are deep thanks to surfaces. Much of the meaning of expanses and worlds depends on thresholds or horizons that define and cover them. Dusha, like a veil, conceals, shields, distances, while seducing one.

In the 1930s, Soviet borders were sealed more tightly, migration into cities was controlled, and elaborate rituals were required to enter buildings (Stites 1992:84). Entering buildings in the 1990s, one still encountered an attendant. Depending on the individual and relations at that workplace, this experience could be one of being denied, interrogated, spied on, or welcomed. The privacy of kitchen table and closed cabinet, the USSR's opaque borders and lore of "enigmatic" and masked folly, deception, and complexity, Omsk's even more rigid impermeability and its map's huge blank spots all implied hidden interiors. Much of the value (positive or negative) of these interiors was determined by the very fact of their hiddenness.

I did not choose Omsk because it was closed, because secrets lived there, or because Dostoevsky had been exiled there; but all these historical facts helped me, as discourses and practices surrounding Omsk itself during the changes of the early 1990s connected so often to those relating to dusha. When I researched Omsk, I did not find much. Despite its size, it was pretty invisible. It had always been a place of military secrets and exile, but, during World War II, military factories and KGB archives were evacuated there. Omsk got big, and foreigners stopped seeing it. Until 1989, the rare foreign specialist visiting the refineries rode in a vehicle with blacked-out windows. Areas were shown to me as ones that "even now foreigners don't see."

Omsk was also hard to see clearly from inside. It was Eurasian, forest-steppe, multiethnic. If in 1836 the philosopher Chaadaev described Russia as a desertlike void and Russians as lost souls, Omsk was often described as a similar nothing: unreal, empty, missing something, even aggressively negative. One woman called it a swamp. People directed me to the "real" Siberia, east to Baikal, north to the taiga. "A navel," one man called Omsk, "geographically in the center but in itself nothing."

After being released from labor camp, Dostoevsky called Omsk "a nasty little town . . . In the summer it is sultry, with sandy wind. In the winter there are blizzards. As for nature, I saw none. It is a dirty little town, military-ridden and to the highest degree degenerate."[4] Mila said nothing had changed. "Omsk is a black hole. [It has] every sort of cultural institution, but it has a very thin layer of culture." She showed three millimeters between two fingers, adding images. "In the far north, south, west, there are strong forces, but here spiritual energy flies away, it can't put down roots."

> If ceilings are low, the window looks out on an industrial landscape, you can say beautiful words to children, but it affects their psyche. Talented people . . . try to create a space around themselves filled with spirituality, but no cultural soil gets made; there's no sum of that energy. Where does it all go? In the capitals there's something in the air. Omsk should be different. Seeds get scattered, but nothing grows; it all remains separate bursts of energy. Legends get created . . . I believe in legends, but legends alone won't save you—I'm speaking of Omsk—If Dostoevsky came back today, I think he'd make exactly the same evaluation. Perhaps he'd also mention what the refineries dump into the air.

Omsk was hard to romanticize, but Dostoevsky and his life story linked Omsk to soul as a constricted-but-vast locus of suffering and a source of works of genius, like the "Dead House" Bakhtin [1984:172] calls "a threshold situation" and "another world." Dostoevsky's years in Siberia were often treated as his passport to Russian soul (see Cherniavsky 1969:204).

At the same time, constriction and suffering were as often said to *preclude* internal vastness: "One hope," Mila concluded, "would be if They took away all borders so normal people could communicate," crowning her mixed imagery with reference to thresholds, the powerful, and normal people. Oleg, like Mila, agreed with Dostoevsky and moved fluidly between contexts to illustrate it:

> Everything went up in a pyramid. It was supposed to be best in Moscow. And where it's better, you know, it's like crap floating in that direction. . . . But as horrible as Moscow is, you go out and there's *something*! What Dostoevsky said is as true now. How can anyone live in this dusty wind?

Omsk, he added, has an empty center. I thought that was rather poetic, but later someone explained why Omsk was the "inverse of other Russian cities." An interval had been maintained around the original fortress for security. When the fortress disappeared, streets were left radiating out from a void that in the early 1990s was partially park with an abandoned heating plant at one end.

---

[4] Dostoevsky 1985a:28, 1, 171: letter to his brother, January 30–February 22, 1854, Omsk.

A Few Thoughts on the Authorities of Body and Dusha

When an acquaintance said I had Russian soul, that "love of Russia came to my body," she did not mean that a spirit had entered an unanimated body. In this case, her use of "body" makes "soul" sound even more real, gives it the authority of the physical world, of nature. This was the case when fear was said to have penetrated deep, into the genes of Omsk exiles and survivors of Stalinism, or when someone described how deep an emotion was by referring to a physical response.[5] Anna Viktorovna said: "A dushevnyi person does not need many words. He feels biocurrents." Grisha called dusha an indescribable, pinching, internal indicator. This kind of "physicality" refers to something extreme and spiritual and commands respect.

Another case where dusha and depth link inexplicability and extremity was when Oleg warned me people wouldn't be able to talk about dusha because "it's inside, in pure feelings." A friend upped the ante: "you can't figure out what's going on here with feelings either, which is why people are turning to ESP, superfeelings." I cited Mila saying that "deeply" or "with dusha" meant "in *all* senses," with one's entire essence. Trying to describe authoritative depth can make people exaggerate.

Ways in which body can be linked to Russian soul is through their mutual pain and in that the flesh has an invisible inside that is one's authoritative center but nevertheless paradoxically unclear and hard to describe. Talal Asad discusses how, in medieval Christianity, body pain was linked to pursuit of Truth: the body is treated as an arena in which truth hides and whence it can emerge. "How art thou to be cured, if thou do not lay bare what things are hidden within thee?" (Asad 1983:306, 311). In one conversation Aleksandr Ivanovich gestured around his chest and called intuition either a channel into dusha or dusha coming out. Both body and soul centers may be associated with truth and and play active roles in imagined transformations.

Spaces of Transformation

A person's spiritual and moral condition is his interior space's hygiene, how things of the outer world pierce him, how his inner world comes out. Feelings may be displayed to their experiencer in a form that somehow implies distance. This may imply that one should somehow get closer to them. One may call a cruel person soulless, but the speaker, hearing his or her

[5] The word *nutro* indicates a visceral center and has the same root as "inside," *vnutri*. It was used in contexts of moral / physical "gut" reaction. Dal''s 1881 dictionary defines *nutro* as: anything's inside; a person's dusha, the spiritual person, his invisible essence; and expanse (*prostor*), "contained within something."

own words' brutality, may shift to the more Christian supposition that a good soul is in there after all, but hidden, locked up, sleeping. People just seem soulless, that is, if you don't care to look deeply enough. A metaphor for dusha offered by ethnographer Sergei Arutiunov indicated this kind of rich center: a book, he said, is paper, glue, ink; but what is its *sense?* "The main thing and simultaneously nothing at all." One may not understand a book right away, he said, but one may come to.

Implied is that "the further in one can look, the more value one sees," that "if something appears in consciousness, it must have emerged from somewhere." This intermingles with beliefs that closed things can and should be opened, that interest, soulfulness, and consciousness open closed things, and that this not only reveals but increases and realizes their value.

Dusha demands conscious display,[6] though its purest form is unclarity or invisibility. Wierzbicka (1989:45) calls "deep" the aspect of dusha of which a person is not aware in him- or herself. However, although the unconscious mind is central to the notion of dusha, extreme depth is problematic. If you can't see any feelings, it's sort of like soullessness.

Zhenia raised his voice. He, his son's godfather, and I sat in his kitchen. "You've seen everything visible. Now I'm going to show you what we have in our dusha. But we crap on it." He appeared, after rummaging, with a cold, spray-painted cardboard frame, a black-and-white mother's brother killed in the Great Patriotic War and, since hanging portraits had gone out of style, stored in an outdoor shed. Holding the portrait but pointing at his own chest, Zhenia said: "*This* is the enigma of the Russian soul." Pointing at his head: "But it's not here." In awareness, I suppose. It was not on the wall either. "Closest to dusha is fatherland, birthplace, isn't it?" he challenged me, referring to the uncle's uniform and death, turning to inform his son, who had wandered in, that he'd have to make a frame for it. Then Zhenia took it into the children's room. The godfather excitedly prompted me: "Look at where he put it!" He put the uncle in the children's glass case. Into focus, hopefully, in them.

Different families' glass cases and different cases in the same home worked differently. A watch I dropped in the children's room and my gifts to them were put in the living-room case, not their own. In this family the living room had different powers from the children's. In placing the uncle in his children's room, Zhenia was trying to uncover or excavate awareness of him in them, to foreground what he felt was too deeply buried in or distanced from dusha. The living-room case seemed more like a way to coopt, appropriate, animate, and socialize unsouled or incoherent things. It was also a heterotopia of liminal things suspended in readiness to be planted, repaired, used up.

[6] Gorer and Rickman's (1949:189–90), Mead's (1955), and other national character statements on Russians' "preoccupation" with the "verbalization of the feelings momentarily possessing them" can be taken in this context.

Dusha, like Taussig's (1987:5,7) "space of death," was where the social imagination kept its metamorphosing images, "a space of transformation" into which one descended to achieve a more vivid sense of life. *Byt* and routine are "soulless" partially because they are "on the surface" and seem to resist change.

A man in his late teens described Omsk life as predetermined, immutable: "A closed space, a narrow path: school, army, family, work." Closedness, emptiness, stagnation were said to make Omsk "unlivable." As in Mila's black-hole speech, life was also "mystically" impossible. The writer Lena reminded me of Dostoevsky's, Mila's, and Oleg's references to air and wind: economic issues, she said, "aren't the problem. It's not not being able to leave, either, because now I can . . . It's something *in the air*. Something mysterious makes it impossible to live here, breaks people."

Showing Our Best Side

If Omsk was a void à la Chaadaev, it was also, if rarely, "nothing" in a mysterious, benevolent sense. Several people mentioned Pasternak's Dr. Zhivago's "wonderful, enigmatic" Russian/Asian brother who was involved with the powers that be and came from Omsk, "out of nowhere" [lit., from under the earth], bearing fairy-tale gifts. When a friend produced a slab of chocolate from a cabinet, he said the same thing I heard in industrial areas: "You didn't see this."

This brings me back to the issue of point of view. If display cases' power hinged on visibility, closed compartments' power was their opacity. Anna Viktorovna's wardrobes issued shoes, papers, linens, vodka, photographs, fine crochet work, sweaters to unravel for yarn, valuables, medicine. She said there were fur pelts there. When toothpaste disappeared from stores Grisha, petulantly, could not believe she had none in there. The opacity of cabinets, root cellars, and wardrobes made them into hats hosts could pull rabbits out of. When Pasha laughed about apartments being small warehouses, it was about how funny it would look all spread out in the open. Supplies were at their most powerful at the moment they appeared.

If You Have Something, Hide It

> The tallest blade of grass, after all, is the one to get cut down.
> Rancour-Laferriere 1995:207

> The Soviet millionaire's principal aim is not to spend money but to conceal it.
> Simis 1982:169

A young man gave a formal definition: "What's on the surface is not what's in dusha and vice versa." Differences between inside and outside can come from protecting one's essence or what is dear. A principle of Soviet life, Andrei said, was "If you have something, hide it." "Don't stick out" averted jealousy, the KGB, the evil eye, and criminals.

It's strange, people said: they can read license plates from ("our" Omsk) satellites, but each of us had to keep secrets. In the 1970s, apartment buildings were built with balconies from which it was illegal to photograph; the landscape they overlooked had secrets in it. Soul is linked to nationalism; patriotism was in the depths. As in the case of Zhenia's uncle's portrait, acknowledgment of war heroism virtually always referred to dusha. Patriotism was also the given reason individual secrecy was demanded in a city where everyone worked in the closed sector or was linked to it by friends and family, and where keeping one's insides in was part of daily life. If the fortress was Omsk's first center, the factories were another.

Andrei said the secrets had been a sacred, patriotic bond, but Kolia, Grisha's friend, said that he had been told to find work anywhere but in a closed factory. A factory worker told me he "gave his soul and part of his health" to a job where he, like everyone, signed vows of secrecy, had security briefings, and could neither go abroad nor have contact with foreigners.

Being different inside from outside is also hypocrisy, as when, as eleven-year-old Vitya told me, someone is decent outside but dirty in his soul. Andrei stressed that many secrets hid not something precious, but abomination, disgrace, disorder, deception. Oleg said the whole System was based on secrets and fear, which led to self-censorship, mistrust, closedness, hypocrisy, betrayal, all forms of being different inside from outside. When Anna Viktorovna tried to stop Grisha from telling me a trivial detail of local corruption, it was also in the interest of "showing our best side," Soviet-style "glossing over grim reality" (Stites 1992:119).

At the Orlovs', glass cases held volumes of literature partially eclipsed by a book on Gagarin, a New Testament, a postcard from me, and portraits of Pushkin, their son, and Zina in the 1960s. This all was upstaged by a plaster rooster and broken clocks. When I moved closer, I froze, noticing Brezhnev flat in the shadows.

Soviets said they wore masks they took off only where official invisibility allowed them to open up. What was in the depths when they opened? Often, unutterable emotion about having been deeply deceived by the profoundly corrupt.[7] Open talk often indexed the value of openness.

If everything was all right, "people would have nothing to say." Lara said dushevnost' was the ability to open up, confide everything you've

---

[7] See Dunham on "deep" talk in novels (1990:80–81). Deep talk is related to open conversation.

accumulated "there" and receive the same sort of treasure in return. Everything that needs to come out is truthlike treasure, even bad things or pain.

This guarded interiority held for power and economics. Circles tightened around the invisible elite, goods and services (Simis 1982:45). People said coverups of industrial disasters could succeed because "it's *Omsk*. Closed city. The mess is easy to hide . . . The KGB, government, and factory directors had privacy to do whatever they wanted." In 1994, I asked Dasha about an odd low construction site. It looked like a metro station, but she called it mysterious. It was supposed to be a factory clubhouse, she said, but when they started building, people saw it was underground and eventually stopped discussing it. Probably it's a shelter, she said, for the elite.

Veiled, power had the right shape to infiltrate dusha. Even now, said an acquaintance in the police force in 1995, all corporate and Mafiia bosses, like the partocrats before them, were invisible, obscured by collectives. No one was visible or accountable. The System was "hard to understand, complicated" because "everything is closed and covered."

One young man implied that depth of discourse itself came from closedness: "Maybe it's not completely fear anymore, maybe someone wants to talk but something *there* still tells him not to. . . . The same political figures want to exploit openness.[8] . . . Also . . . for seventy years everyone was obscure. Now if you talk openly, they still try to find hidden . . . subtext in every word. They break their heads for hours wondering what you meant." Two businessmen proudly discussed, partially with, partially in front of me, using the "skill" of "saying one thing so that you're understood to mean something else" to cheat people.[9] The pleasant intimacy of this devious double-talk is disturbingly similar to soulful communication, as Grisha said, when "you see someone's outside and feel something about his dusha inside."

Secrets moved around without losing secrecy. Petrov, a former partocrat, tallied up Omsk factories for me: petroleum, tires, tractors, chemicals, summing up at 100 percent. Then he paused, grinned a sort of "you know that I know that you know," and added: "But now, of course, everything's open." What Petrov left out he admitted in his oxymoronic metacomment. Our shared secret was that secrets separated us.

---

[8] Openness (*glasnost'*) was sometimes seen as easily manipulated: *Moscow News* in 1992 cited Vadim Bakatin (briefly KGB chief under Yeltsin): "Many sincerely believed it was their duty to cooperate [with the KGB]. . . . All of us were bad. The good ones perished in prison or left. . . . I'm against opening KGB files . . . it plays into the hands of petty politicians."

[9] They defined a half-joking science of deceiving people with this language so murky that even a Soviet with a lot of practice "knows that words mean other than what they mean . . . but what they are hiding . . . is hard to guess" (Sinyavsky 1988:210). See Zinoviev 1990:142.

"Now, of Course, Everything's Open"

> A blank spot (*beloe piatno*) [is] . . . a missing component in
> some . . . order of things, specifically, a blank space on a map. . . .
> In the era of *glasnost'* . . . a suppressed event or name in Soviet
> history. . . . "It is high time that the principles of *glasnost'* were
> fully applied even to the history of the [Communist] Party. It
> must have no blank spots."
>
> Corten 1992:23

A 1983 history of Omsk did not mention the *other* factories any more
than Petrov did. But although residents had always seen them, by 1992
Omsk's blank spots were turning up in the media. My friends began more
clearly enunciating the names of their workplaces. Many who were profiting most from perestroika still strove to preserve the secrecy that gave them
power, but a May 1992 article in the Omsk weekly *Novoe obozrenie* called
the defense industry Omsk's "kernel" and traced the history of military
landholdings in the city center. After "the heavy cross of the defense industry was hung on Omsk's chest" (the honor it received, in other words, was
a cross it bore), military territories inherited from the tsar's army continued
to grow, coming to occupy almost a quarter of Omsk. "A city within a city,"
the article concludes, "is not normal." By 1995, these factories were adver-
tised to foreign investors in English-language brochures.

Whether Omsk people were "open" or "closed" is a useless category for
describing reality, but people liked to argue about it. Some said glasnost
was a destructive hoax unnecessary in Siberia. "You can't send a person farther than Siberia" meant that people there had always had a license to say
anything. The same speakers, however, said that Omsk residents were
closed because of the climate and their "fear genes." One woman said that
when she came to Omsk she had felt that, without foreigners, kindness had
been preserved there. I assumed she was implying that neighborly village
"openness" and "helpfulness" only survives when the circle of participants
is limited. But, she went on, Omsk was the one place her uncle had refused
to give interviews, because of the censorship. "Omsk people are exhaust-
ingly closed and guarded."

Many who said the Soviet system had cramped their internal life were
nevertheless ambivalent about openness. At a 1994 reunion of friends,
Grisha proposed a toast, suggesting we meet every year: "even underground
if we have to—*it's* more interesting that way, anyway." The day he talked
about violins, he said: "It's better if I have to hold some things inside!"
Then he added metaphors of membranes, electronics, doors, and pockets:

> The mystery of your internal world lives inside. You don't want to bring it out
> of its soulful membrane. . . . The mystery can be good. . . . There are also mys-

teries that destroy your dushevnyi harmony. Some people's dushi are not where nature put them, inside where, like that light on your tape recorder there or on some electronic equipment made in Omsk, it tells you things. They say Russians have "wide-open" souls [other expressions are "one's whole soul is on the outside" and "on the street"]. Well, a person's soul *cannot* be thrown open. Unfortunately and fortunately. If it were open, we'd lose our internal world that forms there, that we nurture there, that we can't express. If I turned out all my pockets and walked around, I'd have *nothing*!

Irina said: "Dusha is about my insides, my sufferings, my conscience, my love; dusha is not for display." Tiutchev's poem *Silentium* (1830, tr. Paul Friedrich, 1994) treats dusha's inexplicability and what Wierzbicka calls a tragedy of dusha: it is alive, but only inside.

But opening the closed was a policy and a fashion that took many traditional forms. An emigrant who went back to Russia after a few years in America said the biggest change was that "You can *see* everything! It's all visible!" A 1996 Internet page announced that, imitating the Hermitage's new policy of displaying what had been unseen and opening what had been closed, the Ethnographic Museum had unlocked its storeroom of treasures to reveal its collection's pearls.

Asking big questions and expressing heroic willingness to suffer or display passion, confessions, and revelations still proved one had a soul.[10] On January 23, 1991, I saw an amazing contrast: Moscow TV news was—nothing, really. A mention of the Persian Gulf. A note that Vilnius was calm (when it had *not* been calm there had been *no* news of it).[11] No mention of the currency crisis that had thrown every household into emergency mode. But on the Leningrad channel, the sportscaster, pale with grief and fury, gave a short, expressionless report and launched into a lament for "our poor, miserable money."

A 1992 review of the film *The Russia We Lost* lauds director Stanislav Govorukhin for not aspiring to "American-style" objectivity in his investigation of "the murder of Russia." The film claims that Russian history's mutation into Soviet history "flipped dusha over." "Passion, evidence of . . . heartache, are part of Russian tradition . . . Russia is an enigmatic, unknown country; which is why . . . we live so stupidly." Govorukhin, the review says, "tries to answer questions about who we are, what our mother/land Russia is." But some people, it adds, "do not wish to experience the pain of meticulously hidden facts being made public."

---

[10] A prime example was the TV show *Six Hundred Seconds* (see Stites 1992:190). A November 1992 newspaper article reviewed the first volume of a series, *Unknown Russia: The Twentieth Century*, as heroic. It contained materials from the Moscow Municipal Archives where, reportedly, 90 percent of over eight million files had been sealed: "The authors . . . expose . . . the real situation in a suffering Russia."

[11] The Vilnius situation in January 1991, mentioned in Chapter 5.

Revelatory perestroika reporting was in marked contrast to Soviet news's bland, optimistic party lines and to censored prerevolutionary journalism. It was also increasingly influenced by Western fashion. At this junction, dusha itself became an issue in the media, as evident in examples from the press I have included in various chapters. Clichés appeared in revitalized and newly discovered meanings that ran parallel to their increasingly ironic use.

During and after glasnost some called Stalin's favorite 1949 film, *Kuban Cossacks,* an evil mask obscuring reality. Others remembered it as a ray of happiness in a dark time (Stites 1992:121). This is a classic clash between tactics for achieving soul.

The man who saved Russia in World War II also raped her, even targeting peasant Russia. Another 1949 film, *The Fall of Berlin,* repeats that Stalin gave us life, gave birth to us. Emotion was coopted, penetrated, and informed; life force was implied to be as well.[12] That "I" / "my mother and aunts" / "everyone" cried when Stalin died was remarkably often given as proof that the Soviets had corrupted even kinship-level feeling.

A young man said that the fact that Omsk residents had been shut off from world culture was both good and bad. People who said their eyes were finally open after lifetimes of deceit were repelled by blatant display of ugly truths. In the money chapter I mention the new, "obscene" nakedness of cash. If, as in a previous epigraph, Soviet millionaires' principal aim was "not to spend money but to conceal it," that was not the case with the later-1990s New Russians. "Not everything should be on display," one woman said. "Things are worse now. All the filth that was illegal is now legal. People in power rob us openly now. Formerly they hid it. Nothing is holy." "Holy" implies that if something bad cannot be eradicated, it can at least be suppressed.[13] Many blamed glasnost (which began, of course, with revelations about Stalin) for their pain, as if consciousness of their betrayal was worse than the crimes themselves,[14] as if it was that consciousness that had spat in dusha.

OLEG: To survive, people had to be like that.

DALE: Like what?

[12] Sinyavsky (1988:104) discusses how "When Stalin died, many people thought *everything* had died . . . Stalin had become a synonym . . . for life." See Glazov (1985:30) on the common people's love of Stalin, despite collectivization. Cf. Kempe 1992:199.

[13] Ivanits (1992:39) mentions the many euphemistic names peasants had for the Devil, saying that peasants feared "the devil would appear the moment his name were uttered. . . . The most frequently used designation for 'devil' . . . related to the magic line . . . the unclean force cannot cross."

[14] I do not mean to diminish the experienced effect of the crimes themselves: in 1939, Ol'ga Berggol'ts described in her diary how during her imprisonment, "they extracted my soul, poked in it with dirty fingers, spat in it, sullied it, and then they shoved it back in" (Hellbeck 1998).

OLEG: Suppressed, locked up. In Moscow they had to try not to talk soul-to-soul [*po dusham*]. A person opened up only in familiar company.... But on the periphery, people stayed simple. Siberians—they spat on it all.

DALE: "Farther than Siberia—"

OLEG: "You can't send them." And now we're sick, simply sick.

Andrei said "We were taught that the Party was 'honor, mind.[15] When all this started to come out, inside, in dusha ... [there was] pain.... An abyss appeared, and I left the Party." Oleg often bemoaned current events by gesturing and saying: "In the depths of dusha it's offensive." A question asked was "Why, for the sake of what [did we do it all]?" What is left "underneath," now that it's clear we were deeply deceived? Important things had been rather literally undermined.

Opening, sharing, making explicit any closed thing, in some contexts supremely soulful, in the same and other situations risks injury to dusha as loss of what had lived there. "Where has it all gone?" was a related lament, not only, as in Mila's words, about spiritual energy, but about commodities, natural resources, and fruits of Soviet era enthusiasm, all spirited away into the black hole of someone else's depths by his or her profound deceit.

Another way in which glasnost was performed traditionally is that secrets could be gifts. Gifts are from dusha, so secrets are good ones. That's where they are kept. Anna Viktorovna, reminiscing about how Omsk changed during the war, mentioned the tobacco factory, then had to go answer the doorbell. As she reentered the kitchen, passing me, she leaned and whispered: "and all that rocket [missile] business." Maps drawn for me generously and unnecessarily featured the KGB building. Rapid recitals about Omsk's blank spots were proffered alongside a family secret, a valuable rumor, confession of an emotion, condensed milk, or a souvenir.

Near a village, cutting grass for the cows, I was teasingly called a spy. "Sure, the CIA needs photos of empty steppe." "No. Of the missile silos right *there*."

An old anti-technological theme of Russian dusha, dormant during the Soviet era, reappeared. Williams (1970:580–82) notes, "Gogol had hinted that ['Russian soul'] referred to the ... peasant ... keeping deep within himself that which the gentry was willing to sell." In 1992, newspapers such as *Komsomolskaya Pravda* indicted the Soviets with the same sin. A 1992 TV show proclaimed that the Soviet state had almost killed Russia, and the state's project of electrification, the Volga. Ecological disaster was formulated in the press and conversation as the elite pillaging Russia, "the rape of Russian soul."

---

[15] Andrei omits the word he refers to in this Brezhnev-era slogan attributed to Lenin: "The Party is the honor, mind, *and conscience* of our epoch." Conscience was often called synonymous with dusha; it also hints from inside at moral truths. Other references to this slogan appear in Chapter 11. Paul Easton (1989:50) reports graffiti to the effect that the rock group Aquarium was the "mind and conscience of Soviet youth."

Depth of Meaning and the Meaning of Depth

> Men are regarded as riches enclosed in a worthless shell, and the
> more deeply we penetrate within them, the greater is the treasure
> we discover. But what if there were no treasure?
>
> Michel Tournier

Characteristics of earlier Russian soul—such as strong feelings, the inexpressible, the unlimited, dualism, hyperbole, spontaneity, the unpredictable, the immeasurable, protest, and a sense of mission and potential—were present in 1990s forms, and were revitalized and altered using depth. Dusha implies transcendence and depth through various predications and practices. One involves shared experience. Another touches on suffering, complaining, and ambivalence. Progress still implies [urgency of] penetration toward or emergence from some center. Other predications and practices that imply depth have to do with classifying and treating things:

- as invisible and otherwise opaque, unclearly or incompletely perceived or perceptible, unattainable or distant;
- hyperbolically—things are construed as complex, inexhaustible, vast, intense (especially emotionally), or otherwise infinite; or
- as inexplicable—things defy clear understanding as they are internally contradictory, irrational, antirational, or dual. This includes "not-of-this-world" or carnivalized forms.[16]

The resulting early 1990s depth refused to be confined by spatial definition, a metaphor of scale that vaguely, romantically gestures at infinity. Like Mila's black-hole monologue, dusha weaves a coherence of incoherence out of images of emptiness, failure, partiality, communitas, and "chaos,"[17] a fabric thick with spatially lived "nodes of interconnection" (Turner 1969:42–43).

One mission of "soul," if I may play on Fernandez's (1986:11) "mission of metaphor," is to give form to inchoate pronouns. Dusha clearly uses the form of the inchoate for this. The deep is a culturally sanctioned kind of authoritative inchoate. Moral battlefields and physical spaces are understood in terms of depth. If, as Helms (1988:64) writes, space may express "contrasts between the known, visible, familiar, socially controlled, and morally ordered heartland, and the strange, invisible, uncontrolled, disordered, and morally extreme . . . lands 'beyond,' " in the case of Russian national identity, the heartland itself is strange, invisible, uncontrolled, disordered, and morally extreme.

[16] Bakhtin (1984:157) calls these means for a "generalization in depth" without which life's "most profound layers" could not be located and expressed.

[17] See Fernandez (1986:181, 206–7, passim) and Turner (1969:42–43). I continue this in Chapter 13.

These rhetorical tools were also opportunistically used to reproduce a good internal soul that survives despite external (social) evil. Many value continua strung between poles of inside and outside conflate (see Fernandez 1986:10). Movements between them were seen as *manifestations from somewhere* and *departures to somewhere*.[18] This formal similarity is part of what made tropes of depth so overdetermined and important.

Spatial tropes get their meanings in context, and so, with some accumulation of different contextual associations, they end up as much less clear but much more highly charged images. For example, high and deep, like inner and distant, are not always simply opposed, partially because not only "deep" and "inner," but height and distance, in their ways, are also associated with what is seen as more essential (as Lena said, "dusha is always above everyday life, somewhere *there. Byt* brings it down. . . . to some sort of pettiness"). All four of these terms are multiply associated with essences and depth. Authors stumble on and play with these toys: Erofeev (1990) writes that, since some stores sell alcohol until 11 P.M., if you are not utter scum, by evening you can always rise to some sort of negligible abyss. Dostoevsky wrote that a higher realism would plumb dusha's depths, what Bakhtin (1984:288) called moving into the depths of the heights of consciousness: "The depths . . . are simultaneously its peaks (up and down in the cosmos and in the microworld are relative)."

Habits of imagery related to "alive" centers' openness and closedness show a complicity with dead things. Conflation of depth-related experiences from different contexts into one static, cumulative model, dusha, seems to reveal negative things cohabiting with and dirtying positive ones.[19] A key to soul's complicity with its enemies was its internalizing. Ideally, as much as possible should be taken to heart. Good (one's sense of self, intimacy, cherished information) was hidden. Bad (moral flaws, accidents, corruption, other sources of wealth and power) was hidden. Things were unsaid because they defied formulation or were precious or private, because of fear of persecution, because of stinginess. What was hard to say was deep. Shameful and precious were alternate forms of the sacred. People were united by the fact and action of depth.

Soul also externalizes. It displays, opens, increases, tries to speak. Paradoxically, this may entail sacrificing its definitive mystery. Yet the "transformation of suspicion into knowledge" is always incomplete; "Man's condition is a permanent sickness . . . because he cannot admit the whole truth" (Asad 1983:296–97, 306). The stronger a display of depth, the greater are

---

[18] These are not symmetrical. Consciousness of something's departure is nevertheless a kind of consciousness of the thing.

[19] Although Wierzbicka (1989, 1992) sees the mixing of dusha's meanings in speech as important, and that "things" in dusha can be good or bad, she does not examine the myriad, fascinating accounts, varieties, or pragmatics of sleeping, corrupted, alien, or polluted dushi.

efforts to tear aside the veil and reveal the Platonic true reality.[20] But trying to catch secrets and pursuing soul is falling into their trap. Such hunts are sabotaged.

As Fernandez (1986:10) writes, a clever man can always turn a continuum to his advantage. But such advantages are often double-edged: mixing depth metaphors and internalizing or externalizing in hopes of redemption or progress also provide for the filthiest entering into the sanctuary of the purest. Dirty laundry and skeletons were treated as pearls, exacerbating people's sense that pearls had been cast before swine.

Noticing soul hedging like this made me suspicious of depth. Just as I realized it would be in bad faith to describe other worlds, I tried to resist being seduced by Omsk's and soul's secrets and other depths. I tried to stay on the surface. Containers have facts or scraps of social or personal litter at the bottom, or nothing, or a deeper level. Anyway, as Boym (1994:146) writes, the "secret" is a "fetishized useless souvenir, preserved only for the sake of the game."

Depth is conventional. Depth and centrality are the terms in which many things have power and authority. These values of depth and centeredness are reproduced in everyday practice. Trying to bring things out and elucidate them makes more depth, recapitulates the same forms. I realized that I would be complicit and reproduce them too (since my culture shares this metaphysics to a great extent) unless I could treat deep things as ethnometaphysical, as results of a *belief, not a truth,* that surfaces are explained, governed, determined by, and/or epiphenomenal to what is underlying.

---

[20] See Harries (1968:3, 49, 109, passim) on attempts to "lift the veil." Hellbeck (1998) writes that the Stalin era project of revealing and thereby purifying oneself "depended on the presence of impurities to be overcome. . . . Diarists kept producing new sites of impurity to be exposed."

Story
A Second Soul

In the Generosity story I wrote that although Grisha's soul was drawing him elsewhere, in his soul he knew he belonged in Omsk. It was becoming clear that people had more than one soul.

I began to notice a sort of Soviet caution alternating with openness, straight gestures with sideways glances. And any adult knew when to clam up. Except me.

Oleg clammed up by changing the subject, saying, "We'll talk about that another time." Of course, we did *not* talk about it another time. He said people were afraid because of ignorance as to how certain parts of the System, especially "certain government organs," worked, and that he was less afraid because he knew them from the inside. He also, however, talked at length about the millions killed and the importance of individual caution in protecting friends and family, how that caution and ability to be closed was "in our genes by now. . . . You go over to someone's house, you think: 'We have so many good people!' You go out onto the street, they're completely different. Maybe it's that self-preservation instinct—there were harsh times." "What times?" I asked, provocatively. "What times? Jeez—When there—they say—these repressions. Everyone wants dushevnost', but fear came, people clammed up. You see it in public transportation."

One evening I was at a party. I had met Leonid on my first trip to Omsk and was increasingly classifying him with a few others I had met who could make me strangely verbose, calmly listening while adding nothing. Leonid was also very interested in differences between America and long-closed Omsk, and several times during the preceding months I had casually mentioned to him my feeling of being under surveillance. Each time, he artlessly tripped over arms and legs to change the subject. In short, after a few drinks, I told him how uncomfortable this made me. Drunk, he confusedly answered that it happened because he was very inexperienced at these things. That he was uncomfortable with the subject, that is. We embraced warmly. Twice that evening, clowning KGB, he saluted me across the room. I called him the next evening and asked if he had been offended; he said he hadn't been.

I bumped into him weeks later. In an efficient, businesslike way, with no pretext of genuine interest, he began extracting information as to when I was leaving, what I had been doing, where, with whom. I felt cornered and lied.

I met him again. We smiled, embraced. I did not trust him. When he joked and wished me well I felt reserve. Then I realized: to express reserve was even more unpleasant than the reason for it. It was preferable to make room. Be "open" nevertheless, dushevno style.

What does that mean? Well, to approach him openly, unrestrainedly, "as a human being," with "respect" and "joy." Mistrust becomes a silent, formal limit; otherwise, you are completely open, with all the possibilities and rewards of openness, but for that moment and within limits.

It's like opening a sort of second dusha so you can interact with not wholly trusted people "openly," with dusha. As a basic, decent, interactive behavior, what was required was not any other form of warmth or cordiality, but exactly dushevnost', with its implied everything and its implied depth. A form of "being human" with people one mistrusts but with whom one must work arises. It is hypocrisy and it is religiously hopeful. One wants to admit that we are all imperfect, and that under any circumstances we must (hope to) recognize a fellow man, a live soul. The soulful desire to see soul becomes continuous with hypocrisy and two-facedness.

I return to this. This just shows the clumsy way I struggled with an aspect of the enigmatic, "bottomlessly" vast Soviet soul.

CHAPTER ELEVEN

If You Want to Know a Man, Give Him Power

The essence of the soul is power . . . power, soul, and life become interchangeable categories.

Riviere 1987:426

In 1994 two girls told me about a practice currently strictly observed among children: if they saw a black Volga (the Soviet-era car of powerful regional party members) they had to make a fist and hold it, no matter what, until they saw a person wearing glasses.

Power was presented as really dangerous, as making people soulless: not only not Russian, but not human, and, as I came to see, not "normally" alive. Souls and natures were felt to be on the line in power-related battles of images. I use stories to look at how power is imagined and at the larger lives of other elements I have discussed. Where does power seem to come from? What are its properties? I touch on relations between superiors and subordinates, conditions of soul from various points of view, masks, and ethnic images that parallel those of the powerful.

A Struggle about Soul

Retired seamstress Maria Fëdorovna had Masha and me over for dinner. Maria Fëdorovna's daughter told us about her alcoholic boss, who did no work, got ten thousand a month, and told them, "I have squashed and will continue squashing you." Then Masha talked about her boss's pathological crudeness and cheating lack of respect. She called him mentally ill (*dushevno bol'noi*). He certainly has no kul'tura, answered Maria Fëdorovna.

Maria Fëdorovna's friend, a highly positioned bureaucrat, had also been invited. Masha told me, explaining the cross-class friendship, "They're warm and simple; he *rests* there." Masha kept on badmouthing her despotic, stupid boss after Alexei Stepanovich arrived. He responded by changing the subject, trying to establish a warm, positive mood, reciting poems, proposing toasts to striving, yearning, dusha's highest value; to the way dusha tears at its chains. He told jokes and complimented Russian women, trying, in an odd alternation between soulful *intelligent* and rigid partocrat, to try to keep the atmosphere dushevnyi, to, in fact, establish his soulfulness. Masha's tirades were also, of course, passionate and perfectly within the traditions of dushevnost'. To the end of creating warmth, everyone at some point told a glowing story from the past about sincere gatherings and conversations, trying to illuminate the struggling table and unite the participants in one version of dusha. But Masha's and my presence did seem to keep Alexei Stepanovich from resting.

Bright, cheerful Stalin-era culture, according to many, had been a mask, a system of mystification, an immense "engine of fraud" masking horrors (Stites 1992:95–96).[1] People mentioned hypocritical masks and dehumanizing, isolating masks. Zina Orlova said that with certain coworkers she could never sit like *people*; the mask was always there. But if Alexei Stepanovich's approach was of a genre often called soulless hypocrisy, it was also a way to invoke and activate soul.

As we stood crushed together on the bus home, Masha described Alexei Stepanovich's complexity. His dusha might well have not existed, but look, it's trying to survive: "He has two faces, one for the powerful, and one he shows here. Our director at work has only one face. I think he has no second one." That is, others of rank had allegedly identified with their masks and had been gobbled up by them, but Alexei Stepanovich could still sit with these kind, talented, humble people and rest. That itself was significant. Sitting and resting were usually understood as "together against the boss," the System, Fate; one felt outside of and in defiance of power relations. Once, for example, as Masha, I, and friends sat drinking tea in their workshop, I suggested that their supervisor be invited to join us. "No. That's just not done."

A year later, that supervisor stumbled upon us "sitting." He began to comment on my friends' laziness, but, seeing me, limited himself to a dry remark about the imported German crackers on the table. Masha invited him to join us and intoned the standard "Be our guest, Lev Alexandrovich." He declined. After he closed the door, someone joked that he would fire them. Masha said no; "They're afraid of us."

Lev Alexandrovich's cracker comment challenged the friends' dushevnost' (how could they afford imported luxuries?). Through the crackers he challenged a dushevnost' (their sitting) he would have liked to attack more directly. After this ensued a parody of usual hospitality ritual, "a world inside out," as Bakhtin (1984:173) calls it, in which traditional plots

---

[1] See Dunham (1990:150) on the cultural politic of "soft pedaling of problems"; see Mauss 1985 and Fogelson 1982 on mask imagery in contexts of "differentiated social status."

changed meaning: my friends asked him to join us, as if they meant it (ot dushi); Lev Alexandrovich declined as if their offer had been sincere.[2] In fact, he had had to decline; he would have been out of place. He had had no choice but *not* to sit. His lack of choice was itself a loss of authority. In addition, he had been forced to admit to a power-related lack of respect for my friends (as we have seen, refusal to drink with normal people implies that one considers oneself too high). Lev Alexandrovich challenged my friends' dushevnost' but was forced to behave like a soul-impaired person himself, through their deft revitalization of hierarchy etiquette, "responding in a warm, comradely way" "even if the power treats you coldly" (Sinyavsky 1988:212).

Revenge was had, however, in exactly the same idiom. The director moved to distance this feisty collective from opportunities to make dusha. He hired "his people" and dispersed the friends, some to jobs they did not love. This foregrounded power relations, instilled lack of trust, made life uncozy. It limited people's ability to commune (*obshchat'sia*): new coworkers might be informers, so people could not talk freely, and crossing between shops put them at risk of meeting the director or his flunkies.

A World Inside Out

Russian folk Yuletide mummery, in which people displayed demons, devils, and witches and ritually interacted with their world, was, Veletskaia (1992:62) claims, a Christian-era transformation of proto-Slavic ancestor images into an "unclean force [or spirit]" (*nechistaia sila*). When I participated in an event in which mumming came up against the entities that "held power over life" in 1992, I saw again, among other things, how worlds could "turn inside out" in subtle, spontaneous, contextually specific parodies.

It was Orthodox New Year's Eve, Old New Year, January 13, 1992. Both old and new New Years had reportedly been celebrated ever since the January 1918 changeover to the Gregorian calendar. The village I was visiting, largely Ukrainian ethnic descendants of resettled peasants, with Russians, German ethnics, Kazakhs, and others, was part of a State farm. Emma, a friend of the woman I was visiting, borrowed me for an evening to "show me a tradition" she was trying to revitalize, in which revelers walked from house to house, singing and demanding food and drink. We layered parodies of traditional costume over our coats. One man dressed as a woman; Emma dressed as a man. We rouged on big cheeks and popped out into the driving snow with three bottles of vodka, one for each home in which Emma thought we would spend time.

---

[2] See Bateson 1974:53 on how, by saying the opposite of what he means, the little dog stopped the big dog.

In the first home, Inna, Emma's good friend, served meat pirozhki, chicken, sausage, tomatoes, pickles, and more, then meat soup, cake, and candies. As we were supposed to be going to many houses, it seemed especially excessive. She periodically complained that we did not "respect the hostess's labor." At these words Emma would comically accelerate her eating: "I'll stuff myself and die young!" "I'd rather blow up than let something good go to waste!" "Let my guts burst; it won't show under my shirt!"

The intimacy-generating maxim that "at table you can say anything" was, if not fulfilled, indexed by the recital of "irreverent" (Paxson 1999) political and alcohol-related chastushki.

> Perestroika is my mother
> Breaking even is my dad
> Fuck that kind of family
> I'd rather be an orphan.

> At sunrise the rooster sings
> At noon, Pugachëva[3] does.
> The liquor store is closed,
> Gorbachev has the keys.

The men discussed meat. They had found out that they couldn't sell their own cows, already defrosted for the occasion on the kitchen floor, leading to discussion of by whom and how they were being screwed (city people? the powerful?) and of the disadvantages of private farming (the State farm was about to become a corporation). One man asked me what Jesus' first commandment was. My answer clearly did not matter. "No!" he interrupted, "It's 'Worship no gods other than yourself first.'" Another man said he had it wrong, you're supposed to worship only *God*. The first shot back: "We always worshiped a god: the tsar, Lenin, the State-farm director . . . all a sin, it turns out." After two hours we had drunk all our vodka and more provided by Inna and her husband. We put on our coats and costumes again and, joined by Inna, hit the road.

People never wore shoes indoors. The only exceptions I saw were a tragic situation I mentioned in Chapter 5 and here. We drunkenly violated home after home in grey felt boots caked from the blizzard that was blowing the village waist-deep with steppe snow. At one house we were received warmly, but the family had clearly already retired. They poured us shots of clear alcohol and brought bowls of cold cooked varenniki (Ukrainian dumplings filled with cabbage, meat, white cheese, cherry, berry, or potato). Another home did not answer our taps at the window for a long time. Then a smoky room of young men looked amused but mostly embarrassed as we burst in yelling songs. Further in were their wives. But someone was miss-

---

[3] Alla Pugachëva, a popular singer.

ing, a sign was given, something was understood; there was no lack of politeness, but we were outside again.

At another house the young couple was friendly, but joyful approval of our noise transformed the face of their babushka in a goat-down scarf. Next door, a tired middle-aged couple was a little confused. They hurriedly brought out more and more food, though we said we were full. Emma, drunk, overexuberant reviver of tradition and obnoxious parody of a guest, took a bowl of little nut-shaped pastries filled with sweet cream, transcendently rare in that time of shortage, and dumped them in her pocket. Things got strained and awkward. She quietly took four or five little nuts back out and put them in the bowl, and soon invoked the traditional brevity of such visits.

At some point we entered the home of a Kazakh coworker who, in a different language of hospitality, beaming, sprinkled us with an entire rare bottle of cologne. My companions began yelling for me to say something in English. I was tired of this sort of thing and refused to display my "accent," as they called it. I reached into my bag to get tiny souvenirs instead, but Inna, whom I had met only hours before, stopped me with an iron hand. Drunk, she allowed herself this. I realized I was myself a gift. Gifts I gave were gifts *through* them. My gift-giving was their business. I was annoyed when we left. Emma, trying to calm me down, whispered that they had needed to prove I was American because those people were Kazakhs, Asians, different; "They're so used to deception," she said, "they didn't believe us."

My friends' fluid movement between Russian and Ukrainian only partially masked from me the birth of a whispered, debated plan to present ourselves at the house of the State-farm director, the man earlier listed with Lenin and the tsar as a false idol. Some clearly felt more drawn there than others. I knew that "Bosses do not drink with subordinates," which was violated between midnight and one.

We banged and entered. Visiting family members were drunk and partially introduced. A man in his fifties had his head down on a table. Emma entered. He looked up. She boisterously, mock-rudely asked, "Who're you?"

MAN: I'm from Sakhalin.

EMMA: From *Sakhalin*? Where'd all the red fish go?

MAN: My mother died two months ago—

EMMA: Oi, forgive me, forgive me, I didn't know, I didn't know, I asked, I heard you were from Sakhalin, and just—"Where's the red fish"—

[silence]

How old are you?

MAN: Mama was—you understand—

EMMA: Please forgive me, forgive me, forgive me.

"Red fish" refers to several kinds of salmon, cold-smoked and sliced as an appetizer. Emma's blurted red fish joke referred to shortages of formerly available delicacies. She implied that the guest, being from the far east source of salmon and being, presumably, powerful, must be privy to what was *really* going on, why life had gotten so rotten. Emma's questions, aimed at his complicity in the System, were derailed by his inappropriate references to his mom. Sakhalin's sentence fragments demanded Emma acknowledge his humanity. Having no choice, she indicated her willingness by exaggerated contrition and a rapid reenactment of the conversation, rewinding, reframing it as forgivable, just her clumsy drunk ejaculations, yet, in the process, she *repeated* it all and came to roost on an odd thing to ask a powerful older man: "How old are you?" as if he was an orphaned boy. Each of them, under alcohol's auspices, claimed the right to be broadly irresponsible. Each, as did Masha with Lev Alexandrovich, struggled precisely, armed with their best dushevnost'.

We sat. Drinking began with a toast which, although common, was *very* odd for a first toast and here perfectly outrageous, though no one seemed to care. Emma proposed: "If we have enemies, may they leave us alone!" Everyone knows stronger forms that humbly request that enemies drown or otherwise expire horribly or disgracefully, and are always in (general or specific) reference to hierarchy. Such toasts classify those sitting as on the same side, together. But here, being so marked, it insinuated the exact opposite: that those present were not on the same side.

As in the workshop, people feigned community and groveling respect. The toastmaster's prerogative was used to exact consensus on a private agenda in a moment of ritual dusha. Things were said insincerely, establishing everything as possible inversion or perversion of its usual sense. Things said sincerely were framed as jokes or misdirected. Clichés and dead metaphors, suddenly revitalized, blinked around to see what had awakened them, revealing features of the situation and their own indirection.[4] People resorted to Russian soul's commonplaces, touching base before bouncing off again into dogfights over divergent implications of dusha: "For a Russian, 'Esenin,' that says it all" was unanimously supported, but talk was, as when Lev Alexandrovich entered the workshop, exactly *not* open. Hospitable gestures were made, but meant contrary and subtler things. Veiling was itself meaningful.[5] The right to say anything at table and when drunk was transformed into an equally proverbial tendency in worker-boss relations, to say nothing ("We're silent, they're silent").

The room had become long and full of unfamiliar costumed people; the director's family was confused. A woman clung to me, fawning, peering,

[4] See Coleman (1996) on how "performance reassembles contingent possibilities, bringing forth new and surprising facts."

[5] "As Luke Gibbons argues, . . . the veiling of reference, as well as its multiplicity and complexity . . . gives . . . texts their ability to convey powerful and complex emotions" (Coleman 1996:3).

babbling German, beaming, stroking my hand and arm. Not drunk enough to reciprocate, I offered what turned out to be my last souvenir. She asked unsteadily if the color suited her. As the sloppy commotion continued, the table's far end began assaulting me in tough waves, a barrage from Inna's eyes. I had given to the wrong woman, and now I had to give something else. I eventually gave something of my own to a woman indicated just as nonverbally as the one across from the bewildered director. The air immediately cleared. The director's wife presented me with a plastic box ribbed with flowers that altered queasily with the box's angle to my eyes.

As we were feeling our way to getting up, more revelers burst in. Emma started yelling, allegedly good-humoredly, that we were there first, so *we* were the bosses (*nachal'niki*). They were intruders and couldn't sit. She invoked a rule (made up) that since we were first and had come before midnight (we hadn't), we were the hosts (*My khoziaeva*). They left. Emma had similarly usurped the first toast, which usually belonged to the host or his or her designate. My friends aggressively appropriated traditions and imposed them on what the media and everyday conversations called "the heirs to feudal power." They were empowered to do this by their ability to generously materialize a live American out of a blizzard. Emma showed the director that if the State farm was host to me, *she* was that host. Then she used this power to turn away rival guests to his home.[6]

The woman clinging to me stuck all the way to the door, where I was finally introduced to the director. We tried to have a respectful exchange, but my companions must have had reasons to drag me outside. Going out into the storm, I was overwhelmed by the detailed, brutal, silent messages I had received from Inna, by Russian soul's iron hand, and even more by a whiff of the nature of this power. *Vlast'* is power; *vlasti*, the authorities;[7] they were closer to identical than I was used to. It was bottomless, and bottomless didn't mean anything. Any sense of "sincerity" "under" "masks" was undermined. It was masks all the way down, and they mixed with, sometimes *were* sincerities.

I spent weeks perplexedly bugging Omsk friends to help me figure that night out. I even brought up the topic while sitting and having a drink with an acquaintance and her colleagues, whom I had just met. After I told my State-farm story, the familiar, dreaded paralysis came over the table, and the air got slow and less transparent. Words became sounds in the thick space. Maybe there were some bosses there, I don't know. My hostess broke in coquettishly, saying she could not believe all that made more of an impression

---

[6] In Chapter 7 I discuss the fluidity of who was host, how the entity as representative of which one offered gifts could shift. Emma had allowed Inna to be my hostess, but here she did not relinquish me.

[7] This dates from the 1920s; *vlast'* meant both state power and its exercise by the Party (Fitzpatrick 1992:1).

on me than did her singing, which I had recently heard. I grabbed the dusha-restoring mention of song.

Bakhtin (1984:155) describes how, in Dostoevsky's "deeply carnivalized" "Nasty Story," a man drops in on a lowly subordinate's wedding feast, where he gets drunk, and how everything that follows is built on scandalous inappropriateness. Bakhtin describes disrespect for money, other debasements, boundary transgressions, dethroning, violations of routine, profanation, blasphemy, absurdity, disorder, parodies where things are reborn through inversion, parodies on sacred texts and sayings, scandals, inappropriate speeches, and toying with established norms, "ultimate questions," and utopian images. These all fit an aesthetic and genre of behavior I heard called "very Russian" and "for the soul." This sort of parodic, expansive, ironic dusha includes a healthy dose of violation of everyday warm, supportive dusha.

On Old New Year, as in Dostoevsky, drinking was involved in transgressing boundaries, violating routine, and challenging the hegemony of a world felt to coerce people into living by its laws. There were grotesque costumes, cross-dressing (see Ivanits 1992:8), exaggeration; parodies, inversions, violations of purity. Bakhtin (1984:123) says that in such carnivalized situations the usual distance between people is suspended. This was the case on Old New Year, but, although I saw creative manipulation of cultural elements and meanings by people who, as Dostoevsky says his Gambler does, "rebel against the authorities while fearing them," I saw nothing I would call a new mode "counterposed to socio-hierarchical relationships" (ibid.:171).

Deception, Respect, Despotism

Many of the Soviet elite were children of peasants or urban working class. The old Russian expression *Iz griazi v kniazi*, "Out of the dirt and into princes," refers to those who rise from humble beginnings and forget them. When I told her my story, Mila remarked that in villages they know those in power had come out of the dirt and into princedom, come up from exactly where they themselves were still stuck. That's crushing, Mila said. Makes them drink.

Despite the city's size, many Omsk residents could recite family and career histories of prominent persons (whose parents, grandparents, or great-grandparents had lived next door or worked with one's own). If the regional powerful had forgotten where they came up from, others had not. Although just being American, then and there, had a lot of power that I rarely wanted, I once, at a banquet, unintentionally used it to "remind" a man where he had come up from. When I sat with worker friends rather than at my place at the VIP table, the guest of honor kept coming over, sentimentally saying that *these* were the people he'd always felt the most kinship to, this was where he *came* from.

What sort of path was this transformation from dirt into princes seen as being? How was it traveled? By whom?

People insisted that all bosses must be dishonest, or they would have never climbed up there. "No one open and honest like our Grisha," Nadia added, "could get a position like that."

When I asked "what qualities bring a person to power?" Andrei said: "That's an art. Unknown to us. Maybe we don't know . . . The entire partocracy . . . said one thing from the podium and behind the scenes did the opposite. They said 'work honestly' and were dishonest." Zina continued: "People only come to power with help, some sort of machinations or cronyism. . . . If you get into power on the principle of one hand washing the other, you go up the ladder."

Zina, like many people, could list every Communist Party step in local and national figures' trips up the ladder of power, not rising by virtue of talent or intelligence but, as Zina said, by riding up on bottles opportunely set down, at each step catering to narrow-minded, power-hungry, petty, stupid, uncultured bosses, until they themselves "sat up there, utterly incompetent." Her teenage children could also recite "how one gets to be a boss": "You start as an honest pioneer—." It was not a matter of having talent, Zina said. Opinions would tie you down. These people are good at carrying out orders. They fall in, adapt, and for that they'll "make a killing" (*zhrat'*, the word for animals' eating) in our System.

Zina described the humiliation. Bosses see subordinates as bugs to squash; they try to break them. Andrei said, "Bosses always suppress. That is so deeply ingrained." Words based on crushing or squashing (*dav-*) were especially common in talk about power. When Maria Fëdorovna's daughter's boss said that he had squashed and would keep squashing them, he echoed grammar-book type exercises in tense. Play of this sort predates Communism: Kuprin's antisemitic letter chants that the Jew "has always run, is running, and will run" after his Zion. Current uses of this form more immediately played on Mayakovsky's sacred-sounding "Lenin lived, Lenin is living, Lenin will continue to live"; the first reference of this form is to authority itself. More generally, it refers to victory; an army or sports team might say, "We beat them, are beating them and will continue to beat them!" The boorishness of the boss's declaration bore a finer affront: he was victorious at his audience's expense. He was simply not one of them.

Casual conversation often featured badmouthing individuals in power as well as general indictments of the bosses who "made the porridge[8] we have to eat." Everything the elite did was seen as designed to make things, not

---

[8] The word kasha, a name for any food cooked into porridge, smashed into paste or blended into a disorderly mass, is often used to refer to nonfood, such as social, messes.

just better for themselves, but worse for "normal" people, some of whom were literally living on kasha.

Culture was another "arena in which power ... could be won or lost ... 'power' fought 'culture' for power in culture" (Fitzpatrick 1992:2). The Revolution partially coopted Russian dusha, in part through the coopting of community; the Revolution's goal was to make men brothers (see Sinyavsky 1988:164). Then the Party elite partially coopted the Revolution, positioning themselves as keepers of souls, partially replacing romantic kul'tura by "a mere program for proper conduct in public" (Dunham 1990:22–23; 151, 181).[9] Regional government officials' backgrounds were invoked in skeptical discussions of their qualifications, sensitivity, and link to real culture. My mention of one name was answered by: "Former parto-crat, that says it all." Party + bureaucrat summarized "everything"; the System. Russian and Soviet culture had been lost, some said, when the cultured people had all emigrated or been killed by the uncultured (see Sinyavsky 1988:200–201; for jokes, see Corten 1992:73–74). One man attacked Soviet appropriation of culture, the elite's lack of it and use of it to uncultured ends: "Some people don't think about culture, only about what's good for them. ... That hypocrisy, glorifying their own personality [a use informed by Stalin's cult of personality] at someone else's expense, in the cultural domain, that's considered normal."

"Dusha Rossii," an Omsk festival of culture, featured fine performances and networking: when an official said in a speech that "Art is the face of business," an outraged friend muttered a translation: if these people could dump thermonuclear waste in the city center and get a trip to England for it, they would. "They're restructuring pretty friskily [*shustro*]," he commented, "wherever the wind blows. That's our country for you." Appeals to dusha in the context of cultural events could be effective by claiming to be "more representative of the true national values" (Verdery 1993:180), but, for those unconvinced by calculated uses of terms such as dusha, culture, and friendship, these were seen as crude attempts at exploiting the best and purest. "Soviet culture pulled useful fragments from traditional Russia," Anatolii concluded, "but then they exploited them ... used Russian culture to inspire Russians to acts of heroism. That's Soviet ... Those in power used people's belief for selfish purposes. And now the same politicians are trying to use truth to their own ends again. Glasnost, that is."

So, to recapitulate, people who rise to power, the story goes, are not qualified or intelligent. They are stupid and spiritually stunted.[10] Retired teacher Evgeniia Pavlovna said "It seems to me that People's Deputies' spiritual

---

[9] Evgeniia Pavlovna and others of her generation occasionally implied (though they would never make this statement) that a certain kind of etiquette ("external culture") was continuous with "internal culture," dusha. I did not hear this from anyone under fifty.

[10] Dunham (1990:132) writes that "The vast bureaucratic structure gave birth to a new, systemic kind of *meshchanstvo* ... the soulless, greedy, pompous philistine."

worlds are very narrow." Oleg often referred to himself and childhood friends as children of workers, and often venomously contrasted their values and upbringing to those of children of Party bosses. He elaborated: "It's like crap floating in that direction. To *that*. Both males and females . . . spiritually impoverished. . . . You think it's smart people there at Gosplan? . . . That's a clear part of our system. . . . It's our biggest tragedy that . . . a person's social achievements never depended on his personal qualities."

Since these people are "stupid," their movement up the ladders of power was portrayed as accomplished by cunning (as in the proverb "Cunning is a fool's intelligence") and by fawning obsequiousness and obedience. Evgeniia Pavlovna said: "You compromise yourself to get something from your superiors. You study your boss well." Anatolii, Oleg's young friend, emphasized how this became necessary: "There was always this bootlicking. . . . He who doesn't bend is broken or fired. . . . Part [of the population] adjusts, aligns itself with power; part is subjugated."

Since such individuals could not command respect for their personal qualities, the logic continues, they had to be despots. There is a word (*samodur*) for a stupidly self-indulgent boss who toys with people, making them jump. As Oleg said, bosses issue orders and, having satisfied their need to command, to crush, forget them. While I was speaking to a newspaper editor, a sullen man tried to come in. The editor yelled that he was speaking with a representative of the United States. He explained that after a recent reorganization he had become a boss and this other guy, who had been a coworker and was also thirty-five years old, was "having trouble getting used to it." A partocrat's wife who saw Zina with a stick of smoked sausage asked if she'd bought "sausage-for-the-population" (for the masses, the public) for her dog. Andrei explained: "What she said about our sausage, well, she's just too stupid to understand that you can't say things like that. That visible condescension . . . her husband climbed the ladder, and she does all she can to show we're on different levels."

Mila went to quit. Her boss said he wanted to tell her a joke. Sparrow sits in a yard; a cow craps on her. She climbs out of the stinking pile, labors to clean up. When she is finally fluffy and fresh she flies up, perches on a wire and sings with joy. A passing hawk hears, swoops down and eats her. The moral is, the director said, "Sit where you are, in the crap. Don't chirp." "This is what it means," he concluded, "to have a heart-to-heart talk" (*govorit' po dusham,* implying that they had had an open, soulful chat about the System and thus about his power).

Thus the despotic *samodur* boss has no respect and treats people as not-people. The employees often return the favor. Anatolii mentioned this: "He doesn't consider those under him people. He doesn't respect them. They should do his bidding. He expresses no interest." The emotion one experiences (in dusha) when dusha is ignored, when one is treated as not-human, is hurt, profound offense (*obida*). In Mila's words, "*Obida*—when you're unfairly treated—That's a state, one of the most, I'd say, destructive. . . . For some reason, people are built, at least I am, to suffer injustices very strongly. That feeling, justice, injustice, it's very highly developed."

Most big bosses had offices in which their desk was at the head of a conference table. My interviews with Yurii Yur'evich were at such a table. He told his life story, mentioning at the beginning that the way we were sitting reminded him of a certain interrogation he had performed. He then, not through any conscious conceit, performed his autobiographical narrative in the form of a questionnaire, asking a question, then answering it: "I went to the university, graduated. At that time I had only one desire, one love, investigative work. I thought it was related to the defense of fairness, justice. That is why I loved it and was successful in it."[11] Oleg said: "Only in Russia could slogans of fairness spark a revolution. People believed in it. That's what they sold themselves for. Justice. When all this perestroika began, people trustingly invested their money, and those guys fed it through their companies and either gave it back or didn't. Then people started feeling injured. We are, in general, very trusting."

Offense and soul injury were most often mentioned in contexts of breaches of fairness and corruption of individuals responsible for these breaches. It is play between images of trusting, believing people and images of those same people having felt all along "in dusha" that something was not right. Both descriptions often popped up in one interview segment. For example, in the interview in which he described how trusting Russians were, Oleg said:

> When we all lived immersed in deception, almost everyone knew something was wrong. Communism became a joke. No one had any idea what we were building. A generation of people came, a sad generation, honestly, who believed in nothing . . . *Za chto borolis', na to i naporolis'*, they say.[12] That's a very serious problem for us.

Power supposedly not only crushes and dehumanizes "normal people," it lets them down, betrays, deceives them. Yurii Yur'evich said: "What qualities help a person come to power? . . . Unfortunately, as our history shows . . . the most important of them, including political figures I respect, have the ability to maneuver, to betray their close ones and convictions . . .

[11] Yurii Yur'evich told me: "One man whom I loved . . . practically to this day . . . is—you'll be surprised—Felix Dzerzhinsky. . . . It hurt me when his monument was taken down from the Lubianka. . . . I need more information. I need to— . . . They have to prove to me that he was a villain, a bloody man . . . if they can show that he really—*in his own interest*—did things, for the sake of his career, then I'll accept it."

[12] The original saying is *za chto borolis'*? "What did we fight for?" In social-realist literature, it might be cried out by a veteran of the 1905 revolution who feels betrayed by the provisional government. It is an earlier version of perestroika's "For the sake of *what* (did we do it all)?" In the 1960s, the question of what had been fought for was answered in this popular rhymed saying that glosses as "What we fought for is what we are (now) ripping our flesh on."

for power." "Farewell, Unwashed Russia," a poem by Pushkin, portrays Russia as repeatedly deceived. Late and post-Soviet decrees and projects such as privatization vouchers, currency reforms, and even the dissolution of the Soviet Union were seen as purely manipulative, for personal profit (see Humphrey 1995). Grisha told me:

> I never had a bank account, but Mama saved two thousand rubles in the ten years since she retired. And now, because of Them, there—because there are, after all, guilty parties—but that's the System! Now they say you can buy four kilograms of sausage for that. . . . And they're saying don't worry, you'll be reincarnated and have a hundred more lives. That's propaganda too, fucking bullshit. . . . The order to become a businessman is coming from above too. They're telling me "Grab your piece of the pie." An *order*. All orders have been deceptions. If the government changed the rules once, it can do it again.

Again, the fact that people had sobbed at Stalin's death was offered as evidence of how profoundly they had been deceived.

When I asked, "Has dusha changed recently?" the question was unanimously first interpreted as a question about *deception* (*obman*) and *power* relations! Andrei said:

> Of course, [dusha is] changing. . . . We were profoundly deceived, cruelly. . . . Imagine, I worked my way up from collective-farm worker, was in the Party for twenty years. . . . I served honestly, like a soldier, . . . and suddenly I felt a gap, a failure. . . . I lost interest. . . . I wouldn't *believe* anymore, and my dusha changed. My spiritual world changed completely. On the podium they said one thing, then went into their offices and did the opposite. . . . We were brought up believing that the party was "honor, mind . . ."[13] But we were "population." . . . In the Kremlin there was communism. They got whatever they wanted. . . . The communist idea was a beautifully presented deception. The word "deceit" is most appropriate. A candy can be bad, but if you wrap it up nicely, people want to buy it.

Irina answered my question about change and dusha by exclaiming:

> We sincerely believed that "If you're a good person . . . are useful, work, are honest, you'll become a communist!" Most worked honestly. And imagine, all your ideals are smashed . . . your country torn apart. . . . How can one not grieve that it all turned out like this? Certainly we were deceived, and people are going through a huge, precisely dushevnyi crisis. . . . A dangerous dushevnyi vacuum has formed.

---

[13] See Chapter 10. There is another reference to this slogan below. Steinberg (forthcoming) mentions the salience in the Russian press on the eve of World War I of honor and conscience, insult and humiliation, and of demands to be seen as "human beings," not slaves, machines, or "beasts of burden."

As Oleg said: "There was a lot of lowness, meanness, pure and simple. And now we're sick, simply sick."

There was a parallel, often a confluence, between "Russian" images of Asians, Central Asians, and Caucasians, and the Soviet elite. Both images featured allegations of lack of respect, self-interest, two-facedness, despotism, feudal relations, brutality, and in fact, as the following text shows, these groups often mixed in discourse with reference to offense (*obida*), hurt, "a feeling in dusha." When I complained about rudeness in shops, Oleg quipped: "Remember: you're in *Asia*; Europe ends at the Urals."

> I don't relate too well to those on top right now. Everyone understands those guys are laundering money [twisty gesture]. People feel . . . that again there's this immense deception. We are, after all, maximalists; we want everyone to be fair . . . justice. And there is none. That's a very big problem for us, more or less honest, normal relations. Anger is growing against them. . . . At the markets it's—Asians, Central Asians mostly. They've related to us inhumanly, like cattle . . . and we did so much for them.

Svetlana, lapsing into silence to underscore how degrading it had been, said she tried to forget what she had seen on a State farm: "They say '*Khoziain-barin*'[14]—you're the boss, you do everything you want. And they do. Do they ever. Seventy years, the Party—'Honor and conscience!' It was horrible. . . . We have an eastern-type despotism. It's just like this in the East." Incidentally, I have quoted a number of people mocking the Soviet use of "mind, honor, conscience." In all these cases, only two of the full three terms were cited, a trinity demoted.

Where there is no respect, people are not normal. For example, they are animals. "Caucasians and Asians have acted like animals toward us, no respect at all." In 1994, Zina was calling Caucasians in Omsk "Chechens." In turn, all classificatory Chechens were "beasts." "Killing means nothing to them." Implied, horrifically, is that Chechens may be killed.

Another abnormality is when people are seen as things. Mechanization metaphors for soul loss date at least from the early nineteenth century: "Your soul has turned into a steam engine . . . I see screws and wheels in you but I don't see life' " (Williams 1970:577–79). Stalin proposed that each person was only a screw in the machine, but a 1960s reaction claimed: "We're not screws!" One woman told me that, at work, she respected, could empathize with people. For her bosses, however, she said, their clients were just *material*. At this formulation of people as things, her cousin, who was sitting with us, giggled.

---

[14] Prerevolutionary terms for aristrocratic landholders and serf owners, whose power in their own domain was absolute.

The Powerful as Hosts and Guests: Sweet Vinegar and Smooth Hedgehogs

> Champagne: "The favorite drink of the working class, which it
> drinks through the lips of its finest representatives."
> Dunham 1990:241

Zinoviev (1982:132) writes that "Officials of the Central Committee and the KGB . . . too are human beings . . . inclined to open their hearts and beat their breasts under the influence . . . one must be a Homosos, [15] too, to have real access to the hearts of one's fellow-drinkers." The powerful, however, were always a special kind of guest. Zina and Andrei first introduced me to the Ukrainian expression *na khaliavu*, which means freeloading, getting or eating something at others' expense. One etymology (reported in 1997) points at distribution of free milk (Hebrew, *khalav*) in Odessa. *Na khaliavu* can be a joking synonym for hospitality (being treated to something in a situation where people are more or less equals) or an indictment of privileged people living off normal ones. Zina, who tended to understand all wrongdoing in the idiom of power relations, used it in the second sense. One woman, appalled at how her partocrat neighbors had openly said that they didn't need to grow food, exclaimed: "For them life is a holiday . . . They do everything *na khaliavu*. Our country has been based on bribery for a long time. When someone else pays for it, vinegar is sweet and hedgehogs are smooth."

Zina and others complained about how, as students, they had had to work in superiors' gardens. "They try to live at the expense of someone else's kindness. Our System." "Our System" featured many so-called "feeders" at which the privileged "animals" fattened themselves. The powerful take like guests, *but one doesn't have the privilege of offering*. They are guests with whom one cannot drink.

"Where does it all go?" was a common question. One woman, when I complained about how busy I was, exclaimed: "The System has grabbed you, too! All our life, effort, our work goes off . . . who knows where." Implied was that the elite get it all. "Every person in this system," she contin-

---

[15] Zinoviev abbreviates Homo Sovieticus into *Gomosos,* in the familiar form of Soviet acronyms. It sounds like Homosuck would in English, aggravated by the obscene failure of patriotic imagery of Soviet Man. "Our Soviet Man," as opposed to less perfect forms of life, had been strong, balanced, round-faced, muscular, cleanly-dressed, decent, reliable. They numbered in the imagined millions, yet individuals were usually depicted as only aspiring to Soviet personhood. In the late Soviet era, "Soviet man" took on nuances of *sovok* (dustpan), a jaded, hyperbolically crude person with no higher ideals, frazzled, internally and externally shoddy. Soviet Man, Zadornov said, "gets oddly animated at the mention of the word 'sausage.' " Unable to do a decent day's work, incapacitated by "This Life," Sovki (pl. of *sovok*) compensate with rude behavior and vicious screaming (thanks to Michael Wasserman for helping with this definition).

ued, "should have a memorial put up for him [showing with her hands the tall rectangle] made of solid gold."

Above I mention the parallel and confluence between images of Asians, Caucasians, and the Soviet elite. There are similar cases. Talk about morally defective Russians paralleled talk about ethnic groups seen as that way by nature. Jokes about alleged Ukrainian stinginess, for example, paralleled what was said about partocrat self-interest:

A Russian stewardess brings passengers their meals. One man refuses, saying in Ukrainian (he can't even *speak* Russian!) that he has no money. She consults a Ukrainian dictionary and brings him his meal, exclaiming, "*Na khaliavu!*" The Ukrainian accepts greedily.

Though Ukrainians' image as freeloaders hinged on alleged national stinginess (unlike images of powerful Russians, seen as self-interested because they forget, and thus forfeit, their community membership), the result in both cases is self-interest.

What Jews could be accused of also parallels what Soviet and post-Soviet elite were hated for. Jews' sense of community was seen as exclusive, rather than as helping some people. Their interest was assumed to be *self*-interest. Their alleged cleverness and practicality were seen as calculated, exploitative cunning, not creative "making do." The elite were seen as allied with Jews and sometimes called or assumed to be them. I have mentioned the narrative of Jews having been responsible for the Revolution (see Sinyavsky 1988:8–9, 263–64, 273–75). This, in turn, was used to explain aspects of the Soviet system: "I solemnly announce . . . I will never . . . repeat my sad experiment at moving up in the world . . . To go up that ladder one has to be a kike . . . a faggot forged from pure steel . . . And I am not that kind" (Erofeev 1990:21). "I solemnly announce" recalls the Pioneer pledge's "I solemnly promise." "Pure steel" echoes Lenin's statement that Marxian philosophy is "cast from a single piece of steel." Erofeev's Venichka defines himself against the hierarchy's cold calculation and "Jewish" soullessness.

If bureaucrats, as Masha said, are better at bossing people around than doing things themselves, hate those who can do things, and support only people like themselves, Jews, in some antisemitic lore (Rozanov, in Crone 1978:32), "don't know how to write, but with such a talent for 'being boss' they don't need to." As I showed in Chapter 4, the Jew's assumed lack of respect for the Russian language can be portrayed as coming from his alliance to "his own"; a count against his soul that parallels the elite's auto-alienation from the speaker's community. The elite's community is the System. As Anatolii said, "All bosses, from store purchasing manager . . . to factory director, they're all in it together." Zina repeatedly called this a closed "clan."

When people discussed the powerful's self-interest they referred to a "state of mind" "all Soviets" had been in "all their lives" without noticing it, a state of being deceived, a state people said they had only recently noticed. This often led to the theme of "for the sake of what" everything had been done. Many said that "now we realize" it had all been done in a state in which the powerful had managed to determine and define some of dusha's goals and terms. This realization is important. If (Chapter 2) loss is always going on and always new, some of the newness pertains to impulses of realizations, comings-to-consciousness of loss.

Business people and the monied were, in the early 1990s, also seen as morally equivalent to the powerful: both becoming powerful and going into business are linked to moral degradation. Condemnation of Russian businesses' low quality and fraud paralleled condemnation of the powerful's deceit. The groups also melded together. Anatolii was saying that Russians had become corrupt, oriented toward exchange:

> All stages of Soviet hierarchy were bought and sold. *Everything*— politeness, friendship—came to mean you want something from someone. Everyone assumes you're *not* talking from dusha. If you don't grease [the wheel], you can't ride; it's all for sale. That's the slogan of the System . . . Dusha depends on *byt*, after all . . . The elite's kids, seems like they should be cultured right? But . . . behind their backs it's said that they have no spirit, no humanity. Because in their world, everything is bought and sold . . . Poor children are spiritually richer, more honest, aspire to kind relations.

Voices, Veils, Visibility

Petrov, a former partocrat to whom I had just been introduced, invited me to a banquet for the regional elite. Like many of them, he had grown up in a village. Though princes were supposed to have forgotten their dirty origins, they were often still good at positioning themselves as oppressed and dispossessed, and capitalized on those skills on their paths "up the ladder." On the way to the banquet Petrov tested me to see how naive I was about how things worked. For example, with a pitiful face, he told me his miserable salary (certainly the most insignificant part of his capital). He complained in the voice of Omsk about Moscow just as others complained about him. He said that Moscow did nothing and Omsk did everything, yet Moscow got all the credit, implying that the provinces are to Moscow as the workers are to the bosses. Later on, he said that what was most painful (*obidno*) about the present state of affairs was that "My social welfare: the right to work, rest, health care, education—" he began drunkenly repeating the list of rights guaranteed by the Soviet constitution, forgetting items in the canon, disturbed at forgetting them—then he snapped out of it: "I'm left without all of that." This relatively powerful man spoke fluently in the voice of the oppressed people that has only the value of its losses, a familiar voice lamenting its total lack of protection, how a normal person had "no one to complain to," how "no one will stand up for an honest person."

That day, at, in Petrov's words, the banquet of "the most powerful, biggest people in the region," a woman complained to me about how they, the people, had been deceived by the System for seventy years. While she said this her eyes were oddly locked on mine: "We're in direct contact, these waves of meaning supplement, validate, or contradict my words." Her husband, in contrast, was the finest example I ever met of what I had started thinking of as invisible men. His face was fairly rigid and immobile, I *think*. I somehow never looked at him. He sat across the table; I talked to anyone, but at some point I noticed that a blind spot repelled the casual glance his way. But in a sense everyone there was invisible: although I had been photographing all day, a teenage girl, giggling nervously, dared me to photograph *this* table, "with everyone." I offered her my camera, which made her giggle harder.

Another aspect of the veil around power, an easier one to analyze, was that when moves were made in the System there was no evidence of who made them. The Soviet "rule by telephone," for example: a boss calls and gives an order on the phone. Later, if there is any question, no documents exist. Late 1992 TV ads, mysteriously, featured only the name of a firm but no clue as to products or services offered. People were laughing, confused and angry at what was seen as a typical smokescreen associated with being manipulated, exploited, and deceived.

Although Grisha claimed to abhor masks, he told me that one must maintain guardedly friendly relations with neighbors, neither too close nor too far. "You need them," he said, making a mask with his hand. But masks depended on point of view just as point of view determined dusha's existence or visibility. This is evident in the following segments. The first is with Kazannik, a politician:

> Here, education and dusha, rather than supplementing each other, contradict each other. We lived for seventy years with a double morality. *I* never lived that double morality, but there sometimes was a double morality. A split personality. Person and citizen. A person's dusha was completely different. But . . . using his education he tried to mask his dushevnyi condition. . . . People were sitting on two chairs at once.

"Sitting on two chairs" indicates failure to commit to one idea or value and to sincerely try to embody or achieve it. Not unlike having one's cake and eating it, it is considered a moral error on the verge of hypocrisy. The Orlovs said:

> ANDREI: Zadushevnyi talk, that's when we would talk soul-to-soul (*po dusham*), no one told any lies, everything was exactly—there.
>
> ZINA: Sincere.
>
> ANDREI: Sincere. That's dushevnost'.

ZINA: Dusha and conscience are a person's internal condition with which he communicates. In some sense we, Russians, were raised with a double morality—at home, we take off a certain mask . . . and at work, at school during the stagnation, we had another moral code. Only at home could we afford to say something . . . about our hurt. . . . This led to a permanently critical condition with our consciences, our dushi. Some kind of deal was struck inside a person. . . . A person in our society cannot open himself completely. At work what they know is that I have a responsible attitude to my work. What's going on there, in my dusha, no one's interested. There's constant conflict in my conscience, in dusha, because of this duplicity. A Russian is happy when he can open up, pour out the storms or troubles of his dusha [this refers to a line from a Lermontov poem], share, get advice.

ANDREI: Conscience . . . you have to be faithful to it. . . . I suffered because all *my* sides are the same—home, work, at party meetings. For that, as they say, "they beat me."

Grisha both derided masks and admitted having them. Kazannik and Andrei, saying that everyone was forced to have masks, claimed that they did not have them. One aspect of Kazannik's statement was certainly made in the context of his political career (implying he had never been a Soviet politician). Andrei portrays himself as consistent and conscientious. At the same time, neither implies that he was better than others or that he was not (as all normal people are) split, doubled, constricted and deformed by the System; their words are just caught between different points of view on soul.

Mila and many others described how people had stood on a podium and showed how red and white were opposite, then came down and called red white and white red. If one assumes the mask to be conscious and deliberate, this is hypocrisy. But most admit that it is not that psychologically simple: "When, fifty years ago," Mila said, "people became young pioneers, the necktie, that was all real. By the time we went through it, a lot of it had become a formality." Communist ritual and belief became form and individuals, masks. I have discussed imagery of an immense Soviet mask, "system of mystification," "varnished over" reality (Stites 1992, Dunham 1990). Many people describe Soviet "dualities of mind;" Mead (1955:20) cites Bukharin's 1938 use of the term. Related formulations are Glazov's (1985:11–12) "behavioral bilingualism" ("two grammars of conduct"), and Yurchak's (1997:11, 14) use of the term "cynical subject." Masks were on all sides: on one hand, "The dissident called upon fellow citizens to expose 'the official Lie,' " Yurchak (ibid.:9) writes; on the other hand, "unmasking" was also a canonized Soviet exercise (Zinoviev 1985, 1990).

"Inhuman" political "beasts" "smiled when in their soul they were different, the inverse of a quality I heard predicated of "normal" Siberians: "warm inside, cold outside." Implied is that normal people were faithful while the elite changed masks. Opportunism was the major cited cause of the powerful's "betrayal;" as eleven-year-old Vitya said, "they change allegiances when the other side starts to win." As I show, however, opportunism crept in everywhere. The part of each person that, to survive, had become masked and powerful in a Systemic way was his soul-flaw. One narrative of power can be phrased this way: although rules are hardly ever obeyed, and everyone does what he or she must, there *are* real criminals. As we must absorb their surprises, setbacks, and betrayals, "Our" (victimized) opportunism and "Their" (capricious, traitorous) opportunism make a system that floats on the obstinately unpredictable.

The relatively powerful were more and less visible than normal people, and, correspondingly, freer and less free. People described both the nearly endless license of the very powerful, invisible and protected by the System, and the way the elite were under constant surveillance (see Simis 1982). My friends claimed *both* that (especially "in cities like this") the powerful were hidden and thus could do anything and that the powerful were more watched and had to conform more. For example, people said glasnost was redundant; everyone here had always said what they wanted (well, they might have been asked to say it not quite as loudly). "You can't send a person any farther than Siberia. Only careerists couldn't say whatever they wanted here." Power is power in *this* world, outer freedom, but "Russian people," wrote Aksakov (Rancour-Laferriere 1995:38), "having entrusted all authority in the political sphere to the government, reserved for themselves *life*." The world of dusha is life, *inner* freedom. This interview segment with Maxim shows these two angles:

> *They* lose the sense that they're being watched, so it's a free-for-all. . . . Most bosses, they have inferiority complexes. Why? Well, the system . . . when you feel like every step you take is under surveillance, how you blow your nose is watched, they hear every breath. You start to feel like less than an adequate, full person. The bosses are on strings. . . . Any attempt at independence . . . is punished. They try to insure themselves against responsibility for any decision.

Public Prosecutor Yurii Yur'evich said that dusha *is* conscience; as long as there is conscience a person is a person, a human being. When I asked him about relations between workers and bosses, he answered:

> It all depends on the supervisor's personality. I know directors . . . of big factories who . . . are respected . . . Even during hard times they find ways . . . to support the workers. . . . Why do some people say that a decent person can't become powerful? Well, injustices of power have resonance. A family injustice is secret, but if a director takes an apartment from an underling, he's in the public eye. And lately everything is open. Journalists are not about to write about a normal guy who gets drunk, but if they write that the director of a large factory or a public prosecutor got drunk, it gives the impression that they're all like that. As we say, "The closer to the summit, the more visible."

The "summit" is a tower (with a machine gun).

Perhaps I need not stress that the culture of the more powerful is in most ways that of the less powerful. Power itself is related to soul. As Foucault (1980:96–99) writes, all individuals "are always . . . simultaneously under-going and exercising this power." There are few objectively soulless people; in fact the term "objectively soulless" may be an oxymoron. Power seems to itself be "soulless" and to "kill" dusha in everyone. Those ruled by power, from "inside" or "out," cannot follow their "own" soul's promptings.

Mysteries: The System, Fate, Power

> Only three forces . . . have the power to forever overcome and imprison conscience . . . miracles, secrets, and authority.
> Ivan Karamazov, in Dostoevsky 1982 11:301

> Everything Is Against the Person Here.
> Headline, *Rossiiskaia gazeta,* September, 1992

A man sitting near me at the banquet pointed to the meal, including the only sturgeon I saw between 1990 and 1995, *kumys* (fermented mare's milk), Crimean white wine, chocolate, watermelon, red caviar, and beef. With sneaky glee he said, "Everything—there's *none* of—is here."[16] There was an almost shameless causal connection: it's not there *because* it's here, or almost. As went another punning desecration of a Mayakovsky line I discussed above, the Party was, the Party is, the Party will continue to *eat* (a pun: the infinitive *est'* is both an emphatic way to say "is," "exists," and the infinitive "to eat"). I later talked to Oleg about the banquet. He often deformed the word democrats (*demokraty*) into *der'mokraty*, based on *der'mo*, crap. "Out of the dirt and into princedom," he said, "explains a lot. In the country they relax, talk more cynically, let their masks drop, open their dushi. Like kids, they brag about what they have that others don't."

If the powerful are guests, they are also magicians. Like hostesses, they can magically make things appear and disappear for those they favor. In Chapter 3 we see that talent, a kind of authority, has to do with a domain to which someone has a mysterious, special relationship, interest. The domain may be "good" or "bad," but the relationship is "alive." The politically powerful are familiar with the System.

Given discourse that stresses how helpless normal people supposedly are in face of events blamed on the powerful, power comes to share qualities of fate (*sud'ba*). One man wisely told me that the issue was not *how much* power people had but that there had been an image of unlimited power.

---

[16] Banquets of Party elite and, later, New Russians, resonated with bandit and other world imagery and behavior, soulful except for the exclusivity of it all. See Brooks 1984:184–86 and Ries 1998.

Abuse of power could be presented as not just a social but a cosmic travesty. The connection of legal and illegal is indicated as one of the many things too complex and deep to explain; the System moves in mysterious ways. Although people say that "the powerful grab everything," they also often say "everything goes off who knows where." It hurts, Lara said, that "we live a life ordered not by God but by a corrupt, hidden *human* power."[17] Oleg's friend claimed that normal senses were inadequate for understanding how things work in Russia. I was discussing the early onset of cold weather with a woman in her fifties. She immediately linked the weather to "events" in Moscow; "Even nature feels it. Everything is connected. And who suffers? the people!"[18]

Power Corrupts

> Maybe . . . he is aiming for some sort of Napoleonic goals . . . In that case he might certainly step over himself, across everything he had held sacred, step over his friends.
>
> Lara, Omsk, 1992

Maxim told me that "you get to know a person well only if you and he together—testing a person in a bad situation. They also say that if you want to test a person, give him power. Immediately all qualities of his dusha will appear on the surface." Svetlana also said, after describing her experience with State farm worker-boss relations, "If you want to get to know what a person is capable of, give him power."

Accounts of people refusing powerful posts, though infrequent, were told. Kazannik was the hero of one such story. When Yeltsin appointed Kazannik attorney general, people said that, though he had been honest, becoming part of the government would change things. But Kazannik soon resigned the post in protest. One man not disposed to like Kazannik told me that he had found new respect for him. He called him principled, if too direct (which impractical excess evidenced even more his fine nature).

As he explained this, it dawned on me: individuals' support for political figures was almost always formulated as *respect*, rather than as agreement or disagreement with any specific position! There was a lack of faith in the meaningfulness of any explicit platform; corruption was too "deep," masks too impermeable, invisible threads too tangled. The best criteria for evaluating a person were his or her respectability and apparent conscience. I later heard that Kazannik had started his own party, called Sovest' (Conscience). Stories were more often about the opposite sort of event. One of

---

[17] See chapter 10 and Sinyavsky (1988:103) on secrecy as "the mystery and the magic of Stalin's power."

[18] See Yurchak (1997:9) for a joke to this effect.

Zadornov's comedy routines said that there must be a contagion in the Kremlin, because as soon as someone became a politician he became impossible to understand. In other words, normal people have no access to the language and culture of the empowered, who are ill. Zadornov himself was later suspected of falling ill: in Chapter 1 I mention that when he moved to the building where Yeltsin lived, it undermined his authority as someone who could legitimately laugh at the System in the voice of "our side."

A friend attributed great significance to the fact that her newly wealthy neighbors said they did not need to grow food: they did not even try to seem to be in the same boat as others. Nadia said "A full person will never understand a hungry person; we have that proverb." Masha once said that satiety "eclipses people's brains." The satisfaction of one who rose from the dirt apparently makes him or her forget the voyage. Making things magically appear *for oneself* alienates one from others.

Power and objects of luxury were seen as separating people and even separating "human," "normal" or "simple" people from entities implied to be hardly people at all. This attitude predated Marx, but Soviets were (also) exposed to it in forms such as " 'Money, greed, or mania for wealth . . . *is the community . . . and can tolerate none other standing above it*" (Marx, *Grundrisse*, in Sahlins 1976:6). Objects of luxury and money take the place of community; power replaces soul. Objects do connect people as part of exchange networks, which most people worked fluently and calculatedly. But when people are derisively said to be interested in things, those same things separate people, even into camps of animate and inanimate. The discourse, of course, just as it connects people, separates them. When Kolia was promoted, some old friends, now subordinates, said that he had had that bent to his character for a long time. He seemed, they said, even pleased that some old friends had quit; *there was no one around to remind him of who he used to be.*

The Same People

As Emma and Inna had on Old New Year, Petrov treated me as his attribute the day of the banquet, with eye signals ordering me to his side to be introduced to a people's deputy or other dignitary as "Dale, from the United States, from Chicago"—pretty tiring. Two teenagers and I took a walk. One said that the Party representative at any workplace had been much higher than any boss; "Can you imagine? *Higher.* These people we are here with today." This democracy is a game, she said. They're just waiting to be able to return to business as usual. The Party committee is gone but these people are *the same.*

I found that alleging sameness was a well-used device, and isolated a number of contexts where "They're the same people" was used:

(1) In the "dirt to princes" sense; peasants become bosses.

(2) Similarly, the powerful were *the same* as those they despotically governed, but these "same people" do not admit it. Admitting that one is the same sort of person as others is respect. As Anatolii said, "Respect, that's when the boss is boss on paper, but in fact there's no difference at all. . . . He respects his workers for their dushevnyi, moral qualities. That's normal."

(3) Party elite, underground and criminal worlds were linked: As Zina put it, "The criminal world and the official one . . . somehow join invisibly." The sister of the head of a *mafiia* group told me about the Soviet "two-*mafiia*" structure: one was the "shadow economy," with which Party bureaucrats had had a symbiotic relationship. Occasionally a person in the shadow economy (*tenevik*) was jailed for appearance's sake, but the two systems essentially supported each other. This was described as them being "the same people." Government and *mafiia* were seen as more and more linked as the 1990s proceeded.

(4) "It's the same people" was often said of communists' opportunistic transformation into democrats; "they're restructuring pretty friskily." I was told that on the State farm there had been few changes in who was in power; those in power simply became whoever it was best to be. These "same people" took all the cream and butter before, and they do now.

(5) Many used the "same people" theme to describe lifelong atheists' (sometimes the same elite, sometimes not) transformation into Orthodox Christians. Oleg said that this new religion was just a fashion. "Like people bought crystal in the seventies," he said, "they're buying crosses now. . . . It's *the same people*."

(6) A similar impulse was embodied in an important narrative that claimed that the Soviets were structural heirs to feudal lords' or other prerevolutionary power and relationships. "Nothing has changed" (see Sinyavsky 1988:163). Oleg repeated in countless variations that there had been essentially no change in social relations from feudalism to the present.

. A real bone of contention in all these allegations of sameness is the implication that these people's dushi have gotten stuck. This goes against a basic understanding I have discussed about dusha. The changes in these "same people" are only skin deep or new masks. When it referred to historical periods or belief systems, "the same people" can be understood in terms of a theme I introduced earlier in this book: the evil past was persisting; change had not happened, dusha had not had its impact.

Power Replaces the Soul: "Normal" People, Soulless "People," Vampires

A joke had it that both Brezhnev and Buratino (Pinocchio) received five gold pieces (a reference to Brezhnev's much-ridiculed medals) in the Land of

Fools (See also Banc and Dundes 1990:19, passim). When Soviet leaders went into business, I heard, their already meager brains dried out, which explained "why business here is so moronic." "Our leaders have an inferiority complex; Russian fools," Maxim said, "You know how they call post-Soviets Sovki? This is a *sovok* trait." A teacher cited the expression "Little boss, big head" (*malen'kii nachal'nik, bol'shaia shishka*—*shishka* is a "bump" or pinecone, a bump on the head or the head itself; *bol'shaia shishka* is a big cheese). "Or the other way around, 'little head, big boss.' You know, 'You're boss, I'm a fool; I'm boss, you're a fool.' If you're working, waiting for a promotion, a place in a kindergarten for a child or grandchild, a washing machine . . . you'll just have to be a fool." In other words, the alleged stupidity of the powerful was said to have made the entire country into a Land of Fools.

In the Generosity story I showed how Grisha converted a "stupid Chukchi" joke into a self-referential one about how stupid Russians were to buy into what the current authorities were selling—the whole idea of a market economy. But if everyone was a fool, everyone was also a boss. If a clerk, cleaning woman, or entryway attendant was rude, people said: "Everyone is a little dictator." Almost any social niche endowed one with some fiat (see Simis 1982:76). Oleg called Russia a ladder of increasingly smaller dictators; anyone in charge of anything, feeling the disrespectful way superiors treat him or her, demands the same "respect." The System was everyone, saleswoman to president, taking care of him or herself. In the absence of rule of either law or anything predictable, there was a guarantee only that one would be cheated if one didn't take care of oneself, given that those more hierarchically or even just temporally privileged had already taken theirs. Commodities went through so many hands on the take that all those people seemed to spit in one's face by proxy, through the hideous quality of goods.

Lara said: "You have to close your eyes . . . silence your conscience. No dialogue with your inner self . . . be obedient . . . Look the way they want to see you . . . Power *itself* is not for people, it's for its own sake . . . like all the ways that lead to power." Although Lara proceeded to recite the steps of the ladder, her narrative implies that power relations poisoned all Russians. Power (re-)created souls and society in its image. Though people often implied that the souls of poor, oppressed, simple people were still full of natural kindness and respect, a parallel discourse detailed epidemic diseases of power. As Anatolii put it, "A fawning obsequious kind of politeness that before the revolution existed only in boss-worker relations spread into relations in general. Respect has been bred out of people."

The demands of (those in) power rival dusha's urgent dictates. Power, as Lara implies, takes over the role of demanding, speaking to a person, guiding actions, of the hinting *podskazka*, of interest, passion, inspiration, conscience. *It usurps dusha's structural role.* The internal voice of conscience may not only be silenced, it may be seduced or informed by propaganda.

Listening to power is seen as requiring one to lose sensitivity and consciousness of dusha. The only discussions I heard relating gender to power attributed to women more dusha (sensitivity, caring about others), and occasionally, on this basis, had them soulfully "failing" on the level of power, a traditional form of resistance. For example, Irina said: "Women's dushi are more easily wounded—they take everything on an emotional level. Why are men preferred for managerial positions? Cold mind . . . logic is a man's quality." Many highly placed women, however, seemed to conduct themselves officially as did male Soviet elite, and were called cold, stupid, and corrupt just as men were.

Men may have been seen as better suited to political power than women were, but power was normal for no one. Aleksei Yurchak (1997:4) defines his use of the phrase "normal subject": "a person who . . . learned from experience that he or she could lead a 'normal' enough life—safe, self-manageable, enjoyable . . . provided he/she took no active interest in [the official sphere]." Here again, interest is the key. Withholding interest from the "official" is indeed a gesture of trying to protect one's soul and here is seen as definitive of normalcy. Treating power as *uninteresting* is an attempt to degrade it from a transcendent Other World to a meaningless This World.

Both criminality and power were associated with the possibility that human nature could be absent, as when Yurii Yur'evich told me: "As long as there's conscience, a human being is human. My job is to awaken the human being in a criminal. . . . He should feel that I respect him. . . . I'm punishing the criminal in him, not him as a person. I try to find . . . something good in him." A criminal (or an alcoholic, as Anna Viktorovna indicated) may be found by a soulful, interested person to have a human being in there somewhere. Sinyavsky (1988:183–84) writes, "Every Soviet citizen is . . . a criminal;" but there is apparently a scarier challenge: only "the last of the scoundrels . . . pursue[s] a Party career up the ranks . . . for whom no law is written."[19] Criminality is one thing, but the System has to do with oppositions between *humans* and *nonhumans*. The healing, interested respect Yurii Yur'evich describes is opposed to the "systemic" situation Zina describes, where there were no people, only robots or screws in the machine. Not-normal people, heartless, soulless animals, beasts, treat others inhumanly, and *vice versa*. Simis (1982:299) describes what he calls a general attitude to the Soviet elite: since they are completely corrupt, he writes, when *we* deal with *them* the norms of human morality do not apply. Soullessness is mutual, and notions such as normalcy populate this process. An important glasnost film on Stalin was titled *Monster*. In such usages as this, the distinction between "metaphorically" and "literally" fades.

I once interpreted for a theater director who told a group of Americans that Orthodoxy was the belief system of a people who hold God-given hu-

[19] This plays on the proverb "The law is not written for the fool."

man life supreme to the extent that when five Decembrists were condemned to death "no one in Russia could be found to be executioner or build a scaffold." Now Russia has an elaborate history of executions and killings (see Hingley 1977:3–10), but factual accuracy is beside the point. The director was implying that no one can kill someone they see as a *soul*. Only a "screw," a person of a highly different or, preferably, opposite culture or community (an enemy or someone who holds no interest for you), or a "beast" (itself murderous) can be killed—an entity, so to speak, already inanimate, dead.

The killer is also "dead": a 1996 TV show claimed that Lenin, Stalin, and Kaganovich "became masks behind which there was no longer anything." Hallowell (1960) shows that "the concept of 'person' is . . . not coterminous with human beings" (Fogelson 1982:82–83). Personhood may be lost:

> Depersonalization can eventuate from serious transgression against . . . norms, such as murder or violations of sacred taboos. . . . Witches . . . can assume a human appearance . . . but they are not persons, since they operate outside the constraints of the moral community . . . they are considered to be counterfeit persons. They subsist only by capturing the life essence of others . . . witches are "dead." (ibid.:87)

While many aspects of this sort of witchcraft differ from the Russian case, that personhood can be lost and how it is lost seem similar. A popular notion in the 1990s explained epidemic depression as the agency of energy vampires among strangers, coworkers, or family members. A few people I knew claimed to take steps, such as passing a candle around themselves thrice before going out, to protect themselves from such people, who, according to some, were not necessarily aware that they were vampires and could start all one's vital energy bleeding out by catching one's glance.

The evil eye seems to be related. A woman complained to me that her son and his wife had invited a group of friends over to see their newborn. One should never, she said, show babies. Who knows, someone might have the evil eye without knowing it.[20] Her daughter-in-law, however, drawing on a different version of normalcy, countered that it wasn't normal to not show the child to friends. The evil eye was also blamed for everyday problems in the same breath as the elite were: the two sometimes seemed interchangeable. Similarly, "Energy vampire," notes Stephens (1997:370), in addition to developed literal meanings, "has become a catchword for people with unappealing . . . personalities."

This is linked to images I heard daily of the "blood-sucking" elite's vampire-like preying on others' soulfulness (see also Dicks 1967:637–39;

---

[20] A group of Moscow doctors for whom I was interpreting in Chicago one hot summer was shocked to see a naked baby in public. No Russian mother would expose her child to so many *eyes*. This, they said, explained the "high U.S. infant mortality rate."

Glazov 1985:5 and Kluckhohn 1962:225–26). A 1992 pamphlet by the St. Petersburg School of Spiritual Development of the Personality claims that "Psychic vampirism . . . is a result of Lucifer's fall. . . . When he understood that he would be destroyed as a result of the absence of the divine life force, he began to absorb pure streams of energy from those still connected with God" (Stephens 1997:371). The powerful were felt to have spirited away products both of people's finest work and holiest beliefs, and of the Russian land, into the black hole of their own depths and their own System.

Summary: The Goose Is No Comrade to the Pig

In summary, like witches, those more powerful than oneself were often described as if they had unnatural powers associated with having sold their souls for access into the System. Arguing for the religious foundation of "Soviet civilization," Sinyavsky (1988:113) mentions nostalgia for the Stalin era, when "power was not a soulless mechanism *but a mystery.*" A *real* mystery: the process Mauss describes of the mask's "desacralization" when it began to represent differentiated social status seems not to have been, in this case, complete; issues of political / economic power and sacred spirit interact rather directly.

Sometimes the powerful were equated with fate; how *They* (or the System) forced us to live was not terribly different from how cruel fate did. The elite were "not one of us" and behaved not as "persons." Inadequate emotions, a symptom of soul loss, were predicated (a friend said her partocrat neighbors would go to sleep and not worry where their daughter was). They allegedy felt no empathy because they were not conscious of their dushi, their Russianness, what Sapir called their "elemental humanity." Power corrupted perhaps fundamentally in making people forget or contextually block certain representations from consciousness. Being deaf to dusha's promptings was paramount to losing soul. More evidence that the powerful had done this was that they refused to participate "normally" in exchange and ritual and were successful in "this" world at others' expense. They stole their power from honest, trusting, enthusiastic souls by, as Andrei said, "speculating on the finest words, on the finest dushevnyi qualities." Finally, their opportunism made them centerless masks, liable to betray. Dusha, though it claims inclusiveness, is heavily involved in practices of defining "us" and necessarily makes distinctions.

In this narrative, the powerful are calculating, self-interested individuals who may rise despite absence of intelligence, talent, originality, skill. In these positions they reign with despotism and demand the same false respect they used. As a result, everyone suffers, and social life is governed by these rules. "The normal subject . . . had no other choice but to pretend that the mask was the actual true face" (Yurchak 1997:18). By letting others use one for the wrong set of attributes, by using oneself and others unjustly, one damages one's own dusha and the world's.

Individuals and groups of Russians could be soulless for reasons similar to those by which entire ethnic groups were deemed soulless. Though I never heard it said so directly, by becoming wealthy, powerful, stingy, or insensitive, ethnic Russians seemed to de facto lose their right to be assumed to have a Russian soul. All those touched by power had related illnesses, lowering, corruption, muffling or deviation of vital energy.[21] In Chapter 9 I show how the *krutye* were seen to infect the world so that normal people also had to *krut-*. This is just an example of the general illness related to power. *Krut-* separated people; power supposedly further attacked community by making people forget it.

The powerful were discussed as lacking dusha, but they were often skilled in creating it; what they did with bottles and said at table could be a significant part of how they "climbed the ladder." Like everyone, they had dusha, a dusha also oppressed by power, power wielded by yet others. The admitted ravagers, the shameless powerful bosses, were still trampled, deceived, exploited.

As Oleg said, you feel spiritual closeness with someone you respect. So if you and another person do not have some of the same interests, ways of doing things, cares and values, you will not seem to have dusha to each other. You may know abstractly that a person is dushevnyi or dukhovnyi but you will not experience that together. People with more and less power seem soulless relative to each other on the basis of at least two assumptions: that they have different interests and/or that they have different experiences of everyday life.

Those who have different ways of operating, within the System (those inside or outside relative to the speaker) or outside it (foreigners) are suspected of not having dusha, of having lost it, or of having it deeply hidden, only to be revealed by, at the very least, a good conversation that generates that common experience. Ritual communions may "discover" eclipsed dusha in and to alienated individuals. The "prince" may remember the "dirt" he rose from and speak in that voice. Such situations may also indicate or increase alienation. The issue is mutual comprehensibility or empathy.

These images of the Party elite and the dynamics involved in relations that spawned these images did not disappear with the end of the Soviet era. Many nomenklatura were among the first so-called New Russians. In the mid- to late 1990s, New Russians (a group that might potentially include everyone with more than average amounts of money and some with only average incomes, if they dressed or behaved a certain way) were said to be

---

[21] Dunham (1990:36–37) shows how a person's physical heart could "signal . . . the rift between top and bottom of Soviet society." Ulcers were another "politicized ailment."

soulless,[22] and widely said (see Ries 1998) to have gone from "dirt to prince," to make fortunes in shady, effortless ways, to spend recklessly, ravage the environment, and mangle the Russian language; they are said to be stupid and uncultured, to have no sensibility or scruples, and to be hard to distinguish from mafiosi. So most aspects of the image of the Soviet powerful I heard about were seamlessly transferred to images of the wealthy and the New Russian.

I have examined what power has to do with soul. At the start of this chapter I cited Veletskaia (1992:62) on folk Yuletide ritual interactions with unclean force (or spirit). My acquaintance Emma's revival of these traditions on Old New Year was in a sense more successful than she could have hoped for. Her celebration played with and parodied the very conditions of the persecuted collective soul's reproduction, interacting with real Soviet unclean spirit, what was seen as inanimate and de-animating power.

[22] Ries (1998) cites a joke: Mephistopheles offers a New Russian anything he wants. "How about the biggest bank in Russia?" asks the New Russian. "No problem," answers the Dark One. "What do I have to give you in return?" asks the New Russian. "Just surrender your soul. Sign here on the dotted line." The New Russian frowns and asks, skeptically, "Is that all you want, my soul? I don't get it, what's the catch?"

PART V

TOGETHERNESS

CHAPTER TWELVE

Those Who Poke into My Soul: Dostoevsky, Bakhtin, Love

Thia chapter is mostly about love. Two Russians besides my Omsk friends help me. One is Dostoevsky; the other, the philosopher, linguist, and critic Mikhail Bakhtin, who in the 1920s wrote on moral responsibility and aesthetics and through the long "Stalinist night" worked in exile as a bookkeeper on a Kazakhstan collective farm, taught Russian and literature in Saransk, and wrote on Rabelais and Dostoevsky (Morson and Emerson 1990:xiii–xiv). By the 1970s, his work was becoming the object of admiration and interest in Russia and the West.

Bakhtin wrote that conditions of soul and worldviews cannot be analyzed. People cannot be defined or even fully perceived. They speak in voices and have dialogues. That is how they reveal their life. One can only, Bakhtin writes (1984:68), *relate* to things; "*otherwise they turn to us their objectivized side* . . . fall silent, close up, and congeal into finished, objectivized images."

This is a brilliant description of an aspect of dusha. By treating Bakhtin as a Russian I am in no way implying that his work is relevant only in Russian contexts. But ways in which this virtuoso of his culture translated his Russian soul into theory and practice help me examine both that soul and how one individual pursued his "own" agenda in dialogue with his culture. Bakhtin and Dostoevsky were inspired by similar imagery, and were similarly oriented toward making dusha more alive. Aspects of their work helped me see a great deal about the values and mechanisms of *obshchenie* (communion, communication, interaction) and love. In the previous chapter I show how power and certain kinds of exchange made everyone in the System less able to *see* each other's soul. Here I look at how seeing dusha is life-giving.

Bakhtin, Dostoevsky, and Dusha: A Review

My friend Grisha spoke in voices like those Crone (1978:44), discussing the writer Rozanov, calls the Mentor, the Fervent Mystic, the Confessor, the Prophet, the Buffoon. Points of view, Crone notes, that may stand in opposition to each other. This range and conflict is one reason Grisha's friends and family offered him as a prime example of dusha: soul is where opposites struggle. The more violent this struggle, the more profound a soul is considered to be. Ivan Karamazov's demon invokes an "arithmetic" according to which one dusha in which abysses of belief and of disbelief are concentrated is worth an entire universe (Dostoevsky 1982 12:160).

What was sometimes formulated as mystery, riddle, and enigma was at other times seen as underlying struggle, opposition, paradox.[1] For example, my acquaintance Aleksandr Ivanovich summarized dusha's enigmatic quality by calling it a paradox. Mitya Karamazov says, "You cannot define it, for God gave us only riddles," continuing to say that these "mysteries" and "enigmas" are where opposite shores and contradictions come together (Dostoevsky 1982 11:128). Though the Dostoevskian soul was in itself contradictory, in his so-called "Pushkin" speech (1985b:979) Dostoevsky said that it was exactly and only in the "all-humanitarian and all-unifying Russian soul" that "all European controversies" could be reconciled.

In the 1990s Dostoevsky was still not only associated with but *identified* with Russian soul.[2] His name was a way of referring to soul or guiding conversation toward it. As I mention in Chapter 9, an Omsk actor said that "If you immerse American actors in our Russian life they'll start to know a little better how to act Dostoevsky . . . We cannot explain it . . . no one can. Living a life like ours allows a person to understand something about Dostoevsky." An actress, when it was her turn, listed traditional characteristics of dusha, how it is internally varied, generous, easily made to respond, empathize, and suffer. "In Dostoevsky," she concluded, "each person is caught between heaven and hell." A third actor described how working on Dostoevsky "turns his life inside out": "Dostoevsky . . . doesn't give outer detail; he focuses fully on the heart, the blood. There's always a battle between God and the devil going on. The person in which it's happening swings back and forth like an unpredictable pendulum" (note that the speaker, caught in a metaphor too mechanistic to do justice to soul, made his pendulum unpredictable).

Expanses, worlds, and thresholds between them are among the commonest images in Russian verse; I have shown them in the wider culture as well. Bakhtin (1984:149) shows Dostoevsky concentrating his action temporally

---

[1] Mystery and opposition were both part of dusha from its beginnings (Williams 1970:584). National character and mentality studies of Russia reproduce this imagery as a "programmed" tendency to "oscillate between emotional extremes" or "occupy . . . exclusive positions simultaneously" (Hingley 1977:34).

[2] Cf. Cherniavsky (1969:230) and Williams (1970:584–87) for earlier examples.

and spatially at points of crisis, turning points, thresholds, and catastrophes. Elsewhere, with no reference to Dostoevsky, Bakhtin calls "enclosure within the self" "the main reason for loss of self." What matters, he says, is what takes place on the boundary between consciousnesses (ibid.:287). Such threshold positions depend on life being "drawn out of its usual rut" (ibid.:126).

Extremes, says Bakhtin, protect against systematic explanation. Dusha reveals itself most often (though not only) when people are in extreme positions. Dostoevsky admired Poe, Bakhtin (1984:145) says, for placing his characters in extraordinary positions, "scandalous scenes in which," in Dostoevsky's words, "the 'rotten cords' of the official and personal lie are snapped . . . souls are laid bare . . . and there opens up another—more genuine—sense of themselves and of their relationships."

Conflict and radical difference are taken as meaning that something is transcending logic, undermining explanation, ensuring that things stay "open." Bakhtin combines imagery of separate worlds with a passionate belief in the importance of *openness* and *unfinishedness*. He describes a "polyphony" of unified but incompatible elements, consciousnesses, voices, worlds (ibid.:6,16, 34, passim) that "combine but are not merged." They resolve little, but "reveal new mysteries."

What Bakhtin called dialogue, life that arises between voices, resonates with wider Russian discourses I have looked at. Images of rigid thresholds and borders between worlds inform and are informed by everyday events and talk. These worlds' mutual antagonism keeps them separate and keeps vast wholes from being encompassed by any explanation but "Dusha!"

I argue that dusha, soul, among other things, can be seen as practices centered around beliefs in depth. It is a tool for inverting or negating anything that seems to threaten the infinity of its life. As time passes, it becomes a diagram of aggravated awareness of point of view. As Wertsch (1987:29) writes: "Just when you think you understand [Dostoevsky's characters] they'll . . . do something . . . to demonstrate [their] . . . unfinalizability . . . it is arrogant to think that you can rationally represent . . . human nature." Dusha is condemned on formal principle to never allow itself to be confined, even by expanse or by freedom, for even those are definitions. Dusha is, again, a form labeled formless, "impossible to coherently imagine."

The "reifying devaluation" Dostoevsky felt, Bakhtin (1984:61) notes, "permeating . . . contemporary life," is related to everyday laments that practical life crushes dusha. As part of his personal rebellion against *byt*, Bakhtin focused on "the carnival sense of the world," which, like dusha, definalizes with ambivalence (ibid.:126). Anna Viktorovna said that routine makes dusha tear off from consciousness. Violating routine may make one conscious of soul again.

The carnival aesthetic is evident particularly in everyday talk about the country's disorder (I discuss this in the next chapter). Broad, "antistructural" gestures, debasement, blasphemy, absurdity, "free and familiar contact," alleged disrespect for money, parodies using inversion, scandals, inappropriateness, eccentricity, ultimate questions, and utopian images Bakhtin describes (ibid.:115–18,123–27) all fit an aesthetic and genre of behavior I have shown called "very Russian" and "for the soul." Examples include a doctor I mentioned whose love for making a diagnostic machine's lights blink struck him as the epitome of Russian soul.

Tragic and comic descriptions of internal conflict refer to dusha. Dusha usually appears, as in a Zoshchenko (1981:170–71) story, as soon as contradiction and opposition do. "Lebedev found . . . baptizing [his baby daughter] amazingly unattractive. Nevertheless his dusha was swayed [lit. shuddered] when they put their weight on him, and he, *rent by internal contradictions*, consented." Erofeev's (1990:62) Venichka, trying to express his drunken self to a French couple, parodies his Russianness: "I am dying from internal contradictions." Conscience, as a dusha "synonym," is itself moral struggle, an action retrospectively challenged by subsequent shame, disparate moments met inside a person to quarrel, as Dostoevsky forces his characters to quarrel (ibid.:91).

An emotion called *vostorg* is an excellent example of the coexistence, agitation, activation, and exaggeration of extremes and opposites, embodied in emotion. *Vostorg* means, approximately, rapture. Nearly every character in *The Brothers Karamazov*, at one point or another, is in this state, a state in which "superficial layers" and "masks" fall away, exposing the real "depths."

A note on conversational style. People often made what I thought of as "brave statements." Their bravado, extremity, intonation, and/or timing implied that they were opposing or energetically inverting some given. Brave statements implied that the speaker was in dialogue with or defiance of a larger body of assumptions or some unspoken point of view, anticipating what someone else, the West, or society would say. Bakhtin (1984:211–21) shows Dostoevsky's Goliadkin doing this. "Every thought," Bakhtin (1984:32) writes, "is internally dialogic . . . filled with struggle, or . . . open to inspiration . . . senses itself to be . . . a *rejoinder*."

For example, as I show (Chapter 2), with explanations ranging from religion to economics to politics, everyday life was said to be killing communication and human relations. But then, suddenly, someone would claim that dusha had already died, implicitly challenging listeners to prove him or her wrong. As Bakhtin writes, at such a moment, "Condemning himself . . . [the hero] *insistently peers deep into the other's eyes*, but leaves himself a loophole in case the other should suddenly . . . agree with him . . . and not make use of his *privilege as the other*."

Peering Deep

Although it was said that you could see the effects of social change in people's eyes, if "eyes are mirrors of the soul," as is commonly said, they are fancy glass. When Bakhtin describes how strong points of view help different points of view reveal themselves (1984:67), how extreme and counterfeit last words, shadowed by potential other meanings (ibid.:233), use others' *eyes* to reaffirm life, he describes important cultural practices.

So what *is* this power of others' eyes?

It can be positive or negative. Earlier I discussed how energy vampires were felt to injure people with their glance. Seeing is, in many contexts, both literal and a metonym. Like eyes of the spies of the heart Mitya Karamazov curses (Dostoevsky 1982 11:136), Medusa-like cold, logical or dispassionate "eyes" were felt to immobilize the soul, especially if those eyes passed negative judgement, although images of goodness and adequacy could also finalize. The most common way of referring to someone's presumptuous intrusiveness is to say that he or she is "crawling into one's dusha" (*lezet v dushu*).

Referring to Tiutchev's poem *Silentium*, Bakhtin (1990:133) says that "The *actual* world . . . is an already uttered word . . . So long as the word remained unsaid, it was possible to believe and to hope . . . But when the word *is* pronounced . . . *all* of it is here . . . [It] sounds hopeless." This is amazingly like a quote by Lenin (1960:259–60): "We cannot imagine, express, measure, depict movement without interrupting . . . simplifying, coarsening, dismembering, strangling that which is living. The representation of movement . . . always makes coarse, kills . . . in that lies the ESSENCE of dialectics . . . the unity, identity of opposites."

Bakhtin discussed this "impermissability of some . . . *outside person* penetrating the depths of a personality" (1984:60); as Mitya Karamazov says, "*let no one look so deeply inside as to force me to be utterly perfectly accurate.*" Many images of the life and growth craved by dusha indicate that it emerges exactly from what cannot, must not be expressed or encompassed.

Bakhtin wrote that he could not understand Dostoevsky's "word with a sideways glance" "without a consideration of its formal action." In turn, I cannot write about Russian complaining, brave statements, dusha, or Bakhtin himself and not their formal actions. "Having" dusha, dusha's life, is, from one angle, preserving its alleged openness, creating oppositions and mysteries that cannot be reduced, reconciled, or summarized. It does this by reserving the right to say no, rhetorically creating depths out of which trump cards can be yanked. This formal property may pass for "freedom" or "will."

Depth is made by gesturing at a specific infinity. Like the Hebrew God, these depths must never, out of respect for their transcendence, be fully represented. If anything can be fully known it can be replaced by a conscious, logical model, "reified." Bakhtin called such representations *dead*. Grisha, complaining about the cliché that Russian souls are "wide open," called it disrespectful, indicative of lack of interest. For Bakhtin, interest is also life-giving (1990:13).

Love, Communion

> My friends, our union's full of beauty.
> It's indivisible, eternal, like the soul.
> Pushkin (tr. Michael Wasserman)

> If a dusha is impoverished, it is incapable of love. Damaged.
> Irina, Omsk, 1992

Despite the persistent "Thou shalt not finalize" we find in Russians' perfectly reasonable denial that outsiders can understand their dusha, others' eyes can do more than destroy life. As I have shown, other people are also necessary to give birth to or increase life. I return to the topic of communion (*obshchenie*) that I have discussed throughout.

One day, Grisha listed common sayings and expressions that included dusha. Most had to do with interpersonal relations. For example, many were about attraction:

U menia po nei dusha noet [lit. My dusha tugs (a verb used for nagging pain) after her].

Oni k drug drugu dushami tianutsia [lit. They're drawn to each other with/by their dushi].

Many others related to the status of a relationship:

soitis' / ne soitis' dushami [lit. to get along (or not) with (their) dushi].

Zhili oni dusha v dushu [lit. They lived soul-in(to)-soul].

That attraction and repulsion are related to dusha is not surprising, insofar as primary aspects of dusha relate to emotion, collectives, and solidarities. Kazannik said:

> People drawn to each other are close by their dushevnyi makeup. And the opposite as well; It's unconscious; it's felt in dusha; many people just don't seem pleasant to you. But there are riddles. Simple psychology doesn't understand it. It is exactly dushevnyi makeup that limits and defines one's circle of interaction.

Grisha said: "My dusha is tuned to a given person or situation; in different conditions a violin sounds differently." Intuition tells about loved ones' condition; people are joined at dusha. Public Prosecutor Yurii Yur'evich showed me a poetry book a friend had given him, inscribed "To my comrade in dusha."

I keep returning to interest, a feeling that indicates value. Love or intense interest in something empowers one in relation to it. Sympathy relates to creativity; taking the outside inside oneself gives it life, makes it of the soul;

further *re*-presenting this representation is a particular gift. As in exchange, only others' interest can offer one an exit from one's own limited resources. Again, as Igor said, everyone wants something, but only through someone.

The style of openness infects others with the desire to open up too, to reciprocate. Soulful behavior and *consciousness itself* actively help realize a person's center; focusing on dusha opens it, increases it, increases life. Recognizing *is* realizing.

So interest is sacred; it helps souls realize themselves, gain life and reality.

I have shown ways in which the word *dusha* refers to a site of coexisting enemies, coexisting profanity and purity. Interest can associate virtually any object, event, or sentiment with dusha, overriding a partial definition of dusha as properly the locus of only the purest; the baths, where dusha rests, are themselves such a mixed site; Chapters 10 and 11 show other ways in which dusha becomes a mixture of pure and impure.

Ivan Karamazov says: "I *live*, though in *defiance* of *logic*." Alyosha replies: "Love before logic" (Dostoevsky 1982 11:270–71). Love's advantage over other logics is that it gives life. It includes expansiveness of the kind forgiveness is based on, and so it can embrace both virtuosity and sin, as in my friend Masha's Dostoevskian explanation of drunks' canonical query: "Do you love me? Do you respect me?" "A drunk," Masha said, "wants to hear that you respect him because—look, he's *drunk* but respected anyway; even in that state he's a human being!"

This is important both for the lover, who respects or otherwise identifies another person as human, and for the one so loved. A man at a party drunkenly offered, as proof that dusha had survived perestroika, "I rejoice when I look at you, you're a *person*." Joyfully acknowledging a person's humanity is a proof of or exercise for dusha. Like interest, joy may be felt when one recognizes or encounters soul (in anything).

Grisha "bravely" took simplicity, which he himself admired, out of context in order to condemn simplicity in service of some momentary agenda when he proclaimed that

> A "simple" person is just someone uninteresting to me, with whom I don't come into dushevnyi contact. More interesting is a dusha that burns, howls, contradicts itself. Hungers for something. Nature, it's not to be understood. A person may think he understands . . . nature, but he doesn't understand shit if he can destroy it. . . . A tree can't preach, like I am right now . . . but . . . *if it brings you joy, that means you see dusha in it*. If you pass and feel nothing, its dusha is closed to you.

In Bakhtin's (1990:136–37) version, "It is my otherness that rejoices in me."

Communion, dialogue, is, ideally, life-changing (see Attinasi and Friedrich 1995:38, 42). Bakhtin's work is inspired by the premise of the life-changing and life-giving power of dialogue. In "Author and Hero in Aes-

thetic Activity" (1990) he more or less abandons literature to discuss recip-
rocal soul constitution. By the late 1980s *obshchenie* ("communion") was
being applied to almost any interaction, but even less exalted ones could be
informed by or coopt communion's transformative power. Communion can
be soul-saving, as when Anna Viktorovna said "Dusha does not lose its
spirituality when you commune with people, nature, music."

Bakhtin was committed to describing soul as emerging between people,
the depths as "*outside* [oneself], in the souls of others" (1984:61). Caryl
Emerson (1996:110–11) writes that for Bakhtin, "We know who we are
only because and only when someone has responded to us." Emerson notes
that, in these early writings, Bakhtin devotes much attention to *vision*.

A Dostoevskian version of the Christian "judge not," personified in characters like Alyosha, considers recognizing others' souls in all their *depth*—
that is, in all their sinfulness and goodness—to be most valuable. Dostoevsky, in introducing characters, piles up surprising series of morally
contrasting character traits, avoiding unambiguously positive or negative
characters. Dostoevsky's project was "*to find the man in man* . . . They call
me a *psychologist; this is not true.* I am merely a realist *in the higher sense,*
that is, I portray all the *depths of the human soul*" (Bakhtin 1984:60, 227,
citing Dostoevsky's notebooks).

In this soul-oriented culture, things tend to be valued in terms of their relation to some "deep" center usually associated with emotion. Indifference
or coldness are the greatest offenses as well as prime signs of dusha affliction or loss, more so than rudeness, anger, or even brutality, which still
show that a person is interested, partial, cares. "Indifferent" people are seen
as lacking internal dialogue or as tragically distanced from it. When Mitya
Karamazov "hates but loves at the same time" the strongest negative emotion is a hair's breadth from the best.[3]

"Depth," like Ivan's demon, has its private anti-logic. And as the demon
said, each soul full of conflict is worth a universe. Katerina Ivanovna says
she *sees* Mitya's profound conflicts, which makes her his greatest friend and
advocate (Dostoevsky 1982 v.11:174). And, Bakhtin (1984:86) writes, "It
is precisely to this unfinalized inner core of Raskolnikov" that other *Crime
and Punishment* characters address themselves.

Oleg's friend Anatolii sometimes defined "pure" dusha as a "field between people":

> For example, three strangers on a train. The conversation just doesn't work. A
> fourth enters, and everything changes. You are [your dusha is] drawn to
> him. . . . Dusha is something that unites us all. . . . A friend is a kindred soul;
> another self. . . . When you talk, it's like a mirror. You look at him and see
> yourself. Warmth. One thing together. It's magnetism.

[3] This notion was part of what attracted Dostoevsky to the work of physician/zoologist Carl
Gustav Carus (see Chapter 2).

Although at times Anatolii's version reminded me of Bakhtin's, his dusha-between-people was a mirror, total harmony, like what Kozlov (1995) calls communication at the level of dusha, "talking with one's reflection." Svetlana said, "In friendship a person opens up. In love he should open completely." As Aleksandr Ivanovich said, "In a close circle of friends there appears a feeling of oneness of dusha. He has a little piece there—the same as you have inside . . . we are one thing."

Bakhtin (1990:81–82, 102) disagreed with this crude version. He makes an important distinction, defining soul as the product of powerful "sympathetic" understanding or co-experiencing, "akin to love" but not "pure empathizing." Co-experiencing "does not . . . strive toward . . . totally coinciding, merging . . . because such merging would be equivalent to a falling away . . . of sympathy, of love, and . . . of the form they produced." Emerson (1996:112–13) calls this a revisionist reading of the Christian adage that we should love our neighbor as ourselves: "technically I cannot love my own self . . . it is in this connection that Bakhtin develops his case against the awful temptation and fraudulence of the mirror."

Bakhtin retains interest as the motive force, but "Cognitive and creative forces are never fueled by mirror-reflections but only by . . . interaction . . . love is an urgent curiosity . . . an intensification and concentration of attention that enriches the beloved" (Emerson 1996:112–13).

Here we see Bakhtin in his culture but with his own preferences. He notices that everyday understandings of soul and ideals of dushevnyi empathy and striving to communion, if realized, would undermine the foundations of soul itself.

"I don't like spies and psychologists, at least those who poke into my soul. I don't ask anyone into my soul; I don't need anyone," Dostoevsky's Stavrogin says, in his confession scene. Bakhtin (1984:263–64) points out this "vicious circle" in attitudes toward others. I found this paradox to be endemic (Chapter 10). We need others to see our dusha but cannot tolerate when they try to crawl in there to look. Depths *must* and *cannot* be brought out. The hinting form of some feelings implies distance, thus authoritative authenticity, but this authenticity dictates that one can and ought to get closer, that is, *eliminate* that distance. Bakhtin tries to forge a model of dialogue empowered to create soul without implying that soul's destruction.

The power of individuals to develop each other, give each other life and soul, and the related emphasis on vision do not, of course, appear only in Bakhtin or just in dusha culture. They are ancient and widespread.[4] The theme of openness and soulfulness as contagious, evolutionary, and development-related that runs through my interviews is also, of course, not just Russian.

Although I twice heard theories of congenitally soulless individuals, people who offered these theories also offered contrary explanations: those

[4] See Todorov 1996. I discuss this essay below.

individuals had closed souls because of lack of communion (*obshchenie*) or as a result of interaction (*obshchenie*) with "closed" people. As Bakhtin (1984:287) said, "Absolute death ... is the state of being ... unrecognized." Svetlana said, in fervent, literal belief, that

> A soulless person, ... of course, *has* dusha, but it's closed, in a sac. ... This can start with very little: if a dusha is not surrounded by open dushi, if it's with closed ones, it never opens. If it comes in contact with an open dusha, there can be a break; the dusha can open up. An open dusha *conquers*, develops new territory.

Two different men, in interviews, made clear distinctions between false or surrogate communion and creative, proselytizing, winning over and developing of new dushi. And Lara said:

> Spiritual people gather around themselves ... the same kind of people, who are drawn to them, who interact with them, and become the same way, better and more interesting, near them. Part of being a cultured person is having the ability to organize around oneself at least a minimal circle of communion. ... One must exercise one's dusha. It develops. ... We all do that for each other ... there are things one cannot do for oneself. Sometimes someone you wouldn't necessarily trust responds. On the bus, for example, when you have the instinct that a person needs help, you give up your seat. And then *you* don't feel tired.

This "good thing people can do for each other" may take less elegant forms. Erofeev (1990:56) writes, "One should honor ... the dark of another's soul, one should gaze into it, even if nothing's there, even if there's nothing but crap there—stare into it anyway and honor, stare and don't spit."

Wierzbicka's (1989:52) definition of dusha$_2$ includes the following aspects: "Because of [dusha], a person can feel things. ... Other people can't know what these things are if a person doesn't say it; a person would want someone to know what these things are; because of this part, a person can be a good person." I have shown many ways in which people "with dusha" exactly do *not* need to tell each other things to share them, but that is beside the point; the last attributes of dusha$_2$ in Wierzbicka's list can be seen as telling a story that makes sense only in the light of a theory of *creative love*. This part of a person, the story would go, craves interaction, requires it. Newspaper and magazine "personals" sections during the 1990s were regularly called *Ot vsei dushi* ("From the entire soul") and *Krik dushi* ("Cry of the soul") (*Sel'skaia nov'* 1992 and *Sobesednik* 1992–93, respectively). As Nadia said, "You can't open your dusha to just anyone. Your dusha. But people try to find someone anyway ... You feel better, when you open it, your dusha."

The bringing out and recognition by others of internal parts is how they are realized, how a person becomes his or her best. This is creative love. Becoming one's best includes making others theirs. Wierzbicka does not mention that *by virtue of an identical mechanism, bad souls degrade good ones.*

"They Fall Silent, Close Up, Congeal into Finished, Objectivized Images"

Definalizing others and opening up, I have shown, are social and economic skills. When people "sit" together or otherwise try to see a "human being" in someone, it turns out that all people potentially have soul. *Dusha is always from some point of view, is not subject to context-free definition.* In the absence of shared experiences or the presence of some motivation to do so, there may be a suspicion that the other either has lost dusha or, more charitably, that it is groggy or locked up. On the other hand, the further "into" each other people see, by talking, sympathizing, "eating a pood of salt" together, according to any criteria identifying themselves as members of a group, the more soul appears to them, the more animated others seem. As Bakhtin (1984:59) said, "The genuine life of the personality is made available only through a dialogic penetration of that personality during which it freely and reciprocally reveals itself."

I mentioned earlier how Anna Viktorovna, discussing alcoholics, whom she called "already dead," shifted from a judgment of soulless to a recognition of dusha by remembering that Mussorgsky drank. She then continued describing communion as a window to dusha: "If he was once upon a time an *intelligent*, and that *intelligentnost'* comes from dusha, then you see that. When you start to talk with him, that coarseness of his falls away, and you see that that dusha of his is good. That's why good judges and prosecutors don't give a verdict right away; they look at a person, study his moral, his dushevnyi condition." The husband of a bureaucrat said, in an unusual lexical combination, that his father, a Stalin-era judge, had had a "very strict, good dusha." Of course, many who see themselves as "normal" Russians would categorize the speaker, his beloved father, and his wife as soulless. Public Prosecutor Yurii Yur'evich described how he once found himself faced with "a terrible person who had committed a horrible murder." "I could have shot him. But then you start to work with him and you start to see that somewhere, in his subcortex[5] or somewhere in him, there's still a human being. . . . There are no completely soulless people. . . . If he feels kind relations to himself, his spirituality, I think, can awaken. There are no hopeless people."

Hope and dusha are synonymous here, with love or kindness the active

---

[5] I discuss "subcortex" in Chapter 2.

force. "My job is to awaken the human being in people," Yurii Yur'evich said. "As long as there's conscience, a human being is human." Another time he described his job as "awakening conscience in criminals." "Dusha forces us to suffer about things," he continued. "*It* awakens conscience." Notice: Yurii Yur'evich, the criminals' Other, and dusha alternate as humanizing: in Chapter 11 I cite Y. Y. on his admiration for Dzerzhinsky; he described how painful it was to be expected to perform the opposite function—to revoke, so to speak, Iron Felix's humanity.

Conclusions

It's not so simple as having or not having dusha. Bakhtin was more conscious of that than people I talked to. It is a matter of approaching a person so as to help her or him not "close up and congeal" (1984:68). "*Only purely mechanistic* relationships are not dialogic," Bakhtin (ibid.:40) writes, mechanistic meaning, of course, soulless.

In Bakhtin, people rely on what turns out to be loving (that is, nonfinalizing) finalization for life and future moments of time. Dusha is "a human being's inner life . . . produced . . . shaped and consummated only in the category of the other" (1990:132). Dusha "descends upon me—like grace upon the sinner . . . not through my own powers" (ibid.:100–101). This image of generous, generative dialogue between people is like the Christian God, but the supreme, soul-generating, vitalizing value of interpersonal relations is also familiar from 1990s Russia. Anna Viktorovna's and Yurii Yur'evich's versions imply the same metaphysical beliefs.

Bakhtin found as features of the "idea in Dostoevsky" what I found as attributes of dusha. Both are unfinalized, unanalyzable inner cores of moral issues inseparable from a person's image (1984:86, 96, passim). Both are alive, that is, played out between consciousnesses (ibid.:85–88).

When Bakhtin writes that a true reader of Dostoevsky "senses his consciousness broadening through communication" (ibid.:68) and that "One should learn from Dostoevsky *himself* as the creator of the polyphonic novel" (ibid.:36), he is saying that *we* should focus on how Dostoevsky the person acts, because we too are morally obliged to definalize, to help others become more alive.

Bakhtin tried to infect his audience with dusha and was accepted by some in this spirit. Wayne Booth writes that "Bakhtin's ultimate value [is] . . . a philosophical inquiry into our limited ways of . . . improving—our lives" (Bakhtin 1984:xxv). Emerson (1996:121) notes that Bakhtin "is being read most eagerly in his homeland today not as a literary critic but . . . as a moral philosopher."

Finalization is static, monologic, "dead" (Bakhtin:87–8), what for Dostoevsky (ibid.:59, passim) and some Omsk friends was loss of life, dusha, and other people. Bakhtin tried to do what he saw Dostoevsky as trying to do. What, ideally, dusha does: generate a dialogic feeling for the world (ibid.:265). He lovingly definalizes Dostoevsky's work and represents it to us that way. He helps Dostoevsky's heroes become souls by exposing them as dialogic (ibid.:68), by showing them to be dushi. This is the canonized best one Russian can do for another.

Dostoevsky shows souls as soulful *externally* (resisting finalization by others) and *internally* (uniting opposites). Bakhtin in turn soulfully selects and names in Dostoevsky what is soulful, defies external finalization (dialogue between characters) and internal finalization (hero's and author's losses of unity, the "open-endedness of the polyphonic novel" [ibid.:39]).

Bakhtin writes that Dostoevsky had an "extraordinary artistic capacity for seeing . . . many ambiguous, complex . . . things where others saw one, hearing two contending voices in every one, hearing in every expression readiness to go over to a contradictory" (ibid.:30). Bakhtin shared this capacity, not only regarding Dostoevsky, but in a wider endeavor to show any utterance to be "a contradiction-ridden, tension-filled unity of . . . embattled tendencies" (1981:272).

Bakhtin (1990:100–101) used literature to investigate "the principles of ordering, organizing, and forming the soul." Dostoevsky was the logical object for this loving criticism, and, I suggest, *that love was evolutionary in intent*. Bakhtin contrasts Dostoevskian polyphony to Romanticism and drama (1984:27, 34–35, 201, passim), where "the world must be made from a single piece." "Drama," he argues, "may be multi-leveled, but it cannot contain *multiple worlds*; it permits only one, and not several, systems of measurement" (ibid.:34), whereas Dostoevsky, in Bakhtin's eyes, found "multi-leveledness and contradictoriness" in spirit and society (ibid.:35). In some ways 1990s Russians did too, as I discuss in the next chapter.

But I think Bakhtin was trying to represent the nineteenth-century dusha as striving *beyond romanticism*. He was implying that the romantic soul was not good art. As Karsten Harries (1968:149) writes, "Kitsch pretends to be in possession of an adequate image of man . . . by its very nature bad faith." Polyphonic, loving dusha is an attempt at actively dismantling "inhuman" coherence. Most people, despite irony and dusha's status as cliché, live it fairly romantically, with equally romantic Soviet mutations, but Bakhtin tried to reopen dusha's soul. To what extent did he succeed?

Mitya Karamazov says to Alyosha, "Only God sees the whole picture of my heart" (Dostoevsky 1982 11:144). But, as I mention in Chapter 2, it has been argued that Dostoevsky replaced God by the Russian nation, that "this Russian God was . . . the Russian people . . . The object of myth, they emerge . . . as its propagator" (Cherniavsky 1969:207–8).

But if the category or community of the Russian-souled is circular, it is also somewhat manipulable by individuals in historical context.

The ability to communicate, respect, interest—in short, who is *"ours"*—depends on dusha; this, in turn, depends on the ability to communicate.

God-given soul became Russian soul, and Russian soul Soviet, through this manipulability. Dusha is open to individual exploitation in the name of any number of criteria for community: national, economic, political. Bakhtin tried to use this leeway.

I would like to return for a moment to consciousness, which, though not often called by its name, *soznanie*, was an important implied aspect of many aspects of the culture I have examined. In many ways, as I show in many of these chapters, representation in consciousness *is* life; in other ways, life depends on something evading consciousness' dirty eyes. Strong feelings, phenomena of one's own and others' consciousnesses, the workings of a deity, society, and a category of "unconscious" or "subconscious" all appear in some context as approximately dusha.

Consciousness is consciousness of one thing at a time (a joke says that's why we *have* time, so things don't all happen at once). Consciousness is of different things at different moments, and the conscious person is accordingly different. Awareness that there are many such moments is *hope;* a person cannot be summed up by any one representation.

Dialogue and internal multiplicity give and maintain life, save souls from static, monologic, externalized death. This is fairly consistent with the power of a creator and source of vitality. But what sort of deity is implied here?

It is not under people's control that moments are given and lost. Passing, moments leave a trail of representations and aspects. But if moments are given abundantly, why is dialogic consciousness so desperately needed to save people's animation from being suspended? Hasn't consciousness, with its representations, taken on a lot of power over life and death?

There is evidence of an absence of faith here that time or a higher power will give a new moment of possibilities. In soul culture, there is an implied threat that if one fails to say no, to responsibly hold out for soul and negate, one will be summarized, destroyed.

Both creation of oppositions and resistance to structure are necessary to the dialogic practice of dusha, which abhors reification while creating it, playing on both teams. As Bakhtin (1984:235) says about "loopholes," dusha itself tends to reduce inner life to "a search for [one's] own undivided voice." This Platonic safari after deeper coherence is spoiled by the loophole itself. Voices clash in search of a "final, truly adequate" word (ibid. 56, 166), a search sabotaged by the same negating impulse that gave birth to it, the hero *"living* by . . . [his] capacity to outgrow . . . and render untrue . . . any . . . definition . . . *not* [having] yet uttered his ultimate word" (ibid.:59).

Bakhtin, in a sophisticated way, himself steals the word's finality. Tragic circularity and efforts to recombine form, content, worlds, consciousness, and unconsciousness, are inseparable from dialogue's life-giving power. So in this sense, he failed. But he epitomizes engaged, individual brilliance in a culture where multileveled complexity and clash are master tropes, where life and soul reveal themselves in dialogue, where others' otherwise evil eyes have a particular power and duty to *love*: to see and not see, penetrate to the depths, not *too* deeply. One might say that Bakhtin lovingly tried to bring "life" to aspects of his culture, in particular, to popular notions of self and community, that must have seemed to be degraded, absolutized versions of themselves.

CHAPTER THIRTEEN

We Lost Some Neatness

If this is a system, it's a very nervous one, this system.
                                                Erofeev 1995:284

Sistema means no system at all.
                                                Lara, Omsk, 1992

Traditional Western prohibitions against mixing metaphors and eclecticism feed off criteria and principles related to those used to judge sanity and morality in individuals and the coherence, unity, and autonomy traditionally expected of structures, systems, and paradigms, as well as realism in visual imagery (see Pesmen 1991). These criteria and principles are systematically conflated, and together distinguish what we respect from what we ridicule. Thomas Kuhn (1970:4, 91, passim) and Stephen Pepper (1942:104, 106, passim) each argue that eclecticism appears inevitably in situations of "development," "transition," and in "worlds" felt to be "out of joint." Both eclecticism and mixed metaphor have been called *infertile* and *sterile*: the consensus is that life rarely results from flawed unions. "No . . . combination of the legs of one specimen and the wings of another will ever move except as their fabricator pushes them about," writes Pepper (1942:112).

Mixers of metaphor and eclectics have historically been classified as inspired, inaccurate, impassioned, confused, unifiers, jokers, outlaws, fools, and everyone despite him- or herself—all images I found in post-Soviet discourses of national and ethnic character, identity, and culture. In the early 1990s, time and space in Russia *were* fragmented, messy, and mixed. People were often startled by it and often mentioned it. I found these notions of coherence in descriptions of past and current Russian shortages of "reality," "nature," "life," "truth," "validity," "morality," "form," and "civilization," and images of riddles, hybridity, paradox, mystery, lack of clarity, monstrousness, and chaos.

At the same time, these "imperfections" were regularly coopted as positively valued aspects of national character. A physician for whom I interpreted in 1995 in Chicago sprinkled her comments about how things were in Russia with the refrain "That's our Russian dusha, too." Her examples of Russian soul were everyday messes and ordeals resulting from corruption and mismanagement. She even called declining respect for the Russian language "our Russian soul," adding that you have to live *this* life a long time to understand that dusha. In this chapter I examine pragmatics of and categories involved in discourses of Russian anti-coherence. I begin with a short discussion of abomination.

A Mighty Deformity

> In 1917 ... Korolenko wrote ... : "the Russian soul has no skeleton ... or we have too little of it."
>
> Sinyavsky 1988:259

Mixed metaphors have been called "impure unions." Metaphors join in matrimony not only two terms but visualizable worlds in which those terms appear (Pesmen 1991). "Taking up a cross-scent" or making "impure unions" once a metaphor is begun seems to adulterously abandon a world of potentialities. Those who change models midstream are often themselves seen as morally shifty and/or as suffering multiple vision when they, in Horace's words, engender snakes with doves. After several such leaps, critics move from moral censure to ontological motion sickness, calling mixed metaphor disgusting, nauseating, spoiled. Mixed metaphor is also seen as logically invalid, whereas a good, unmixed metaphor has been called "one of the safest guides through the labyrinth of *truth*" (J. R. Lowell in Hunt 1891:103).

Historically, the only technique to avoid such monstrous abomination is to "surrender one's thoughts to the *picture* suggested until it is wrought out as far as needed" (Tompkins 1897:311), that is, visualize it. What mixed metaphors show looks absurd or improper according to certain fairly specific (nonModern) habits and styles of visual representation that demand one point of view on things behaving traditionally in one space, light, and atmosphere. Prohibitions against mixed metaphors and eclecticism reveal clearly how what is called reality is a matter of habit and habitual ideals. Realism, Nelson Goodman writes, is "an honorific term" determined, as Karsten Harries (1968:145) writes, by interest. What seems meaningful seems to promise or deliver something in the context of some ideal. But what Goodman (1978:20) calls our "passion for one world" is satisfied variously for different purposes at different times; we are always shifting models. Fernandez (1986) also discusses how implications of any predication made on the world never get completely worked out. We constantly move from model to model, neither noticing our opportunistic flexibility nor including it in what we call real. What tickles about mixed metaphor is less that it violates habitual ways of thinking than that it makes us notice them. By making us notice shiftiness, juxtapositions, and jumps we do not usually notice, mixed metaphor shatters our enchantment and wilts our belief in the picture's reality.

Robert Barrett (1987) writes that the Western ideal of a "person" with a grasp of "reality" implies that this individual should be autonomous, integrated, and unbroken. A similar ideal pops up in Russian discourses, yet "Russians" and many who have spent time around them often simultaneously indict themselves as a group for not living up to these ideals and value markedly opposite ideals. Descriptions of Russian national character and "insane" life invoke ill-formedness, schism, formlessness, and disorientation, defects that characterize many images of the Romantic soul, often portrayed in literature, philosophy, and everyday talk as a place where opposites struggle. Dusha often, apparently, manifests itself in situations such as "conscience," when one is pained by "internal" inconsistency. As I have discussed, souls are felt to be alive insofar as they are unresolved.

Culture, Africans, and *Papuasy*

> Why is there no AIDS in Russia?
> Because AIDS is "the Disease of the Twentieth Century."
>   Joke heard in 1992

A historically and still-popular explanation for allegedly "schizophrenic" Russian psyche, land, and "System" was that "Eastern and Western elements conflict" there (Berdiaev 1960:8). Chaadaev, in his 1836 *Philosophical Letter*, used this argument to claim that Russians were lost souls with a borrowed culture. The same argument was also invoked to explain dusha's supposed restlessness, craving for revelation and inspiration, and tendency to be "extreme." Soviet ethnography often referred to another image of Russia as hybrid and internally heterogeneous: *dvoeverie*, syntheses of pre-Christian and Christian beliefs.[1] Bolonev (1992:73) cites a Siberian ethnographer on the persistence of "ancient pre-Christian chaos."

Though most Omsk residents seemed proud to participate in Siberian vastness, they also opposed their so-called "uncivilized" "Eastern" System to what was civilized, cultured, Western. "Scratch a Russian, you'll see a Tatar" explained many ways in which Russians were supposedly only skin-deep "civilized." Speakers then often upped the ante: Svetlana said "We have an Eastern-type despotism . . . only *there* they have a sense of propor-

[1] See Balzer 1992 for Soviet ethnographic studies and Balzer's contextualizations of *dvoeverie*.

tion, measure, borders. Here—it's whatever you can get away with. *Russia*: enigmatic to the point of no return [boundlessness, *bespredel'nost'*]!"[2]

In daily life, flawed or absent coherence was often attributed to this "boundlessness." If a troubled career or multiple talents were evidence of the scale and potential of one person's soul,[3] Russian character and Russia herself were, like the Eurasian landscape, understood, inhabited, and presented in narratives, jokes and remarks as too vast to be virtuous, neat, rational, or stable, Russia's vital expanses and expansiveness allegedly dooming any efficiency or attention to detail on her territory. In 1992, I overheard someone say that "Omsk region is as big as a European state, and we're living any old way" (*kak popalo*). Defining Russian soul, Dostoevsky (for example, in *The Gambler* 1982:333) ridicules French "elegance." Berdiaev rhapsodizes about how "The West is conciseness; everything favors the development of civilization . . . [but] Russian soul . . . corresponds to the immensity, the vagueness, the infinitude of Russian land." "For this reason," he continues, "Russian people have found difficulty in achieving mastery over these vast expanses and reducing them to orderly shape" (1960:9). Jarintzov's romantic 1916 version alleges that few Russians cared about details of everyday life, leading to "the absence in Russia of spick-and-span households [and to] . . . disorderliness in the arrangements of one's time."

Lara said: "That spaciousness (*prostor*) tires me out. Spaciousness. With a sort of indeterminacy. It's hard for me to incorporate, to learn to live with that space." Mila said:

> That Russian flamboyance (*razmakh*) . . . people tried to set up their projects on a grand scale. . . . A sense of spaciousness, the unembraceability of it all, and from there on to all the positive and negative aspects. Positive is the desire . . . to do everything broadly . . . to live on a great scale . . . to the very edge of consciousness. And then the negative . . . when you have too much of everything, you can't approach things very rationally. You can't assimilate—the scale of what is laid before you. . . . Siberia is the site of an extreme version. . . . Unfinished projects and angles result. That's among our character traits. . . . We lost some neatness, some order.

Both internal conflict and sublime scale imply "wholes" that cannot be trivialized by what Bakhtin called monologic explanation. This sort of approach can be found in medieval Orthodox hesychasm's prioritizing of irrational over rational. Aspects of what Turner (1969) calls liminality are coopted as a soul that uses passion, parody, pollution, drink, inferiority,

[2] An increasingly popular one-word summary of "it all" was *bespredel* (*bes-*, without; *predel*, limits), originally prison slang for the end-of-the-world chaos of a prison rebellion.

[3] Mixed metaphor and eclecticism have widely been considered common in great or otherwise marginal people; "Bergson saw in . . . prophets and great artists . . . evolutionary potential . . . not yet . . . externalized and fixed in structure" (Turner 1969:108–9).

complaining, and foolishness to invert, negate, or shift at any perceived threat of classification. This results in a picture of human internal complexity and multifacetedness, where structural and formal "problems" are fundamental to life.

This relates to individual "culture" as well as national. Since the eighteenth century, varied and changing meanings of *kul'tura* have been intimately linked to meanings of dusha.[4] Plavil'shchikov said that Russians' "absence of formal learning, joined to a rich intelligence, held limitless promise" (Rogger 1960:274–75). Although people I interviewed respected education, they also stressed its limits. Zina said: "A *kul'turnyi* person is not necessarily educated; it's a person who remains a person with a capital P. Humane. Culture can come from many factors: education, and genetics, upbringing, family traditions." In this sense of culture (like Sapir's [1960] *genuine* culture), a *kul'turnyi* person is a dushevnyi person.

Evgeniia Pavlovna said: "A dushevnyi person may have very little education . . . but is . . . sensitive. He doesn't need many words. He feels dusha. . . . Our peasants . . . they were fundamentally dushevnyi. That is a fundamental property, I think, of a Russian." Mila marveled that uneducated people could have "a fine, innate understanding of the beautiful. Where do people get that kind of gift?" Lara said: "A *kul'turnyi* person has come to know a lot, but I wouldn't say he necessarily graduated from universities. He's more likely to be someone who worked a lot on himself." Kazannik did not exclude education from his definition of a *kul'turnyi* person, but noted that "Education has been used to be devious" and foregrounded dushevnost': "A *kul'turnyi* person has an education . . . But he is also a person who has recognized all the pain of his people, and who tries . . . to respond to it."

Education could be presented, if a speaker found it interesting to do so, as anti-soulful in the sense that it could be imagined to shape and thus limit dusha, depriving it of its formless potential. At the other extreme, though Anna Viktorovna said that a *kul'turnyi* person was "drawn to knowledge," she also included, unlike younger people I spoke to, good breeding and culture in conduct and attire, elements of what Dunham (1990:22–23) calls *kul'turnost'*. Fitzpatrick (1992:218) describes *kul'turnost'* as "contrasted with being uncultured, uncivilized, 'dark,' and 'backward' . . . *Kul'tura* was something that one naturally possessed; *kul'turnost'* was . . . purposefully acquired." This sort of culture, like education, could be externally obtained. There was no mystery about how one came to have it.

When I said I was studying Russian culture, people almost always grinned and asked me to let them know if I found any, implying that any or all of the "cultures" I mention above (prerevolutionary intellectual and

---

[4] See Dunham (1990); Humphrey (1995); Fitzpatrick (1992); Stites (1992); Rogger (1960); and Cherniavsky (1969).

folk, Soviet high and coopted folk, manneredness, or natural, soulful culture) were absent. Related was the discourse of civilization. Among other meanings in everyday speech, "uncivilized" (*netsivilizovano*) could refer to absences of bourgeois comforts, moral order, rule of law, rule of anything predictable. Andrei Sinyavsky notes that the Revolution brought about no new life but rather a world where light bulbs and garbage pails were important and a "normal, civilized" way of life nonexistent. This is a "normal" similar to that implied by, for example, 1990s TV coverage of domestic issues in which anchormen contrasted "normal, civilized" countries like polite, easy, orderly Czechoslovakia (See how well *their* currency reform went!) with us, Russia, the Wild East, wild because of its stage in cultural-economic evolution or by nature. But the same speakers would often go on to express scorn or ridicule for politeness, ease, and order (as insincere, naive banality). Whereas long before the nineties, "normal life" and "civilization" could imply material comfort, many Russians who called themselves "normal" simultaneously appealed to the value of their poverty.

Wild—unmannered—inconsiderate—insensitive to others—evil—animal was a path of association often traveled (not necessarily in that order). For example, a reason given for a Mexican soap opera's popularity in Russia was that "They relate to each other politely, like human beings; here people have become *animals*." Former Marxists found themselves and neighbors accumulating capital in the most primitive ways, and blamed the Revolution, Stalin,[5] or Gorbachev.

Although for decades African students had attended Moscow's Friendship of Nations Lumumba University, there had been no Africans in closed Omsk. Africa often appeared in 1990s Russians' discourses of themselves as "primitive." They also called themselves uncivilized, Chukchi, primitives, monkeys, and *papuasy*.[6] When Soviet lack of manners was targeted, "Africans," "monkeys," "Papuans," and "wild" were interchangeable. Two mothers I knew often yelled at their unruly children: "What are you, a Chukcha?" And Oleg's wife often "apologized," "We're backwards, we're monkeys," though she did not seem disturbed by it. This backwardness was set up to be coopted, as when her husband called post-Soviet poverty "African" and went on to favorably contrast Russian spirituality to African. A family of such comments referred to Soviet infrastructure and *khaltura*. *Khaltura*'s first meaning was work "on the side," but it was long used to indicate shoddy workmanship. "Even in Africa," which originally meant "everywhere" (as in "Even in Africa people fall in love"), had become common in remarks such as "Even in Africa public transportation is better than in Omsk." An Omsk newspaper in 1992 featured a front-page

---

[5] See Banc and Dundes (1990:125) for a joke portraying Stalin as the Master of Chaos.

[6] Soviet children had read of the travels of Russian ethnographer Nikolai Miklukho-Maklai (1846–1888) in New Guinea, whence popular awareness of *papuasy*. Stocking (1992:231) notes the presence of the "European dream of the Noble Savage" in Miklukho-Maklai's writing.

cartoon of a white man in spiky hair, grass skirt, and beads at a lectern, saying: "Comrades, I was in Africa. . . . Africa is living better than we are."

Africa was often used for what Leerssen (1996) calls auto-exoticism.[7] This involved "dialogic relationships . . . towards one's own utterance . . . if we somehow detach ourselves . . . speak with an inner reservation" (Bakhtin 1984:185). If, as Elias (1994:3) writes, "civilized" and "uncivilized" express Western self-consciousness, when Russians auto-exoticized it was partially in this voice of Western self-consciousness, partially in one responding to it, German *Kultur*[8] against the "external shell" of *Zivilisation*, in turn answered by Russian and Soviet voices emphasized according to speaker and context.

Ekzotika was often mentioned in a widespread sense: Foucault (1970) uses Borges's "Chinese encyclopedia" to show how juxtaposed points of view, though labeled exotic and foreign, make us aware of our own thought's limitations. A saleswoman remarked to me that for Americans to come to Omsk must be like Omsk natives going up to the taiga to see how people live there: "*Ekzotika!*" A similar, facetious comment was *Servis na grane fantastiki*! (Service [here] verges on science fiction). Everyday absurdities and disorder shock people in ways similar to how the exotic shocks them; their comments at such moments reflect this.

I noticed another meaning of "primitive" when a curator asked me if her exhibit on Omsk history looked like African art. When I expressed surprise, she explained: "We make everything ourselves, out of nothing, paint every bit of cloth, scrounge for every scrap of paper."

So "uncivilized" implied lacks of systematicity including: doing everything oneself; using "magic" to collage new things (door hinges) out of bits of old ones (strips of tire), significantly called *nothing*; and being governed by self-interest. These structural flaws were opposed to a "cultured" ("rational") division of labor in which things and people are used for their "real" purposes and do what they lawfully, logically ought to; and situations governed either by rule of law or by something larger than individual caprice.

Unsystematic unpredictability is "wild"; when Simis (1982:225) writes that corruption in a district hospital is more "civilized," he implies that *systematic* bribery is more civilized than unsystematic. Bricolage (Levi-Strauss 1962:16–17) in Russia, as elsewhere, evidenced what was felt to be broken structure. "Russia" (*Rossiia*) became a synonym for such dearths of healthy structure. Once, in Evgeniia Pavlovna's lavatory, just as I noticed that there

---

[7] "A mode of . . . representing oneself . . . in terms of an anomaly, a riddle, a question, a mystery" (Leerssen 1996:37–38). Taylor (1996) calls this self-irony in a context that also resonates with the Russian case; he cites Irish saying, "It may confuse you; it confuses us even more." Lloyd (1993) calls Irish texts too hybrid even for Bakhtin's model of multivocality (and uses an adultery metaphor for hybridity similar to mine [Pesmen 1991]).

[8] Like *Kultur*, kul'tura refers to much of what Russians claim to value most "in their own being," including innate or acquired tact, warmth, interactive skills, and creativity. An "innate" version claims that these things are natural, or at least entirely internalized.

was no toilet paper, I heard a piece of torn newspaper rustling under the rest-room door and my hostess' voice saying "Russian style!" As a young engineer said, "In one word, *Russia*. Where everyone is engaged in what he should not be engaged in."

As in Orthodoxy, where this world is seen as "nothing," "a shadow, a dream," grueling late and post-Soviet conditions were often called "not *real* life": "This life has been upset to the point where one can hardly call it a *life*" (Sinyavsky 1988:189). Yet surface messiness and lack of structural elegance or viability were often taken as indicating integrity "elsewhere," *internal* integrity. As Mila said, virtuosity is not dushevnyi and dusha is not virtuous: "Depth matters, not surfaces." Epithets indicating such attitudes to Russia's holy disorganization and complexity were such exclamations as "Russia," "Soviet Union," "Siberia," and "Asia."

Land of Miracles, Land of Fools

> A rabbit is trapped, but because of various shortages it can't be cooked; eventually it's let loose and runs off crossing itself and muttering, "Hail CPSU! Hail CPSU!"
>
> Joke heard in 1991

Rhetoric, poetics, and style texts occasionally condone mixed metaphors when they express or generate a mood we are to attribute to a speaker or a situation. In other words, a domain may be fractured if it is to be experienced formally, as representative of disorder *itself*. Thus when Hamlet ponders taking arms against a sea, critics, loathe to indict Shakespeare with mixing metaphor, have argued that Hamlet is impassioned, distracted, confused, all states in which metaphors are mixed and that supposedly characterize the prince's fragmented internal "space." Such hypothetical spaces defy us to understand "where we stand," as Foucault (1970:xvi) says, the site on which these things' propinquity would be possible. The sanity of the "space" is the concern, and Russia is such a site. The freshly former Soviet Union, as the "*Pole Chudes*" cartoon map I mention on page 69 shows, was such a site. "Only in Russia, only *here* could things work like this."

The writer Maxim told me that the mentality behind the popular phrase "Land of Fools" (*strana durakov*) was born of the Petrine reforms: "If you change too fast," he said, "people don't understand. We all became Russian fools." His dating is hardly definitive; an origin legend of Russia from the Primary Chronicle (A.D. 862), valued by Slavophiles and cited to me in the 1990s, is that quarreling Slavic tribes invited an outsider to come rule them because they themselves were incapable of making order. The "fool for Christ's sake" also predates Peter.

But Maxim's use of two points of view is astute: as I have discussed, Russian nationalists formulated an inexpressible, unlimited, unmannered, unpredictable, immeasurable collective soul in opposition to supposed European rational virtues, imagery that was newly reappreciated in the early 1990s. When someone indicated an individual's or the country's chaos or crudeness, labeled Russia or any part of it "theater of the absurd" or "circus," or displayed appreciation of the aesthetic that Bakhtin (1984:134) says erases barriers between genres, systems of thought, and styles, a voice that valued coherence was both implied and refuted "in a word."

I have mentioned newspaper article headlines that referred to the current Russia as a land or field of miracles, a mysterious place, and a land of fools. Examples are *Chudo Rossii* (The Miracle [or wonder] of Russia, 1992 *Nasha Rossiia*), *Neizvestnaia Rossiia* (Unknown Russia, Omsk local paper, 1992); and *Zagadochnyi bilet* (The Enigmatic Bill, a take-off on *kaznacheiskii bilet*, treasury bill), about rapidly changing, varied, and confusing currency (*Oreol*, Omsk, 1992). An article in the national newspaper *Komsomol'skaia pravda* titled "Long live Russian carnival, senseless and merciless!" discussed clowns, jesters, and fools in Russian history.

These were proud, bitter quips on national character and the limits of one's control over life in a country whose jokes about itself included:

> In Moscow a foreigner falls into a construction pit, breaking a leg. He wants to sue [at this point many Soviets already laughed, in reference to their incredible lack of such recourse]. The foreigner tells the judge that "in civilized countries" there are little red warning flags marking construction sites. The judge thinks, then asks the foreigner how he entered the USSR. "By train." "Didn't you see a big red flag on the border?"

Passing a playground in central Omsk, a friend marveled at absurd metal structures that, like all monuments to "our system's" degrading incompetence, were, he said, "good for nothing but for little kids to trip over." He grinned. "But they really *trip*, from the depths of their soul." Then we passed a factory. My friend told me that some process involving warheads at that factory regularly registered on radiation therapy gauges at a nearby oncological center and vice versa. "No joke," he said. "Russia."

In a Word, *Sistema*

I have discussed the importance of profane, blunt, or rude phrases and the significance of their condensed brevity. Such talk was "saying it *in Russian*." Like curses, the comments "Russia!" and "Soviet Union!" were powerful, condensed, stood on their own, communicated more than they said. This also is not new: Jarintzov (1916:67–68) describes the depth and vastness evoked by "the one syllable *Rus'*" [the old name for Russia].

A friend's family laughed uproariously whenever anyone said either the word *beskul'tur'e* (lack of culture) or *bezdukhovnost'* (lack of spirituality).

They explained: a comedian had told of how his performance in a small city had been disrupted by a drunk who eventually loudly attributed his behavior to "The sticks. The provinces. No *culture*. No *spirituality*. *Shit*!" The humor here hinges on consecutive evocation of contexts and meanings, their juxtaposition as synonyms, and a snowballing in which "Each new word . . . more exact and more execrable than the one before," explains and compounds it, as Sinyavsky (1988:220–21) says of a similar construction.

An important member of this genre was *Sistema* (the System), often used in such phrases as our system or our Soviet system. Dunham (1990:176) discusses the Stalinist use of *sistema*, including the phrase "the 'system' of a novel," meaning its "intrinsic structure." Lara called the System "no system at all." Mila called it "hard-boiled and soft-boiled at the same time." Others called it monstrous[9] or kasha or *vinegret* (a party salad of chopped or shredded vegetables). Yurchak (1997:25) writes that Soviet ideology ceased to be a system that "represented reality in a believable way." Sinyavsky (1988:xi) called the System "so novel and extraordinary that . . . even those who grew up within it . . . see it as a sort of monstrosity or alien environment—one, however, in which they belong." If these descriptions implied an unsystematic, weird, broken System, their *form* condensed, encapsulated, pointed at and valued the inchoate coherently, pointed at mess and inexpressibility neatly.

Russia and dusha do have their forms of unity or tidiness: on the radio in 1992, a writer discussed a book that helped him "bring his soul to order."

That outsiders could not possibly "understand" (or agree) with what the form of formlessness implied was a theme in everyday talk and comedic routines.[10] When I worked as a translator for Americans, their Russian host once opened up the comment "Russia!" for their benefit by adding the usually implicit word "paradox." An American picked up on this and subsequently explained some peculiarity as an "American paradox." Her host laughed, but, perhaps, politely, as if this transnational communion was about as meaningful as one he might have with a parrot. However, though immersed in "our life" and "System," Russians have long claimed that they themselves understand neither the System nor their soul: A. V. Nikitenko in 1867 claimed that "Russian spirit," though a commonplace, was "a great, meaningful essence," a meaningful essence that, however, neither he nor anyone else understood (Cherniavsky 1969:196).

As I have mentioned, words' meanings tended to be "very hard to express" when their meaning varied greatly with context—varied subtleties of disparate experiences can be summarized cleanly only by the word. Such

---

[9] Turner mentions the association of liminality with monstrosity (1969:95). In Chapter 11, I discuss how souls coopted by power are monsters.

[10] See Bakhtin (1984:164) on "reduced laughter," an "aesthetic relationship to reality [that cannot] be translated into logical language . . . could grasp . . . a phenomenon in the process of change." In the early 1990s the comic Zadornov marveled at how only Soviets understand Soviet jokes, at the inventiveness mandated by "our life," and at "monstrous" Soviet shop clerks who "lack the muscles and brains to smile." Cf. Yurchak (1997) on laughing at Soviet life.

words were all, like dusha, condensed and deceptively thingy. But even without "understanding," by using or correctly responding to such dense, wry comments, people shared consensus on the meaningfulness, the interest of their mess. Frequent comments were on how interesting or jolly (*vesëlaia*) the country was. As a friend said: "What a fun country ours is, always in reverse."[11] Nothing ever gets done, it was said, because "Ivan is sick, then Sasha goes on vacation, then Kolia goes on a binge; it's interesting here!"

In 1992, I asked an acquaintance "Everything OK (normal)?" He answered: "It's *never* normal here; every workplace is the country in miniature." Later I asked a friend what was happening in his workshop; he shrugged: "In the shops it's like it is in the entire country." When I stopped by that workshop myself, I quoted him. Everyone laughed, but said no, it's worse in the shops—it's a madhouse. Zinoviev's 1980 novel *Zheltyi Dom* (translated as *The Madhouse*) relies on the same metaphor for a scholarly institute and Russia.

Another epithet for the situation was *marazm* (senility), funny in the way a doctor called the hospital's "sterilizing" room the funniest place of all. Calling a context a psychiatric hospital or "not normal" implied that no one present, no Russian, could escape suffering in that community. This "laughing in the face of horror" (Bakhtin 1984:168) affirmed entire tragicomic narratives unnecessary to formulate because they were suffered together. On the TV news in 1992, after describing an official decision and its mysterious nonfulfillment, the news anchor commented that such a thing would be incomprehensible in the "Wild West," but, he said, addressing his audience with intimate irony: "You and I understand the mysterious Russian soul better."

Not only was Russia mythologized as a site of ideal disorder and monstrous abomination, but juxtaposed objects, tactics, economic systems, and styles were as heterogeneous and visible as newly gilded onion domes nestled up against rusty hammers and sickles. Exclamations of "Russia" or "Russian soul" explained how nuclear disasters were hushed up, how an entrance to a public toilet could be by metro token through blinking turnstiles, or how the cost of humanitarian aid could be exorbitant at kiosks that also offered toxic instant coffee, underwear, American-flag T-shirts, cigarettes, condensed milk, condoms, newspapers of varied dates, and bottles with misspelled English outside and stolen industrial alcohol inside. Leather miniskirts in mink berets stepped over drunk quilted peasant jackets in dogfur hats outside rotting concrete apartment blocks looming over ornately carved houses with antennas twisted to match the carving, houses exchanged for cars by workers paid in canned meat, shoes of useless sizes, and plastic sheeting. The train to Omsk once stopped in the middle of the

---

[11] This "in reverse" is related to quips that everything in Russia is done through the butt, "ass-backwards."

night in a town in the Urals where crowds of men and women who took their pay in crystal stood selling shot glasses, chandeliers, and crystal swans in the darkness. On TV church leaders solemnly blessed, one woman exaggerated, "boats, musicals, whorehouses." In late 1991, the radio asked how the same Supreme Soviet could declare both the October Revolution (or November coup) and Christmas national holidays. In 1992, television advertising featured a Proctor and Gamble ad for products no Omsk acquaintance of mine had ever seen, followed by a description of someone's lost dog. A firm called "Children's World" plugged automotive parts. Thirty seconds of dead airtime followed, capped by congratulations on someone's anniversary. In spring, a radio show began: "We congratulate those who are celebrating May [International Worker's Day], and congratulate those who are not celebrating what ought not to be celebrated." People jokingly greeted each other with the slogan "Peace, Labor, May!" and laughingly offered the Easter response: "Truly, He is risen!" Shops were not privately owned, but prices varied and taxes appeared and vanished according to alleged laws that changed often and secretly.[12] Calculators were used to add prices, registers produced a receipt, and an abacus was used to figure change given in bus tickets or individual wooden matches. A bookstore sold cassette tapes, cognac, and eyeshadow, and then one morning it was closed and crates of rare oranges were carried out. Overnight, street corners sprouted pyramids of ketchup; the next day there was only one bottle, lying at a village market between a pair of socks and a pig's head.

A firm dealt in chemicals, wheat, knitting machines, boots, and aluminum-related products. On its office coffee table sat a large metal valve, full of milk, being tested for leaks. A partner went to Moscow to buy aubergine-colored wool coats and returned with Soviet military watches with "Operation Desert Shield" faces. Time was fragmented as people forgot where they were going to queue up for whatever was available and debated planting their gardens using astrology or almanacs and then used both; leaving, between all the systems, precious few auspicious days on which to replant their baby tomato plants.

This texture can be explained as a by-product of socioeconomic conditions, change, and a shortage economy, but I rarely heard sociological explanations invoked either in the media or by individuals. Some things that surprised me, such as collections in glass cases, were never mentioned, but most of the heterogeneity I have just listed was both called to my attention and discussed in situations where no foreigner was involved. Other comments and headlines I cite also confirm that the idiom of surprise was regularly chosen over less interesting ones.

---

[12] For example, in December 1991 a so-called "Gorbachev" 5 percent tax, which for a brief time had been tacked on, vanished; in a few days rumor had it that a new 28 percent tax had been instituted but was already included in prices. See Humphrey 1996 on private ownership during this time.

Although "this reality of ours" or "That's our (Soviet) system" explained when things looked funny or did *not* work, the System had an equally mysterious invisible hand: "Bosses stole and stores were empty, but somehow we got approximately what we needed." I describe how a table set for guests condensed people's life stories, talents, temperaments, opportunism, and luck in buying, hoarding, sharing, gardening, canning, stealing, bartering, bribing, and calling in debts. Yet when women worked the system to materialize meals, people called them magicians, speaking in the voice of naive observers who see only shocking results in a "Land of Miracles." Techniques were so varied it was hard to believe a meal could condense it all. Having to invent ways to get things done was part of what was implied when Russians talked about how they *krutilis'*. When a friend and I tried to bribe someone, he nervously assured the bribee that I, although from Chicago, *iz Chikago*, was "completely Russian". He meant that I understood the System. When planes flew empty, but you couldn't buy tickets; then flights were so full, people sat on the floor, but Aeroflot was not fulfilling its plan, and forms used to report the number of passengers appeared in toilet paper holders; when a torn-up building opened into a spotless bathhouse, people said "the System," "Land of Miracles!" or offered another, similarly terse explanation.[13]

The same woman who asked me if her exhibit looked like African art asked, "Doesn't our enigmatic Russian soul frighten you?" and went on to describe Stalinist horrors and repression. This, she said, "is in our genes." As the corrupt, unsystematic System began to disintegrate, many who had hated and suffered in it still complained that dusha was dying. Abominations, irrationalities, and new versions of the System had ready places in discourse. "That's our Russian dusha too," as the Moscow physician sardonically punctuated her descriptions of absurdity and abomination.

As adults were modifying the Stalin-era term *sistema,* it was, remarkably, being adopted by "hippies" to describe their *counter*culture (this process began in the seventies and eighties; See Rayport Rabodzeenko 1998). *Sistema* was semiotically hardy enough to gain in scope of reference, increasingly widely used by youth groups as it was used increasingly richly to refer to post-Soviet messes. Often discussed as dusha's loathsome nemesis, it had enough of the right stuff to be coopted and revitalized as newly dushevnyi.

This implies a transformed, surviving dusha; but one man told me: "Dusha has to do with belief. Formerly it was in God, then . . . in the party and a bright future . . . but now," he said, launching a special Omsk military industrial lament: "People have no command center . . . *An organism that's*

---

[13] I was often told that to understand Russian dusha, I had to read Il'f and Petrov. This had both to do with *krut-* imagery and the sort of stories that made Russia "the Land of Miracles." See Simis (1982:127) and Wolfenstein in Mead and Metraux (1953:431) for more examples.

lost its steering is like a missile with no guidance system ... Dusha has lost something. Dusha now has no belief, no orientation except economic."

The Return to the Whole and the Containing of Multitudes

A traditional argument against mixed metaphor is that it is confusing; it takes too much work to unify the different images. But the work required by mixed imagery can be seen and used positively. Art that lacks dissonance, lacks tension, displays no glitch in "the union between conception and execution," may be considered bad art (Harries 1968:75–76). Similarly, Basso (1976, passim) and others (Coleman 1999) have shown that ill-formedness and enigma can be "powerful instruments of expression." Fernandez (1982, 1986) describes how, in their sermons, Bwiti knowledgeable ones mixed metaphors, "cross-referencing domains" and encouraging movement "between text and context," creating "spaces" where, "by condensation, by extension and expansion ... and by the performance of metaphoric predications," aspects of what was felt to be broken cultural life were apparently reconciled.

Russia's changing state also featured "challenging sources of incoherence" in the face of which individuals systematically wove images of emptiness, failure, incompletion, "the forces of disorder," and communitas into identity, a fabric made dense by conflation of different definitions and contexts into the condensed unity of overdetermined words like soul, system, or Russia. These "nodes of interconnection between planes of classification" (Turner 1969:42–43), like those in Bwiti sermons (Fernandez 1982:571–72), *suggested* rather than *stated clearly*, achieving a sense of seeming incoherence seemingly reconciled by an apparently higher principle.

Conclusions

Now this portrays realistic pictures of wholes in their best light: these integrations "help." But such pictures also have an element of what Harries (1968:75–76, 149) calls kitsch; by offering solace in a simplified image of humans and groups as even potentially coherent, they can be seen as being, I suggest, in bad faith. As Adorno (1974:50) says, inverting Hegel's dictum, "The whole is the false." Harries (1968:150–51) writes that transformation of traditionally transcendent, therefore vague ideals into something finite "makes dogmatism imperative," taking as an example the Third Reich's uses of kitsch. Lloyd (1993:89, 98–99) calls kitsch "a virtually inevitable consequence of [cultural nationalism's] aesthetic programme," its "monologic desire." The coherence without which common sense refuses to confer the "honorary" title of real and meaningful is, I suggest, kitsch. It only soothingly appears to reveal identity, a kind of identity that often leads to struggles over hegemony and to murder. The formation of cultural or psychological wholes felt to be authoritative and "real" is fully continuous with how identity is politicized and made violent.[14] Wholes and identities engineered, for example, by exaggeration and generalization of contiguities, through opposites and negation, and through indiscriminate use of spatial models are, I believe, *made* to be manipulated.

Since I began this chapter with more widespread senses of coherence, I want to articulate one way in which my critique in these chapters has been directed to some extent at my own soul and cultures in which I am complicit. Absolutized partial models for identity, continuity, and coherence of souls, selves, identities, individuals, families, blood kin, groups, and nations reproduce spatialized worlds in the image of reason. If Russian soul can be this sort of kitsch, so can others, and in related ways. Still, these reassuring coherences are only temporary. "Worlds' " stabilities are always threatened by history and other surprises.

One of soul's tactics is to coopt daily life by denying it reality, affirming depth and solidarity in a potlatch of self-defamation. Jesse Jackson was quoted during the 1992 American presidential campaign as saying he would visit Russia when everything started to improve. A Russian anchorwoman paused to comment, with smug pride, that if Jackson waited for *that*, he'd never come. In a joke from that time,

> Mitterand, Bush, and Yeltsin find themselves before God. Mitterand asks when things will be OK, *really* OK, in France; God replies, "fifty years." Mitterand bursts into tears and leaves. Bush asks when things will be OK, *really* OK, in the United States. God answers, "One hundred years." Bush bursts into tears and leaves. Yeltsin approaches and asks God when things will be OK, *really* OK, in Russia. God thinks, bursts into tears and leaves.

Some of the "size" of dusha that makes it seem to defy reckoning exploits the fact that people and groups are fleeting moments, impulses, tropes, identities, approaches, and practices. What is selected and foregrounded as dusha carries with it the distilled richness associated with the whole; terms dominated by dusha share this reference and power. But what if the notion of the "whole" gets its "vastness" from something everyday and unappreciated: people's multiplicity *over time*? In this sense, soul is what human flexibility and incoherence look like or become in interaction with a hegemonic model of the center, of depth.

---

[14] Tambiah's (1968:189–90) description of how magic creates a "realistic picture of the whole" strikes me as remarkably similar to how he shows ethnicity constructed and made violent (1996).

Dusha reifies and idealizes inchoate pronouns and phenomena, making them possible to visualize and represent, giving them a clear form (what Fernandez [1986:11] calls the mission of metaphor). The form it gives, however, is the form of the unclear, unformed, and transcendent. In critique and complicity dusha searches for coherences and rebels against them, timeless Platonic wholes, complete with the futile project of capturing them.[15]

I have cited an Omsk friend saying that we only become aware of soul when life causes us pain. For Peirce, "The subject or self is only a moment . . . when . . . habit is interrupted by the surprising facts of the world" (Coleman 1996). Our habits of "reality," what we label *that by which we are persuaded*, are very much based on images from within one moment. The sense of soul seems to be to some extent modeled on such moments of value-laden consciousness, generalized, again, in the image of reason. Assuming it to be a single "thing" leads to a sense that it must be such a painfully huge, deep thing, more messed up than God is powerful, that a simple word marking the spot has to be enough.

[15] Emerson (1996:117–18) writes of "Bakhtin's . . . delight at . . . multiplicity and unmanageability." "Bakhtin implies that we cripple ourselves . . . by seeking truth in a hypothetical, static state of Being. It is precisely the absence of such preexistent order . . . that obligates us to attend so carefully to particulars."

PART VI

CONCLUSIONS

Two Discussions
Semantics and National Character / Homo Sovieticus

Semantics and National Character

I return now to two approaches from which Russian soul has been approached in the past, to give a brief sense of how this study relates to them and to recapitulate a few ways in which it differs.

Dusha was embodied by different dominants at different times, and all the time people and those words and images were "reciprocally educating each other" (Peirce in Singer 1984:55). Informed by history, power, belief, and economics, the late and post-Soviet soul was involved in the occurrence of specific miracles, mysteries, and hopes. With perestroika-era discrediting of Soviet ideologies and a widespread sense of loss, the "spiritual" gained new vitalities and forms. Obsolete and dated words changed, increased in frequency, and some, such as *obshchenie*, were displayed in wider usages. Old themes such as the pollution of pure souls were revitalized. In the course of creative, grueling Soviet winding one's way "through people," twistiness and complexity, already part of Russian dusha, were enriched. As *Sistema* increasingly richly referred to the late and post-Soviet condition in terms of incoherence, internal struggle, and contradiction, *Sistema* became increasingly like Russian soul. None of these factors and meanings are easily accessed or reflected in studies that focus exclusively on semantics or that focus on describing a mentality or national character.

Much in Wierzbicka's (1989, 1992) study of dusha is supported by evidence and analysis in this book. This book also reveals shortcomings of a purely semantic approach. As I have said, Russian soul must be seen as a historically and individually contingent repertoire of options, limitations, and practices. The project of defining a limited set of souls or meanings of soul looked increasingly flawed as I noticed how dusha's meanings opportunistically interacted and blurred. This led to thoughts not only about dusha's meaning but about its relationship to meaning (I discuss these further in the Conclusion). I have discussed some aspects of Wierzbicka's study; I will touch on a few more here.

Wierzbicka cites Tsvetaeva's "I am my soul—my perception of it," claiming that there is no implication that feelings, emotions, and thoughts in dusha, hidden unless one reveals them, may be hidden to the "insider" as well (1989:51). Though the category of unfelt feelings is a queasy one for me, my data show beyond a doubt that belief in the possible existence of a closed or sleeping dusha, hidden to the "insider," is very important to beliefs in and practices of soul. Dusha's relative and changing visibility are a key to many aspects of its culture.

Wierzbicka says that other people cannot know what is in dusha if a person does not say it. This does reveal some tendencies of dusha, but it also suffers from lack of ethnography. It is clear that people experience communions that are affirmed by condensed, silent, "intuited," or gestural representations, and that those interactions are exactly about and with dusha. Such shared knowledge also indicates ways in which dusha does not just belong to an individual but unites people in everyday ways and, like the Christian God, is where all people are simply one. Dusha is never from one point of view and cannot be defined out of context, and Wierzbicka's study overlooks this.

"A person would want [another] to know what . . . things [in dusha] are" is an aspect of Wierzbicka's definition of dusha$_2$ I would say that a person with a "good" or "open" dusha, minimally "in contact with it," would indeed want that. But no one is always (seen as) such a person. Furthermore, although Wierzbicka sees the mixing of meanings of dusha in speech as important, and includes the possibility of bad things being in dusha, dusha's genre requires examination of exactly *how* bad, sleepy, possibly dead, corrupt, or polluted dushi get to be that way and how they come to be *seen* as that way.

Wierzbicka describes dusha's breadth generously, but it is still narrowed down. She maintains that one cannot feel surprise in dusha. Everyone I asked about this disagreed, saying that one can feel anything in dusha as long as the feeling is "strong," "deep," "with all of one" (or, I'd add, underneath a surface of something else). Wierzbicka mentions that "*Dusha* is . . . a symbol of pricelessness." One can go farther: dusha is linked to pricelessness's constituent aspects, value and limitlessness, and this relationship is far from only "symbolic." Another not-"just-symbolic" aspect Wierzbicka misses are the specific interrelations of body and dusha, such as ways in which physicality offers proof of, strengthens, and is a locus of dusha. Without looking at these, we miss seeing the ways in which "internal" representations can *be* life.

⌒

Studies of Russian "character," "mind," and "mentality" go back, according to Hingley (1977:18), to an account written by Baron Sigismund von

Herberstein after serving as the Holy Roman Emperor's ambassador to Muscovy in the 1500s. Although the term "mentality" is still sometimes used, "national character" studies were most popular from the 1940s to the 1960s. But if I argue against the premises of such studies, the horse I am beating is perhaps not as dead as it may seem to some who see these approaches as long-abandoned. Despite strong thoretical arguments against "essentialization" and classical social-scientific categories, including "culture," our descriptions of individuals and groups often continue to be shaped by normative expectations of the visual and static and systematic, especially when we are talking like people and not like scholars. I have said that these categories are disrespectful and disguise as much as they reveal. Here I touch on a few sample topics that both appear in national character-type studies (by Russians and by non-Russians) and are treated in this book in order to briefly indicate how different approaches to and assumptions about human beings can result in different meanings being derived from similar phenomena.

For this discussion I chose an arbitrary beginning point, my category of "expansiveness," from which a number of topics follow in a chain. Dostoevsky (for example, in what is called his "Pushkin" speech [1985b]), may have been first to formulate Russian soul's "universal compassion." It has since been mentioned countless times by authors without[1] and within[2] Russian culture. A number of authors, acutely, have noted how volatile this inclusive compassion is: Gorer and Rickman (1949), for example, attribute to Russians "deep warmth and sympathy for all whom (at a given time) they consider as 'the same as' themselves" and of the expectation of "hostility from all who are 'different.' " Mead (1955) sees them as tending to "assume the coexistence of both good and evil in all individuals . . . an expectation that friends could behave like enemies was combined with an expectation that this behavior could be reversed." However, these authors, by finding "trait" to be a proper description and "tendency" adequate, miss entirely that these are *practices* of manipulating and negotiating personhood, individual and all sorts of group identities and affiliations, and economic and political realities through the imagery of expansiveness, an expansiveness not separate from what Dicks (1967:638, 643) reifies as a "drive" or "need" to acquire "more space."

Hingley (1977)[3] wants to avoid national character studies' "universalizing and essentializing" pitfalls. His book is generous, informative, and specific, but fails to avoid the pitfalls. For example, in his study of "the Russian

---

[1] See Sapir (1924:313) on how Russians only take "elemental humanity" seriously; Mead (1955) attributed to otherwise "rigid" Russians "a strong countertendency to establish complete equality among all human souls and to wipe out all social distinctions"; versions can be found in Turner (1969) and Friedrich (1979). I mention a few more and discuss Sapir's use of these images in the Epilogue.

[2] Such as Erofeev's, Kuprin's, Chekhov's, and others I cite.

[3] See also Ries 1997:24–25, n. 7.

mind" ("the" is symptomatic of the problem), he offers astounding statistics on Russian territorial expansion, but uses them as support for reproducing Russian self-characterizations (some of which can be true), such as the link between expansive Russian land and mentality (ibid.:29–30), without examining the contexts, genre, or phenomenological status of terms such as expansive.

I have examined social and cultural contexts for phenomena that can create impressions and observations such as Kluckhohn's (1962:214–15) about "the [Russian] people" being "warmly human, tremendously dependent on . . . affiliations, labile, nonrational, strong but undisciplined, and needing to submit to [both hateful and essential] authority" and Dicks's (1967:638, 643) that the Russian "always needs direct, spontaneous, heart-to-heart contact and communication, a sense of being loved and belonging, and he respects that need in others"; "loves . . . total investment of strength and feeling" and "is distressed by distant hauteur, formalism, and bureaucratic protocol and hierarchy." I have also shown that concepts such as "depth," "heart," "total investment," and "respect" imply specific meanings and practices.

Examining meanings, practices, and genres of terms such as "civilization" and "depth" makes statements such as Sapir's (1924:313–14) that Russians resist "subordinating the depths of personality" to institutions and civilization seem very vague. Similarly, Gorer and Rickman's (1949:189–90) claim that Russians "pay little attention to order, efficiency and punctuality" must be put in some very specific context to mean anything, especially since most Russian homes are tidy.

Gorer and Rickman's (1949) description of Russians as "preoccupied with exploration and verbalization of feelings possessing them" and Mead's (1955) and others' that "little distinction was made between thought and deed" can be taken in the context of values of representations such as emotions or feelings occurring "in" or emerging "from" persons. Statements of intention, offers, and lies were neither just thoughts nor just words but were seen as generous impulses coming out of dusha, thus already valuable acts. I have discussed such actions' social powers; in the Conclusion I treat representations' believed-in and lived powers.

Kluckhohn (1962:214–15) summarized the then-current "national character drama . . . being played out in the USSR" as centering on pairs of opposed tendencies or tactics. This is directly related to the image of Russian soul as internally contradictory (though, of course, linguistic models of contrastive sets, perhaps another influence on Kluckhohn, are not only Russian). More recently, Mikheyev (1989:634–35) writes:

> It is a long-standing tradition to deem Russia . . . an "unintelligible country." . . . At the core of this riddle is, no doubt, the Russian national character, the so-called "mysterious Slavic soul," . . . such a bizarre combination of oppo-

site qualities that it hardly lends itself to any rationally plausible interpretation. . . . The problem . . . [is] trying to integrate all the possible explanatory concepts into a single coherent structure.

Mikheyev finds the concept of mentality to be an adequate coherent structure; it is only adequate, however, if one is looking for a core or single structure underlying something conceived of as a riddle. "Mentality" is simply unsuited to show anything else.

In the same vein, more can be understood about Russian suffering than Rancour-Laferriere gets at with his diagnosis of a masochistic "slave-soul." It is certainly true that "Russians do not merely suffer." But when he continues (1995:5) that Russians "have concocted for themselves a veritable cult of suffering" and "tend to injure . . . defeat . . . humiliate . . . or sacrifice themselves unduly" (ibid.:7), he appeals to his own culture's standard of psychological normalcy, opposed to a "cult" (implying "primitive" behavior) Russians have "concocted for themselves" (a derisory phrase standing in for most workings of culture, society, and individual). Rancour-Laferriere uses *dusha* but does not examine it, an examination that might have contextualized and thereby challenged his central notion; dusha and the Western, psychological soul are old cronies.

Glazov (1985:18–19) writes that Soviets do not trust foreigners,

as from [the ordinary Russian's] point of view they are made from another sort of stuff altogether. Their language is not "ours," not Russian. They do not have a Russian soul. He cannot drink vodka with them, or talk in a friendly way about everything in the world, including troubles. . . . And even if a foreigner [called *chuzhoi*, not-ours] speaks Russian, how could he understand the realities of life in the Soviet Union.

This reflects details of many Russians' thoughts about foreigners, but practices related to solidarity and otherness show it to be desperately impoverished conceptually. What Glazov sees as dependable "facts," "things Russians think," are common results of individual negotiations that may occur in myriad situations, from ones involving foreigners all the way to issues relatives and neighbors dealt with daily.

Sinyavsky, in his thoughtful 1988 *Soviet Civilization*, shows continuities between Russian and Soviet cultures, to the point of calling the USSR a renamed Russian empire. But because he, like these other authors, does not include the parts of the dusha "myth" with which he agrees in his list of "metaphysical principles of the system," his categories remain static. For example, though Sinyavsky says that "national character, . . . 'popular soul' and its psychology, is a mystery" (1988:258), and takes as his goal rather to examine Soviet civilization and how dusha changed during the Soviet era, he ends up (ibid.:233, 258–61) both arguing that "Soviet civilization cut the cord of cultural continuity" and describing Soviets in terms of "tendencies of the Russian national character," "the composite of the Russian soul."[4] Russian and Soviet souls clearly share terms and descriptions; but if this is Sinyavsky's position, in what way did the Soviet era cut cultural continuity? And if Russian and Soviet souls are that similar, did the Soviets really touch dusha? Sinyavsky depicts dusha both as dead and simultaneously as the same old Russian one (both everyday Russian assumptions).

If, as DeVos (1968:15) writes, national character studies simply assume culturally inculcated elements held in common by members of a particular state, one might agree: many people living in the same place share many things. The present study reports the continuing salience of discourse and other phenomena that national character and mentality studies drew on. But even if all Russians said and did the same things, describing them in such terms would be misleading. If one does not examine the phenomenological status, processes, conditions, and practices implied by and involved in terms and concepts one shares with the culture studied, entire sets of meanings are missed.

Some writers on national character note that Russians object to their diagnoses (e.g., Gorer and Rickman 1949, Kluckhohn 1962:214). There are nonpsychological reasons for this. One is that dusha is not a thing, so "meanings" and "characteristics" discovered by purely semantic, national character, and mentality studies are victims of the same reification as the word *dusha*, victims of stunted understanding of their own genre. Such formulations' theoretical ability to do justice to their authors' often excellent data is amputated.

Again, without examining the flexibility with which images, discourses, and practices were manipulated by individuals and groups, adapted to historical contingencies, and related to each other, one cannot see how spatialized depth, transcendence, and centralization organized meaning. If we do not question that people and other mysteries are organized around centers, we have no choice but to look deeper and for static sets of qualities. Depth is a belief.

Homo Sovieticus

I show descriptions of Russian nationalist soul and national character and rituals involved in Russianness being transformed into the 1990s. Writer Alexander Zinoviev, in his 1982 novel *Homo Sovieticus,* writes a late Soviet-souled Underground Man, a bitter, ambiguous émigré speaking out in a journal-like "report." I will briefly use this work of literature to help sum up some aspects of late Soviet and early post-Soviet dusha.

---

[4] Sinyavsky's (1988:258–61) outline of that soul includes patriotism, "mystical devotion to something vast, vague, . . . inexplicable"; shapelessness, "somewhat amorphous, not completely formed"; "universal compassion"; and "satisfaction from the fact of being Russian. . . . Notions such as *svoi* (one's own) and *chuzhoi* (alien), *nashi* (ours) and *ne nashi* (not ours)."

According to Zinoviev, the Soviet soul's life depends on others: "The soul of the Homosos lies in his participation in collective life" (p. 84). Traditional communions ("eating, drinking, shouting . . . Nothing we say is in any way binding") that helped soul pour out and defied metering of time (which "isn't money. It doesn't even exist") could be facilitated by state socialism (pp. 65, 140–41). Such behavior, as well as dialogue with others or oneself, relates to what Homosos calls a "stereotype of behavior" by means of which Soviet man transcends truth, error, and primitive, rigid, Western "convictions" (p. 11). While sitting, everyone, even criminals, "officials of the Central Committee, the KGB" were "human beings," could be found to have souls. One must be a "Homosos" to have access to the hearts of one's fellow-drinkers, but once exposed, these "hearts" made available information and other things money could not buy (p. 132).

Zinoviev's hero holds the West in contempt, setting up Russian superiority by ambivalent Fëdor Karamazov-like buffooning tactics: "If they call us *Homo Sovieticus* . . . I will go a bit farther . . . *Homosos* . . . a fairly disgusting creature" (pp. 32–33). Homosos's rejection of the West is tempered and torn by curiosity and love. His alleged superior scale and internal paradox (p. 33) are direct inheritances from dusha.

The notions of consciousness (*soznanie*) and self-consciousness (*samosoznanie*) have important Soviet histories. Historically contingent Marxist class consciousness supposedly had the power to transfigure individuals' actions into ones that potently, accurately engaged the world with a transformative power. There was also a notion of conscious Bolshevism, themes of self-analysis, and "taking a look at oneself." Zinoviev's hero portrays Russians as absorbed in a self-consciousness that prevents them from ever being a virtuous anything, even themselves. His irony and parody when he calls Homosos the highest product of civilization, universal, capable of any frightfulness, possessing every virtue, naive, simple, Nothing, Everything, God and Devil (p. 199) show a late Soviet dusha suffused with *self-consciousness of exactly Russian soul*.

Homo Sovieticus laughs at his own passionate creativity, which, by eschewing meticulous precision and by omitting parts, discovers more elegant mechanical solutions than the West. If these solutions for some reason do not work well in the everyday sense, that's all right: his inattention to picky detail is under divine protection. In hindsight, none of it matters anyway (p. 18). Homosos is in a state of grace by virtue of his Russian soul.

If Homosos' unfathomability is in part due to the inadequacy of mere words ("there is as yet no adequate terminology" [p. 55]), foreign words are altogether useless: "You can't translate Russian problems into foreign languages" (p. 10). If historically, the West was seen as incapable of understanding Russia partially because the West had inadequately suffered, the Soviet era upped that ante: "What's normal life for us is from the Western viewpoint . . . nighmarishly difficult. . . . This is where our superiority lies"

(p. 49). Where suffering is emphasized, one might expect to (and does) find the virtue of loss and poverty (p. 202).

Zinoviev's Homo Sovieticus is especially shifty when an outside eye tries to define him. The narrator claims that if the West ever loses a war to the USSR, it will lose precisely because of the clear image of Soviet man created by Western special services and sovietologists on the basis of conversations with Soviets (p. 39), conversations even the genre of which they cannot possibly understand because of their lack of flexibility. Soviet society itself tends toward "indeterminacy, fluidity, mutability, block- and multi-think" as well, "jelly-like units [that] form a jelly-like whole . . . a society of chameleons; and so the whole resembles a kind of giant chameleon" (p. 74). This is exemplified in a section on *iskrennost'*, sincerity (pp. 52–53; see also pp. 11, 16), in which I recognized what, at the time, I awkwardly described as a "second soul":

> Sincerity has no meaning when applied to . . . Homosos. . . . Everything depends on the circumstances in which [he] exhibits his qualities. . . . There is nothing in him which could be called genuine, because "genuineness" is only one of a number of . . . possibilities. . . . But everything in him is natural in the sense that it corresponds with the concrete conditions of his life. . . . Homosos . . . would be glad to be [sincere], but he can't, because he considers that he is always sincere . . . if he is ready to change one sincerity into another from one minute to the next, this isn't a sign of insincerity.

When we see the fluidity and context dependence of "genuine" and sincere, it is clearer how Homosos's innermost, individual center is bound up with power: "Was I a collaborator with the KGB? . . . Homosos doesn't collaborate. . . . *He himself participates in power*" (p. 53). Power inheres in soul, and masks go all the way down: "I knew that my . . . [unmasking] was only a bit of theatre. But . . . it was genuine, because all the actors played their roles correctly and naturally. . . . I was mortally wounded" (p. 87). This is not, of course, newly Soviet (see Crone 1978:17); neither is it Russia-bound: this "crown of creation," writes Zinoviev, is simply "human"—any reader can find Homosos in him or herself (pp. 199–200).

Conclusions

We include internal feelings as part of dusha, like love, hate, envy, empathy, fear. *That whole positive to negative range* we call dusha. Dusha is like another sense organ. A person sees the world through the prism of dusha. Everything depends on what kind of dusha that person has.

Anatolii, Omsk, 1992

I summarize and distill some of the chapters' results here but repeat very few examples. I must again stress that the cosmology I am describing is what I found, not what I would have chosen to find. It is, in ways I have no control over, my cosmology as well, but I am not presenting this picture of the world in a spirit of admiration.

In Omsk I heard that a soul, entering a body, makes it alive. Russian soul, dusha, was also about life. Discourse of how soul was experienced and understood included constant mention of life and increase, intensification, and decrease, withering, of life (connected to the waxing and waning of soul or someone's contact with it). One might provisionally call this soul a force, property, or ways of behaving experienced as alive. This is synonymous with having a tendency to "expand" itself and "broaden" other things, and is opposed to what was often called "this" or "everyday" life, considered to be less alive, deadening, not *life*.

Dusha was felt to be starved or fed, and as growing or shrinking, strengthening or weakening accordingly. Individuals, types of people, and modes of action *with* or *for* dusha were distinguished from those that threatened to decrease or damage it. People or actions could work for or against dusha (a polarity no doubt exaggerated by the fact of speakers focusing on it; I assume that there are more neutral experiences that were not formulated).

A particular enemy said to be killing soul was *time*, usually mentioned as an extension of "this" life and "this" world. It was malicious, constricted, ravaged, perverted time defined by shortage and friction; defined as not subject to individual control, against people, full of what was meaningless, not interesting, not loved. Time's and this life's actions on soul were formulated spatially, as lowering and cramping dusha, maximizing surfaces rather than depths, exposing soul to and forcing it into predictable patterns. This was accompanied by a morally charged range of spatial perversions and limitations.

Suffering was said to develop, increase, sensitize, *and* deaden and harden soul. It was felt to unite people except when it was felt to separate them. When pain was too great, a person's soul could be described as getting sleepy, covered up, coming to "contain" almost nothing or even alien things related to the cause of pain.

Depth was an expanse assumed to extend away from a "surface" of perception. I found practices of believing in and valuing depth in a wide range of contexts. Practices of depth imply values and continua related to bringing things from one inner, outer, conceptual, or cosmological order to another. Surfaces were often valued in terms of what they were assumed to "express" about depths. Some implied deep centers were positively and others negatively appreciated, defined as they were separated, by contingent values and natures. Their complex relationships and formal similarity were part of what made cultural quality spaces defined by depth and surface so overdetermined and important.

In this metaphysics, life, that which animates, makes more like soul, is inseparable from what I call *representation*. Life force is implied to have two positions in relation to consciousness (the "surface of perception" I mention above). On one hand, soul implies strong conscious representation, in which case a "deader" dusha is covered over, locked up, hidden deeper. On the other hand, depth, as in the Freudian belief in the existence of "deeply repressed feelings," also implies exactly what is *not* clearly consciously represented. In this universe, deeper implies both *more* and *less* soulful.

A mechanics metaphor helps here; again, it is similar to the sense of the world Freud translated into psychological theory. We supposedly feel life force only when it is, like kinetic energy, moving. Potential life force, though unfelt, is assumed to have the same qualities, only suspended in the future. Unconscious, generative depths are absent as kinetic, but are potentially represented or imagined. Potential is experienced either as belief in domains that coexist with this one, or as incomplete, unclear representation. "Deeper" and "higher" imply either more potential or more tracks left by past movement. Such "tracks" may be valued as much as is potential; as emotion-charged experience and memory (that is, part of dusha), they themselves generate representative life force. This is how any change of state may increase a sense of life, and even suffering may "deepen" and enliven dusha by how it "damages" it.

⌒

The legendary romantic futility of trying to pin down Russian soul and peer into its depths is enforced, reproduced and embodied by it formally.

Classifying, treating, or understanding things as unclearly or incompletely perceived, attracting, concealing, inexplicable, complex, internally contradictory, irrational, unattainable, distant, or inexhaustible characterized them as marking depths, "other domains" where something essential was believed to reside. Clear representation of these other domains' otherness is usually considered impossible to fully achieve. Such other "worlds" were believed to be inhabited by experiences not fully experienced, unfelt feelings; they were also believed to be the source of creative works and actions from the soul or heart.

The difference between *inner* worlds and *other* worlds could be minor; both were characterized by maximal difference from the everyday and were ideally expansive enough to generate or encompass anything. If soul was one's internal world, cities, countries, rooms, furniture, acts of communication, artworks, people, and other entities seen as framed or bounded, such as distant places, times, dreams, realities, or lies could also be called and treated as worlds. Speakers and agents might move fluidly between these contexts.

Dusha increases life by taking representations *in* (called soul) and by bringing representations *out* (called soul). Dusha was both distanced worlds and the process or tool of communicating with them. An increase of awareness was called dusha and was understood as something moving *outward* or *inward*; what calls soul to mind increases soul and often is it.

What is treated and spoken of as dusha's voice, though rarely considered audible, is felt to take forms that seem to confirm a model of emergence from a distant, highly valued space, and seems to challenge people to go deeper or bring meaning out. The content and relative clarity of "emergences" and the ease of their "emergence" are taken as defining an individual soul's nature or condition. Promptings from "within" were assumed to be ideally truthful, benevolent, and / or omnipotent, but they were not always. Although the assumed content of dusha (or of worlds dusha mediates) was ideally better, healthier, and more generative, bad things did end up in or affect the depths. For example, negative things gained access by being hidden, unclear, nonverbal, or extreme or by causing emotion or interest, that is, by being formally like dusha.

Most elements of deep, romantic Russian soul had reproduced, revitalized and modified 1990s forms. This dusha implies transcendence and depth (and vice versa) through various predications and practices. One is shared experience. Another is generalized protest and ambivalence. Others have to do with classifying and treating things:

- with reference to *invisibility* and other opacities: things are unclearly or incompletely perceived, unattainable, or distant.
- with *hyperbole*: things are construed as highly complex, inexhaustible, vast, intense, or infinite.
- with reference to *inexplicability*: things defy clear understanding, as they are internally contradictory, irrational or antirational, or dualistic.

⌒

Statically, dusha is treated as a center where *all life is one*. Dynamically, soul "unites us all." Individuals' sensitivities to and faith in this are obscured to greater or lesser degrees.

Each person has context-dependent relationships to soul's continua and quality spaces, positioning him- or herself in them, inhabiting, embodying, enacting them idiosyncratically. There were also historically specific ways of coopting various soulfulnesses and incorporating social change into dusha culture and vice versa. Very un-soulful (when looked at generically) attitudes, could, at a given moment, be (called) dusha or dushevnye, and virtually any action might be done in such a way as to be classifiable as for dusha by someone. Suffering, poverty, feasting, riches, and pleasure are all called "for" dusha; *dusha is an individual's relationship with something*.

This relationship may include what is described as an "internal" impulse or pressure that people respond to idiosyncratically. Russians may be assumed to all have soul, which tries to bring "that" world into "this" one, but what helps one person "open" at a given moment may be unique or opposite of what would satisfy another.

A person seen as having a more restructured, corrupted, or diminished dusha may be described as, like all souls, striving to create expansiveness and inclusiveness, but failing to the extent of spreading corruption just as dusha spreads life. That is, the condition of dusha, one's way of enacting it, tends to be contagious, to reproduce itself. If souls bring more of their kind into the world, by the same token, artifacts can vitalize, propagate truth or life, or devitalize, make more evil.

The soul of a discipline, language, or medium is its potentials, conditions, principles, manipulabilities; intimacy with some*thing*'s or some*one*'s dusha leads to being (like) a creator, working well with it, speaking for it. Art, as it itself comes from deep or far, is supposed to touch one profoundly or greatly. Representations emerging through people may communicate, represent those other worlds in others or call them out of others. Some people are seen as having strong, open channels for *that* world to flow through. Others have healthy but painfully narrow outlets. Others have no developed outlets and can be broken or strangled by their soul. Certain people could be seen as conduits for Russian soul without even "having" it. These are just examples of possible descriptions.

Education and effort were often thought of as developing innate channels more than as actually giving birth to them. Another point of view claims that talent itself comes from contact with other souls. The Marxist principle that true value is created by work becomes continuous with the idea that work and talent are engendered by love and interest, which emanate from the depths, seat of values and affinities. The idea that talent is God-given and that it is the result of effort or upbringing may alternate; the ideas that love is the result of effort and that effort is the result of love may alternate in one person's words or in different contexts and people. This parallels alternating ideas that dusha is given to everyone and that it is developed and nurtured; they are dusha-life seen from different contexts, for different purposes, in different spirits. Facility, effort, and achievement have limited authority unless they are linked to something more mysterious, in this case, love.

A "healthy" relationship to some place in or out of oneself is something all people need and can have, or perhaps some people cannot, as they have too little interest, desire, or hope (left), or perhaps they have it, but in relation to an unhealthy place. These other worlds are *necessary;* need from "within," but need; so that a person without contact with a vital other world may well be assumed to have a high chance of physically dying. Physical and spiritual are linked by the way representation is treated as life force. I return to this.

Some terms that alternate with *dusha* are spiritual world (*dukhovnyi mir*), internal world (*vnutrennyi mir*), soul-makeup (*dushevnyi sklad*), complex of subconscious experiences (*kompleks podsoznatel'nykh perezhivanii*), subcortex (*podkorka*), and psyche (*psikhika*). Words, notions, images, or gestures that condensed many apparent opposites, domains of life, and situations on some current playing field of authority, mediated among individuals, social conditions, and values, could become associated with dusha, and could be said or implied to be "one and the same" as dusha or "synonymous" with it. Such things can be sites of ritual dusha or metaphors for dusha, related to it, informed by it, intrinsic to its reproduction.

Some things I heard called "synonyms" or "one and the same" as dusha were:

- Internal contradiction and contradictory things.
- Life, usually human.
- Hope. "Where" to find hope for individuals can be "where" to find soul.

- Conscience.
- Breadth, increasing scale, and propagating scale. Russians may be seen as participating, to the extent they have dusha, in their motherland's vast creativity.
- Russia (land of miracles). Patriotism and other versions of love of this land are also dusha.
- Sincerity (transformative, community-generating "openness").
- The vast Russian land. Exporting natural resources (petroleum products, lumber, diamonds, etc.) was central in perestroika / early post-Soviet capitalism. Much discourse regarding betrayal and prostitution of soul was in terms of sale and rape of the land. What was done to one was done to the other.
- Music. As representing what words could not and as linked to emotion, music formally shared dusha's goals and was a good channel and form for it. Talent or love for even non-Russian music was often taken as a sign of an alive soul.
- The Russian language, the best linguistic channel for dusha, especially in the forms of literature and poetry (formally even closer to dusha, as its "body," "spirit," and "sense" were felt to resonate). Language could also metonymically confirm and participate in the sense that "we" can communicate with and be understood by *ours*, but not by *not* ours. Profanity could also be soul; in passionate, oppositional impulses, elliptical representations understood by Russians, "strong language" got things off one's chest.
- A person, a human being. Without dusha, one is an animal, machine, or monster.
- Intuition, impulses, premonitions, and inspiration: dusha's voice, representations from elsewhere.
- Fluency in the culture, habits and knowledge of "the right thing to do," even, in certain versions, etiquette, might be called intuition or soul. Similarly, rituals, activities or processes tied to generation of Russianness / humanity, such as drinking, hospitality, the steam baths, and conversation, could be "dusha."
- Interest, which evidenced and could associate anything to dusha. Interest indexed value (of any sort) and motivated connections between people, including economic ones (as the difference between interest and *self*-interest could be forefronted or finessed). People were widely seen as corrupted in this way, by something that seemed alien to the speaker (such as money) becoming part of dusha. Experiencing interest or joy could be becoming conscious of dusha (in or outside of oneself).
- The unconscious. What was assumed to exist, although it was not experienced, could be *life* and soul insofar as it was understood as too vast or deep to be encompassed by one (conscious) moment. This could be conceived of as a generative "source."

- Friendship, love, consideration, compassion, kindness, tact, generosity, openness (whatever happened to draw people "closer," decreasing "distance" between them).

Things could be considered necessary and/or sufficient for dusha, such as understanding, suffering, or living in the Soviet Union; as indications of soul, such as unclarity, talent, simplicity, complexity, interest; or as signals of soul's absence, such as alienations, abuses of hierarchy, cruelty, stinginess, and other forms of calculation. *Dusha, emotion, depth, and centeredness* were conflated or otherwise co- or mutually defined and determined.

Idiosyncratic, spontaneously generated tropes for dusha I heard included my tape recorder, its indicator lights, its tape; a violin's soundpost, missile guidance systems, a sense organ, a prism. Beloved individuals, both personal acquaintances and historical figures, writers, musicians, artists, performers, and political leaders, becoming associated with one aspect of dusha, could be linked to dusha itself. In a chain that illustrates the possible promiscuity of these elements, Dostoevsky, in part due to his characters' passion and internal conflict, was equated with Russian soul; dusha, in turn, was often said to be gotten only through understanding "how *we* live;" understanding Dostoevsky was called a key to understanding Soviet dusha; and living a life like this was seen as helping understand Dostoevsky.

Individuals, like Bakhtin (who had a dushnevnyi agenda on dusha itself and created formally and informationally dusha-like categories) and my friend Grisha (who tried to embody Romantic dusha and was mentioned by acquaintances as a prime example of aspects of dusha), have idiosyncratic ways of relating to dusha.

This shows how topics I have discussed and new ones can be dominated by dusha and, as such, when they themselves appeared in a situation or discourse, it in turn might be understood in terms of dusha culture.

Exchange raised issues both of dusha and possible opposition of interests and a state of mind that has forgotten that *people are one in dusha*. Dusha united people, taking advantage in many ways of people's lack of logical coherence, for example, by a shifty ritual management of consciousness.

There is a widespread sense that speaking something's name invokes it. Representations are, in some sense, given a power related to existence. What one mentions, displays, sees, matters. People could be responsible for providing a stage for dusha. The explicit image of economics, for example, was unacceptable and threatening at some times and for some people; one way to control such imagery was to attenuate speaking of cash and to attenuate having visual and observed contact with it. Formalism, etiquette, embarrassment, drinking, time, imprecise calculation of debts, and eclectic barter were tools that helped blur images of exchange enough for an aesthetical sense and set of practices called dusha to affect economic value. Taking advantage of the breadth and flexibility of terms such as *helping, interest, friendship, culture,* and *dusha* also helped transform business (through people) into community (through people) and vice versa. These terms' formal similarity and associated behaviors were used to purify, mask, exploit, and to allow people to act in ways that allowed for more than one interpretation. Emphasizing community involved formulating experiences according to an aesthetics of "complex invisible threads" connecting "friends." Soviet dusha's rituals mediated between generosity, shortages, and market pressures; this System, systems held in tension by dusha, was sometimes seen as having elements of an invisible hand.

Personal identity in such a situation included repertoires of what one could do for and through others and skills in creating good feelings, sometimes but far from always evaluated according to variously determined criteria of "genuineness." If dusha was practices of increasing a contextually determined kind of life, then hospitality, generosity, help, kindness, and conscience, the first associations with Russian Siberian character, represented dusha.

Soul made one want to respond, to answer, and apparently *automatically* responded on feeling warmth, witnessing need, or identifying another soul by trying to make things good for others. It warmed people (made them more alive). Offering from the "bottom" of dusha implied agreeing to be such a conduit; some people examined themselves to see if they were doing this; others focused on exercising their ability to perform the rituals persuasively. Ways of being dushevnyi used by individuals to define themselves included obeying traditional soulful rules, modifying them, and breaking them.

Drinking, a dominant of hospitality rituals, was a privileged context for spirit-related activities; alcohol's importance had profound implications for economies, from household to state. Drinking's property of always saying something about a person's soul in part related to how it could facilitate "emergences" into consciousness. In this way as well as in how it seized and defined time and space, drinking could be seen as humanizing. Drinking also, however, when it replaced community, becoming an end in itself, could indicate, reveal, or cause absence of dusha, often attributed to absence of *hope.* To be humanizing, drinking must remain a protesting, magically generative, uniting path, a connection of some sort, for example, between people.

‹౨⁀

As ways to unify kinds of interest and transform them into each other, as a medium of mutual understanding, affecting consciousness, and sometimes enjoyable, hospitality and actions involving alcohol can be seen at their best as earnest attempts at socially, culturally, and economically acknowledging human multiplicity and incoherence. They were also often just powerful tools for trying to assert the hegemony of one version of dusha. In both cases, these tactics were often seen as attacked and damaged by events of perestroika and what followed.

‹౨⁀

Practices such as hospitality, drinking, and generosity were also used to categorize souls along individual, national, regional, directional, and historical axes.

Russian soul could be seen as encoded in "blood" or "genes," and some people had strict criteria to discern subtle behavioral signs of "genuine" dusha, but the volatile way communities were made and remade left the possibility for non-Russian Soviets and people raised in dusha culture or even briefly engaging in it to persuade others that they had Russian soul. So one might say that human interaction was a key to Russianness, humanity, and life; and indeed, shortages of it were said and implied to cause physical illness and soul damage.

Different degrees and proof of understanding were needed for someone to be deemed animated by different people. The diversity of criteria for animation was mediated by, for example, how life experience and social conventions could be called "very deeply" ingrained and emotions "deeply felt."

If the "expansive" and "emotionally egalitarian" Russian soul included tools to find some seed of sleepy or wounded dusha in even the worst criminal or alien, in any specific situation there were blind spots, defects in an observer's ability to forgive, *see*, represent soul. If understanding and human contact "revealed" soul, being *not one of us* was validated by *lack* of understanding. Any difference in experience, character, or approach to life might become the source of generalizations. So if lack of mutual understanding was rarely formulated as dramatically and brutally as soullessness, all lacks of understanding had the seeds of soullessness. If at a given moment people find no common interests, tactics, cares and values, class, economic bracket, citizenship or ethnicity, it's hard to find dusha. Anything that foregrounds such issues, including individual and collective acts of exclusion, tends to make people notice other such contexts.

❧

Soul always implies more than one point of view. For example, for an "outside" audience (however ephemerally defined or fluidly negotiated), "spaces" were generative; for an "insider," opacity provided privacy, an "internal" freedom, perhaps used to accumulate potential emergences. Things could bear dusha when given; but another gift hostesses gave that guests could never provide for themselves were moments of abundance, license, and warmth, representations of a world outside everyday life, time, and space. In any such interpersonal "openness," offering images of over-abundant "everything" and convincing others to accept them could create relatedness, though sharing representations of poverty and hardship could do the same.

❧

Moral and aesthetic values attributed to outside and inside, appearing and disappearing, were absolutely context-dependent. Their conflation into one static or cumulative model, soul, seems to reveal abomination: negative cohabiting with and polluting positive *inside*. Dusha culture in history resulted in a conscious representation of invisible threads intertangling good with evil, ideal with actual, and everything with the material. One key to this was soul's life-giving internalizing. The good was hidden and the bad was hidden. The good was understood as cherished deep inside and the bad was felt to be taken to heart. Sharing the same internal position, they came to share more. Inside and outside defined both soul and its antitheses. Since certain words, notions, images, or gestures could, at a certain national or personal moment, become (like) dusha, these things, getting "deep in," could become impostor souls, their foreign agendas empowered by dusha's authority and laws.

❧

Like exchange, political power, seen from various points of view, reveals much about the semantics and pragmatics of dusha and larger lives of its rituals and images. The implied rational narrative of power and soul runs like this: power infiltrates and replaces dusha, (re-)creating society in its own image, as "the [sociopolitical] System." *Sistema* and soul were formally similar. Usurping dusha's structural role, power subverted and coopted its terms, forms, and tools; it coopted culture and habits both of attenuating representations of exchange and of positing different things inside and outside, coopted hiddenness, invisibility, complexity and depth, including imagery of magic. Powerful people, it was said, stole from honest, trusting, enthusiastic souls by speculating on and shifting the meanings of the finest words, best impulses, and most soulful qualities.

Authority of any sort, like talent, implied some specific domain to which an individual had an "alive" relationship such as interest or love. A person could be governed by different *spirits*; a center, something peripheral, or a corrupted center. Power was represented as obtained by one or another form of selling one's soul for something else or allowing something foreign access to dusha. People willing to make (or unable to not make) this deal did so by following institutionalized pathways and obeying "external" demands. Power corrupted by making people not listen, forget, block things from their consciousness, blocking out, in particular, other communities to which they had belonged. This made them (seem) soulless; being deaf to soul's representations was, approximately, losing soul.

Evidence that the powerful had diminished dusha was that they were often seen as not participating "normally" in exchange and ritual. Respect, like interest, was a mandate to make contact with something or to treat someone as a human being. The powerful supposedly "didn't drink" with "normal" people and played one-sided roles in hospitality, feeding off the System. Inadequate emotions and loyalty on the part of the (centerless) elite were also predicated.

Having become calculating, insensitive, deceptive, and self-interested, the story goes, powerful people began living *inside* the System. They kept their power not through "real" authority but by demanding the same fawning tribute they had used. They were freer and less free, more and less visible than normal people, because their vital force belonged to the System, they were familiar with the System; their community was under its sign.

Again, however, soul's visibility and invisibility were relative; it was construed and reconstrued. Semantic and sentimental shiftiness allowed people to negotiate community by indicting others for less than soulful motivations; solidarity was formed against those with "less" dusha. Including oneself or others in the category of normal people could diminish the sense of corruption: they were victims of the System. The elite, of course, were often very skilled in creating and manipulating soul, and so could be presented (by themselves or by anyone interested in exercising or displaying a compassionate, universalizing soul) as souls also exploited by power, in the structural position of dusha, normal, animated in relation to even higher powers.

The attenuated consciousness seen as involved in getting power (unlike another choice of how to see things, the consciousness-management involved in "friendly" exchange) was considered bad and connected to a "state of mind" all Soviets were said to have been in. Those seen as doing things in the wrong spirit were implied to make the world such that "normal" people were also forced to live by the sword. Crookedness, brutality, self-interest, and masks spread like a social infection *and like dusha*. If dusha is the ability to unite, masks and crookedness were negative life forces. "Masks" both shielded humanity and dehumanized, distanced. Sometimes, mask was all that seemed to be left.

Dusha was used to define groups but claimed a spirit of inclusiveness. Situations seen in terms of power and economics (and treating situations in these terms) threatened exclusivity, (in)comprehensibility, cruelty, and stagnation. Thus social life was seen as governed by a system that treated normal people as *not*-people, making them sick. Those ruled by power in any capacity (often called animals or less than human) suffered muffling, shrinking, perversion, distortion or deviation of dusha. In other words, differential power made groups alienate each other into similarly infected notpersons who could call each other soul-dead, license to further hurt each other.

Seeing a person as soul-dead could imply a problem with the observer's own soul (his or her inclusive compassion). It was more dushevno to charitably moderate the judgment into one of a groggy, locked-up, sleeping, distorted, injured, withered, or dirty soul or one hidden from the person him- or herself. A final, serious verdict that someone's dusha was dead was to no one's advantage except in a case of securing license to kill people; no one can kill a soul. An important image of inanimacy is that of machinery—finished, explicable structures with nothing emergent. In a machine, nothing is transformed, only worn down, by virtue of force moving through it. It creates at its own expense. Dusha, on the contrary, is generative, gets better through use, and cannot be fully explained. Only a machine, a person of a group seen as opposing one's own, a "beast," or a "monster" can be killed—an entity in fact already soul-dead.

❧

If soul injury was related to people becoming less able to see soul, communication, love, and joy involved seeing *more*. Others' eyes could be loving, positive, and life-giving or logical, dispassionate, negative, deadening. As dusha is always from some point of view, dusha could be eclipsed or ignored, revealed, discovered, or injured by representation in others' eyes. It is not so simple as *having* or *not having* dusha; it is a matter of *approaching* a person in such a way that dusha is visible. The further "into" each other people see, talking, sympathizing, sharing difficulty or other togetherness, the more soul appears to consciousness, the more animated others seem.

Conventions of "open" soulful behavior and consciousness itself were active in realizing the value of the center. Focusing on dusha, recognizing it, opened it, increasing it, increasing life. Other people could do this for one. Interest helps souls realize themselves and others, gain life and reality; indifference is soul death. Love, like interest, helped one see or act toward someone or something without finalizing. Interest and joy were emotions often experienced on (respectively) suspecting and recognizing what one accepted as soul.

I have discussed how both good and bad were brought "in." A similar distinction was often made between kinds of assumed "emergence" from the depths or representation in consciousness. Some appearances are characterized by things experienced as being still submerged to infinite depths or inextricably dissolved in mystery, enigma, and contradiction. These are treasures to be displayed and shared. Other things, such as "bad things" "leaving," seem to have finite roots and appear to consciousness "on the way out." People may treat things of the first category as things of the second; this is *finalizing*, representing things in such a way as to cut off their depths. Mistaking things of the second category for things of the first sacralizes the profane.

In the context of generosity I discuss notions and rituals of *everything*. "Everything" is a dusha dominant. If some cultures stress the existence of several differently named souls in an individual, dusha's wide semantic / practical range leads to overdetermination of one word. Wierzbicka (1989:52) describes dusha as including "virtually all aspects of a person's personality: feelings, thoughts, will, knowledge, inner speech, ability to think"; Bakhtin defines the depths of dusha as the "sum total of all higher ideological acts." I often heard it called simply "all of a person." As a result of the weaving of everyday life and history into "dusha" and "dusha" into everyday life, *dusha* is overdetermined, not only in relation to the person but in relation to its own definition. For example, as often as dusha was presented as anti-practical, anarchic, or passionate, it was connected to calm warmth and stability. Things gain the authority of transcendence or depth by carrying definitions from different contexts back into a word's apparent unity. And vice versa: dusha and depth carve the world into categories that, projected onto experience over time, are betrayed and betray themselves. This sort of violation of ideology through psychological shiftiness and human multiplicity and incoherence is made a source of value by being encoded into an image of soul as a vast locus of paradox: the greater the internal struggle, the more "profound" the soul; the more it suffers, the more it lives.

What is selected and foregrounded as soul, dusha, carries with it the distilled richness associated with the whole; terms and practices dominated by dusha share this reference and power. I have suggested, however, that the notion of the whole may be stealing some of its "vastness" from something less romantic, something utterly everyday and unappreciated: people's multiplicity and incoherence over time. In this case, soul can be seen as *what the phenomena of human flexibility and incoherence look like or become when molded by belief in a hegemonic model of an integrated center, of depth.*

᭡

Descriptions of Russian national character and fragmented, messy Soviet and post-Soviet life, time, and space were often in terms of riddles, hybridity, paradox, mystery, unclarity, monstrosity, and chaos. These implied violations of habitual, spatially understood notions of coherence that are intrinsic to habitual meanings of reality, nature, life, truth, validity, morality, form, and civilization. "Uncivilized," for example, could imply lacks of systematicity including messiness, lack of division of labor, collaging new things out of bits of old ones, and situations governed by self-interest. Flawed Russian national coherence was auto-exoticized as interesting, uncivilized, Eastern, Wild-Western; as metaphorically African, Chukchi, Papuan, or simian. As with early Russian soul, such discourse coopted these "defects," partially in the name of potential and partially as implication that broad inattention to picky detail was under divine protection and would not really matter in the end. The late and former USSR's richly described lacks of life and reality indicated both unviability and internal, deeper, future integrity, life, and reality.

A genre of comments indicating these simultaneous attitudes toward everyday life's holy weirdness, messiness, irrationality, disorganization, inefficiency, complexity, and incoherence included epithets such as Russia!, Soviet Union!, Siberia!, Asia! and Russian soul! The form of such nouns, like dusha, condensed, encapsulated, indexed, and valorized incoherence coherently, pointed neatly at messiness and inexpressibility, in a form (only) those who could understand could understand. An important member of this genre was *Sistema!*, which implied exactly *un*systematic, contradictory, weird, broken; "a monstrosity or alien environment" in which, however, "one belonged" (Sinyavsky 1988:xi).

If I drop the terms "synonym" or "one and the same" so often volunteered in my interviews and consider dusha as Fernandez sees metaphor, as giving form to the inchoate, *dusha clearly uses the form of the inchoate to* weave a coherence out of images of emptiness, failure, partiality, incompletion, communitas, and disorder, a fabric made dense by the polysemy of inside, outside, and other spatially imagined and lived "nodes of interconnection between . . . planes of classification" (Turner 1969). But it is, by form, a rationalized coherence.

If routine made dusha "tear off from consciousness," violating routine could bring it back in. Dusha's life depended on practices of ambivalence, on preserving unresolvedness by creating oppositions and mysteries that could not be reduced, reconciled, or summarized. This could pass for "freedom" or "will." Like the Hebrew God, the depths must never be diminished by being fully represented. Something fully seen, it is assumed, can be replaced by a logical, conscious model.

Dusha, life, can be seen as appearing moments of consciousness in conjunction with beliefs that things potentially conscious already exist somewhere. This spatializes time: that consciousness is consciousness of different things at different moments should guarantee that a person cannot be summed up by any one representation. There is evidence, however, of an absence of faith that time will give birth to a new moment. The spatialized soul feels that if it fails to demand a new, different, better moment, it will be summarized and destroyed.

Thus both *creation* of and *resistance* to structure are necessary to the practice of dusha, which abhors reification while creating it, as Bakhtin says, reducing inner life to a search for one's own undivided voice.

Dusha points at a question or worldview crystallized around oppositions: conscious and unconscious, represent[-able,-ed,-ation] and unrepresent [-able,-ed]. Soul is partially an attempt to come to grips with the uncontrollable, abundant nature of time by coopting moments as emergences from "deep spaces." Depth is in part spatialization of future and past.

The deep is a culturally valued, appropriated, displayed kind of inchoate, one where *size and space try to absorb and reflect the variety offered in time*; things are made into these sorts of situations by virtue of their participation in dusha's depth, that is, its specific relation to consciousness. The "size" of human soul that makes it transcend definition comes partially from the fact that a person is not a whole but moments, impulses, tropes, identities, approaches, practices. Assuming them to be emerging from somewhere leads to a sense that that whole must be inexhaustible, inexpressibly huge.

Having considered more figurative aspects of dusha, I'll go in the other direction. Physicality emphasizes spirituality in cases where something is said to have become deeply encoded, penetrated into people's genes, or when someone describes how deep an emotion is by describing a physical response. Reference to the body could strengthen dusha by asserting that it partakes of nature's authority. Body is linked to soul through their mutual pain, by sensations and feelings, and in the invisible inside of flesh that, though nothing can be closer to a person's center, is unclear, defies adequate description, and "feels" better than it speaks. Both body and soul centers may be associated with truth and and play active roles in imagined transformations during which truths or bad things enter or emerge.

At critical moments, faded metaphors may be activated, mediating changes in bodies and experience, altering people's relationships with each other and the world (see Fernandez 1986, 1974 and Jackson 1983). Although perestroika was just such a crisis, tropes always unnoticeably fade

and revive, and people live by versions of cosmologies those tropes participate in. Reality is determined by such determination of life.

Anthropologists have discussed the "very real" efficacity of metaphor in
ritual. I want to make it clear that in the picture I am describing, this goes
beyond the Austinian (1962) sense of words doing things. Tropic representations are, in this worldview, not separate from other representations; and
representation is life and soul. Soul may be valued above physical life or
may be metaphysically above physical life. The body, the physical, space,
may absorb time; symbols, signs, representations becoming soul and life.
Wierzbicka (1989:52) writes that, given dusha's richness and scope, it is not
surprising that in the opposition body / soul, dusha is commonly seen as
more important and identified with the person as a whole. I would go farther: because the representing soul *is* life, it may include the physical or be
indistiguishable from it.

If the vitality power and economic relations weaken and kill was not always separate from the vitality creativity or love represent, and those were
not totally separate from physical life, power was not only "soulless" in the
sense of "cruel"; it could damage or chase soul away. Physical vitality could
be damaged by "soulless" things and people. The "more significant life"
people craved was approximately the same as there being less difference between physical and symbolic life. Physical and spiritual are not opposed but
multiply interrelated; metaphor can be continuous with literal. The meaning of life Russians were supposed to be interested in finding was related to
the literal life of meaning.

∽

A final note on perestroika and early post-Soviet dusha. As I discuss in the
Introduction, in the course of Soviet history there was increasing lack of
clarity as to to what and to whom "Russian" referred. This was aggravated
by the way Russian-souledness could be opportunistically negotiated and
predicated of anyone who seemed, even fleetingly, human. Along with a rise
in various ethnonationalisms and the advent of glasnost, a demand, in effect, to "open up," the late 1980s and early 1990s saw a burgeoning of interest in and use of the terms *dusha* and *russkaia dusha*. Terms and rituals
involved in soul and "Russianness" were, for a time, transformed, revitalized, newly literal, and important.

I have discussed suffering's association to the community of Russian-
souled. "This" world is felt to isolate people, make them unable to be kind,
weaken spirituality. Yet often, only when it begins to crush do people notice
dusha. During perestroika, it crushed: exchange, self-interest, and the horrors of Soviet history took consciousness's center stage. Glasnost's "open,"

inescapable, representations were, as a result, blamed for loss of dusha. They also saw an odd renaissance of the term.

In January 1991, Leningrad Television's program *Fifth Wheel* used "We are all passengers on the same ship" as a nationalist metaphor. But Oleg once jokingly said he'd rather be a foreigner so Russians could afford to be nice to him. People in the bus, he said, for example, seemed to "have no way to be anything but animals to each other." Russians' very togetherness in boat and bus seemed to render politeness a hypocritical farce, though the association of kindness, empathy, and suffering to community sometimes seemed to be a contender for the job of saving that soul. In 1998, poet and political candidate Viktor Krivulin reportedly said: "We are united today by pain, which is bigger than politics . . . Politics . . . has become the art of spitting on the soul" (*The Chicago Tribune*, November 22, 1998). The writer Lena told me:

> Suddenly, unexpectedly, I started to sense warmth. Before, you got on the bus—negative energy—someone shoved you—"You damned communist!" Like that, to the point of utter idiocy. But now, in the bus, even if it's quiet—suddenly a wave of warmth comes at you, nothing's said, but they *feel* for you, understand you, share your views. Two years ago people assumed they would be happy millionaires . . . and on the bus they were animals to each other. When everyone finally understood that we'll never get rich, that anyone who could already had, we understood that our children share a fate. The boys will become racketeers, the girls prostitutes. And now we are ready to come together. Dusha is waking up after all. My neighbor in public transportation, in line, I know he's in the same position.

Here Maxim interrupted: "Those who aren't in the same position aren't on the bus but in *Toyotas*!" Lena continued: "The cruelty began around 1989. Before that we expected the best. Then we realized nothing good was coming, and we began to ask whose fault it was. Now we see—we're all in one boat and it's floating out to sea."

Increasingly, as the 1990s progressed, dusha's salience in discourse seemed to me to diminish. The vigorous revitalization of the term *dusha* that I discuss in the Introduction began to fade. By the mid-1990s I heard and read much less about dusha. It is very possible that, had I asked the same questions of the same people five years later, I would have gotten somewhat different responses.

Epilogue
Non-Russian Souls

> We, the Russians, are . . . once more the most interesting phe-
> nomenon on earth . . . like a novel whose ending none of us
> knows.
>> Sinyavsky 1988:273 on the sensation caused by perestroika

A similar-looking phenomenon does not necessarily mean the same
thing in different situations, or even have meaning in similar ways.
As I say in the Introduction, however, when cultures have been intimately related, similarities can be powerful heuristic tools. Looking at Russian soul has revealed many things pertinent to other cultures. It is a local
version of something. Most West Europeans and Americans share many of
Russian soul's ancestors, and, as I have discussed, Russian soul became
"Russian" in collaboration with and opposition to other imageries and
philosophies. Images of Russian soul were also reappropriated by Europeans and responded to in their self-definition.

My discussion of national-character studies looked at one kind of non-
Russian treatment of Russian soul. Here I take American and other material
of the same categories and dates as my Russian data (mostly twentieth-century, including very recent philosophy, media, everyday speech, and popular
culture) to, first of all, briefly indicate how souls in them resonate with ones
I have described. I do not trace these images historically (in Chapter 1 I cite
a few studies that do), but begin with evidence that they are shared. Sec-
ondly, I use these similarities to show some special meanings and *uses* of
Russian soul *outside* Russia.

Even before Russians used prevailing definitions of primitivism to pro-
claim their superiority over the West, Rogger writes, Rousseau "revealed an
almost Slavophile streak when he deplored in the *Social Contract* Peter's attempts to make his subjects into Germans or Englishmen" (1960:127–28).
If German romanticism helped Russians see themselves as an individual nation with a mission, Williams (1970:573) claims that, "European intellectu-

als critical of bourgeois society, in turn, found the Russian attack . . . a confirmation of their own malaise, and readjusted their social criticism with the help of . . . Russian literature." The international exchange involved in Russian soul and the national-soul notion in general was not one-way, but cyclical (ibid.:588), or, more precisely, multidirectional; it was among European intellectuals dissatisfied with the cynicism, secularism, prosperity, and power of the Victorian era and with imperialism and World War I that, Williams writes, the myth of the Russian, the Slavic, or the myth of a dearth of soul in Europe was kept alive between 1880 and 1930.[1]

It has even been argued that it was during the same period and as a direct result of European awareness of "Russian soul" and contact with Russian literature and philosophy that "the West" took on aspects of its current meaning: GoGwilt (1995:50) claims that the terms "East" and "West" owe much to the Slavophile-Westerner debate and to a later "reaction against the Bolshevik Revolution which . . . redefined the nineteenth-century idea of Europe in the distorted image of Russian intellectual debates."

Russians may notice others' fingerprints on dusha: Mila and Lara both told me that the idea of Russian soul came, to some extent, from the West. Western interest in Russia, they each told me, was born of readings of Tolstoy and Dostoevsky and exposure to their uses of dusha and images of Russians; Russians then reabsorbed this Western image of themselves.

Berdiaev argues that "He who understands Dostoevsky . . . has assimilated an essential part of the Russian soul" (Williams 1970:586). Dostoevsky's continuing influence on non-Russians is undeniable. GoGwilt (1995:45–46) writes:

> Responding to Aksakov's extreme rejection of European literary models, Dostoevsky . . . argued: ". . . Have we not experienced [European ideals, views and influence] as part of our own lives? . . ." Dostoevsky . . . points to a complexity of cultural identification captured . . . in his fiction . . . the cue to the construction of a new concept of "the West." The suggestion that "our Russian view" can transform . . . has a political dimension which . . . accounts for much of the fascination for Dostoevsky among Western European readers. . . . The rhetoric of the "Russian soul" had an immense impact. . . . Whether as political threat or intellectual excitement, this challenge was read in Dostoevsky's fiction as a far-reaching imaginative unsettling of European cultural and historical identity.

One example is the prewar (and persisting) Dostoevsky cult in Germany. And an English diplomat, Maurice Baring (Williams 1970:586), translated Dostoevsky's concerns into his own version of Russian soul as a symbol of the innate goodness and innocence of a non-Western people. Goodness and

---

[1] Toynbee claimed in 1934 that Lenin was symbolic of the reaction of the Russian soul against Western civilization (See Williams 1970:587–88 on differences between the meaning of Russian soul in Russia and Europe).

purity are still often predicated of Russian soul; witness a 1998 Stolichnaya vodka ad in the American media, hailing, "The purest glacial water, the purest winter wheat. A vodka as authentic as the soul of Russia."

Walter Schubart, a Balt in Switzerland, wrote in 1938 that the West had "robbed the human race of its soul" and that Russia would give it back (cited in Williams 1970:587). Stephen Lapeyrouse, in 1990, cites Schubart:

> Russia is the only country which can . . . redeem Europe—for the simple reason that toward all vital problems she assumes an attitude which is diametrically opposed to that of all European nations. Out of the depths of her unique suffering . . . Russia is able to bring a deeper knowledge of . . . the meaning of human life to the other nations. The Russians possess the spiritual qualities . . . we are lacking . . . [to] reunit[e] a divided mankind and . . . creat[e] the perfect . . . human being.

Then Lapeyrouse, in 1990, in full agreement with Schubart's 1938 formulation, quotes a 1990 *New York Review*[2] article expressing the same ideas. He cites Berdiaev that "The structure of the Russian soul is . . . completely different . . . The more penetrating minds of the West realize this . . . and are attracted by the puzzle it presents" (ibid.:131). Lapeyrouse admiringly calls Russian soul "a tremendous tension, a great struggle between extremes, a profound contrast in their inner and outer lives, between 'heaven and earth' " (ibid.:36). If the Russian soul image is still alive in the West, it is because it was formed in interaction with issues very important in the West.

Like Lapeyrouse, Valentin Tomberg, a Russian of Baltic German extraction, expounds on the Dostoevskian "wisdom of suffering." I cite Tomberg on how suffering is never merely "personal"; it heralds "something new," "the unity of mankind." He opposes happy "American" to tragic but true "Russian" film endings to claim that Americans relate to suffering as to something senseless, shameful. He uses nineteenth-century author Prentice Mulford to exemplify the "American" position that by ignoring the negative, suffering can be eliminated (Tomberg 1994 [1931]:43–44). Opposite in one sense, what Tomberg sees as "American" is similar to "Russian" in that they equally depend on what I have discussed as a link between representation and existence. At the same time, suffering clearly *is* highly valued in the West, partially in "Western" forms (e.g., Weber 1992[1930]), partially in forms more similar to those linked to Russian soul. It is noteworthy that, if Tomberg himself was not fully "not-Russian," his 1931 essay was considered current and interesting enough to publish in America in 1994. In January 1999, *The Chicago Tribune* called suffering and hardship (in the form of a lot of snow) "good for man's soul," in that it challenges people to innovate.

Soul imagery is still reproduced in Russian self-presentations to Westerners; my interviews are filled with such statements, and they have been abun-

---

[2] By Timothy Garton Ash; vol. 37, no. 2 (1990); Lapeyrouse 1990:119.

dant in the American media: a 1997 *New York Times* article cites a Russian calling the Bolshoi Ballet best because "We have the special soul, the very Russian essence that you can find nowhere else." The last line of a 1994 *Chicago Tribune* article on the Yenisei River's destruction cites a local person claiming that bringing back the thaw "would be like rediscovering a vital part of Siberia's soul."

One specific association with Russian soul shared by Europeans, Americans, and Russians has to do with order and disorder. Things "Russian" or post-Soviet are represented in American media as problematic, deep, and verging on chaos. A 1998 *Chicago Tribune* front-page article depicts Russia sinking in "crisis that knows no bottom"; a 1994 *Tribune* headline reports, "Sunny Days Give Russia Fragile Calm: Deep, Abiding Problems Still an Undercurrent." Another headline screams: "Nonsense and Crisis: Russia Spins into Chaos." This article, by Howard Witt, delivers familiar imagery: "It has been another . . . schizophrenic week in Russia, a land without law, logic, or equilibrium where anything and everything can be both true and false, all at the same time." The classic example is, of course, Churchill's assertion that the actions of Russia are "a riddle wrapped in a mystery inside an enigma" (1939, cited in Gilbert 1983:50).[3]

In terms of depth and essence, I mentioned Kozlov's 1995 invocation of the nesting doll as "perfect symbol of the Russian character;" Kay (1997:80) uses similar imagery, of the Russian woman as a *matrëshka* with a deep and solid core.

Far from everything in Russia is couched in terms of dusha; nor is soul never thought about in the West, but Westerners sometimes get a Slavophile streak and claim this. In a 1997 *Chicago Tribune* article, an American doctor, Juliette Engel, described how she felt Russian air to be thick, full of life, chaotic, and full of immaterial heart. Then she went farther: "In Russia, every medical problem is couched in terms of the human soul, which we never think about in the West," disregarding soul in favor of order, rationality, time consciousness, and a tendency to treat things mechanistically and materially.

If the West and Russia are often presented by non-Russians in terms of time, order, the known, money, and systematicity as opposed to chaos, heart, mystery, nurturing, and soul, Virginia Woolf, in "The Russian Point of View," shows how available the idea of Russian soul could be (at that time) for the English. Woolf sees Russian prose as suffused with "something" so adamant that it survives both the ravages of translation and foreign readers' lack of understanding. That something, "the chief character in Russian fiction," is *soul*. This soul says, according to Woolf, "Learn to make yourselves akin to people . . . not with the mind . . . but with . . .

---

[3] In *Siberian Odyssey: A Voyage into the Russian Soul,* journalist Kempe claims, romantically, to have penetrated to the *unfathomable breadth and depth* of the heartland and seen the *narod* living its real life. But when his translator teases him about looking for the Russian soul, Kempe (1992:304) admits that his romantic quest had been "preposterous."

love." Woolf (1925:245) sees this epitome of "Russianness" said with "simplicity . . . [and] the assumption that . . . the chief call upon us is to understand our fellow-sufferers"; this shared "deep sadness" produces a "sense of brotherhood" (ibid:246). Woolf finds that focusing on issues such as the soul's health makes "the horizon widen" and "the soul gain an astonishing sense of freedom" (ibid:249). She says that Dostoevsky's "formless" soul,[4] unconnected to intellect, "diffuse . . . seething whirlpools . . . which hiss and boil and suck us in," desiring only to torturedly "talk, reveal, confess" (ibid:250), is utterly alien to the English (though she clearly appreciates it). This soul makes people "at the same time villains and saints" who love and hate with a passion that renders everything else unimportant (ibid:251). Nobles, like simple people, are "vessels of this perplexed liquid, this cloudy, yeasty, precious stuff, the soul . . . not restrained . . . overflows . . . mingles with the souls of others" (ibid:252–53).

One also finds negative valuations of these images of antisystematic chaos: as part of a conservative reaction against communist Russia, GoGwilt (1995:44) argues, " 'Western civilization' [came to] be constructed as the historical heritage to be defended against . . . Russian nihilism" which, according to Max Müller, "would extinguish the light of civilization by stifling it, then plunge back into chaos" (ibid:47–48).[5]

For Rilke, "Slavic soul" implied "a capacity not only to suffer but to find meaning in suffering" (Williams 1970:586). This suffering is agreed upon, but is sometimes understood differently than it was by Woolf and Rilke. Rancour-Laferriere labels it masochism (though a *Times Literary Supplement* review [Chamberlain 1995] notes that Rancour-Laferriere fails to draw the "positive conclusion" that "suffering . . . has a dignity and a Christian value beyond masochism"). Yi-Fu Tuan, in an unpublished 1996 essay, calls suffering the principal element of Russian soul, describes how, in its absence, souls may perish, and then markedly suggests that that perishing is *good*:

> My father and I . . . share a common admiration for Russia. . . . Something to do with space . . . my shorthand for large virtues such as generosity, and depth, by which I mean the Russian soul . . . a profound understanding of common humanity, expressed in literature and music. . . . We have all heard about the Russian or Slavic soul, but no one speaks of the American soul. Perhaps for soul to develop, one had to suffer and Americans . . . did not. . . . Let's just hope that as the Russians prosper they . . . *will* lose their soul.

[4] Woolf may exaggerate "formlessness" in part because she is describing translated works, in which content survives better than form. Though themes of anarchy can be important in soul-related discourse, formal aspects of art tended to be problematic only if they were felt to be poorly integrated. Dusha was best represented by works whose "form" was felt to be holistically inseparable from or in significant relation to its "content."

[5] GoGwilt (1995:48) shows how Enlightenment principles "were redefined in terms of a new cultural and political identity. 'Nihilism,' associated with Russian thought, allows for a (confused) cultural identification between Western Europe and Enlightenment against Russia."

But Americans *do* speak of their souls. *Soul* appeared in thousands of American book titles, magazine covers, and article headlines in the 1990s. Even cases where soul is not mentioned in the body of the writing are significant: soul sells. *Newsweek* in 1997 noted increasing interest in American soul:[6] "Dying to write a best seller? Just put 'soul' . . . in the title. Since 1994, when Thomas Moore's *Care of the Soul* began its 150–week run of the New York Times best-seller list, there have been nearly 800 books published on the soul of this and the soul of that." Nice statistic on a moribund cliché! A 1997 *Chicago Tribune* article, "Soul Food: Thomas Moore and a Host of Authors Tell Us Why We're Unhappy," says:

> When . . . *Care of the Soul* was published . . . America exhaled en masse upon reading its first words: "The great malady of the 20th century, implicated in all of our troubles and affecting us individually and socially, is loss of soul" . . . loss of soul, Moore wrote, is . . . emptiness, meaninglessness, vague depression and yearning for fulfillment . . . complaints he heard repeatedly from his therapy clients.

Moore says: "Now you see the word 'soul' everywhere . . . This notion of soul as something beyond psychology and beyond technology . . . speaks to that desire to reach deeper. There is a spiritual hunger." Soul sells by implying familiar, valued notions.

Francis Crick's 1994 *The Astonishing Hypothesis: The Scientific Search for the Soul* deals with consciousness as the essence of humans. Soul also often refers to essences of nations such as contemporary or traditional values, as in *Time* magazine's 1995 cover story, "Are Music and Movies Killing America's SOUL?" (the word *soul* does not appear in the article at all). Modernity's soullessness can be fought by means of community: columnist Mary Schmich wrote in 1998: "It may seem anachronistically romantic . . . but when I watch network TV I feel I'm gathered with other viewers around the . . . hearth . . . The soul-sucking activity of TV-watching feels better when it is done with other souls." A 1997 *Chicago Tribune* article on the Chicago Bulls basketball team suggests an animated political community: "Every town wants a team that is true to its soul."

A *Tribune* article by Bob Greene states: "In 1993, whatever 'well regulated Militia' the Founding Fathers had in mind has been replaced by an anarchistic, unregulated army of soulless and homicidal morons . . . This country is dying." Parallels to early post-Soviet articles on the *mafia* are clear. An interesting juxtaposition is a 1997 *Tribune* commentary, "Battling for the Soul of the NRA," which indicts the condition of the soul of an entity that chose the second amendment of one soul as its own soul.

---

[6] This article reviews James Hillman's *The Soul's Code,* on "the power of myth" . . . our "Invisibles," a "something," a "defining image that each of us is born with . . . a particular . . . destiny . . . Hillman would have us imagine [the soul] as our core identity battling for . . . expression."

In another display of contending souls, the summary paragraph of a 1997 *Time* article on cloning, "Can SOULS be xeroxed?" muses:

> The cause of . . . empathy wouldn't be that your inner life was exactly like your clone's (it wouldn't be) . . . seeing that familiar face . . . would remind you that you . . . were essentially the same. . . . You might even feel you shared the same soul. And in a sense, this would be true. Then again, in a sense, you share the same soul with everyone.

In a 1997 *Chicago Tribune* examination of media coverage of an apparently racially motivated beating, Eric Zorn writes: "Taunts and accusations make good TV, briefly satisfy the soul, and may help rally the troops . . . but they harden the hearts of those at whom they are aimed." *Satisfying* the soul, as in Russian, does not necessarily *soften* or *open* it and may be explicitly linked to intergroup politics and cruelty.

As is clear from international appreciation of Dostoevsky, internal conflict, enigma, and extremity are characteristic of soul elsewhere: Francis Ford Coppola, discussing the character of Kurtz in *Apocalypse Now*, said he "wanted a character struggling with the extremities of his soul." A 1997 article by Mary Schmich on a novelist's suicide concludes: "The mind of another person is the greatest mystery of all," a "mind" version of the "dusha" proverb.

American news articles about Russia display a surprising frequency of the word *soul*. For example, a 1994 *National Geographic* photo caption reads: "Battered souls line up in Kiev for registration as Chornobyl invalids." This particular usage of soul would be equally possible in English in reference to Central Americans, Palestinians, Israelis, or Africans, but it seems far from as probable. A 1997 *Chicago Tribune* article concluded that skater Oksana Baiul had to "stop living with artifice and return to what was once natural and essential, the skating that lifted her soul from a tormented past and transported those who watched to places where dreams are all sweet." A 1995 *Time Magazine* cover story, "The Rape of Siberia," begins with a soul-chilling fog.

A 1999 *Chicago Tribune* article calls a Leningrad Zoo orangutan a sensitive soul. If the Western press tends to use the word *soul* in reference to Russians (*most* broadly defined) in contexts in which it would have been less likely to have been used for others, *mere contact* with the "spirit of Russia" may incur uses of *soul* in reference to *anyone*. A 1994 *Chicago Tribune* article by Howard Witt on American astronauts merely *training* in Russia calls them "hearty and worldly souls."

A popular culture exposition of soul in America is a 1994 cartoon by Matt Groening in which an older creature is asked by a younger one what the soul is. He flounders in a familiar way: "That's a tough one . . . the soul is sort of like, you know, your inner spirit . . . it's the best part of you . . .

uh . . . inside you . . . this thing . . . it's this . . . deep . . . your deepest . . . feelings . . . your heart . . . in you . . . it's, uh . . . it's your life force."

American souls, like Russian, are often mentioned at moments when they are felt to be liable to betrayals: an April 1999 *Chicago Tribune* article titled "There Are Those Trusting and Trustworthy Souls" tells of flirting with and skirting betrayal by a partner.

A 1998 book review by Chauncey Mabe discusses a novel that "engages the soullessness of life in an age in which everything is . . . sold." The image of American soul infiltrated with economic self-interest relates to the pragmatics of American soul somewhat as the image of pure, altruistic Russian soul relates to its practice. Both certainly involve superimposed voices, as when, on Chicago public radio in 1997, Aaron Freeman summed up the morality of buying for $16 a silk jacket made by slave labor in China by shouting: "We're Americans! We're consumers to the core of our little souls!" A multi-voiced 1998 Volkswagen ad in the *New Yorker* announces that "If you sold your soul in the 80s, here's your chance to buy it back."

Sahlins (1976:215–16) writes that in Western society, "Even . . . in what is sometimes called 'life' as opposed to 'work' . . . there enters a . . . reflection . . . of the relations of production . . . money is to the West what kinship is to the Rest. It . . . assimilates every other relation." Within the vast range of versions this leaves room for, one would expect that relations between money and soul in America would be radically different from Russian ones. Although they are, there are similarities: a 1997 *Chicago Tribune* article claims that "driven by greed, CIA spy Aldrich Ames sold his soul . . . to the KGB for $2.5 million."

Etiquette surrounding "filthy lucre" existed in 1990s Anglo-American culture. There were also similarities in how "work" was not "life." In America, a friend and I were once asked to "help out" on a project with the understanding that we would be compensated. When we were not, my friend broached the subject. The person apologized, saying she had not paid us because we had seemed to enjoy ourselves. A clear distinction is evident between something interesting or pleasurable and things money is seen as appropriately entering.

Interest, sentiment, and making others comfortable play important roles in and bridge all sorts of relations: "When inferiors extend their most lavish reception for visiting superiors, the selfish desire to win favour may not be the chief motive; the inferior may be tactfully attempting to put the superior at ease by simulating the kind of world the superior is thought to take for granted" (Goffman 1959:30).

I will offer a few examples from work of non-Russian scholars. One is anthropologist Victor Turner's (1969:127–28) notion of *communitas*, which includes openness, life, the "existential quality" of relations between "the whole man in his relation to other whole men . . . sacred . . . because it transgresses or dissolves the norms that govern structured and institutionalized relationships and is accompanied by experiences of unprecedented potency." Turner (ibid.:110–11) sees Dostoevskian characters and "holy beggars" as figures "who strip off the pretensions of holders of high rank . . . reduce them to the level of common humanity." "Liminal entities may be represented as having nothing" (ibid.:95), are "inferior or 'marginal', yet represent what . . . Bergson . . . called 'open' as against 'closed morality' . . . [and] what David Hume has called the 'sentiment for humanity.' " Turner agrees with Bergson that "prophets and great artists," whose work expresses "élan vital, or evolutionary 'life-force' " and who "strive with a passionate sincerity to rid themselves of the clichés associated with status incumbency and role-playing and to enter into vital relations" may reveal "potential in mankind which has not yet been externalized and fixed in structure." Turner's choice of Russian examples is significant: dusha coopted liminality and became linked to life, holism, openness, potential, marginality, passion,[7] and values of statuslessness, poverty, and "antistructure" outside Russia.[8]

And there is anthropologist and linguist Edward Sapir's "Culture, Genuine and Spurious" (1924). Sapir says that Russians resist seeing humans as representative of types or statuses and resist subordinating the "depths of personality" to institutions and civilization; he finds Russians disposed to genuine religion and sincerity and to making virtuous use of literature and music (1960:313–14). This is all familiar national-character imagery, but then Sapir proceeds to earnestly, in his own voice, draw on this Russian imagery to subtly define a "genuine culture" that brings a "sense of inner satisfaction" rather than other benefits, including economic. A "mediocre person moderately gifted with the ability to express his aesthetic instincts . . . in his own sincere and humble way (to the neglect, it may be, of practically all other interests)" may be, Sapir (ibid.:323) writes, more "cultured" than an educated but "flat" person who has never brought "his interests into direct relation with . . . the innermost shrine of his personality," linking that personality to that of his culture's "great minds and hearts" and "unfolding" it (ibid.:324). Sooner or later, Sapir (ibid.:331) concludes, "we shall have to get down to the humble task of exploring the depths of our own consciousness and dragging to the light what sincere bits . . . we can find. These bits will not always be . . . pleasing, but they will be genuine." Virtually every phrase of this touches on imagery I have discussed in above chapters.

I mention many references to the power of others' eyes in "Russian" culture. Tzvetan Todorov (1996) traces thought on others' eyes from Aristotle

[7] Both Western and Russian writers tend to describe Russians as "obsessed"; for example, with culture (Corten 1992), reflection on the self (Steinberg forthcoming), and material goods, even fashion (Lipman 1998:98).

[8] The work of Erving Goffman (1959:64) displays notions similar to those I have shown in Russia. He cites Santayana on how "living things in contact with the air must acquire a cuticle," how man "has crystallized his soul . . . offered up his life . . . and we become . . . masks," and the "bureaucratization of the spirit" required to "give a perfectly homogeneous performance at every appointed time."

to Rousseau. Rousseau distinguishes humans from animals by virtue of a "faculty of attaching . . . to beings who are foreign," a practice that makes us " 'extend and reinforce the feeling of our being' . . . inscribing . . . the need for the other's gaze in the very definition of man." Adam Smith was greatly influenced by Rousseau: access to humanity by virtue of a gaze exchanged with another "plays . . . a central role . . . Smith's description of our dependence on the other is permeated with visual terms" (ibid.:5). Hegel, in turn, says that man does what is necessary for self-preservation but also "aspires to a recognition of his value which can come to him only from the gaze of others" (ibid.:9).

On the topic of life and love, many non-Russian texts display similarities to Russian examples. I have shown relations of dusha to externalizing, including how creativity is understood as expression, a folk theory that is part of a widely shared cosmology. I have cited Asad (1983) on pain and truth in medieval Christian ritual, which displays clear elements of the same metaphysics found in psychoanalytic theory.

John Dewey, in *Art as Experience*, distinguishes between *living* and just surviving, between life and "the humdrum." In his examination of creativity, Dewey (1934:6; emphases mine) writes that "Everything that *intensifies the sense of immediate living* is an object of intense admiration." He finds that expansion or growth, spurred by contact with opposition and conflict, result in higher-powered, more significant life (ibid.:14). Being "fully alive" is "active and alert commerce with the world" as opposed to "being shut up within one's own private feelings . . . *Experience in the degree in which it is experience is heightened vitality*" (ibid.:19). In Omsk, Anna Viktorovna said that "Dusha does not lose its life when a person interacts with music, others, literature"; art, Dewey writes, is "a remaking of the experience of the community" (ibid.:81).

Dewey proposes *interest* as more fundamental than any talent or medium: an intelligent mechanic, he writes, interested, finding satisfaction in his work, caring for his materials and tools, is artistically engaged. In Russia this is relating to something "with dusha," "putting soul into it." "When excitement about subject matter goes deep . . . a store of attitudes and meanings . . . are aroused into activity . . . become conscious thoughts and . . . emotionalized images" (ibid.:64–65). Dewey wants to offer an alternative to the Platonic model of having been distanced from the source of life and meaning, but his version exhibits signs of the same metaphysics; for example, the striving life that moves everything springs from internal need (ibid.:58).

Aspects of Charles S. Peirce's relation of signs to connection-making, community, consciousness, and life can be seen as brilliant readings of a metaphysics of which dusha is a version. Strikingly similar to the picture I formulated with help from Omsk friends is how Peirce uses depth, distance, and even potential energy (CP §7.553) as metaphors for semiosis, calling consciousness a bottomless lake in which ideas are suspended at different depths . . . the deeper ideas are, the more work . . . [is] required to bring them to the surface. This virtual work . . . is the negative of the 'potential energy' . . . that feature of the image which corresponds to the . . . vividness of the idea. Or we may see that the potential, or depth, represents the degree of . . . attention . . . requisite to discern the idea at that depth.

Semiosis is related to issues of space and time, the value of representation, and representation's link to life and soul. In a section on *Musement*, Peirce writes: "Everything which is essentially a Sign [is] . . . the Sign's Soul, which has its Being in its power of serving as intermediary . . . Such, too, is a living consciousness, and such the life, the power of growth." Peirce says that any habit or lawfulness has the form of a symbol; "so anything the least bit *real* has the same . . . form as any human symbol. That is why there is no absolute distinction between matter and mind in Peirce's philosophy. Or between mind and body" (Steve Coleman, personal communication, 1997).

Peirce writes that "Whenever we think, we have present to consciousness some . . . representation . . . We ourselves . . . appear as a sign" (in Singer 1984:58). "Man is a sign" is a literal statement. When I realized that my Russian material suggested that life was linked to representation, I felt that shock. Singer (ibid.:55–56) waffles, calling it a metaphor. It is *not* only a metaphor.

Peirce, like Dewey, stresses interest as a live connection with wholes, "continuity of mind":

an immediate attraction for the idea itself, whose nature is divined before the mind possesses it, by the power of sympathy . . . This mental tendency may . . . affect a . . . community in its collective personality, and be thence communicated to such individuals as are in powerfully sympathetic connection with the collective . . . It may affect a private person directly, yet so that he is only enabled to apprehend the idea . . . by virtue of his sympathy with his neighbors. . . . It may affect an individual . . . by virtue of an attraction it exercises upon his mind. . . . This is . . . due to the continuity between the man's mind and the Most High (CP §3.307).

Singer (1984:65) writes that for Peirce, "The boundaries of personal identity . . . depend on the social and cultural 'outreach' of a particular individual's consciousness." This variable outreach is similar to variable dusha. Peirce condemns the "nineteenth-century Gospel of Greed" according to which "progress takes place by virtue of every individual's striving for himself . . . and trampling his neighbor," and uses the Gospel of John to explain the same "Evolutionary Love" (CP §1.287–304) I showed in Bakhtin and in everyday uses of *dusha*:

Hatred and evil are mere imperfect stages of . . . love and loveliness. . . . Suppose, for example, that I have an idea that interests me. . . . I love it; . . . It is not by dealing out cold justice to . . . my ideas that I can make them grow. . . . Love,

recognizing germs of loveliness in the hateful, gradually warms it into life. . . .
The gospel of Christ says that progress comes from every individual merging his
individuality in sympathy with his neighbors. . . . Love cannot have a contrary,
but must embrace what is most opposed to it, as a degenerate case of it.

Which is one thing dusha is a way of trying to do and what it does, with
varied results, politically, spiritually, economically.

Now, as I do with my Russian material, I turn to *de*humanizing. In American courts, when the question is guilt/innocence or capital punishment/life
in prison, rhetorical efforts of defense and prosecution usually rotate precisely around whether the defendant is a *human being* (with a childhood,
family, and/or extenuating circumstances that allow one to, even distantly,
empathize with or understand him) or a soulless, cold-blooded animal.
Only a "killing machine" or savage beast can be destroyed; killing a *soul*
would be killing something *with which one is oneself continuous*.

What's more, a court may feel empathy when shown evidence of the accused's *own* ability to sympathize, to see soul. A 1997 *Chicago Tribune* article reported that on the witness stand O. J. Simpson portrayed his ex-wife
"more as a troubled soul than a . . . party animal." As per the logic I show
in Chapter 12, if Simpson saw *her* soul, i.e., felt compassion, implied is that
he could not have killed her and that his soul should also be seen (recognized [Hegel], considered [Rousseau], attended to [Smith], sympathized
with and warmed into life [Peirce]; etc.). Aristotle, according to Todorov
(1996:2), "left this . . . formulation: 'The man who is incapable of being a
member of a community . . . because he is sufficient unto himself, does
not . . . belong to the city-state . . . is either a brute or a god' (*Politics*,
1253a). Animals and gods are self-sufficient."

෧

Yi-Fu Tuan, in the essay I cite above, makes one exception in regard to
"soulless" Americans: "The one . . . streak of depth or soul in American
culture emerged from African-American experience," implying that political
enfranchisement and relative prosperity will eliminate that soul. Dale Peterson examines parallels between African-American and Russian "souls" and
claims that African-American "soul" (in the sense of self-conscious identification) was influenced by Russian soul and formed along parallel Herderian
links to music and literature. He shows in DuBois's *The Souls of Black Folk*
an "implication . . . that the striving in the souls of black folk is best expressed and best heard in . . . song" (Peterson 1992:753).[9] Peterson notes
that DuBois's descriptions resonate with Turgenev's (see Chapter 4 epi-

---

[9] A parallel in Irish discourse is how poetry, song, and music may be felt to be more suited
than prose to "express" what's "inside." See Coleman (1999) on how "people couldn't express
their views orally so they had to put it in verse."

graph); singing, transcendent in its relation to sorrow, invokes depths of passion under and through a cracked surface, fire, and vast steppes. Imagery Peterson mentions in others' work and/or reproduces himself includes: sorrow songs' "misty wanderings and hidden ways;" native soil and earthy peasant roots out of which soulful expressions emerge; critique of rationality; formerly invisible meaning emerging from enigmatic "spaces" invisible to many, becoming visible and significant to the world; and spaces and bodies that condense oppositional, higher value, double consciousness, and warring ideals.

Peterson claims that Bakhtinian discourse analysis is apt for and has strongly influenced interpretation of African-American literary work: "the counter-language of 'soul' giving voice and visibility to a hidden humanity" (ibid.:751). "The message of Russian souls and black folk is expressed in a literature that is always already double-voiced" (ibid.:757). I have not studied African-American soul's relation to Russian soul and limit myself to one example: a 1998 *Chicago Tribune* article by Michael Eric Dyson, "Wayward Soul of the Black Church," shows a fluid merging, as in the Russian case, of religious and ethnic meanings of soul with everyday ethical and moral issues.

Wierzbicka (1992) compares English *soul* and *mind* to *dusha*. In this chapter I show more ways in which soul, in current and recent Anglo-American (and other) usages, relates to uses of *dusha*. In partial summary, *soul* and *dusha* are both used:

- when depth and indescribability are implied or invoked;
- when expansive and expanding "life force" is intended;
- in reference to nature and the land;
- in relation to suffering;
- in reference to an "inner world";
- in reference to *essences* of people, countries, cities, ethnic groups, other collectives, and anything else;
- in citing or implying authenticity and/or purity;
- in referring to and/or evoking something felt to be universal, shared, and uniting people;
- in referring to and/or evoking kindness and compassion or in opposition to cruelty;
- in referring to and/or evoking extremity, contexts of life and death, and intense struggle;
- when aspects of modernity, such as the market or mechanization, are opposed, resisted, or counteracted; and
- when materialism, hierarchy, or power are opposed, resisted, or counteracted.

Both soul and dusha

- are centers of values that can be stolen, corrupted, and deviated;
- may be internally complex;
- can harden and soften;
- can open and close, be exposed (alive) or encapsulated (insensitive); and
- may be "listened to" or "heard" or not, and are "voices" assumed to be benevolent.

In contexts of sincerity, theatrical and mask tropes are often used for both, and tropes drawing on vision are also pervasive in both cases. As with Russian dusha,

- healing truths of all sorts are believed to emerge from the American soul's depths, a transgressive movement that can increase a range of kinds of life;
- emotional, representational, and physical depths are often mutually or reciprocally defined;
- feeling or thinking "deeply" is fundamentally valued as an indicator of soul, yet this depth may indicate something understood as "so deep" that nothing about it is felt or thought;
- issues of consciousness and unconsciousness are linked to soul.

Souls tend to be mentioned more in America, as in Russia,

- when they are just opening;
- when they are felt to be threatened, betrayed, or dying; and
- when they are needed to co-opt, oppose, or evoke any of the above-listed elements and qualities.

Alongside their spirit of capitalism, many Americans share a "Russian" sense that violating routine or rebelling against diseases of time imposed by "the world" can bring soul back into consciousness, increasing and spreading kinds of life. This alone is enough to indicate Americans' continuing engagement in a worldview related to the one I have described.

In English-speaking countries, at least, as in Russia, "Where there's life, there's hope."

❦

Russian soul's best defenses from the "destructive gaze" of what Dostoevsky called spies and psychologists are right there in its international reputation as an internationally known symbol and insipid commonplace. As what romantic foreigners come in search of and receive from Russians willing to speak in a romantic voice, as what drunks talk about, as a cliché, *russkaia dusha* has been both too deceptive and too familiar and visible for tastes that assume that what is *on the surface* is less interesting and farther from "real truth" than what is "deep." I have examined this partially in order to question it, trying to not to be more complicit with beliefs I have described than I have been forced to by their similarity to my own inheritance. I have done this by starting to examine and question depth, coherence, transcendence, and spatialized centralization as ways of organizing meaning and the sense of life, and by looking at not only at the meaning of soul but at soul's relationship to meaning.

The history of Russian soul, the way Russian writers and imagery are invoked when certain topics are discussed by non-Russians, to the extent of *Russian* even standing for *soul* in certain cases, together with clear parallels between notions of soul and life in Russia and the West, suggest that these results might be good heuristic tools for examining other notions of soul, creativity, and senses of human life. I hope that they can also serve as they have served me; as ways to examine my own everyday metaphysics and critique it, for what that is worth, given the physical, material, and spatial tenacity of habit.

Bibliography

Adorno, Theodore. 1974. *Minima Moralia*. Translated by E. F. N. Jephcott. New York: NLB.

Asad, Talal. 1983. Notes on Body Pain and Truth in Medieval Christian Ritual. *Economy and Society* 12, 3:287–327.

Attinasi, John, and Friedrich, Paul. 1995. Dialogic Breakthrough: Catalysis and Synthesis in Life-Changing Dialogue. In *The Dialogic Emergence of Culture*, edited by D. Tedlock and B. Mannheim. Urbana: University of Illinois Press.

Austin, J. L. 1962. *How to Do Things with Words*. Cambridge, Mass.: Harvard University Press.

Bakhtin, Mikhail. 1981. *The Dialogic Imagination*. Austin: University of Texas Press.

Bakhtin, Mikhail. 1984. *Problems of Dostoevsky's Poetics*. Minneapolis: University of Minnesota Press.

Bakhtin, Mikhail. 1990. *Art and Answerability: Early Philosophical Essays of M. M. Bakhtin*. Translated by Vadim Lapunov. Edited by M. Holquist. University of Texas Press Slavic Series. Austin: University of Texas Press.

Bakunin, Mikhail. 1980. *On Anarchism*. Montreal: Black Rose Books.

Baldaev, D. S., Belko, B. K., and Isupova, I. M. 1992. *Slovar' tiuremno-lagerno-blatnogo zhargona: rechevoi i graficheskii portret sovetskoi tiurmy*. Moscow: Kraia Moskvy.

Balzer, Marjorie Mandelstam, ed. 1992. *Russian Traditional Culture: Religion, Gender, and Customary Law*. Armonk, N.Y.: M. E. Sharpe.

Banc, C., and Dundes, Alan. 1990. *You Call This Living? A Collection of East European Political Jokes*. Athens, Ga.: University of Georgia Press.

Barrett, Robert. 1987. Schizophrenia and Personhood. Manuscript.

Basso, Keith. 1976. "Wise Words" of the Western Apache: Metaphor and Semantic Theory. In *Meaning in Anthropology*, edited by K. Basso and H. A. Selby. Albuquerque: University of New Mexico Press.

Bateson, Gregory. 1972. *Steps to an Ecology of Mind*. New York: Ballantine.

Berdiaev, Nicolas. 1947. *The Russian Idea*. London: The Centenary Press.

Berdiaev, Nicholas. 1955. *The Meaning of Creativity*. Translated by Donald A. Levine. New York: Harper.

Berdiaev, Nicholas. 1960. *The Origin of Russian Communism*. Ann Arbor Paperbacks for the Study of Marxism and Communism. Ann Arbor: University of Michigan Press.

Bernshtam, T. A. 1992. Russian Folk Culture and Folk Religion. In *Russian Traditional Culture*, edited by M. M. Balzer. Armonk, N.Y.: M. E. Sharpe.

Bolonev, F. F. 1992. Archaic Elements in the Charms of the Russian Population of Siberia. In *Russian Traditional Culture*, edited by M. M. Balzer. Armonk, N.Y.: M. E. Sharpe.

Bourdieu, Pierre. 1990. *The Logic of Practice*. Translated by R. Nice. Cambridge: Polity Press.

Boym, Svetlana. 1994. *Common Places: Mythologies of Everyday Life in Russia*. Cambridge, Mass.: Harvard University Press.

Brooks, Jeffrey. 1984. *When Russia Learned to Read*. Princeton, N.J.: Princeton University Press.

Cajkanovic, Veselin. 1996. Magical Sitting. In *The Anthropology of East Europe Review*: De Paul University. Translated by Marko Zivkovic.

Carrithers, Michael. 1985. An Alternative Social History of the Self. In *The Category of the Person,* edited by M. Carrithers, S. Collins, and S. Lukes. New York: Cambridge University Press.

Chaadaev, Pyotr Yakovlevich. 1969. *Philosophical Letters and Apology of a Madman*. Knoxville: University of Tennessee Press.

Chamberlain, Lesley. 1995. A Suffering People. *Times Literary Supplement*, December 22, 1995.

Chekhov, Anton P. 1985. *Pripadok*. Moscow: Pravda.

Cherniavsky, Michael. 1969. *Tsar and People: Studies in Russian Myths*. New York: Random House.

Christian, David. 1987. Traditional and Modern Drinking Cultures in Russia on the Eve of Emancipation. *Australian Slavonic and East European Studies* 1, 1:61–84.

Cienki, Alan. 1998. Straight: An Image Schema and Its Metaphorical Extensions. *Cognitive Linguistics* 9, 2:107–49.

Coleman, Steve. 1996. Sentiment, Entelechy, and Text in Irish-Language Song Tradition. Paper read at American Anthropological Association National Meetings, San Francisco.

Coleman, Steve. 1999. Return from the West: A Poetics of Voice in Irish. Ph.D. dissertation. Department of Anthropology, University of Chicago.

Condee, Nancy. 1996. The Second Fantasy Mother, or All Baths Are Women's Baths. In *Russia/Women/Culture*, edited by H. Goscilo and B. Holmgren. Bloomington: Indiana University Press.

Corten, Irina H. 1992. *Vocabulary of Soviet Society and Culture: A Selected Guide to Russian Words, Idioms, and Expressions of the Post-Stalin Era, 1953–1991*. Durham, N.C.: Duke University Press.

Crick, Francis. 1994. *The Astonishing Hypothesis: The Scientific Search for the Soul*. New York: Simon and Schuster.

Crone, Anna Lisa. 1978. *Rozanov and the End of Literature: Polyphony and the Dissolution of Genre in Solitaria and Fallen Leaves*. Wurzburg: Jal-Verlag.

Dal', Vladimir. 1882. *Tolkovyi slovar' zhivago velikoruskago iazyka*. St. Petersburg: Izdanie Knigoprodavtsa-Tipografa M. O. Vol'fa.

DeVos, George A. 1968. National Character. In *International Encyclopedia of the Social Sciences*, edited by D. L. Sills. New York: Macmillan and The Free Press.

Dewey, John. 1934. *Art as Experience.* New York: Minton, Balch, and Co.

Dicks, Henry V. 1967. Some Notes on the Russian National Character. In *The Transformation of Russian Society: Aspects of Social Change since 1861,* edited by C. E. Black. Cambridge, Mass.: Harvard University Press.

Dostoevsky, Fëdor. 1980. *Polnoe sobranie sochinenii v tridtsati tomakh.* Vol. 21. Leningrad: Nauka.

Dostoevsky, Fëdor. 1982. *Sobranie sochinenii v dvenadsati tomakh.* Vol. 11–12: *The Brothers Karamazov.* Vol. 3: *The Gambler; Notes from the Dead House.* Moscow: Pravda.

Dostoevsky, Fëdor. 1985a. *Polnoe sobranie sochinenii v tridtsati tomakh.* Vol. 28. Leningrad: Nauka.

Dostoevsky, Feodor M. 1985b. *The Diary of a Writer.* Translated by Boris Brasol. Salt Lake City: Gibbs M. Smith.

Dovlatov, Sergei 1991. *Zona/Kompromiss/Zapovednik.* Moscow: PIK Nezavisimoe izdatel'stvo.

Dreizin, Felix. 1990. *The Russian Soul and the Jew: Essays in Literary Ethnocriticism.* Studies in Judaism. Lanham, Md.: University Press of America.

Dunham, Vera S. 1990. *In Stalin's Time: Middleclass Values in Soviet Fiction.* Durham, N.C: Duke University Press.

Eagleton, Terry. 1996. Talk on Adorno at The Red Stripe Seminar. St. Patrick's College, Maynooth, Ireland.

Easton, Paul. 1989. The Rock Music Community. In *Soviet Youth Culture,* edited by J. Riordan. Bloomington: Indiana University Press.

Elias, Norbert. 1994. *The Civilizing Process: The History of Manners and State Formation and Civilization.* Translated by Edmund Jephcott. Oxford: Blackwell.

Emerson, Caryl. 1996. Keeping the Self Intact during the Culture Wars: A Centennial Essay for Mikhail Bakhtin. Paper read at Living Together Alone, University of Virginia, Charlottesville, Va.

Erofeev, Venedikt. 1990. *Moskva-Petushki, i pr.* Moscow: Izdatel'stvo "Prometej" MGPI im. V. I. Lenina. Translated by H. William Tjalsma as *Moscow to the End of the Line* (1980, Evanston, Ill.: Northwestern University Press).

Erofeev, Venedikt. 1995. *Ostav'te moiu dushu v pokoe: Pochti vsë.* Moscow: Izdatel'stvo "Kh. G. S."

Fernandez, James W. 1974. The Mission of Metaphor in Expressive Culture. *Current Anthropology* 15 (2):119–45.

Fernandez, James W. 1982. *Bwiti: an Ethnography of the Religious Imagination in Africa.* Princeton, N.J.: Princeton University Press.

Fernandez, James W. 1986. *Persuasions and Performances.* Bloomington: Indiana University Press.

Fitzpatrick, Sheila. 1992. *The Cultural Front: Power and Culture in Revolutionary Russia.* Ithaca, N.Y.: Cornell University Press.

Fogelson, Raymond D. 1982. Person, Self and Identity: Some Anthropological Retrospects, Circumspects, and Prospects. In *Psychosocial Theories of the Self,* edited by B. Lee. New York: Plenum Press.

Foucault, Michel. 1970. *The Order of Things: An Archeology of the Human Sciences.* New York: Random House.

Foucault, Michel. 1980. *Power/Knowledge: Selected Interviews and Other Writings.* New York: Pantheon Books.

Friedrich, Paul. 1978. *The Meaning of Aphrodite.* Chicago: University of Chicago Press.

Friedrich, Paul. 1979. *Language, Context, and the Imagination: Essays by Paul Friedrich*. Stanford, Calif.: Stanford University Press.

Friedrich, Paul. 1986. *The Language Parallax*. Austin: University of Texas Press.

Friedrich, Paul. 1994. Translation of Tiutchev's *Silentium. The InterGalactic Poetry Messenger*.

Friedrich, Paul. 1996a. The Tragedy of Shame: Anna Karenina. Paper read at Slavic Forum Conference, University of Chicago.

Friedrich, Paul. 1996b. The Culture in Poetry and the Poetry in Culture. In *Culture/Contexture: Explorations in Anthropology and Literary Studies*, edited by E. V. Daniel and J. M. Peck. Berkeley: University of California Press.

Friedrich, Paul. 1997. *Music in Russian Poetry*. New York: Peter Lang.

Froianov, I. A., Dvornichenko, A. Iu., and Krivosheev, Iu. V. 1992. The Introduction of Christianity in Russia and the Pagan Traditions. In *Russian Traditional Culture*, edited by M. M. Balzer. Armonk, N.Y.: M. E. Sharpe.

Gerhart, Genevra. 1974. *The Russian's World: Life and Language*. San Diego: Harcourt Brace Jovanovich.

Gilbert, Martin. 1983. *Winston S. Churchill*. Vol. VI. Boston: Houghton-Mifflin.

Glazov, Yuri. 1985. *The Russian Mind since Stalin's Death*. Vol. 47: *Sovietica*. Dordrecht: D. Reidel Publishing Company.

Goffman, Erving. 1959. *The Presentation of Self in Everyday Life*. New York: Penguin Books.

GoGwilt, Chris. 1995. True West: The Changing Idea of the West from the 1880s to the 1920s. In *Enduring Western Civilization: The Construction of the Concept of Western Civilization and Its "Others"*, edited by S. Federici. Westport, Conn.: Praeger.

Goodman, Nelson. 1978. *Ways of Worldmaking*. Indianapolis: Hackett Publishing Company.

Gorbachev, Mikhail. 1987. *M. S. Gorbachev: Izbrannye rechi i stat'i*. 4 vols. Moscow: Izdatel'stvo politicheskoi literatury.

Gorer, Geoffrey, and Rickman, John. 1949. *The People of Great Russia: A Psychological Study*. London: The Cresset Press.

Greenfeld, Liah. 1992. *Nationalism: Five Roads to Modernity*. Cambridge, Mass.: Harvard University Press.

Gromyko, M. M. 1992. Traditional Norms of Behavior and Forms of Interaction of Nineteenth-Century Russian Peasants. In *Russian Traditional Culture*, edited by M. M. Balzer. Armonk, N.Y.: M. E. Sharpe.

Grossman, Gregory. 1986. A Note on Reform, Money, and Administrative Supremacy. In *Stagnation or Change in Communist Economies?* edited by K. C. Thalheim. London: Centre for Research into Communist Economies.

Handelman, Stephen. 1995. *Comrade Criminal: Russia's New Mafiya*. New Haven, Conn.: Yale University Press.

Hansen, Erik. 1993. Living Conditions on the Kola Peninsula. Oslo: FAFO SOTECO.

Harakas, Stanley Samuel. 1990. *Health and Medicine in the Eastern Orthodox Tradition*. New York: Crossroad.

Harries, Karsten. 1968. *The Meaning of Modern Art*. Edited by J. Wild. Northwestern University Studies in Phenomenology and Existential Philosophy. Evanston, Ill.: Northwestern University Press.

Hauner, Milan. 1990. *What Is Asia to Us?: Russia's Asian Heartland Yesterday and Today*. London: Routledge.

Hellbeck, Jochen. 1998. Laboratories of the Soviet Self: Diaries from the Stalin Era. Ph.D. dissertation. Columbia University.

Helms, Mary. 1988. *Ulysses' Sail: An Ethnographic Odyssey of Power, Knowledge, and Geographical Distance.* Princeton, N.J.: Princeton University Press.

Hingley, Ronald. 1977. *The Russian Mind.* New York: Charles Scribner's Sons.

Hirschman, Albert O. 1977. *The Passions and the Interests: Political Arguments for Capitalism before Its Triumph.* Princeton, N.J.: Princeton University Press.

Hivon, Myriam. 1994. Vodka, the 'Spirit' of Exchange. *Cambridge Anthropology* 17, 3.

Holisky, Dee Ann. 1989. The Rules of the Supra: or How to Drink in Georgian. *Annual of the Society for the Study of Caucasia* 1:22–40.

Humphrey, Caroline. 1995. Creating a Culture of Suspicion: Consumers in Moscow: A Chronicle of Changing Times, at The Centre for History and Economics. (Version subsequently published as Creating a Culture of Disillusionment: Consumption in Moscow, a Chronicle of Changing Times, In *Worlds Apart,* edited by Daniel Miller. New York: Routledge. pp. 43–67.)

Humphrey, Caroline and Hugh Jones, Stephen, eds. 1992. *Barter, Exchange, and Value: An Anthropological Approach.* Cambridge: Cambridge University Press.

Hunt, Theodore W. 1891. *The Principles of Written Discourse.* New York: A. C. Armstrong and Son.

Il'f, Il'ia, and Petrov, Evgenii. 1984. *Dvenadsat' stul'ev.* Tashkent: "Ukituvchi".

Ivanits, Linda J. 1992. *Russian Folk Belief.* Armonk, N.Y.: M. E. Sharpe.

Jackson, Michael. 1983. Thinking through the Body: An Essay on Understanding Metaphor. *Social Analysis* 14:127–49.

Jakobson, Roman. 1956. Two Aspects of Language and Two Types of Aphasic Disturbance. In *Fundamentals of Language,* edited by R. Jakobson and M. Halle. The Hague: Mouton.

Jakobson, Roman. 1987. *Language in Literature.* Cambridge, Mass.: Belknap.

Jarintzov, Madame N. 1916. *The Russians and Their Language.* Oxford: Blackwell.

Jowitt, Ken. 1983. Soviet Neotraditionalism: The Political Corruption of a Leninist Regime. *Soviet Studies* 35, 3:275–97.

Kay, Rebecca. 1997. Images of an Ideal Woman: Perceptions of Russian Womanhood through the Media, Education, and Women's Own Eyes. In *Post-Soviet Women: From the Baltic to Central Asia.* edited by M. Buckley. Cambridge: Cambridge University Press.

Kempe, Frederick. 1992. *Siberian Odyssey: A Voyage into the Russian Soul.* New York: Putnam's Sons.

Kim, Yulii. 1990. *Tvorcheskii vecher: proizvedeniia raznykh let.* Moscow: Izdatel'stvo Knizhnaia Palata. Translated in 1991 by Dale Pesmen for The Milwaukee Repertory Theater.

Kluckhohn, Clyde. 1962. *Culture and Behavior: Collected Essays of Clyde Kluckhohn.* Glencoe, Ill.: The Free Press of Glencoe.

Kozlov, Gera. 1995. The Russian Matryoshka, or How to Understand the Multi-Tiered Psychology of Russians. *Surviving Together: A Quarterly on Grassroots Cooperation in Eurasia* 13, 4.

Kristeva, Julia. 1980. *Desire in Language: A Semiotic Approach to Literature and Art.* New York: Columbia University Press.

Kuhn, Thomas. 1970. *The Structure of Scientific Revolutions.* Chicago: University of Chicago Press.

Kuprin, A. I. 1909. Letter to F. D. Batiushkov.

Lapeyrouse, Stephen Ludger. 1990. *Toward the Spiritual Convergence of America and Russia: American Mind and Russian Soul, American Individuality and Russian Community, and the Potent Alchemy of National Characteristics*. Santa Cruz, Calif.: self-published.

Leake, C. D. 1963. Good-Willed Judgment on Alcohol. In *Alcohol and Civilization*, edited by S. P. Lucia. New York: McGraw-Hill.

Ledeneva, Alena V. 1998. *Russia's Economy of Favors*. Cambridge: Cambridge University Press.

Leerssen, Joep. 1996. *Remembrance and Imagination: Patterns in the Historical and Literary Representation of Ireland in the Nineteenth Century*. Cork: Cork University Press.

Leifer, A. E. 1984. *Dostoevskii i Omsk: Glavnyi zal omskogo literaturnogo muzeia imeni F. M. Dostoevskogo*. Edited by I. A. Makarov. Omsk: Omskoe oblastnoe upravlenie kul'tury, Omskii gosudarstvennyi ob"edinennyi istoricheskii i literaturnyi muzei F. M. Dostoevskogo.

Lemon, Alaina M. 1996. Indic Diaspora, Soviet History, Russian Home: Political Performances and Sincere Ironies in Romani Cultures. Ph.D. dissertation. Department of Anthropology, University of Chicago.

Lenin, Vladimir Ilich. 1960. *Philosophical Notebooks*. Vol. 38: *Collected Works*. London: Lawrence and Wishart.

Levada, Yu. A., et al. 1993. *Sovetskii prostoi chelovek: Opyt sotsial'nogo portreta na rubezhe 90–kh*. Moscow: Mirovoi Okean.

Levi-Strauss, Claude. 1962. *The Savage Mind*. Chicago: University of Chicago Press.

Lewin, Moshe. 1990. Popular Religion in Twentieth-Century Russia. In *The World of the Russian Peasant: Post-Emancipation Culture and Society*, edited by B. Eklof and S. Frank. Boston: Unwin Hyman.

Lipman, Masha. 1998. Fade to Red? Style in the Land of Anti-Style. *The New Yorker*, September 21, 1998. pp. 106–13.

Lloyd, David. 1993. *Anomalous States: Irish Writing and the Postcolonial Movement*. Dublin: Lilliput.

Lotman, Yurii, and Ouspensky, Boris. 1984. *The Semiotics of Russian Culture*. Edited by A. Shukman. Ann Arbor: Michigan Slavic Contributions (1).

Marx, Karl. 1978. The German Ideology. In *The Marx-Engels Reader*, edited by R. C. Tucker. New York: W. W. Norton.

Mauss, Marcel. 1967. *The Gift: Forms and Functions of Exchange in Archaic Societies*. New York: W. W. Norton.

Mauss, Marcel. 1985. A Category of the Human Mind: The Notion of Person; the Notion of Self. In *The Category of the Person*, edited by M. Carrithers, S. Collins, S. Lukes. New York: Cambridge University Press.

Mead, Margaret. 1955. *Soviet Attitudes towards Authority: An Interdisciplinary Approach to Problems of Soviet Character*. New York: William Morrow.

Mead, Margaret, and Metraux, Rhoda. 1953. *The Study of Culture at a Distance*. Chicago: University of Chicago Press.

Mikheyev, Dmitry. 1989. The New Soviet Man: Myth and Reality. In *The Soviet Union and the Challenge of the Future*, vol. 2: *Economy and Society*, edited by A. Shtromas and M. A. Kaplan. New York: Paragon House.

Minenko, N. A. 1992. Daily Life and Holidays of the Siberian Village in the Eighteenth and First Half of the Nineteenth Centuries. In *Russian Traditional Culture*, edited by M. M. Balzer. Armonk, N.Y.: M. E. Sharpe.

Mirsky, D. S. 1949. *A History of Russian Literature*. New York: A. A. Knopf.

Morson, Gary Saul, and Emerson, Caryl. 1990. *Mikhail Bakhtin: Creation of a Prosaics*. Stanford, Calif.: Stanford University Press.

Muldoon, Paul. 1973. *New Weather*. London: Faber and Faber.

Munn, Nancy D. 1986. *The Fame of Gawa: A Symbolic Study of Value Transformation in a Massim (New Guinea) Society*. Cambridge: Cambridge University Press.

Paxson, Margaret. 1998. The Festival of the Holy Trinity (Troitsa) in Rural Russia: A Case Study in the Topography of Memory. *Anthropology of East Europe Review* 16, 2:59–64.

Paxson, Margaret. 1999. Configuring the Past in Rural Russia: An Essay on the Symbolic Topography of Social Memory. Ph.D. dissertation. University of Montreal.

Peirce, Charles Sanders. 1931–35, 1958. *The Collected Papers of Charles Sanders Peirce*. Edited by C. Hartshorne and P. Weiss (Vols. I–VI) and A. W. Burks (Vols. VII–VIII). Cambridge, Mass.: Harvard University Press.

Pelevin, Victor. 1998. Moscow Dynamo. In *Granta* 64 (Winter 1998).

Pepper, Stephen. 1942. *World Hypotheses*. Berkeley: University of California Press.

Pesmen, Dale. 1991. Reasonable and Unreasonable Worlds: Some Expectations of Coherence in Culture Implied by the Prohibition of Mixed Metaphor. In *Beyond Metaphor: The Theory of Tropes in Anthropology*, edited by J. W. Fernandez. Stanford, Calif.: Stanford University Press.

Pesmen, Dale. 1993. Ashkenazim (Russian, Ukrainian, and Belorussian Area). *Encyclopedia of World Cultures*. Boston: G. K. Hall and Co.

Pesmen, Dale. 1998. *The Russian Soul: Ethnography and Metaphysics*. Ph.D. dissertation. Department of Anthropology, University of Chicago.

Peterson, Dale E. 1992. Justifying the Margin: The Construction of "Soul" in Russian and African-American Texts. *Slavic Review* 51, 4:749–57.

Pipes, Richard, ed. 1961. *The Russian Intelligentsia*. New York: Columbia University Press.

Platz, Stephanie. 1996. *Pasts and Futures: Space, Time, and Armenian Identity, 1988–1994*, Ph.D. dissertation. Department of Anthropology, University of Chicago.

Polanyi, K., Arensberg, C. M., and Pearson, H. 1957. *Trade and Markets in the Early Empires*. Glencoe, Ill.: Free Press.

Propp, V. Ia. 1995. *Russkie agrarnye prazdniki*. St. Petersburg: Izdatel'stvo "Azbuka."

Pushkareva, N. L. 1992. The Woman in the Ancient Russian Family (Tenth to Fifteenth Centuries). In *Russian Traditional Culture*, edited by M. M. Balzer. Armonk, N.Y.: M. E. Sharpe.

Rancour-Laferriere, Daniel. 1995. *The Slave Soul of Russia: Moral Masochism and the Cult of Suffering*. New York: New York University Press.

Rayport-Rabodzeenko, Jennifer. 1998. *Creating Elsewhere, Being Other: The Invented Spaces and Selves of St. Petersburg Youth, 1990–1995*. Ph.D. dissertation. Department of Anthropology, University of Chicago.

Riasanovsky, Nicholas V. 1984. *A History of Russia*. New York: Oxford University Press.

Ries, Nancy. 1991. The Power of Negative Thinking: Russian Talk and the Reproduction of Mindset, Worldview, and Society. *Anthropology of East Europe Review* 10, 2:38–53.

Ries, Nancy. 1997. *Russian Talk: Culture and Conversation during Perestroika.* Ithaca, N.Y.: Cornell University Press.

Ries, Nancy. 1998. The "New Russian" as Social Critique: Its Features and Implications. American Anthropological Association National Meetings, Philadelphia.

Riordan, Jim, and Bridger, Sue, eds. 1992. *Dear Comrade Editor: Readers' Letters to the Soviet Press under Perestroika.* Bloomington: Indiana University Press.

Riviere, Claude. 1987. Soul: Concepts in Primitive Religions. In *The Encyclopedia of Religion*, edited by M. Eliade. New York: Macmillan.

Rogger, Hans. 1960. *National Consciousness in Eighteenth-Century Russia.* Cambridge, Mass.: Harvard University Press.

Rose, Richard, and McAllister, Ian. 1993. Is Money the Measure of Welfare in Russia? Glasgow: Centre for the Study of Public Policy, University of Strathclyde.

Sahlins, Marshall. 1976. *Culture and Practical Reason.* Chicago: University of Chicago Press.

Santayana, George. 1922. *Soliloquies in England and Other Soliloquies.* London: Constable.

Sapir, Edward. 1960 [1924]. *Culture, Language, and Personality.* Berkeley: University of California Press.

Schnirelman, Victor, and Komarova, Galina. 1997. Majority as Minority: The Russian Ethno-Nationalism and its Ideology in the 1970–1990s. In *Rethinking Nationalism and Identity: the Struggle for Meaning and Order in Europe*, edited by H.-R. Wicker. New York: Berg.

Sergeev, R. B. 1981. *Omsk.* Moscow: Sovetskaia Rossiia.

Shaliapin, Fëdor Ivanovich. 1960. *Shaliapin.* Vol. 1. Moscow: Gosudarstvennoe izdatel'stvo "Iskusstvo".

Shishkov, Viacheslav. 1953. *Ugrium-reka.* Kuibyshevskoe Knizhnoe Izdatel'stvo.

Shukshin, Vasilii. 1992. *Kalina Krasnaia.* In *S. Shukshin: Sobranie sochinenii v 5 tomakh*, edited by A. Fedoseeva-Shukshina. Ekaterinburg: Ural'skii rabochii.

Simis, Konstantin M. 1982. *USSR: The Corrupt Society: The Secret World of Soviet Capitalism.* Translated by J. Edwards and M. Schneider. New York: Simon and Schuster.

Singer, Milton. 1984. *Man's Glassy Essence: Explorations in Semiotic Anthropology.* Bloomington: Indiana University Press.

Sinyavsky, Andrei. 1988. *Soviet Civilization: A Cultural History.* Translated by Joanne Turnbull. New York: Arcade Publishing.

Smith, Adam. 1976. *The Wealth of Nations.* Chicago: University of Chicago Press.

Smith, Adam. 1982. *The Theory of Moral Sentiments.* Indianapolis: Liberty Classics.

Solzhenitsyn, Alexander. 1980. Speech to Harvard on its 327th Commencement (June 8, 1978). In *Solzhenitsyn at Harvard*, edited by R. Berman. Washington, D.C.: Ethics and Public Policy Center.

Steinberg, Mark D. forthcoming. *Proletarian Imagination: Self, Modernity, and the Sacred in Russia's Time of Crisis and Revolution.*

Stephens, Holly DeNio. 1997. The Occult in Russia Today. In *The Occult in Russian and Soviet Culture* edited by B. G. Rosenthal. Ithaca, N.Y.: Cornell University Press.

Stites, Richard. 1992. *Russian Popular Culture: Entertainment and Society since 1900.* Cambridge: Cambridge University Press.

Stocking, George W., Jr. 1992. *The Ethnographer's Magic and Other Essays in the History of Anthropology.* Madison: University of Wisconsin Press.

T. D. 1925. On the Use of Metaphors. *Blackwood's Edinburgh Magazine* 18:719–23.

Tambiah, S. J. 1968. The Magical Power of Words. *Man*:175–208.

Tambiah, Stanley. 1996. Lecture at the University of Chicago.

Taussig, Michael. 1980. *The Devil and Commodity Fetishism in South America*. Chapel Hill: University of North Carolina Press.

Taylor, Lawrence. 1996. "The Sea, Oh, the Sea": The Ironic Dimension in Irish Culture. Paper read at American Anthropological Association National Meetings, San Francisco.

Teffi. 1991. *Nostal'giia: Rasskazy, Vospominaniia*. Leningrad: Izdatel'stvo Khudozhestvennaia Literatura.

Timasheff, Nicholas S. 1946. *The Great Retreat: The Growth and Decline of Communism in Russia*. New York: E. P. Dutton.

Todorov, Tzvetan. 1996. Living Alone Together. Paper read at Living Alone Together, University of Virginia, Charlottesville, Va.

Tomberg, Valentin. 1994 (1931). The East European Conception of Suffering. *Gnosis*, Spring 1994:43–45.

Tompkins, Arnold. 1897. *The Science of Discourse: A Rhetoric for High Schools and Colleges*. Boston: Ginn.

Tournier, Michel. 1969. *Friday*. Translated by Norman Denny. New York: Pantheon.

Tucker, R. C. 1987. *Political Culture and Leadership in Soviet Russia*. New York: W. W. Norton.

Turner, Victor. 1969. *The Ritual Process: Structure and Anti-Structure. Lewis Henry Morgan Lectures, 1966*. Ithaca N.Y.: Cornell University Press.

Veletskaia, N. N. 1992. Forms of Transformation of Pagan Symbolism in the Old Believer Tradition. In *Russian Traditional Culture*, edited by M. M. Balzer. Armonk, N.Y.: M. E. Sharpe.

Verdery, Katherine. 1993. Ethnic Relations, Economies of Shortage, and the Transition in Eastern Europe. In *Socialism: Ideals, Ideologies, and Local Practice*, edited by C. M. Hann. London: Routledge.

Verdery, Katherine. 1996. *What Was Socialism, and What Comes Next?* Princeton, N.J.: Princeton University Press.

Vitaliev, Vitali. 1998. The Last Eighteen Drops. *Granta* 64 (Winter 1998):181–94.

Vlasov, V. G. 1992. The Christianization of the Russian Peasants. In *Russian Traditional Culture*, edited by M. M. Balzer. Armonk, N.Y.: M. E. Sharpe.

Vygotsky, Lev S. 1962. *Thought and Language*. Cambridge, Mass.: MIT Press.

Ware, Kallistos. 1987. Eastern Christianity. In *Encyclopedia of Religion*, edited by M. Eliade. New York: Macmillan.

Weber, Max. 1992 (1930). *The Protestant Ethic and the Spirit of Capitalism*. London: Routledge

Wertsch, James. 1987. Cultural and Historical Interpretations of Soviet Nuclear Policy. Paper read at Nuclear Policy, Culture and History, University of Chicago.

Whorf, Benjamin Lee. 1956. The Relation of Habitual Thought and Behavior to Language. In *Language, Thought, and Reality*. Cambridge, Mass.: MIT Press.

Wierzbicka, Anna. 1989. Soul and Mind: Linguistic Evidence for Ethnopsychology and Cultural History. *American Anthropologist* 91:41–58.

Wierzbicka, Anna. 1992. *Semantics, Culture, and Cognition: Universal Human Concepts in Culture-Specific Configurations*. New York: Oxford University Press.

Williams, Robert C. 1970. The Russian Soul: A Study in European Thought and Non-European Nationalism. *Journal of the History of Ideas* 31:573–88.

Wilson, Andrew, and Bachkatov, Nina. 1992. *Russia and the Commonwealth A to Z.* New York: HarperCollins.

Woolf, Virginia. 1925. *The Common Reader.* New York: Harcourt, Brace.

Yurchak, Alexei. 1997. The Cynical Reason of Late Socialism: Power, Pretense, and the Anekdot. *Public Culture* 19, 2.

Zaitsev, Igor, ed. 1990. *Soviet Rock.* Moscow: Progress Publishers.

Zinoviev, Alexander. 1982. *Homo Sovieticus.* Translated by Charles Janson. Boston: Atlantic Monthly Press.

Zinoviev, Alexander. 1990. *Perestroika in Partygrad.* (Russian title: *Katastroika.* Translated by Charles Janson.) London: Peter Owen.

Zinoviev, Alexander. 1995. *Russkii Eksperiment: Roman.* Moscow: Nash Dom— L'Age d'Homme.

Zoshchenko, Mikhail. 1981 (1938). *Izbrannoe.* Leningrad: Lenizdat.

Index

Aesthetics, 6, 9, 190n, 204, 239, 265, 293, 314, 316; Bakhtin, 267–68, 288–89n; of money, 127, 130, 136

Absurdity, 53, 67, 91, 121, 171, 177, 206, 239, 267, 281, 286–88, 292

Adaptation. *See* Change

Africa, Africans, 14n, 48, 154–55, 282–86, 292, 320

Alcohol, drinking, 170–188, 239; alcoholism, 86n, 170–77, 186, 257, 275; bottles as currency, 180–81; and community, solidarity, 18, 86, 109, 157, 165, 171–74, 178–82, 181–82, 184–88, 206, 234, 246, 305, 314; and consciousness, 180–81; as dominant of Russianness and dusha, 9, 13, 53, 171, 177–79, 181–82, 185–87, 312–14; as exchange-related, 134, 170, 180, 185–88, 290, 314; with foreigners, 182–83, 303; and gender, 166, 174–75, 178–79; historically, 9, 176–79, 185–88; and humanity, 18, 55, 136, 169, 175–77, 187, 257, 275; 314–15; jokes and lore, 177–78, 182, 235; and *kul'tura*, 176; open talk and "letting go," 53, 92–93, 122, 150, 162, 167, 170–88, 230, 237, 305; resistance, 171, 183, 314; rituals, 157, 165, 171–75, 183, 185–86, 235; shortages, Gorbachev's war against, 167, 170, 177, 180; snacks, 174–75, 178; and time, 171–71, 178; toasts, 171–75, 183–85, 237; transformations, "magic," 136–37, 168, 177–81, 185–88, 228, 282–83,
314–15; varieties, 178, 180; —, beer, 26, 102, 106, 173–76, 214; —, "cognac," 202, 291; —, homebrewed, 150, 170, 173, 175, 178–80; —, liqueurs, 173; —, mislabeled, 179, 290; —, vodka, 27, 68, 98, 106, 114, 158, 167, 171–88, 203, 234–35, 303, 326; —, wine, 30, 120, 152, 158, 173–74, 179; in village, 100, 175, 177–79, 186, 239. *See also* Food; Power; Steam baths; Tea

Altruism and selflessness, 65, 137, 151, 164, 204, 331. *See also* Generosity; Nobility

Ambivalence, 8, 227, 267, 305, 309, 320; and *krut*, 196; about money, success, 126–32; about openness, 223

America, Americans: American/Russian contact, 132, 135, 148–50, 160, 179, 196, 236, 238–39; can't understand, 47, 58, 195–96, 266, 289; goods, 27, 45, 97, 148–49, 215; images, 37, 100–102, 106–7, 148; as *krutoi*, 195, 201, 205; as opposed to Russia, 14n, 40, 117, 120, 128–29, 150, 162, 181, 224, 286, 294; as other world, 63–65, 132; shares aspects of dusha, 4, 324–38. *See also* English language

Animals, 23, 25, 29, 113, 156–57, 173; animals' souls, 15n, 113, 156. *See also* Beastliness; Tropes

Anthropology: complicity, 6, 13, 229, 294, 303, 338; ethnography, 4–19, 57, 62, 300; method, 9–15, 37, 62, 211–12,

349